Discover
Honolulu,
Waikiki & O'ahu

Contents

Throughout this book, we use these icons to highlight special recommendations:

 The Best...
Lists for everything from beaches to wildlife – to make sure you don't miss out

Local Knowledge — Local experts reveal their top picks and secret highlights

 Detour
Special places a little off the beaten track

 If you like...
Lesser-known alternatives to world-famous attractions

These icons help you quickly identify reviews in the text and on the maps:

Beaches   **Eating**

Sights   **Drinking**

Sleeping   **Information**

This edition wri

Sara ~~Benson~~

Lisa Dunford

Contents

Plan Your Trip

On the Road

In Focus

Survival Guide

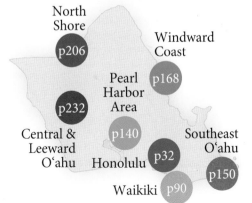

This Is Oʻahu

Landing at Honolulu's airport plunges you into the urban jungle, but relax, it's still Polynesia. Even among downtown high-rises, you'll find capital-city power brokers in breezy aloha shirts. By day, inspect royal feathered capes and ancient temple carvings, then swizzle mai tais while slack key guitars play at Waikiki Beach after dark.

There's another side of the island: the 'country,' where farms and dirt roads lead deep into a Hawaiian heartland. On some wild, rugged and nearly deserted beaches, sea turtles still outnumber surfers. Set your watch to island time as you cruise past the Windward Coast's emerald valleys, rustic ranches and roadside shrimp trucks, or lose yourself on the rural Waiʻanae Coast.

Don't dismiss Oʻahu as a transit point en route to the Neighbor Islands. Take a closer look and you'll uncover a lifetime of adventures. Surf the Banzai Pipeline's giant waves, hike atop knife-edged *pali* (cliffs), dive in Hanauma Bay's giant fishbowl, windsurf or kayak to uninhabited islands off Kailua Bay, and be back in Waikiki for sunset hula. No worries, *brah*.

Oʻahu, like Honolulu-born President Barack Obama, is proud of its multicultural heritage. The nerve center of the archipelago brings you face to face with Hawaii as it really is, not just a postcard fantasy. All over this island, nicknamed 'The Gathering Place,' pulses the Hawaiian lifeblood, from ancient heiau (stone temples) to sacred hula dances and chants. Boisterous festivals keep diverse traditions alive.

Spam, surfing, hula, pidgin, rubbah slippah – these are just some of the touchstones of everyday life floating in the middle of the Pacific Ocean. People are easygoing, low-key and casual, bursting with genuine aloha and fun. You'll feel welcome whether you're a surf bum, a honeymooner or part of a big *ʻohana* (extended family) with grandparents and kids tagging along.

> On some wild, rugged and nearly deserted beaches, sea turtles still outnumber surfers.

Boats docked on Lanikai Beach (p181), near Kailua
ANN CECIL /LONELY PLANET IMAGES ©

O'ahu

PACIFIC OCEAN

158°15'W 158°00'W

Kahuku Point

North Shore

Turtle Bay

Kawela

Malaekahana Beach

11 Sunset Beach

Kahuku

Kulalua Point

Pupukea (552ft)

La'ie

Waimea Bay **7** Pupukea

Kaua'i Channel

7 Waimea

Kamehameha Hwy

Hau'ula

Pua'ena Point

Pu'u Ka'inapua'a (2361ft)

Mokule'ia Beach Park

Kaiaka Point

10

Hale'iwa

21°35'N

Ka'ena Point

13

Dillingham Airfield

Waialua

Kamehameha Hwy

Ka'ena Point State Park

Yokohama Bay

Makua Military Reservation

Ko'olau

Pu'u Ka'aumakua (2681ft)

Kukaniloko Birthstones State Historic Site

Mt Ka'ala (4020ft)

Schofield Barracks Military Reservation

Wahiawa

Schofield Barracks Military Reservation

Wai'anae Coast

Kepuhi Point

Kane'aki Heiau

Makaha Valley

Wai'anae Range

Kolekole Pass (1724ft)

Wheeler Army Airfield

Range

Makaha

Lahilahi Point

Kunia

Mililani

Kamehameha Hwy

Kane'ilio Point

Wai'anae

Lualualei Naval Reservation

Kunia Rd

Ma'ili Beach Park

Ma'ili

Ma'ili Point

Pearl City

Kea'iwa Heiau State Recreation Area

Nanakuli

Hawaii's Plantation Village

Waipahu

Pearl Harbor

8

Kahe Point & Tracks Beach Park

Makakilo

Farrington Hwy

Hawaiian Railway Station

US Naval Reservation

Nimitz Hwy

Hickam Air Force Base

21°20'N

Kapolei

Ewa

Honolulu International Airport

'Ewa Beach

Mamala Bay

South Shore

Barbers Point

PACIFIC OCEAN

ELEVATION

4000ft
3000ft
2000ft
1000ft
500ft
0

N

0 ————————— 10 km
0 ————————— 5 miles

158°15'W 158°00'W

15

Top Experiences

15 O'ahu's Top Experiences

Sunset Hula at Waikiki Beach (p127)

Every night at beachfront resorts, bars and shopping malls you can stumble upon legendary O'ahu musicians strumming their slack key guitars and ukuleles or singing *ha'i* (a style of falsetto) and Hawaiian chants, while hula dancers in swaying skirts perform subtle hand movements and patterned footsteps. After sunset, tiki torches are lit and the conch shell blown at Kuhio Beach Park, where you can watch a free show that's surprisingly not just for tourists – it's a way of keeping Hawaiian traditions alive.

1

Diamond Head (p155)

Jutting into the ocean, this extinct volcanic crater – where ancient Hawaiians once sacrificed humans to war god Ku – is Honolulu's best-known landmark. Every day hundreds of visitors stomp up the trail, leading through a 225ft-long tunnel and past concrete bunkers to the summit. The reward is panoramic views of the Pacific and Honolulu's cityscape. View from Diamond Head

Snorkeling at Hanauma Bay (p162)

With turquoise waters ringed by the remnants of an ancient volcano, this is O'ahu's most loved snorkeling spot. Cradled along the island's southeast shore, legally protected Hanauma Bay offers a giant outdoor fishbowl to splash around in, plus a coral reef that's thousands of years old. Pull a snorkel mask over your eyes – you'll be amazed by the diversity of sealife visible just below the surface of the nature preserve's glimmering waters. If you're lucky, a green sea turtle will paddle by.

Bishop Museum (p54)

Sometimes it's a challenge to find remnants of the ancient Hawaiian ways that flowed on this island for more than 1000 years before Captain Cook arrived. That's what makes the Bishop Museum such a rich cultural and natural-history store-house. Inspect rare artifacts such as the feathered cloak worn by Kamehameha the Great and fearsome *ki'i akua* (carved temple images), then step inside O'ahu's only planetarium and gaze at the same stars that guided the first Polynesian voyagers to this archipelago, the planet's most remote.

The Best...
Beaches

WAIKIKI BEACH
O'ahu's most buzzing all-around beach scene. (p94)

ALA MOANA BEACH PARK
Join the locals taking their morning swim. (p36)

KAILUA
Pick your beach pleasure: walking, kayaking, windsurfing or sunbathing. (p179)

KO OLINA LAGOONS
Four postcard-perfect beaches with palm trees, calm water and sunset views. (p247)

SUNSET BEACH
Watch the pros surf when the big winter waves come out to play. (p213)

The Best...
Hikes

MANOA FALLS
Family-friendly waterfall
hike in the hills above
Honolulu. (p58)

MAKIKI VALLEY & MANOA CLIFFS
More magical forest hikes
with skyline views. (p58)

DIAMOND HEAD
Tried-and-true military trail
to a volcanic summit with
360-degree views. (p155)

MAUNAWILI
Take your pick of a waterfall trail or a coastal-view
trek. (p173)

KA'ENA POINT
A flat former-railbed hike
between craggy cliffs and
pounding shore. (p260)

Kailua Beach Park (p179)

5

The clouds gather on the
horizon, but it's a calm morning. You put your kayak in at
Ka'elepulu Canal and paddle
out. As you look back over the
water that fades from cobalt
to azure (or is that electric
blue?), you see the golden arc
of sand and the ridges of the
green Ko'olau Mountains in
the distance. You enjoy every
moment because you know
by afternoon those clouds
will arrive with the wind, and
it will be kitesurfing time at
Kailua Beach Park.

ANN CECIL/LONELY PLANET IMAGES ©

END OF
PAUOA FLATS
TRAIL

6 Hiking Around Mt Tantalus (p58)

You don't have to leave Honolulu behind to find a natural escape thanks to footpaths winding into the lofty Ko'olau Range. Take the kids on a walk to Manoa Falls, or press on up a steep ladder of tree roots to Nu'uanu Valley Lookout where a gap in the peaks reveals the lush Windward Coast. No matter which trail you choose, you'll get a free lesson in Hawaiian natural history, walking past hulking banyan trees, fragrant guava and musical bamboo groves where honeycreepers flit between flowers. Hiker on Pauoa Flats Trail, Nu'uanu Valley

KARL LEHMANN/LONELY PLANET IMAGES ©

Waimea Bay (p218)

Waimea Bay is one of the most polyglot places on O'ahu. The gorgeous deep-blue bay has attracted attention since outsiders first hit the shore in 1779. Back then the area had a large Native Hawaiian population. The valley is now a park and the beach the domain of visitors. In winter, the waves rise so high that it's international surfers and their fans who are most attracted.

USS *Arizona* Memorial (p144)

A hush settles over the group as you disembark onto the memorial. It's hard not to be moved by the realization you are standing over the watery grave of more than 1000 sailors. Roughly half of the US servicemen who died during the Pearl Harbor attack on December 7, 1941, were killed on the USS *Arizona*. An optional audio tour recounts survivor tales, but switch it off until you get back to dry land. This sacred place is best experienced in silence.

Honolulu's Chinatown (p43)

An anchor's throw from Honolulu Harbor, the crowded streets of Chinatown possess more history than any other place on Oʻahu. Nineteenth-century whalers whooped it up in bars and brothels, while plantation-era immigrants made their way into island society by putting down roots. Today this pan-Asian neighborhood keeps evolving, with art galleries, creative restaurants and hip nightspots. It's small enough to walk around in a morning, with a tasty break for dim sum or noodles.

The Best...
Ocean Adventures

SNORKELING AT HANAUMA BAY
Schools of tropical fish in an aquamarine preserve. (p162)

BODYSURFING AT SANDY BEACH PARK
Crashing waves for experts only. (p166)

KITESURFING AT KAILUA
Catch the wind on a sailing wakeboard. (p181)

STAND-UP PADDLING IN HALEʻIWA
Ride the Anahulu River. (p222)

SURFING OFF PUAʻENA POINT
North Shore breaks for beginners. (p221)

WHALE WATCHING ON THE WAIʻANAE COAST
Spot a leviathan in winter. (p253)

Matsumoto's Shave Ice (p225)

Why would someone stand in such a long line for shave ice? Maybe it's the exotic, homemade flavors such as *li hing mui* (salty dried plum) and coconut cream. Maybe it's the ice cream and azuki beans. Or maybe it's the history. The building dates to the 1920s, but it wasn't until 1951 that Japanese immigrant Mamoru Matsumoto opened his grocery here. Shave ice quickly became the best seller when introduced in the 1960s. Today his son runs the store and, on a hot day, he sells more than 1000 serves of shave ice.

The Best...
Views

Surfing the North Shore (p213)

11

Phantoms, Freddyland, Backyards, Rocky Point, Log Cabins. Not only every beach, but every break on the North Shore has a name. You've heard of the Banzai Pipeline, one of the world's most perfect barrel rides, but aficionados know how the surf hits on every reef. The shore breaks around Sunset Beach are some of the most famous. Though you may get a little action in fall and spring, winter is prime time for the epic waves – several world-class competitions are held here between December and February.

Surfers on Sunset Beach

Helena's Hawaiian Food (p76)

12

Doesn't look like much, right? Just another strip-mall storefront with a lei painted around the doors. But inside the kitchen waft the aromas of Hawaiian soul food – *kalua* (underground-pit cooked) pig, sour poi, steamed *laulau* (meat or fish wrapped in leaves) bundles, *lomilomi* (minced with tomato and onion) salmon and *pipi kaula* (beef jerky) – all made from the family recipes of Helena Chock, a James Beard Award winner. Her grandson now runs the joint, and Honoluluans still crowd the tiny parking lot, ducking inside to grab takeout for an impromptu luau.

Hiking to Ka'ena Point (p260)

Trekking along this easy ocean-side trail, you'll almost certainly spot wildlife. If you're lucky you'll see an endangered monk seal bathing on the volcanic rocks below. If not, look closely for them once you hit the nature reserve at the island's tip. They'll be the black 'rocks' that are more rounded and smooth than angular and pockmarked. High above, frigates and other seabirds fly by. Keep your eyes peeled in winter: you may spot a humpback whale in the distance.

Shopping in Waikiki & Ala Moana (p133)

Forget hula dolls and coconut bikinis. You can pick up unique Hawaiiana and souvenirs – from hand-crafted ukuleles and koa wood carvings to tropical skirts and flip-flops – in the malls and boutiques of Waikiki and Ala Moana. Detour down Kapahulu Ave to Bailey's Antiques and Aloha Shirts, full of modern reproductions and vintage prints, including neon designs from the swingin' 1960s.

LINDA CHING/LONELY PLANET IMAGES ©

Shangri La (p156)

In the shadow of Diamond Head, the former mansion of billionaire tobacco heiress Doris Duke is a sight for art lovers and celebrity hounds. From its exterior this tropical hideaway looks plain and unassuming, but inside it's a treasure house of antique ceramic-tile mosaics, carved wooden screens and silk tapestries, all embraced by meditative gardens with ocean vistas. Touring Shangri La feels as intimate as reading Duke's private journal.

The Best...
Island Cuisine

ALAN WONG'S
Hawaii Regional Cuisine from a Honolulu-raised kitchen star. (p69)

LEONARD'S
Get your *malasadas* (Portuguese doughnuts) hot from the oven. (p125)

ROY'S WAIKIKI BEACH
Top-notch island bistro for evolutionary fusion food. (p119)

SIDE STREET INN
Jovial sports bar where chefs chow down after hours. (p71)

TED'S BAKERY
Classic plate-lunch fare at its finest. (p214)

POKE STOP
Take some of the island's freshest seafood to go. (p245)

O‘ahu's
Top Itineraries

PACIFIC
OCEAN

TURTLE BAY

SUNSET BEACH 18   19
                        20 KAHUKU
           17   WAIMEA   21 LA‘IE
LANIAKEA BEACH 16
           15 HALE‘IWA

KA‘ENA POINT
STATE PARK
24

                    22 KUALOA

           14 WAHIAWA

O‘AHU

                              KAILUA
                                 23

              6
         PEARL   BISHOP
         HARBOR   MUSEUM   MANOA VALLEY   KOKO
                        7   5   HEAD
                                              REGIONAL
    HONOLULU 3 - 4 9   PARK
                              HAWAI‘I KAI
    WAIKIKI 1 - 2   8   12   13
    DIAMOND HEAD   8   10   11
                        SHANGRI   HANAUMA
PACIFIC   LA   BAY
OCEAN

● **Waikiki to Pearl Harbor** Four days
◗ **Diamond Head to Makapu‘u** Two days
● **Wahiawa to Turtle Bay** Two days
● **Kahuku to Ka‘ena Point** Two days

Waikiki to Pearl Harbor

4 DAYS

The Battleship *Missouri* Memorial, also an interactive museum

ANN CECIL/LONELY PLANET IMAGES ©

① **Waikiki Beach** (p94)

Bronze your bod for two days on this world-famous resort strip, stretching from **Fort DeRussy Beach** to **Sans Souci Beach Park**, a secret snorkeling spot.

② **Kuhio Beach Park** (p95)

After you've put up your surfboard each day, watch the sun sink into the Pacific and lie back on your beach mat for the free **Hawaiian music and dance show**.

③ **Downtown Honolulu** (p37)

On day three, take the bus to tour **'Iolani Palace**, browse the **Hawai'i State Art Museum** and ascend the **Aloha Tower**.

④ **Chinatown** (p43)

Walk in the steps of 19th-century whalers from Honolulu's harbor to historic Chinatown. The bustling streets are crammed with open-air markets, lei shops, art galleries, antique stores and eateries.

⑤ **Manoa Valley** (p52)

For the afternoon, shake off the urban grit and head for the hills. Wander among tropical plants in the **Lyon Arboretum**, then hike with the kids to **Manoa Falls**.

⑥ **Pearl Harbor** (p144)

On your fourth day, get up early to visit O'ahu's stirring WWII sites, starting with the sunken **USS Arizona Memorial**.

⑦ **Bishop Museum** (p54)

In the afternoon, get lost in Polynesia's top-ranked anthropological museum, where artifacts fill the **Hawaiian Hall**.

● ● ● ● ● ● ● ● ● ● ● ●

🡒 THIS LEG: 55 MILES

2 DAYS

Diamond Head crater with Honolulu in the distance

MARK A. JOHNSON/CORBIS FLIRT/ALAMY ©

⑧ Diamond Head (p155)

Start day five with an early-morning hike up an extinct volcanic crater, scrambling through a spooky tunnel for summit views extending from *mauka* (the mountains) to *makai* (the sea).

⑨ Honolulu Museum of Arts (p49)

Head back downtown to this exquisite, globally minded art museum. Break for lunch at the courtyard **Honolulu Museum of Arts Cafe**.

⑩ Shangri La (p156)

With advance reservations, board a minibus back toward Diamond Head to tour Doris Duke's former mansion, today a trove of Islamic art.

⑪ Hanauma Bay (p162)

On the next day, if you really want to go face-to-mask with schools of rainbow-colored fish and green sea turtles, visit this crescent-shaped bay. Show up early to avoid the crowds.

⑫ Hawai'i Kai (p159)

For lunch, chow down at **Kona Brewing Company**, grab healthy takeout for a picnic outdoors by the beach from **Kale's Natural Foods** or scoop up homemade ice cream from **Bubbie's**.

⑬ Koko Head Regional Park (p164)

Cruise by car down O'ahu's southeast coast. Roadside stops include **Halona Blowhole**, surf-pounded **Halona Cove**, the bodysurfers' hangout of **Sandy Beach** and the lighthouse trail up windy **Makapu'u Point**.

○ **THIS LEG: 35 MILES**

Wahiawa to Turtle Bay

2 DAYS

KARL LEHMANN/LONELY PLANET IMAGES ©

Hwy 803 from Hale'iwa to Wahiawa running between pineapple fields, heading toward Wai'anae Range

⑭ **Wahiawa** (p237)

On day seven, drive from Honolulu to the North Shore via slow-and-scenic **Kunia Road**. Stop at **Dole Plantation** to get lost in the pineapple maze or go on a garden tour.

⑮ **Hale'iwa** (p220)

Spend some time that afternoon wandering among the Hale'iwa town shops at **North Shore Market Place** or taking a stand-up paddling lesson. For dinner, **Hale'iwa Cafe** has creative island cuisine starring local produce.

⑯ **Laniakea Beach** (p220)

The next morning you might have some luck spotting *honu* (sea turtles) at Laniakea Beach.

⑰ **Waimea** (p218)

Just down the road is **Waimea Valley**, where you can stretch your legs walking through an 1800-acre park filled with native flora and swim beneath **Waimea Falls**. As you leave, be sure to admire the stunning **Waimea Bay**.

⑱ **Sunset Beach** (p213)

'**Ehukai Beach Park**, aka Banzai Pipeline, is definitely worth a stop. As is **Ted's Bakery**, for a plate lunch and pie. Afterwards, hit **Sunset Beach** for some sunbathing and surf watching.

⑲ **Turtle Bay** (p210)

There's time for one more swim in the sheltered cove before sunset cocktails at **Turtle Bay Resort**.

· ·

🡒 THIS LEG: 42 MILES

2 DAYS

Roadside shrimp truck, Kahuku

KARL LEHMANN/LONELY PLANET IMAGES ©

20 Kahuku (p204)

Turtle Bay to Kahuku is less than 5 miles, but on day nine wait to depart so you can have lunch at one of the famous Kahuku shrimp trucks like **Giovanni's**. Save room for some Kahuku-grown corn, too.

21 La'ie (p202)

Unless you have an extra day to spare, skip the **Polynesian Cultural Center** on this tour. Just know that the interpretive shows and luau are worth coming back for someday.

22 Kualoa (p197)

Meander down the coast, pausing at any beaches or roadside stands of interest. Fans of *Lost* and *Jurassic Park* will want to stop at **Kualoa Ranch**, where several scenes were shot. Continue on to **Tropical Farms** to buy some flavored macadamia nuts and other Hawaiian-made products.

23 Kailua (p178)

End your day in Kailua, where you'll spend two nights. You have to stop at the **Kalapawai Market**, a landmark grocery store, for a picnic to take to **Kailua Beach**. While there, watch the windsurfers and kitesurfers, or rent a kayak and take off on your own. The next morning you'll hear the guava pancakes at **Cinnamon's Restaurant** calling.

24 Ka'ena Point State Park (p258)

Those feeling in need of some downtime should stay by the beach in Kailua. Energetic sorts should take a day trip across O'ahu. The reward? A stunning coastal hike to **Ka'ena Point**, the tip of the island, with excellent animal-spotting potential en route.

THIS LEG: 85 MILES

Get Inspired

Books

○ **Shark Dialogues**
(1995) Honolulu-born
Kiana Davenport's
multigenerational novel
spans the decades from
Western contact through
to the plantation era.

○ **House of Thieves**
(2005) Local author Kaui
Hart Hemming's short
stories about upper-class
families in Hawaii.

○ **Hotel Honolulu** (2001)
Paul Theroux's satirical
tale about a washed-up
writer managing a run-
down Waikiki hotel.

○ **Legends and Myths of
Hawaii** (1888) King David
Kalakaua magically mixes
history with mythology.

○ **Best of Honolulu
Fiction** (1999) Sixteen
years of island stories.

Films

○ **The Descendants**
(2011) An O'ahu father
(George Clooney) comes
to terms with family after
his wife's critical accident.

○ **Blue Hawaii** (1961) Elvis
Presley on Waikiki.

○ **Tora! Tora! Tora!** (1971)
Dramatization of the Pearl
Harbor attack.

○ **Highwater** (2009)
Action-filled doco about
the Triple Crown surfing
competition.

○ **50 First Dates** (2004)
Romantic comedy filmed
near Moli'i Fishpond.

♫ Music

○ **Gabby** (1991)
Legendary slack key
guitarist and vocalist
Gabby Pahinui.

○ **Hana Hou** (1995) Auntie
Genoa Keawe's classic
Hawaiian melodies.

○ **Generation Hawai'i**
(2006) Lyrical, modern
Hawaiian album from
Amy Hanaiali'i.

○ **IZ in Concert: The
Man and His Music**
(1999) O'ahu-born Israel
Kamakawiwo'ole live on
vocals and ukulele.

○ **Kamahiwa** (2005)
A collection of Keali'i
Reichel's local tunes.

Websites

○ **O'ahu Visitors Bureau**
(www.visit-oahu.com)
Island's official site.

○ **Hawaii Visitors and
Convention Bureau**
(www.gohawaii.com)
Great activity info.

○ **Alternative Hawaii**
(www.alternative-hawaii.
com) Indie travel website.

○ **Honolulu Weekly**
(http://honoluluweekly.
com) Best area event and
music calendar.

Short on time?

This list will give an instant
insight into the country.

Read *Growing Up Local*, an
anthology from Honolulu-
based Bamboo Ridge press,
sheds light on what it means
to be from the island.

Watch TV's *Hawaii 5-0*, the
remake, offers viewers a
modern-day look at Hono-
lulu's sights and sounds.

Listen *Facing Forward* is the
all-time best-selling album by
legendary Hawaiian musician
IZ (Israel Kamakawiwo'ole).

Log on The Aloha Shorts
(www.hawaiipublicradio.
org/alohashorts) podcast
introduces you to the
island's actors, play-
wrights, musicians and
poets.

Surfing at Sandy Beach (p166), Koko Head Regional Park
ANN CECIL /LONELY PLANET IMAGES ©

O'ahu Month by Month

Top Events

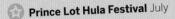

 Aloha Festival September

Triple Crown of Surfing November

Prince Lot Hula Festival July

Hawaii International Film Festival October

 **'I Love Kailua' Town Party** April

 # January

Tourist season gets underway as mainlanders escaping less temperate climes arrive en masse. This is typically the rainiest month of the year.

Chinese New Year

Around the time of the second new moon after the winter solstice, usually between mid-January and mid-February, Chinatown in Honolulu celebrates the lunar New Year with more than a week's worth of lion dances, firecrackers, street fairs and parades.

 # February

Humpback whales migrate past the island from December through May, but February is one of the best times to spot them. Valentine's weekend is booked solid at resorts.

 # March

It's still winter elsewhere, so it's still peak season on O'ahu. Note that college students take spring break in March or April, making things even busier.

Honolulu Festival

Music, dance and drama performances at various venues in Honolulu and Waikiki take place for three days in mid-March. The Asia Pacific cultural festival also features an arts-and-crafts fair and a grand parade followed by a fireworks show.

 # April

Winter rains abate about the same time as the tourist crush does. Any

(left) Children playing saxophones at the Aloha Festival, Waikiki

JOHN BORTHWICK /LONELY PLANET IMAGES ©

time after Easter is a low-key, and possibly lower-priced, time to visit the island.

Waikiki Spam Jam

One of Waikiki's wackiest street festivals is held on a day in late April. The Spam Jam celebrates the state's favorite meat product. Try Spam served as sushi, in spring rolls, atop nachos, in tacos, mixed with pasta – even as a popsicle flavoring.

'I Love Kailua' Town Party

A giant block party takes over Kailua town's main street one Sunday in April. Local bands and hula schools turn out to perform, while the community's artists vend their wares and area restaurants cook up a storm.

May

May Day, the first, is Lei Day in Hawaii, when the beautiful ancient tradition of stringing together and wearing tropical flowers, leaves and seeds is celebrated.

June

Calmer, summer currents prevail; it's relatively safe to assume you can swim instead of surf on the North Shore.

Pan-Pacific Festival

Expect outdoor hula shows and *taiko* drumming as part of the early-June Asian and Polynesian performing-arts showcase in Honolulu and Waikiki. Don't miss the huge *ho'olaule'a* (celebration) block party and parade that takes place along Kalakaua Ave.

King Kamehameha Celebrations

The state holiday, King Kamehameha Day, is June 11. A ceremony at the king's statue in Honolulu is followed by a parade and a street party. Later in the month, a hula festival is held in his majesty's honor (p62).

July

Towns around the island welcome Independence Day, July 4, with fireworks and festivities. Family summer vacation travel is at a peak around the holiday, as are lodging prices.

Prince Lot Hula Festival

On the third Saturday in July, one of O'ahu's premier Hawaiian cultural festivals features noncompetitive hula performances at Moanalua Gardens in Honolulu. The former royal retreat setting provides an even more graceful, traditional atmosphere.

August

Sunny weather continues nearly everywhere. On Statehood Day, the third Friday of the month, some celebrate, some protest – but everyone takes the day off work.

Hawaiian Slack Key Guitar Festival

Lay out a picnic blanket at Waikiki's Kapi'olani Park and enjoy free Hawaiian guitar and ukulele shows. The island's top performers take the stage, plus there are food vendors and an arts-and-crafts fair in the park.

September

Tradewinds blow in, but the temperature is still ideal, making it an excellent time for those without kids in school to explore the island – sans crowds.

Aloha Festival

Begun in 1946, the Aloha Festival is the state's premier cultural festival, an almost 10 day-long tribute to all things Hawaiian. The signature events are Waikiki's royal court procession, block party and floral parade. Affiliated activities may take place elsewhere across the island.

Hawai'i Food & Wine Festival

Island star chefs Roy Yamaguchi and Alan Wong co-host three days of fabulous food and wine. Events in Honolulu and beyond highlight the local bounty and may include gala dinners, farm-to-table tastings, traditional Hawaiian feasts, luncheon discussions, and wine-, chocolate- and coffee-pairing sessions.

October

Travel bargains abound during one of the year's slowest times for visiting O'ahu.

Hawaii International Film Festival

Screenings of imported Pacific Rim, Asian, mainland American, European and even a few Hawaii-related films roll at venues in Honolulu and Waikiki. This highly-regarded event is popular, so book tickets ahead. For full schedules, see www.hiff.org.

Halloween

In the days and weeks leading up to and including Halloween, October 31, look for themed performances, haunted houses, costume contests and local festivals. Attractions such as the Dole Plantation in central O'ahu, the Polynesian Cultural Center on the Windward Coast and the Hawai'i Nature Center in southeast O'ahu get into the act by hosting spooky events.

November

Surfers of the world descend on the North Shore at the beginning of the epic winter wave season. It can get cool at night, so bring a sweater.

Triple Crown of Surfing

This world-class surfing competition takes place from mid-November to mid-December at the North Shore's Hale'iwa Ali'i Beach Park, Sunset Beach and 'Ehukai Beach Park. The actual start date depends on the surf. So be ready, and bring your binoculars!

December

Despite the occasional chill, Santas all over the island are putting on their best aloha shirt and shorts. Early on, locals have the place to themselves; Christmas and New Year's bring crazy-high prices and crowds.

Honolulu Marathon

On the second Sunday in December, the Honolulu Marathon attracts more than 25,000 runners (more than half hailing from Japan), making it one of the world's top 10 largest marathons. Runners trace a route from downtown Honolulu to Diamond Head.

Christmas

The island celebrates Christmas all month long. Many communities host parades, including a floating regatta originating at Hawai'i Kai Marina. Honolulu City Lights starts in early December with a parade and concert and finishes with fireworks for the New Year.

Far left: Women performing a hula during Christmas festivities **Below:** Surfing champion Kelly Slater at a Triple Crown of Surfing event on the North Shore

(FAR LEFT) DOUGLAS PEEBLES/CORBIS © (BELOW) SYLVAIN CAZENAVE CORBIS ©

Need to Know

Language
English, Hawaiian and pidgin.

ATMs
Very common.

Credit Cards
Required for vehicle rentals; widely accepted at hotels but not all other lodgings.

Visas
For Visa Waiver Program (VWP) countries, visas are not required for stays of less than 90 days.

Cell Phones
Carrier Verizon has the best network; international travelers need multiband phones.

Wi-Fi
Not all lodgings have wi-fi; some have wired connections (fees may apply). Look for wi-fi hot spots in hotel lobbies and cafes (purchase required).

Internet Access
At public libraries with a card (nonresidents $10).

Directions
Makai means 'toward the ocean'; *mauka* means 'toward the mountain.'

Tipping
Tip 18% to 20% at restaurants and bars; minimum $2 for valets, hotel maids or porters.

When to Go

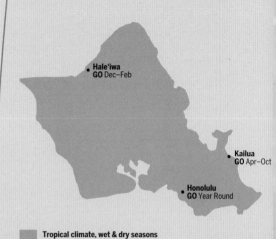

Hale'iwa
GO Dec–Feb

Kailua
GO Apr–Oct

Honolulu
GO Year Round

■ Tropical climate, wet & dry seasons

High Season
(mid-Dec–mid-Apr & Jun–Aug)
- North Shore has winter waves; surf comps in full swing
- Whales migrating
- Book rooms and activities far ahead
- High lodging prices, high occupancy
- Rainiest time of the year

Shoulder
(Jun–Aug)
- Dry, hot weather
- Waves picking up in Waikiki, tame on North Shore
- Early starts best for hiking
- Visitor spike due to school summer vacations

Low Season
(mid-Apr–May & Sep–Oct)
- Lodging rates drop, bargaining may be possible
- Airfares at their lowest
- Crowds few
- Weather still temperate

Advance Planning

- **Three months before** Make flight and lodging reservations. If you plan to travel during the winter holidays or in July and August, book at least six months ahead.
- **Two weeks before** Reserve in-demand activities such as tours, boat trips, and tickets for Valor in the Pacific National Monument, Polynesian Cultural Center and Doris Duke's Shangri La.
- **One week before** Make reservations for any top restaurants where you hope to dine, especially in Waikiki and Honolulu.

Your Daily Budget

Budget (less than $150)

- Waikiki hostel: $25–35
- Walk to the beach
- Buses and a taxi or two to get around
- Mostly self-catering and plate lunches, occasional evening meal or drinks out

Midrange ($150–350)

- Waikiki budget hotel or Kailua vacation rental: $90–160
- Car rental for a couple of days
- Activities like surfing or stand-up paddling
- Restaurant meals as well as food-truck fare

Top End over ($350)

- Full-service resort room
- Top chef-made meals
- Whale-watching tours, activity rentals, spa services

Exchange Rates

Australia	A$1	US$1.06
Canada	C$1	US$1.01
Europe	€1	US$1.32
Japan	¥100	US$1.20
New Zealand	NZ$1	US$0.82
UK	£1	US$1.59

For current exchange rates see www.xe.com

What to Bring

- **Light, waterproof jacket** For tropical windward showers and wind-whipped, cloud-shrouded *pali* (cliffs or mountains).
- **Shoes with traction** When trails get muddy, flip-flops (thongs) just don't cut it.
- **Dive certification** Bring card and logbooks if you're going to take the plunge. Snorkel sets are easily rented or borrowed.
- **Sunglasses and sunscreen** Come on, you know you'll be spending time at the beach.
- **Aloha spirit** This is the islands, man. Slow down and hang loose.

Arriving on O'ahu

- **Honolulu International Airport (HNL)**

Airport shuttle To Waikiki $12, to Kailua $40, to Hale'iwa $80

Taxi To Waikiki $35 to $45, 25 to 45 minutes

Car Via Hwy 92 (Nimitz Fwy/Ala Moana Blvd) to Waikiki

Bus Routes 19 and 20 to Waikiki (one carry-on bag only per person) $2.50, 45 to 80 minutes

Getting Around

- **Car** Consider skipping the car if you're staying in Waikiki, otherwise a rental is almost required ($35 to $60 per day).
- **Bus** More than 100 routes, but not always convenient. Some popular parks and sights are beyond reach. Circle Isle buses (52 and 55) circumnavigate O'ahu.
- **Bicycle** Not practical for islandwide travel; recommended for getting around the North Shore and in Kailua on the Windward Coast.

Accommodation

- **Hotels and condos** Mostly available in Waikiki, also a few in Honolulu. Price depends on location, view and room size.
- **Vacation rentals and B&Bs** This is where you'll be staying if you leave the city behind. Expect full kitchens and beach gear, but no hot breakfasts are included.
- **Resorts** Outside Waikiki, the only resorts are at Ko Olina in leeward O'ahu and on the North Shore at Turtle Bay.

Be Forewarned

- **Swimming in wild, non-regulated waterfalls** Hazards include falling rocks and leptospirosis.
- **Car break-ins** Absolutely do not leave anything visible in a rental car. Car break-ins are common. Hiding things in the trunk is only effective if you do so before getting to your parking spot.
- **Beaches** Do not leave valuables on the beach while you swim; slippers and towels are usually left alone.

Honolulu

Here in Honolulu, away from the crowded haunts of Waikiki, you get to shake hands with the real Hawaii. A boisterous Polynesian capital, Honolulu delivers an island-style mixed plate of experiences. Eat your way through the pan-Asian alleys of Chinatown, where 19th-century whalers once brawled and immigrant traders thrived.

Gaze out to sea atop the landmark Aloha Tower, then sashay past Victorian-era brick buildings, including the USA's only royal palace. Ocean breezes rustle palm trees along the harborfront, while in the cool, mist-shrouded Ko'olau Range, forested hiking trails offer postcard city views.

At sunset, cool off with an amble around Magic Island or splash in the ocean at Ala Moana Beach, a rare beauty in the middle of the concrete jungle. After dark, migrate to Chinatown's edgy art and nightlife scene. You won't even miss Waikiki, promise.

'Iolani Palace, Hawaii's official royal residence until 1893 (p37) **33**

Honolulu Itineraries

One Day

1 **'Iolani Palace** (p37) Start your journey through time at this brightly restored 19th-century royal palace, today also a protest symbol for Native Hawaiian sovereignty activists.

2 **Mission Houses Museum** (p39) Tour Hawaii's first Protestant settlement, which set off a tidal wave of arrivals across the islands throughout the 19th century.

3 **Kawaiaha'o Church** (p40) A solid, imposing, Gothic-style church made of priceless coral rock signaled that O'ahu's missionaries were here to stay. Keep your eyes open for royal and colonial ghosts in the cemetery out back.

4 **Hawai'i State Art Museum** (p39) Sate your artistic side with visions of Hawaii's multicultural society and heritage, from abstract paintings and landscape photographs to mixed-media and found-art collages. Then stop downstairs for a gourmet island plate lunch at **Downtown**.

5 **Chinatown** (p43) Poke around fragrant lei stands and animated open-air markets, or join the locals for lunch at a pan-Asian kitchen. Afterward hound the galleries and antiques stores, or meditatively visit traditional incense-burning temples and the botanic garden.

6 **Aloha Tower** (p41) Stroll over to the harborfront and take the elevator straight up this art-deco landmark, which welcomed every visitor landing on O'ahu before the jet age arrived in 1935. Grab sunset drinks with ocean views or listen to live Hawaiian music at **Chai's Island Bistro**.

➡ THIS LEG: 2 MILES

Three Days

1 Bishop Museum (p54) At this first-rate Polynesian anthropological museum, marvel at ancient Hawaiian artifacts such as *kahili* (royal staffs) and King Kamehameha's feathered cape. Kids can go nuts in the interactive science hall.

2 Helena's Hawaiian Food (p76) Get a taste of Native Hawaiian and infused immigrant food traditions at this storefront kitchen, where you can custom-order your own mini luau plate for a picnic.

3 Lyon Arboretum (p52) Take a walk on the wild side (literally – the walking paths are mostly unmanicured) at this verdant tropical reserve, with a hidden waterfall at the back.

4 Manoa Falls (p58) Although the Tantalus–Round Top scenic drive looks tempting, Honolulu's memorable skyline views are best earned with your own two feet, so pull on those hiking shoes.

5 Honolulu Museum of Arts (p49) The next morning, visit downtown's most prestigious art museum, which also sponsors film screenings and leads tours of **Shangri La**. Fork into market-fresh fare at the courtyard cafe.

6 Ward Warehouse (p84) Stock up on island-made souvenirs, arts and crafts, and Hawaiiana books and music.

7 Ala Moana Regional Park (p36) Swim laps or simply laze on the golden sands, then wander **Magic Island** at sunset.

8 Ala Moana Center (p85) Head upstairs to the boisterous **Mai Tai Bar** for live island-style music. Nearby streets are filled with under-the-tourist-radar chowhound haunts for dinner and late-night drinks.

● THIS LEG: 15 MILES

Honolulu Highlights

1 Best Beach: Ala Moana Regional Park (p36) Wide, sandy beach where Honolulu residents go for swimming, surfing, beach volleyball and picnicking.

2 Best Museum: Bishop Museum (p54) Visit the three-story Hawaiian Hall full of royal artifacts, then catch a kid-friendly planetarium show.

3 Best Hike: Manoa Falls (p58) Take the whole family on this cool, shady upland forest hike in Makiki Valley.

4 Best Nightlife: Chinatown (p81) Ground zero for Honolulu's art, club and hipster scenes.

5 Best Shop: Native Books/Nā Mea Hawai'i (p84) This inspiring independent bookstore and made-in-Hawaii souvenir shop is also a community gathering spot.

Manoa Falls
DOUGLAS PEEBLES/CORBIS ©

Discover Honolulu

History

In 1793 the English frigate *Butterworth* became the first foreign ship to sail into what is now Honolulu Harbor. In 1809 Kamehameha the Great moved his royal court from Waikiki to Honolulu ('sheltered bay') to control the vigorous international trade taking place there, but it didn't replace Lahaina on Maui as the official capital of the Kingdom of Hawai'i until 1845.

In the 1820s Honolulu's first bars and brothels opened to crews of whaling ships. Hotel St, a lineup of bars and strip joints a few blocks from the harbor, became the city's red-light district. Christian missionaries began arriving around the same time, presumably for different purposes. Today, Hawaii's first missionary church still stands just a stone's throw from the royal palace.

In 1893 a small group of citizens, mostly of American missionary descent, seized control of the kingdom from Queen Lili'uokalani and declared an independent republic, imprisoning the queen in downtown Honolulu's 'Iolani Palace. After political machinations and backroom deals that reached Washington DC, Hawaii was formally annexed by the USA in 1898. For more about O'ahu's history, see p266.

Beaches

ALA MOANA REGIONAL PARK   Beach

(Map p70; 1201 Ala Moana Blvd; P)
Opposite the Ala Moana Center shopping mall, this city park is fronted by a broad, golden-sand beach, nearly a mile long and buffered from passing traffic noise by statuesque shade trees. Swimmers should be aware that at low tide the deep channel that runs the length of the beach can be a hazard – formerly a boat channel, it drops off suddenly to overhead depths. Ala Moana is hugely popular, yet big enough that it never feels too crowded. This is where Honolulu residents come to go running after work, play beach volleyball and enjoy weekend picnics. The park has full facilities, including lighted tennis

Statue of King Kamehameha the Great (p41)
JOHN BORTHWICK/LONELY PLANET IMAGES ©

courts, ball fields, picnic tables, drinking water, restrooms, outdoor showers and lifeguard towers.

The peninsula jutting from the southeast side of the park is **Magic Island**. High school outrigger-canoe teams practice here in the late afternoon when school's in session. In summer it's a hot surf break. Year-round, you can take an idyllic sunset walk around the peninsula's perimeter, within an anchor's toss of sailboats pulling in and out of neighboring Ala Wai Yacht Harbor.

KAKA'AKO WATERFRONT PARK Beach
(off Map p70; www.hawaiistateparks.org; end of Ohe or Kolua Sts, off Ala Moana Blvd; P) Near downtown, little Kaka'ako feels far away from the urban jungle. Built over a former landfill, this grassy, hilly park attracts experienced surfers in the morning and picnickers in the afternoon. Inline skaters roll along the rock-fringed promenade, offering clear views of Diamond Head and Honolulu Harbor. It's not a safe swimming beach, but **Point Panic** is a killer body-surfing break. Other tricky breaks let you watch expert board surfers up close. Limited facilities include restrooms, drinking water and picnic tables. Buses 19, 20, 42 and E CountryExpress! each stop about a half-mile walk from the waterfront park.

 Sights

Honolulu's compact downtown is just a lei's throw from the harborfront. Nearby, the buzzing streets of Chinatown are packed with food markets, antiques shops, art galleries and hip bars. Between downtown and Waikiki, Ala Moana has Hawaii's biggest mall and the city's best beach. The University of Hawai'i campus is a gateway to the Manoa Valley and the Mt Tantalus green belt. A few outlying sights, including the Bishop Museum, are worth a detour.

The tourist epicenter of Waikiki is officially contained within the boundaries of Honolulu but is covered in its own comprehensive chapter (see p94).

Downtown

This area was center stage for the political intrigue and social upheavals that changed the fabric of Hawaii during the 19th century. Major players ruled here, revolted here, worshipped here and still rest, however restlessly, in the graveyards. Today, stately Victorian-era buildings are reflected in the black glass of modern urban high-rises.

TOP CHOICE **'IOLANI PALACE** Palace
(Map p46; info 538-1471, tour reservations 522-0832/23; www.iolanipalace.org; 364 S King St; grounds admission free, adult/child 5-12yr guided tour $20/5, self-guided audio tour $12/5, basement galleries $7/3; 9am-4pm Mon-Sat, guided tours every 15min 9-10am Tue & Thu, 9-11:15am Wed, Fri & Sat, self-guided tours every 10min 9am-4pm Mon, 10:30am-4pm Tue & Thu, noon-4pm Wed, Fri & Sat) No other place evokes a more poignant sense of Hawaii's history. The regal palace was built under King David Kalakaua in 1882. At that time, the Hawaiian monarchy observed many of the diplomatic protocols of the Victorian world. The king traveled abroad meeting with leaders around the globe and received foreign emissaries here. Although the palace was modern and opulent for its time, it did little to assert Hawaii's sovereignty over powerful US-influenced business interests, who overthrew the kingdom in 1893.

Two years after the coup, the former queen, Lili'uokalani, who had succeeded her brother David to the throne, was convicted of treason and spent nine months imprisoned in her former home. Later the palace served as the capitol of the republic, then the territory and later the state of Hawaii. In 1969 the government finally moved into the current state capitol, leaving 'Iolani Palace a shambles. After a decade of painstaking renovations, the restored palace reopened as a museum, although many original royal artifacts had been lost or stolen before work even began.

Visitors must take a docent-led or self-guided tour (no children under age five) to see 'Iolani's grand interior, including re-creations of the throne room

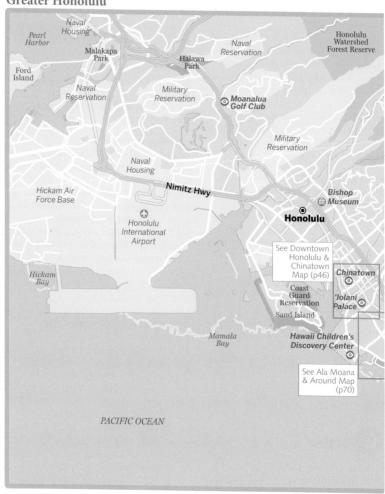

and residential quarters upstairs. The palace was quite modern by Victorian-era standards. Every bedroom had its own bathroom with flush toilets and hot running water, and electric lights replaced the gas lamps years before the White House in Washington, DC, installed electricity. If you're short on time, you can independently browse the historical exhibits in the basement, including royal regalia, historical photographs and reconstructions of the kitchen and chamberlain's office.

The palace grounds are open during daylight hours and are free of charge. The former **barracks** of the Royal Household Guards, a building that looks oddly like the uppermost layer of a medieval fort, now houses the ticket booth. Nearby, a domed **pavilion**, originally built for the coronation of King Kalakaua in 1883, is still used for state governor inaugurations. Underneath the huge **banyan tree**, allegedly planted by Queen Kapi'olani, the **Royal Hawaiian Band**

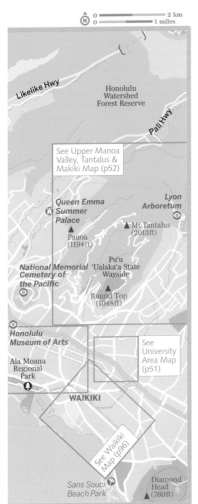

art museum brings together traditional and contemporary art from Hawaii's multiethnic communities. The bite-sized museum inhabits a grand 1928 Spanish Mission Revival–style building, formerly a YMCA and today a nationally registered historic site. Upstairs, revolving exhibits of paintings, sculptures, fiber art, photography and mixed media are displayed around themes, such as the island's Polynesian heritage, modern social issues or the natural beauty of land and sea. Hawaii's complex confluence of Asian, Pacific Rim and European cultures is evident throughout, shaping an aesthetic that captures the soul of the islands and the hearts of the people. Drop by at noon on the last Tuesday of the month for free 'Art Lunch' lectures or between 11am and 3pm on the second Saturday for hands-on Hawaiian arts and crafts, often designed with kids in mind.

MISSION HOUSES MUSEUM Museum
(Map p46; ☏447-3910; www.missionhouses.org; 553 S King St; grounds admission free, 1hr guided tour adult/child 6-18yr & college student with ID $10/6; ☺10am-4pm Tue-Sat, tours usually 11am, noon, 1pm, 2pm & 3pm) Occupying the original headquarters of the Sandwich Islands mission that forever changed the course of Hawaiian history, this modest museum is authentically furnished with handmade quilts on the beds and iron cooking pots in the stone fireplaces. You'll need to take a guided tour to peek inside any of the buildings.

Walking around the grounds, you'll notice that the first missionaries packed more than their bags when they left Boston – they brought a prefabricated wooden house, called the **Frame House**, with them around the Horn. Designed to withstand New England winter winds, the small windows instead blocked out Honolulu's cooling tradewinds, which kept the two-story house hellaciously hot and stuffy. Erected in 1821, it's the oldest wooden structure in Hawaii.

The 1831 coral-block **Chamberlain House** was the early mission's storeroom, a necessity because Honolulu had few shops in those days. Upstairs are hoop

gives free concerts on most Fridays from noon to 1pm, weather permitting.

Call ahead to confirm tour schedules and reserve tickets in advance during peak periods.

FREE HAWAI'I STATE ART MUSEUM Museum
(Map p46; ☏586-0900; http://hawaii.gov/ sfca/HiSAM.html; 2nd fl, No 1 Capitol District Bldg, 250 S Hotel St; ☺10am-4pm Tue-Sat, 5-9pm 1st Fri of the month) With its vibrant, thought-provoking collections, this public

barrels, wooden crates packed with dishes, and the desk and quill pen of Levi Chamberlain. He was appointed by the mission to buy, store and dole out supplies to missionary families, who survived on a meager allowance – as the account books on his desk testify.

Nearby, the 1841 **Printing Office** houses a lead-type press used to print the first bible in the Hawaiian language.

FREE KAWAIAHA'O CHURCH Church

(Map p46; www.kawaiahao.org; 957 Punchbowl St; ⏱usually 8am-4pm daily, worship service 9am Sun) Nicknamed 'Westminster Abbey of the Pacific,' O'ahu's oldest church was built on the site where the first missionaries constructed a grass thatch church shortly after their arrival in 1820. The original structure seated 300 Hawaiians on *lauhala* mats, woven from hala (screwpine) leaves.

This 1842 New England Gothic–style church is made of 14,000 coral slabs, which divers chiseled out of O'ahu's underwater reefs – a weighty task that took four years. The clock tower was donated by Kamehameha III, and the old clock, installed in 1850, still keeps accurate time. The rear seats of the church, marked by *kahili* (feather staffs) and velvet padding, are reserved for royal descendants today.

The **tomb of King Lunalilo**, the short-lived successor to Kamehameha V, is found at the main entrance to the church grounds. The **cemetery** to the rear of the church is almost like a who's who of colonial history: early Protestant missionaries are buried alongside other important figures, including infamous Sanford Dole, who became the first territorial governor of Hawai'i after Queen Lili'uokalani was overthrown.

FREE ALI'IOLANI HALE Historic Building

(Map p46; www.jhchawaii.net; 417 S King St; ⏱8am-4pm Mon-Fri) The first major government building ordered by the Hawaiian monarchy in 1874, the 'House of Heavenly Kings' was designed by Australian architect Thomas Rowe to be a royal palace, although it was never used as such. Today, this dignified Italianate structure houses the Supreme Court of Hawai'i. Go through the security checkpoint at the main entrance on the ground floor

Chinatown Cultural Plaza (p45)

JON HICKS/CORBIS ©

Island Insights

You may notice that Hawaii's state flag is quartered, with the Union Jack in the top left corner next to the flagpole (you can see one in downtown Honolulu's historic capitol district). But Hawaii was never part of the UK. Kamehameha the Great simply thought the Union Jack would add an element of regal splendor to Hawaii's flag, so he took the liberty of adding it. The flag's eight horizontal red, white and blue stripes represent the eight main islands. Today Native Hawaiian sovereignty activists often choose to fly the state flag upside down, a time-honored symbol of distress.

and step inside the **King Kamehameha V Judiciary History Center**, where you can plop yourself into the judge's chair inside a restored 1913 courtroom, then browse thought-provoking historical displays about martial law during WWII and the reign of Kamehameha I.

Out front, a bronze **statue of Kamehameha the Great** faces 'Iolani Palace. Often ceremonially draped with layers of flower lei, the statue was cast in 1880 in Florence, Italy, by American sculptor Thomas Gould. The current statue is a recast, as the first statue was lost at sea near the Falkland Islands. It was dedicated here in 1883, just a decade before the Hawaiian monarchy would be overthrown. The original statue, which was later recovered from the ocean floor, now stands in Kohala on the Big Island of Hawai'i, where Kamehameha I was born.

FREE **STATE CAPITOL**   Notable Building
(Map p46; ☎586-0178; 415 S Beretania St; ⏰8am-4:30pm Mon-Fri) Built in the architecturally interesting 1960s, Hawaii's state capitol is not your standard gold dome. It's a poster child of conceptual post-modernism: two cone-shaped legislative chambers have sloping walls to represent volcanoes; the supporting columns shaped like coconut palms symbolize the eight main islands; and a large encircling pool represents the Pacific Ocean surrounding Hawaii. Visitors are free to walk through the breezy, open-air rotunda and peer through viewing windows into the

legislative chambers. Pick up a self-guided tour brochure on the 4th floor from Room 415.

In front of the capitol is a highly stylized **statue of Father Damien**, the Belgian priest who lived and worked with victims of Hansen's disease who were exiled to the island of Moloka'i during the late 19th century, before later dying of the disease himself. In 2009, the Catholic Church canonized Father Damien as Hawaii's first saint after the allegedly miraculous recovery from cancer in 1988 of a Honolulu schoolteacher who had prayed over Damien's original grave site on Moloka'i.

Pointedly positioned between the capitol and 'Iolani Palace is a life-size bronze **statue of Queen Lili'uokalani**, Hawaii's last reigning monarch. She holds a copy of the Hawaiian constitution she wrote in 1893 in an attempt to strengthen Hawaiian rule; 'Aloha 'Oe,' a popular song she composed; and 'Kumulipo,' the traditional Hawaiian chant of creation.

FREE **ALOHA TOWER**   Landmark, Lookout
(Map p46; www.alohatower.com; 1 Aloha Tower Dr; ⏰9:30am-5pm; P) Built in 1926, this 10-story landmark at Pier 9 was once the city's tallest building. In the golden days when all tourists to Hawaii arrived by ship, this pre-WWII waterfront icon – with its four-sided clock tower inscribed with 'Aloha' – greeted every visitor. These days hulking cruise ships still disembark at the

terminal beneath the tower. Take the elevator to the top-floor tower observation deck for 360-degree views of Honolulu and the waterfront, then peek inside the cruise-ship terminal to see colorful nostalgic murals depicting bygone Honolulu. Self-parking costs $3 (weekends or after 4pm $5).

FREE **HONOLULU MUSEUM OF ARTS AT FIRST HAWAIIAN CENTER**   Art Gallery
(Map p46; www.honoluluacademy.org; 999 Bishop St; ⏰8:30am-4:30pm Mon-Thu, to 6pm Fri) First Hawaiian Bank's high-rise headquarters also houses the downtown gallery of **Spalding House** (p52), featuring fascinating mixed-media exhibits of modern and contemporary works by artists from around Hawaii. Even the building itself features a four-story-high art-glass wall incorporating 185 prisms. Free guided gallery tours typically meet at noon on the first Friday of the month while exhibitions are being held.

WASHINGTON PLACE   Historic Building
(Map p46; ☎586-0248; http://hawaii.gov/gov/about/washington-place; 320 S Beretania St; donations welcome; ⏰tours by appointment only Mon-Fri) Formerly the governor's official residence, this colonial-style mansion was built in 1846 by US sea captain John Dominis. The captain's son became the governor of O'ahu and married the Hawaiian princess who later became Queen Lili'uokalani. After the queen was released from house arrest inside 'Iolani Palace in 1896, she lived here until her death in 1917. A plaque near the sidewalk is inscribed with the lyrics to 'Aloha 'Oe,' the patriotic anthem she composed. For tours, call at least 48 hours in advance and bring photo ID. Visitors may not carry anything larger than a purse onto the property, now a national historic landmark. Photography is not allowed inside the house.

FREE **ST ANDREW'S CATHEDRAL**   Church
(Map p46; ☎524-2822; www.saintandrewscathedral.net; Queen Emma Sq; ⏰usually 9am-5pm

daily, tours usually 11:50am Sun)
King Kamehameha IV, attracted by the royal Church of England, decided to build his own cathedral in Hawaii. Friends with Queen Victoria, he and his consort, Queen Emma, founded the Anglican Church in Hawaii in 1861. The cathedral's cornerstone was laid in 1867, four years after the death of the king, who died on St Andrew's Day – hence the church's name. The architecture is French Gothic, utilizing stone and stained glass shipped from England. Historical tours usually meet by the pulpit after the 10:30am worship service on Sunday, but call ahead to confirm. For a free lunchtime concert, the largest pipe organ in the Pacific is sonorously played every Wednesday starting at 12:15pm.

Chinatown

The location of this mercantile district is no accident. Between Honolulu's busy trading port and what was once the countryside, enterprises selling goods to city folks and visiting ship's crews sprang up in the 19th century. Many of these shops were established by Chinese laborers who had completed their sugarcane-plantation contracts. The most successful entrepreneurial families have long since moved out of this low-rent district to wealthier suburbs, making room for newer waves of immigrants, mostly from southeast Asia.

The scent of burning incense still wafts through Chinatown's buzzing markets, fire-breathing dragons spiral up the columns of buildings and steaming dim sum awakens even the sleepiest of appetites. Take time to explore: wander through nouveau art galleries and antiques stores, consult with a herbalist, rub shoulders with locals over a bowl of noodles, buy a lei and take a meditative botanic garden stroll.

Island Insights

The tradition of giving lei to visitors to O'ahu dates to the 19th-century steamships that first brought tourists. In the heyday of cruise-ship tourism, passengers were greeted by local vendors who would toss garlands around the necks of *malihini* (newcomers, or foreigners). It was believed that if passengers threw their lei into the sea as their departing ship passed Diamond Head, and the flowers of the lei floated back toward the beach, they'd be guaranteed to return to Hawaii someday.

TOP CHOICE CHINATOWN MARKETS   Market

(Map p46; www.chinatownhi.com) The commercial heart of Chinatown revolves around its markets and food shops. Noodle factories, pastry shops and produce stalls line the narrow sidewalks, always crowded with cart-pushing grandmothers and errand-running families. An institution since 1904, the **O'ahu Market** (145 N King St) sells everything a Chinese cook needs: ginger root, fresh octopus, quail eggs, jasmine rice, slabs of tuna, long beans and salted jellyfish. You owe yourself a bubble tea if you spot a pig's head among the stalls. At the start of the nearby pedestrian mall is the newer, but equally vibrant, **Kekaulike Market** (Kekaulike St, btwn King & Hotel Sts). At the top end of the pedestrian mall is **Maunakea Marketplace** (1120 Maunakea St), with its popular **food court** (p69).

FOSTER BOTANICAL GARDEN   Garden

(Map p46; ☎522-7066; www.co.honolulu. hi.us/parks/hbg/fbg.htm; 50 N Vineyard Blvd; adult/child 6-12yr $5/1; ☺9am-4pm daily, guided tours usually 1pm Mon-Sat; P) Tropical plants you've only ever read about can be spotted in all their glory at this botanic garden, which took root in 1850. Among its rarest specimens are the Hawaiian *loulu* palm and the East African *Gigasiphon macrosiphon*, both thought to be extinct in the wild. Several of the garden's towering trees are the largest of their kind in the USA. Oddities include the cannonball tree, the sausage tree and the double coconut palm capable of producing a 50lb nut – watch your head! Follow your nose past fragrant vanilla vines and cinnamon trees in the spice and herb gardens, then pick your way among the poisonous and dye plants. Don't miss the blooming orchids. A free self-guided tour booklet is available at the garden entrance.

HAWAII THEATRE   Historic Building

(Map p46; ☎528-0506; www.hawaiitheatre. com; 1130 Bethel St; tours $10; ☺tours usually 11am Tue) This neoclassical landmark first opened in 1922, when silent films were played to the tunes of a pipe organ. Dubbed the 'Pride of the Pacific', the theatre ran continuous shows during WWII, but the development of Waikiki cinemas in the 1960s and '70s finally brought down the curtain. After multi-million-dollar restorations, this nationally registered historic site held its grand reopening in 1996. To peek at its trompe-l'oeil mosaics and bas-relief scenes of Shakespearean plays, take a one-hour guided tour, which offer insights about the theater's history and architecture, and a demonstration of its lauded pipe organ. Call ahead to confirm tour availability.

FREE KUAN YIN TEMPLE   Temple

(Map p46; 170 N Vineyard Blvd; ☺usually 7am-2pm) With its green ceramic-tile roof and bright red columns, this ornate Chinese Buddhist temple is Honolulu's oldest. The richly carved interior is filled with the sweet, pervasive smell of burning incense. The temple is dedicated to Kuan Yin, bodhisattva of mercy, whose statue is the largest in the interior prayer hall. Devotees burn paper 'money' for prosperity and good luck, while offerings of fresh flowers and fruit are placed at the altar. The large citrus fruit stacked pyramid-style is pomelo, a symbol of fertility because of its many seeds. Respectful visitors welcome.

CHINATOWN CULTURAL PLAZA
Mall

(Map p46; cnr Maunakea & N Beretania Sts; ⏰24hr) Inside this utilitarian modern mall, covering almost an entire city block, traditional acupuncturists, tailors and calligraphers work alongside travel agencies and dim-sum halls. In the small open-air central courtyard, elderly Chinese light incense before a **statue of Kuan Yin**. Down by the riverside, a **bronze statue of Chinese revolutionary Dr Sun Yat-sen** stands guard while senior citizens practice tai chi after dawn and play checkers and mah-jongg all afternoon long.

FREE IZUMO TAISHA
Shrine

(Map p46; 215 N Kukui St; ⏰8am-5pm) Across the river, this Shintō shrine was built by Japanese immigrants in 1906. It was confiscated during WWII by the city and wasn't returned to the community until the early 1960s. The 100lb sacks of rice that sit near the altar symbolize good health. Ringing the bell at the shrine entrance is considered an act of purification for those who come to pray. Thousands of good-luck amulets are sold here, especially on January 1, when the temple heaves with people from all around O'ahu who come seeking New Year's blessings.

LUM SAI HO TONG
Temple

(Map p46; 1315 River St) Founded in 1899, the Lum Sai Ho Tong Society was one of more than 100 societies started by Chinese immigrants in Hawaii to help preserve their cultural identity. This one was for the Lum clan hailing from west of the Yellow River. The society's Taoist temple honors the goddess Tin Hau, a legendary child who rescued her father from drowning and was later deified. Some claim to see her apparition when they travel by boat.

What makes Honolulu's Chinatown unique? It's a multicultural Chinatown. The sights, sounds and smells, even the architecture of the buildings, are a unique East-West blend. It's still gritty but has an authenticity that rings true.

How did the arts scene evolve in Chinatown? The area had been in decline since the 1940s, when the sailors left. The Hawaii Theatre (p44), now beautifully restored, was a porn movie house, with drug dealers on the corners. In the 1980s, pioneers like the Pegge Hopper Gallery (p83) arrived. Then we [Arts at Marks Garage; p83] came in and started attracting an audience, with artists having their show openings here.

What's your mission? We're trying to be an authentic counter-balance to Waikiki by dedicating shows, exhibits and performances to contemporary Hawaiian cultural life perspectives. It's all about building a homegrown arts ecosystem, being surrounded by small-scale, local businesses that attract artistic and creative types.

How can visitors connect with the Chinatown arts scene? First Friday (p81) is an awesome way to get initiated and see all the hot spots. Also check in on our artists' lofts (www.chinatownartistslofts.com), in a secret courtyard with a koi pond, tall palm trees and a brick building that survived the Chinatown fires of the early 1900s.

Any other neighborhood highlights? Morning in Chinatown is all about fresh fruits and veggies at the markets (p44), plus lei shops. Maunakea Marketplace (p65) has an amazing ethnic mix of food from a wild cross-section of immigrants to Hawaii.

Downtown Honolulu & Chinatown

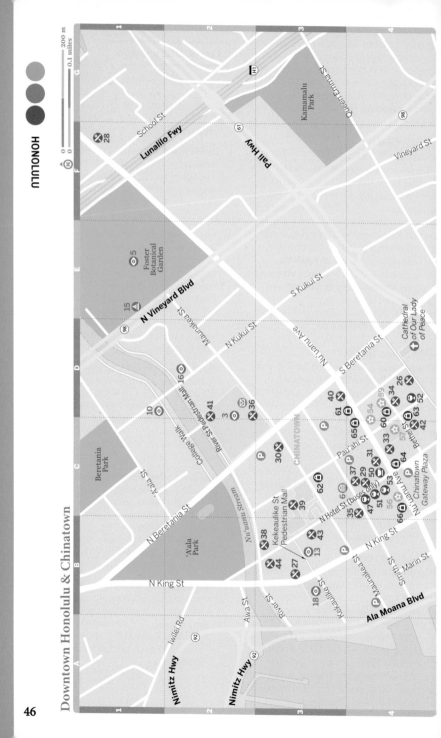

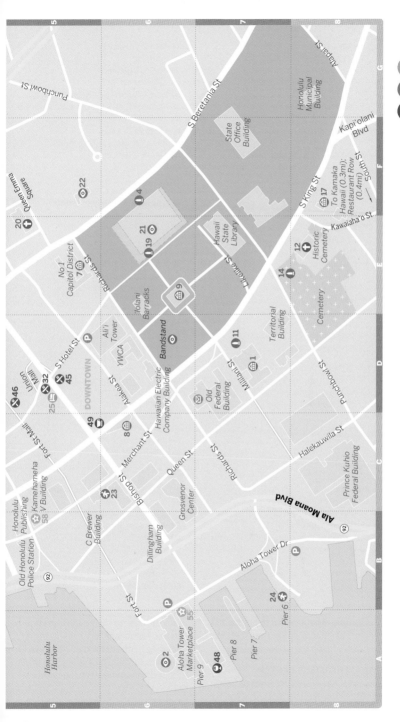

HONOLULU

Punchbowl St

Queen Emma Square

20 ✚

22 ◉

S Beretania St

State Office Building

Honolulu Municipal Building

Alapai St

Kapi'olani Blvd

S King St

To Kamaka Hawaii (0.3mi); Restaurant Row (0.4mi) South St

17 🏛

Kawaiaha'o St

4 ◗

21 ◉

19 ◗

No1 Capitol District

7 🏛

Richards St

'Iolani Barracks

Hawaii State Library

S Hotel St

Ali'i Tower

YWCA

Bandstand ◉

Theatre St

9 🏛

12 ✚ Historic Cemetery

14 ◗

Cemetery

P

DOWNTOWN

Union Mall

25 ✖

32 ✖

45

49 ◗

8 🏛

Alakea St

Hawaiian Electric Company Building

Merchant St

Old Federal Building

Milliani St

11 ◗

Territorial Building

1 🏛

Punchbowl St

46 ✖

Fort St Mall

Honolulu Publishing

Kamehameha V Building

58 ★

23 ✚

Bishop St

Queen St

Richards St

Grosvenor Center

Halekauwila St

Prince Kuhio Federal Building

Old Honolulu Police Station ⊗

C Brewer Building

Dillingham Building

Ala Moana Blvd

⊗

Fort St

P

Aloha Tower Dr

P

2 ◉

Aloha Tower Marketplace

55 ★

48 ◗

Pier 9

Pier 8

Pier 7

24 ✚

Pier 6

Honolulu Harbor

Honolulu Harbor

Downtown Honolulu & Chinatown

The temple is not open to the general public, but you can still admire the colorful exterior from the sidewalk below.

HAWAI'I HERITAGE CENTER Museum
(Map p46; ☎521-2749; 1040 Smith St; admission $1; ⏰9am-2pm Mon-Sat) Local volunteers with family ties to the community run this friendly gallery that displays changing historical and cultural exhibitions about O'ahu's Chinese and other ethnic communities. For the center's guided historical walking tours of Chinatown, see p61.

Ala Moana & Around

Ala Moana means 'Path to the Sea' and its namesake road, Ala Moana Blvd (Hwy 92), connects the coast between Waikiki and Honolulu. Although most people think of Ala Moana only for its shopping malls, **Ala Moana Regional Park** (p36), which happens to be O'ahu's biggest beach park, makes a relaxing alternative to crowded Waikiki.

TOP CHOICE HONOLULU MUSEUM OF ARTS
Museum

(Map p70; ☏ 532-8700; www.honoluluacademy.org; 900 S Beretania St; adult/child 4-17yr $10/5, 1st Wed & 3rd Sun of the month free; ☺10am-4:30pm Tue-Sat, 1-5pm Sun, also 6-9pm last Fri of the month; P ♿) This exceptional fine-arts museum may be the biggest surprise of your trip to O'ahu. The museum, dating to 1927, has a classical facade that's invitingly open and airy, with galleries branching off a series of garden and water-fountain courtyards. Stunningly beautiful exhibits reflect the various cultures that make up contemporary Hawaii, include one of the country's finest Asian art collections, featuring everything from Japanese woodblock prints by Hiroshige and Ming dynasty–era Chinese calligraphy and painted scrolls to temple carvings and statues from Cambodia and India. Another highlight is the striking contemporary wing with Hawaiian works on its upper level, and modern art by such luminaries as Henri Matisse and Georgia O'Keeffe below. Although the collections aren't nearly as extensive as at Honolulu's Bishop Museum, you can still be bewitched by the Pacific and Polynesian artifacts, such as ceremonial masks, war clubs and bodily adornments.

Plan on spending a couple of hours at the museum, possibly combining a visit with lunch at the **Honolulu Museum of Arts Cafe** (p73) or a tour of **Shangri La** (p156), Doris Duke's enchanting estate. Admission tickets are also valid for same-day visits to **Spalding House** (p53). Check the museum website for upcoming special events, including gallery tours and art lectures; film screenings (p84) and music concerts (p83) at the **Doris Duke Theatre**; **ARTafterDARK (www.artafterdark.org)** parties with food, drinks and live entertainment on the last Friday of some

Courtyard ceramics display at the Honolulu Museum of Arts

months; and family-friendly arts and cultural programs on the third Sunday of every month.

Four-hour validated parking at the Museum of Arts Center at Linekona lot, diagonally opposite the museum at 1111 Victoria St (enter off Beretania or Young Sts), costs $3 (flat rate after 4pm $4). From Waikiki, take bus 2 or 13 or B CityExpress!.

University Area

In the foothills of Manoa Valley, the neighborhood surrounding the University of Hawai'i (UH) Manoa campus feels youthful, with a collection of cafes, eclectic restaurants and one-of-a-kind shops. You'll probably pass through here en route to the Manoa Falls trailhead and the university's Lyon Arboretum.

UNIVERSITY OF
HAWAI'I AT MANOA   University
(Map p51; 956-8111; www.uhm.hawaii.edu; 2500 Campus Rd; P) About 2 miles northeast of Waikiki, the main campus of the statewide university system was born too late to be weighed down by the tweedy academic architecture of the mainland. Today, its breezy, tree-shaded campus is crowded with students from islands throughout Polynesia. The university has strong programs in astronomy, oceanography and marine biology, as well as Hawaiian, Pacific and Asian studies.

Campus Center (956-7236; Room 212; usually 8:30am-4:30pm Mon-Fri) is your departure point for free one-hour **walking tours** of campus, emphasizing history and architecture. Tours usually leave at 2pm Monday, Wednesday and Friday; no reservations are necessary, but check in 10 minutes beforehand at the ticket, information and ID office upstairs. Ask for a free *Campus Art* brochure, which outlines a self-guided walking tour of outdoor sculptures and other works by notable Hawaii artists.

A short walk downhill, the **John Young Museum of Art** (956-3634; www.outreach. hawaii.edu/JYMuseum; Krauss Hall, 2500 Dole St; admission free; 11am-2pm Mon-Fri, 1-4pm Sun) features 20th-century Hawaii painter John Young's collection of artifacts from the Pacific islands, Africa and Asia, mostly ceramics, pottery and sculpture. Although it's just two rooms, it's worth a quick visit.

On the east side of campus, the **East-West Center** (944-7111; www. eastwestcenter.org; 1601 East-West Rd) aims to promote mutual understanding among the peoples of Asia, the Pacific and the US. Changing exhibitions of art and culture are displayed in the **EWC Gallery** (Burns Hall; admission free; usually 8am-5pm Mon-Fri, noon-4pm Sun). Spy the petite Japanese teahouse garden and royal Thai pavilion outside. The center regularly hosts multicultural programs,

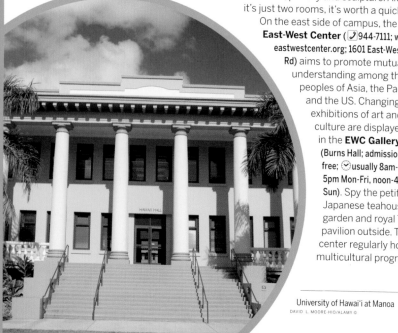

University of Hawai'i at Manoa
DAVID L. MOORE-HIO/ALAMY ©

University Area

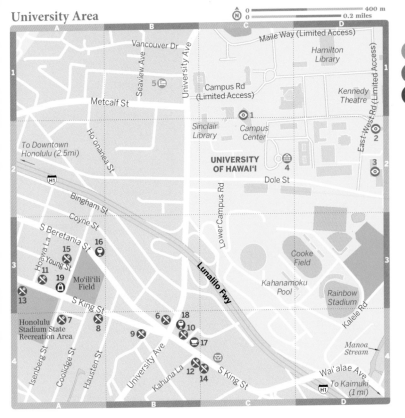

University Area

Upper Manoa Valley, Tantalus & Makiki

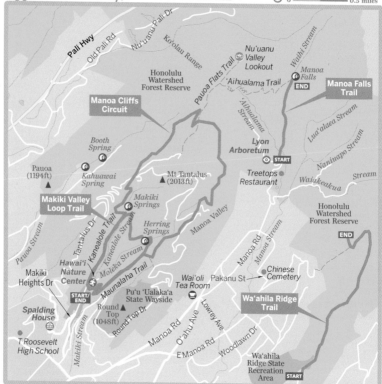

including lectures, films, concerts and dance performances.

On-campus parking costs $5 (before 4pm on weekdays $4). From Waikiki or downtown Honolulu, take bus 4; from Ala Moana, catch bus 6 or 18.

Upper Manoa Valley, Tantalus & Makiki

Welcome to Honolulu's green belt. Roads into the verdant upper Manoa Valley wind north of the UH Manoa campus, passing exclusive residential homes and entering forest reserve land in the hills above downtown's high-rises. It's a peaceful place to commune with nature, especially at the arboretum and on family-friendly hikes to Manoa Falls and along Wa'ahila Ridge (see p57).

Further west lies Makiki Heights, the neighborhood where President Barack Obama spent much of his boyhood. A narrow, switchbacking road cuts its way up into more forest reserve lands in the Makiki Valley above. Offering skyline views, this 10-mile **Tantalus–Round Top scenic drive** climbs almost to the top of Mt Tantalus (2013ft), passing swank homes along the way. Although the road is one continuous loop, the west side is called Tantalus Dr and the east side, Round Top Dr. Branching off the loop road is a network of hiking trails (see p57).

LYON ARBORETUM · Garden

(Map p52; ☎988-0456, tour reservations 988-0461; www.hawaii.edu/lyonarboretum; 3860 Manoa Rd; suggested donation $5, guided tour

$5; ◷8am-4pm Mon-Fri, 9am-3pm Sat, guided tours usually 10am Mon-Fri; P) Beautifully unkempt walking trails wind through this highly regarded 200-acre arboretum managed by the University of Hawai'i. It was originally founded in 1918 by a group of sugar planters looking to experiment with growing native and exotic flora species to restore Honolulu's watershed and test their economic benefit. This is not your typical overly manicured tropical flower garden, but a mature and largely wooded arboretum, where related species cluster in a seminatural state. For a guided tour, call at least 24 hours in advance.

Key plants in the Hawaiian ethno-botanical garden are *'ulu* (breadfruit), *kalo* (taro) and *ko* (sugarcane) brought by early Polynesian settlers; *kukui,* once harvested to produce lantern oil; and *ti,* which was used for medicinal purposes during ancient times and for making moonshine after Westerners arrived. It's a short walk to Inspiration Point, or keep walking uphill for about 1 mile along a jeep road, then a narrow, tree root–ridden path to visit seasonal 'Aihualama Falls, a lacy cliff-side cascade (no swimming, sorry!).

From Ala Moana Center, catch bus 5 toward Manoa Valley and get off at the last stop, then walk about half a mile uphill to the end of Manoa Rd. Limited free parking is available.

SPALDING HOUSE
Museum
(TCM; ☎526-0232; www.honoluluacademy.org; 2411 Makiki Heights Dr; adult/child 4-17yr $10/5, 1st Wed of the month free; ◷10am-4pm Tue-Sat, noon-4pm Sun; P) Embraced by tropical sculpture gardens, this art museum occupies an estate house constructed in 1925 for O'ahu-born Anna Rice Cooke, a missionary descendant and wealthy arts patron. Inside the main galleries are displayed changing exhibits of paintings, sculpture and other contemporary artwork from the 1940s through to today by international, national and island artists. A lawn pavilion holds the museum's most prized piece, an environmental installation by David Hockney based on sets for *L'Enfant et les Sortilèges,* Ravel's 1925 opera. Downstairs, a modest courtyard cafe serves light lunches, including romantic picnic baskets for two (reserve ahead by calling ☎523-3362).

Tickets are also valid for same-day admission to the **Honolulu Museum of Arts** (p49). From Waikiki, take bus 2, 13 or B CityExpress! toward downtown Honolulu and get off at the corner of Beretania and Alapa'i Sts; walk one block *makai* (seaward) along Alapa'i St and transfer to bus 15 bound for Pacific Heights, which stops outside Spalding House.

Lyon Arboretum

Mr Obama's Neighborhood

During the 2008 race to elect the 44th president of the United States, Republican vice-presidential candidate Sarah Palin kept asking the country, 'Who is Barack Obama?' It was Obama's wife, Michelle, who had an answer ready: 'You can't really understand Barack until you understand Hawaii.'

Obama, who grew up in Honolulu's Makiki Heights neighborhood, has written that 'Hawaii's spirit of tolerance...became an integral part of my world view, and a basis for the values I hold most dear.' The local media and many *kama'aina* (those who were born and grew up in Hawaii) agree that Hawaii's multiethnic social fabric helped shape the leader who created a rainbow coalition during the 2008 election.

Obama has also said Hawaii is a place for him to rest and recharge, as he has done with his family every winter after assuming office. Back in 1999 he wrote: 'When I'm heading out to a hard day of meetings and negotiations, I let my mind wander back to Sandy Beach, or Manoa Falls... It helps me, somehow, knowing that such wonderful places exist and I'll always be able to return to them.'

If you want to walk in Obama's boyhood and presidential footsteps on O'ahu, here are some places you can visit:

○ **Manoa Falls** (p57)

○ **Alan Wong's** (p69)

○ **Kapi'olani Beach Park** (p99)

○ **Rainbow Drive-In** (p125)

○ **Waiola Shave Ice** (p125)

○ **Hanauma Bay** (p162)

○ **Sandy Beach** (p166)

○ **National Memorial Cemetery of the Pacific** (p56)

○ **Nu'uanu Pali State Wayside** (p172)

○ **Olomana Golf Links** (p176)

MANOA HERITAGE CENTER
Temple, Garden

(988-1287; www.manoaheritagecenter.org; adult/child & student $7/free; ⊙tours by appointment only; P) Hidden on a private family's estate, the centerpiece of this unique site is a stone-walled agricultural heiau (temple) surrounded by Hawaiian ethnobotanical gardens, which include rare native and Polynesian introduction plants. Take your turn playing *konane* (a Hawaiian version of checkers), then follow the path downhill to learn how taro was traditionally farmed. Walking tours are led by volunteers and staff eager to share island lore and Hawaiian traditions. Try to call at least a week in advance for tour reservations and to get directions. No walk-ins can be accommodated, to protect both the historic site and the resident family's privacy.

Greater Honolulu

BISHOP MUSEUM
Museum

(Map p38; 847-3511; www.bishopmuseum. org; 1525 Bernice St; adult/child 4-12yr $18/15; ⊙9am-5pm Wed-Mon; P) Like Hawaii's version of the Smithsonian Institute in Washington, DC, the Bishop Museum showcases a remarkable array of cultural and natural history exhibits. It is often ranked as the finest Polynesian anthropological museum in the world. Founded in 1889 in honor of Princess Bernice Pauahi Bishop, a descendant of the Kamehameha dynasty, it originally housed only Hawaiian and royal artifacts.

The recently renovated main gallery, the **Hawaiian Hall**, resides inside a dignified three-story Victorian building. Displays covering the cultural history of Hawaii include a *pili* (grass) thatched house, carved *ki'i akua* (temple images), *kahili* (feathered royal staffs), shark-toothed war clubs and traditional tapa cloth made by pounding the bark of the paper mulberry tree. Don't miss the feathered cloak once worn by Kamehameha the Great, created entirely of the yellow feathers of the now-extinct *mamo* – some 80,000 birds were caught and plucked to create this single adornment. Meanwhile, upper-floor exhibits delve further into *ali'i* (royal) history, traditional daily life and relationships between Native Hawaiians and the natural world.

The fascinating two-story exhibits inside the adjacent **Polynesian Hall** cover the myriad cultures of Polynesia, Micronesia and Melanesia. You could spend hours gazing at astounding and rare ritual artifacts, from elaborate dance masks and ceremonial costumes to carved canoes. Next door, the **Castle Memorial Building** displays changing traveling exhibitions.

Across the Great Lawn, the eye-popping, state-of-the-art multisensory **Science Adventure Center** lets kids walk through an erupting volcano, take a minisubmarine dive and play with three floors of interactive multimedia

exhibits. The Bishop Museum is also home to O'ahu's only **planetarium**, which highlights traditional Polynesian methods of wayfaring (navigation), using wave patterns and the position of the stars to travel thousands of miles across the open ocean in traditional outrigger canoes, as well as modern astronomy and the cutting-edge telescope observatories atop Mauna Kea on the Big Island. Shows usually start at 11:30am, 1:30pm and 3:30pm daily except Tuesday, and are included in the museum admission price.

A **gift shop** off the main lobby sells books on the Pacific not easily found elsewhere, as well as some high-quality Hawaiian art, crafts and souvenirs. Check the museum website for special events, including popular 'Moonlight Mele' summer concerts, family-friendly Hawaiian cultural festivities and after-dark planetarium shows (buy tickets online or make reservations by calling ☎848-4168 in advance).

From Waikiki or downtown Honolulu, take bus 2 School St-Middle St or B CityExpress! to the intersection of School

Inside the Bishop Museum
MARC SCHECHTER/PHOTO RESOURCE HAWAII/ALAMY ©

St and Kapalama Ave; walk one block *makai* (seaward) on Kapalama Ave, then turn right onto Bernice St. By car, take eastbound H-1 Fwy exit 20, turn right on Houghtailing St, then take the second left onto Bernice St. Parking is free.

FREE **NATIONAL MEMORIAL CEMETERY OF THE PACIFIC** Cemetery
(Map p38; www.cem.va.gov/cems/nchp/nmcp. asp; 2177 Puowaina Dr; ⊙8am-5:30pm Sep 30-Mar 1, 8am-6:30pm Mar 2-Sep 29, 7am-7pm last Mon in May; P) About a mile northeast of downtown Honolulu and surrounded by freeways and residential neighborhoods is a bowl-shaped crater, nicknamed the Punchbowl, formed by a long-extinct volcano. Hawaiians called the crater Puowaina ('hill of human sacrifices'). It's believed that at an ancient heiau here the slain bodies of *kapu* (taboo) breakers were ceremonially cremated upon an altar.

Today the remains of ancient Hawaiians sacrificed to appease the gods share the crater floor with the bodies of nearly 50,000 soldiers, many of whom were killed in the Pacific during WWII. The remains of Ernie Pyle, the distinguished war correspondent who was hit by machine-gun fire on Ie-shima during the final days of WWII, lie in section D, grave 109. Five stones to the left, at grave D-1, is the marker for astronaut Ellison Onizuka, the Big Island astronaut who perished in the 1986 *Challenger* space-shuttle disaster.

Even without the war sights, Punchbowl would be worth the drive up for the plum views of the city and Diamond Head. After entering the cemetery, bear left and go to the top of the hill, where there's a sweeping ocean-view lookout. Special events held at the cemetery include Memorial Day ceremonies to honor veterans and a traditional Easter sunrise Christian service.

From Waikiki, take bus 2, 13 or B CityExpress! toward downtown Honolulu and get off at Beretania and Alapa'i Sts. Walk one block *makai* along Alapa'i St and transfer to bus 15 Pacific Heights, which stops near the entrance at the corner of Puowaina Dr and Ho'okui St, then walk uphill for approximately 15 minutes. If you're driving, take the H1 Fwy westbound to the Pali Hwy – there's a marked exit on your right almost immediately as you start up the Pali Hwy. Then carefully

National Memorial Cemetery of the Pacific

ILENE MACDONALD/ALAMY ©

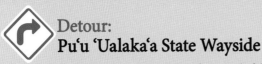

Detour:
Puʻu ʻUalakaʻa State Wayside

For a remarkable panorama of Honolulu, take a scenic drive or cycle up into the mountains to find this tiny roadside **park** (Map p52; www.hawaiistateparks.org; admission free; ⊙7am-7:45pm Apr-early Sep, to 6:45pm mid-Sep–Mar; P). Atop a volcanic cinder cone now taken over by the forest, sweeping views extend from Kahala and Diamond Head on the far left, across Waikiki and downtown Honolulu to the Waiʻanae Range on the far right. To the southeast is the University of Hawaiʻi, easily recognizable by its sports stadium; to the southwest you can peek into the green mound of Punchbowl Crater. The airport is visible at the edge of the coast, and Pearl Harbor beyond. The park entrance is about 2.4 miles up Round Top Dr from Makiki St, then another half-mile to the lookout, bearing left at the fork.

follow the signs through winding, narrow residential streets.

QUEEN EMMA SUMMER PALACE
Museum

(Map p38; www.queenemmasummerpalace.org; 2913 Pali Hwy; adult/child $6/1; ⊙9am-4pm; P) In the heat and humidity of summer, Queen Emma (1836–85), the wife and royal consort of Kamehameha IV, used to slip away from her formal downtown Honolulu home to this cooler hillside retreat in Nuʻuanu Valley. Built in Greek Revival style, the exterior recalls an old Southern plantation home, with its columned porch and high ceilings. Inside are a repository of regal memorabilia and period furniture that looks much as it did in Emma's day. Gracious docents from the Daughters of Hawaiʻi society show off the cathedral-shaped koa cabinet that displays a set of china given by England's Queen Victoria, brightly colored feather cloaks and capes once worn by Hawaiian royalty, and more priceless antiques.

To get here, take bus 4 from Waikiki, the university area or downtown Honolulu, or bus 56, 57 or 57A from Ala Moana Center. Be sure to let the bus driver know where you're going, so you don't miss the stop. By car, look for the entrance on the northbound side of the Pali Hwy (Hwy 61), near the 2-mile marker.

 Activities

You could spend days enjoying the solitude of the forests and peaks around the city. Some of Oʻahu's most popular hiking trails lead into the lush, windy Koʻolau Range just above downtown. For more details about these hikes and to find even more trails, visit the helpful government-run **Na Ala Hele Hawaii Trail & Access System website** (http://hawaiitrails.ehawaii.gov). For guided and group hikes around Oʻahu, many of which depart from Honolulu, see p311.

For Honolulu's best ocean swimming, head to **Ala Moana Regional Park** (p36). There are intermediate-level surf breaks just off Ala Moana, while those off **Kakaʻako Waterfront Park** (p36) are for advanced surfers and bodysurfers only.

UNIVERSITY OF HAWAIʻI RECREATION SERVICES
Outdoors

(Map p51; ☎956-6468; Campus Center; www.facebook.com/UHMRecServ) The University of Hawaiʻi at Manoa offers a variety of inexpensive outdoor sports, 'leisure classes' and group activities that are open to the public, from hiking ($10) and kayaking ($30) excursions around Oʻahu, to half-day introductory bodyboarding ($20) and learn-to-sail classes ($25). Advance

The Best...
Rainy Day Activities

1 Bishop Museum (p54)

2 Honolulu Museum of Arts (p49)

3 'Iolani Palace (p37)

4 Hawai'i State Art Museum (p39)

5 Ala Moana Center (p85)

sign-up is required; check class schedules online or call ahead to register.

GIRLS WHO SURF
Surfing, Stand-up Paddling

(Map p70; ☎772-4583; www.girlswhosurf.com; 1020 Auahi St; ⊗8am-6pm) Award-winning girl-powered surf and stand-up paddling (SUP) lessons are given around Honolulu, with free hotel transportation to/from Waikiki. For surfboard, bodyboard and SUP rentals, delivery to Ala Moana Beach costs an extra $10.

MANOA FALLS
Hiking

(Map p52; 🚶) Honolulu's most rewarding short hike, this 1.6-mile round-trip trail runs above a rocky streambed before ending at a pretty little cascade. Tall tree trunks lining the often muddy and slippery path include *Eucalyptus robusta*, with soft, spongy, reddish bark; flowering orange African tulip trees; and other arboreals that creak like wooden doors in old houses. Wild orchids and red ginger grow near the falls, which drop about 100ft into a small, shallow pool. Falling rocks and the risk of leptospirosis (a waterborne bacterial infection) make even wading dangerous (no swimming, sorry). It's illegal, not to mention unsafe and foolhardy, to venture beyond the established viewing area.

On public transit, take bus 5 Manoa Valley from Ala Moana Center or the university area to the end of the line; from there, it's a half mile walk uphill past Treetops Restaurant to the trailhead. By car, drive almost to the end of Manoa Rd, where a privately operated parking lot charges $5 per vehicle. Free on-street parking may be available just downhill from the bus stop, but obey any posted parking restrictions to avoid being ticketed and towed.

NU'UANU VALLEY LOOKOUT
Hiking

(Map p52) Just before Manoa Falls, the inconspicuous **'Aihualama Trail** starts to the west of a chain-link fence and scrambles over boulders. The trail quickly enters a bamboo forest with some massive old banyan trees, then contours around the ridge, offering broad views of Manoa Valley. Another mile of gradual switchbacks brings hikers to an intersection with the **Pauoa Flats Trail**, which ascends to the right for more than half a mile over muddy tree roots to the spectacular **Nu'uanu Valley Lookout**. High atop the Ko'olau Range, with O'ahu's steep *pali* (cliffs) visible all around, it's possible to peer through a gap over to the Windward Coast. The total round-trip distance to the lookout from the Manoa Falls trailhead is approximately 5.5 miles.

MAKIKI VALLEY LOOP & MANOA CLIFFS CIRCUIT
Hiking

(Map p52) A favorite workout for city dwellers, the 2.5-mile **Makiki Valley Loop** links three Tantalus-area trails that are usually muddy, so wear shoes with traction and pick up a walking stick. The loop cuts through a diverse tropical forest, mainly composed of nonnative species introduced to reforest an area denuded by the 19th-century *'iliahi* (sandalwood) trade. Keep watch for the tumbledown remains of ancient Hawaiian stone walls and a historic coffee plantation.

Starting just past the **Hawai'i Nature Center** (p65), the **Maunalaha Trail** crosses a small stream and climbs over a giant staircase of tree roots, passing Norfolk pines, banyans and taro patches. Behind are views of Honolulu's skyscrapers and harbor. After 0.7 miles, you'll reach a four-way junction: continue uphill on the 1.1-mile **Makiki Valley Trail**, which traverses small gulches and gentle streams bordered by patches of ginger and guava trees while offering glimpses of the city below. The 0.7-mile **Kanealole Trail** begins as you cross Kanealole Stream, then follows the stream back to the base yard. This trail leads down through a field of Job's tears; the pearly, bead-like pseudocarps (false fruit) of this tall grass are sometimes used for making lei.

A more adventurous 6.2-mile hike beginning from the same trailhead leads to sweeping views of the valley and the ocean beyond. This **Manoa Cliffs Circuit**, aka the 'Big Loop,' starts on the same Maunalaha Trail. It then follows the 0.75-mile Moleka Trail and connects across Round Top Dr with the Manoa Cliff Trail, which intersects with the Kalawahine Trail. You can detour to the right on the Pauoa Flats Trail up to the **Nu'uanu Valley Lookout**. From the lookout, backtrack to the Kalawahine Trail, which connects via the Nahuina Trail with the Kanealole Trail, leading back down to the forest base yard.

The starting point for both hiking loops is the **Makiki Forest Recreation Area base yard** (Map p52; 2135 Makiki Heights Dr), less than half a mile up Makiki Heights Dr from Makiki St. Where the road makes a sharp bend left, keep driving straight ahead through a green gate into the base yard. Park along the shoulder just inside the gate or in a small unpaved parking lot, then follow the signs and walk along the rolling hillside path to reach the main trailheads further inside the base yard.

From downtown Honolulu, take bus 15 Pacific Heights and get off near the intersection of Mott-Smith and Makiki Heights Drs by Spalding House, then walk half a mile southeast down Makiki Heights Dr to the base yard. From Waikiki, take bus 4 Nu'uanu to the corner of Wilder Ave and Makiki St, then walk 0.3 miles northeast up Makiki St, veering left onto Makiki Heights Dr and continuing another 0.4 miles uphill to the base yard.

WA'AHILA RIDGE TRAIL Hiking
(Map p52) Popular even with novice hikers, this boulder-strewn trail offers a cool retreat amid Norfolk pines and endemic plants, with ridgetop views of Honolulu and Waikiki. Rolling up and down a series of small saddles and knobs before reaching a grassy clearing, the 4.8-mile round-trip trail covers a variety of terrain in a short time, making an enjoyable afternoon's walk that even families with older children might enjoy. Look for the Na Ala Hele trailhead sign beyond the picnic tables inside **Wa'ahila Ridge State Recreation Area** (Map p52; www.hawaiistateparks.org; ☺7am-7:45pm Apr-early Sep,

Hiking the Manoa Falls trail
KARL LEHMANN/LONELY PLANET IMAGES ©

to 6:45pm mid-Sep–Mar; P), at the back of the St Louis Heights subdivision, east of Manoa Valley.

If you are traveling by car, turn left off Wai'alae Ave onto St Louis Dr at the stoplight. Heading uphill, veer left onto Bertram St, turn left onto Peter St, then turn left again onto Ruth Pl, which runs west into the park. From Waikiki, bus 14 St Louis Heights stops at the intersection of Peter and Ruth Sts, which is about a half-mile walk from the trailhead.

ATLANTIS ADVENTURES   Whale Watching

(Map p46; ☎800-548-6262; www.atlantisadven tures.com; Pier 6, Aloha Tower Dr; 2hr tour adult/ child 7-12yr from $74/37) From late December through early April, Atlantis runs whale-watching cruises with an onboard naturalist on the *Navatek I,* a high-tech catamaran designed to minimize rolling, usually departing at noon daily. Rates include a light breakfast or a lunch buffet. Reservations are essential; book online for discounts, or look for coupons in free tourist magazines available at the airport and around town.

BIKE SHOP   Bicycle Rental

(Map p70; ☎596-0588; www.bikeshophawaii. com; 1149 S King St; rental bikes per day $20-85, car racks $5; ⏰9am-8pm Mon-Fri, 9am-5pm Sat, 10am-5pm Sun) Rents a variety of high-quality bicycles and can give you maps of cycling routes to match your skill level. Road cyclists looking for an athletic work-out should pedal the Tantalus–Round Top scenic loop (p52).

MOANALUA GOLF CLUB   Golf

(Map p38; ☎839-2311; www.mgchawaii.com; 1250 Ala Aolani St; green fees $30-40; ⏰by reservation only Mon-Fri) The oldest golf course in Hawaii was built in 1898 by a Protestant mission-ary family. It's a fairly quick par-72 course with an elevated green, straight fairways and nine holes that are played twice around from different tees. The eighth hole has killer views of Diamond Head.

ALA MOANA REGIONAL PARK   Tennis

(Map p70; 1201 Ala Moana Blvd) Municipal park has 10 free first-come, first-served public tennis courts. If you hit balls during the day, you can cool off with a dip in the ocean afterwards; if you come at night, the courts are lit.

Honolulu golf course

DAVID L. MOORE-HIO/ALAMY©

Island Insights

O'ahu has an endemic genus of tree snail, the *Achatinella*. The island's forests were once loaded with these colorful snails, which clung like gems to the leaves of trees. They were too attractive for their own good, however; their spiral shells were collected for lei-making, and hikers also started collecting them by the handful. Even more devastating has been the deforestation of their native forest habitat and the introduction of an exotic cannibal snail and predatory nonnative rodents such as mongoose. Of O'ahu's 42 *Achatinella* species, less than half remain today – and all but two are endangered.

 Courses

**NATIVE BOOKS/
NĀ MEA HAWAI'I** Arts, Culture
(Map p70; ☏596-8885; www.nativebookshawaii.
com; Ward Warehouse, 1050 Ala Moana Blvd;
P) Community-oriented bookstore, art
gallery and gift shop hosts free classes,
workshops and demonstrations in hula
dancing, Hawaiian language, traditional
feather lei making and *lauhala* weaving, ukulele playing and more. Call for
schedules and to check if pre-registration
is required.

 Tours

Guided walking tours of Chinatown are
peppered with historical insights and take
you to a few places you'd be unable to
visit by yourself. Just west of Ala Moana
Regional Park, sunset sails, dinner cruises
and party boats leave daily from Kewalo
Basin. More expensive guided tours may
include transportation to/from Waikiki
and advertize various specials in the free
tourist magazines available at the airport
and around town.

ATLANTIS ADVENTURES Boat
(Map p46; ☏973-1311, 800-548-6262; www.
atlantisadventures.com; Pier 6, Aloha Tower Dr;
dinner cruise adult/child 5-12yr from $121/69;
👶) Atlantis rolls out lunch buffet and
sunset dinner cruises aboard the *Navatek
I*, a sleek catamaran (for winter whale-

watching tours, see p60). Book ahead
online for discounts.

**ARCHITECTURA
WALKING TOUR** Walking
(Map p46; ☏628-7243; www.aiahonolulu.org;
4th fl, 119 Merchant St; tours $10; ☺usually
9-11:30am Sat) Led by professional archi-
tects, these historical-minded walking
tours will literally change your perspective
on downtown Honolulu's capitol district.
Reservations required.

HAWAII FOOD TOURS Van
(☏926-3663; www.hawaiifoodtours.com;
from $99) Designed by a former chef and
restaurant critic, this four-hour lunchtime
tour samples Chinatown's holes-in-the-
wall, island plate-lunch stops, beloved
bakeries, crack-seed candy shops and
more. Reservations are essential.

HAWAI'I HERITAGE CENTER Walking
(Map p46; ☏521-2749; 1040 Smith St; tours
$5; ☺9:30-11:30am Wed & Fri) Leads low-
cost historical guided walking tours of
Chinatown, beginning at the center's
storefront museum.

 Festivals & Events

Some of Honolulu's biggest festivals spill
over into Waikiki (see p108).

CHINESE NEW YEAR Culture
(www.chinatownhi.com) Between late January and mid-February, Chinatown's

The Best...
Annual Festivals & Celebrations

1 Pan-Pacific Festival

2 Chinese New Year

3 Honolulu Festival

4 Prince Lot Hula Festival

5 Hawaii International Film Festival

swirling festivities include a parade with lion dances and crackling firecrackers.

GREAT ALOHA FUN RUN   Sports
(www.greataloharun.com) A popular 8.15-mile race from the harborfront Aloha Tower to Aloha Stadium on the third Monday in February.

HONOLULU FESTIVAL   Arts, Culture
(www.honolulufestival.com) Three days of Asian-Pacific cultural exchange with music, dance and drama performances, an arts-and-crafts fair, a parade and fireworks, all in mid-March.

LANTERN FLOATING HAWAII   Culture
(www.lanternfloatinghawaii.com) On the last Monday in May, the souls of the dead are honored with a Japanese floating-lantern ceremony after sunset at Magic Island in Ala Moana Regional Park.

PAN-PACIFIC FESTIVAL   Arts, Culture
(www.pan-pacific-festival.com) Three days of Japanese, Hawaiian and South Pacific entertainment in early June, with music, dancing and *taiko* (traditional Japanese drumming) at Ala Moana Center.

KING KAMEHAMEHA HULA COMPETITION   Dance
(www.ticketmaster.com) One of Hawaii's biggest hula contests, with hundreds of dancers competing at downtown's Neal S Blaisdell Center in late June.

QUEEN LILI'UOKALANI KEIKI HULA COMPETITION   Dance
(http://web.mac.com/kpca) Children's hula troupes from throughout Hawaii take over the stage at the Neal S Blaisdell Center in mid-July.

PRINCE LOT HULA FESTIVAL   Dance
(www.moanaluagardensfoundation.org) The state's oldest and largest noncompetitive hula event invites Hawaii's leading hula *halau* (schools) to the royal Moanalua Gardens on the third Saturday in July.

HAWAII DRAGON BOAT FESTIVAL   Sports
(www.gohawaii.com) Colorful Chinese dragon boats race to the beat of island drummers at Ala Moana Regional Park in late August.

HAWAII FOOD & WINE FESTIVAL   Food
(www.gohawaii.com) Star chefs, sustainable farms and food lovers come together for a weekend of wining and dining in September.

TALK STORY FESTIVAL   Storytelling
(www.honolulu.gov/parks/programs) Story-tellers gather at Ala Moana Regional Park over a long weekend in mid-October; Friday is usually spooky stories.

HAWAII INTERNATIONAL FILM FESTIVAL   Cinema
(www.hiff.org) This celebration of celluloid packs the city's movie theaters with homegrown and imported Pacific Rim, Asian, mainland American and European films for 11 days in late October.

KING KALAKAUA'S BIRTHDAY   Culture
(www.honolulu.gov) Festive Victorian-era decorations and a concert of traditional monarchy-era music by the Royal Hawaiian Band at 'Iolani Palace on November 16.

HONOLULU MARATHON   Sports

(www.honolulumarathon.org) The USA's third-largest marathon runs from downtown Honolulu to Diamond Head on the second Sunday of December.

 Sleeping

Almost a dead zone after dark, downtown Honolulu doesn't have much in the way of accommodations. Most visitors sleep by the beach at Waikiki (see p109).

ASTON AT THE EXECUTIVE CENTRE   Condo Hotel $$$

(Map p46; 539-3000, 877-997-6667; www.astonhotels.com; 1088 Bishop St; ste/1br from $250/300; P ❄ @ 🛜 ♨) Honolulu's only downtown hotel is geared for business travelers and extended stays. Large, modern suites with floor-to-ceiling windows get kitchenettes, while one-bedroom condos add a full kitchen and washer/dryer. A fitness center, heated lap pool and complimentary continental breakfast round out the executive-class amenities. Free lobby wi-fi and in-suite wired internet. Parking $22.

ALA MOANA HOTEL   Condo Hotel $$$

(Map p70; 955-4811, 866-956-4262; www.outrigger.com; 410 Atkinson Dr; r/ste from $149/279; P ❄ @ 🛜 ♨) Looming over the Ala Moana Center mall and convenient to the convention center, this high-rise offers bland hotel rooms without island flavor. Upper floors may have straight-on views of the beach – request the Waikiki Tower for a lanai (balcony). You'll share the check-in line and fitness facilities with jet-lagged executives and airline crews. In-room wired internet is free, but lobby wi-fi costs extra. Parking costs $20.

OHANA HONOLULU AIRPORT HOTEL   Hotel $$

(836-0661, 866-956-4262; www.ohanahotelsoahu.com; 3401 N Nimitz Hwy; r from $99; P ❄ 🛜 ♨) If you need to be next to the airport (although Waikiki hotels are only a 20-minute taxi ride away), this nondescript chain sleeps underneath the noisy freeway. Rates include infrequent 24-hour airport-shuttle service, free lobby wi-fi and in-room wired internet access. Parking $20.

Floating lanterns drift in the water as the sun sets

DWIGHT MORITA/ALAMY ©

HOSTELLING INTERNATIONAL (HI) HONOLULU Hostel $

(Map p51; ☎946-0591; www.hostelsaloha.com; 2323-A Seaview Ave; dm $20-23, r $50-56; ⏰reception 8am-noon & 4pm-midnight; P @ 📶) Along a quiet residential side street near the UH Manoa campus, this tidy, low-slung house just a short bus ride from Waikiki has same-sex dorms and basic private rooms kept cool by the tradewinds. Some students crash here while looking for apartments, so it's often full. It has a kitchen, a laundry room, lockers and two free parking spaces.

Eating

You might sleep and play in Waikiki, but you should definitely eat in Honolulu. In fact, if O'ahu weren't so far away from the US mainland, you'd hear a lot more buzz about this multiethnic chowhound capital. During **Restaurant Week Hawaii** (www.restaurantweekhawaii.com), usually happening in mid-November, dozens of locally owned restaurants offer serious discounts for dining out, including prix-fixe dinner menus.

Downtown

Weekday cafes for office workers and students abound downtown. The Aloha Tower Marketplace has breezy waterfront tables for sunset drinks and *pupu* (appetizers). Heading toward Ala Moana, Restaurant Row has hot spots that come and go.

TOP CHOICE **HIROSHI EURASIAN TAPAS** Fusion $$

(off Map p46; ☎533-4476; www.hiroshihawaii.com; Restaurant Row, 500 Ala Moana Blvd; shared plates $10-16, mains $26-30; ⏰5:30-9:30pm; P) A serious player on the Honolulu culinary scene, chef Hiroshi Fukui puts a Japanese twist on Pacific Rim fusion style, from crab cannelloni swirled with miso sauce to smoked *hamachi* (yellowtail) with a garlicky habanero pepper kick. Order foamy tropical martinis and fresh-fruit sodas at the bar, or duck next door to vivacious Vin, an Italian tapas and wine bar, or mod Bonsai, a sushi, sake and *shōchū* bar. Make reservations for dinner. A pay-parking garage is available.

DOWNTOWN Local $$

(Map p46; www.slowdowntown.com; 1st fl, 250 S Hotel St; mains $10-16; ⏰11am-2pm Mon-Fri, also 5:30-9:30pm on 1st Fri of each month) Hidden on the ground floor of the Hawai'i State Art Museum, this arty cafe is a downtown outpost of Kaimuki's trendy Town (p77). Market-fresh salads, soups and sandwiches bend culinary barriers – savor lotus-root chips, *'ahi* (tuna) club sandwiches and steamed guava cake. Reserve ahead or grab a gourmet plate lunch from the 'ASAP' takeout counter.

Sashimi from Hiroshi Eurasian Tapas

C.DOUGLAS PEEBLES PHOTOGRAPHY/ALAMY ©

Honolulu for Children

o For grassy picnicking lawns, endless sand and calm waters, take the kids to the beach at **Ala Moana Regional Park** (p36), which has lifeguards and outdoor showers to wash the sand off little feet.

o The **Bishop Museum** (p54) has educational diversions for kids of all ages; a planetarium chronicles the stars that guided ancient Polynesians to Hawaii, while the Science Adventure Center lets youngsters walk through an erupting model volcano.

o In the basement of the **Honolulu Museum of Arts** (p49), seek out the interactive arts-and-crafts center for creative families.

o Drive up into the Manoa Valley to visit the wide-open **Lyon Arboretum** (p52) or make the family-friendly hike to **Manoa Falls** (p58).

o **Hawai'i Nature Center** (Map p52; ☎955-0100; www.hawaiinaturecenter.org; 2131 Makiki Heights Dr; program fees $5-20; ℗) Inside the woodsy Makiki Forest Recreation Area, this nonprofit community education center conducts family-oriented environmental programs and weekend hikes (reservations strongly recommended).

o **Hawaii Children's Discovery Center** (off Map p70; ☎524-5437; www.discoverycenter hawaii.org; 111 'Ohe St; adult/child 1-17yr/senior $9/7/8; ☺9am-1pm Tue-Fri, 10am-3pm Sat & Sun; ℗) With plenty of aloha, this hands-on community play space, designed for tots and young schoolchildren, is the place to go on a rainy day.

HUKILAU Local $$
(Map p46; ☎523-3460; www.dahukilau.com/honolulu; 1088 Bishop St; mains lunch $11-16, dinner $12-20; ☺11am-2pm & 3-9pm Mon-Fri) Underground at downtown's high-rise hotel, this tiki-themed sports bar and grill serves an aloha-shirt-wearing business crowd. Huge salads, sandwiches and burgers aren't as tempting as only-in-Hawaii specialties such as miso butterfish, kimchi (Korean seasoned vegetable pickle dish) and *kalua* (cooked in an underground pit) pig saimin (noodle soup), *'ahi poke* (cubed raw fish mixed with *shōyu*, sesame oil, salt, chili pepper, *furikake*, *'inamona* or other condiments) salad and happy-hour *pupu*. Live music on most Friday nights.

VITA JUICE Health Food $
(Map p46; www.freewebs.com/vitajuice; 1111-C Fort St Mall; snacks $3-6; ☺7am-5pm Mon-Fri; ☞) Flooded with Hawai'i Pacific Universi-ty students, this orange-walled juice and smoothie bar takes the concept of 'brain food' seriously. Healthy ingredients range from Amazonian acai and Tibetan goji berries to green tea and ginseng.

 'UMEKE MARKET & DELI Supermarket, Deli $
(Map p46; www.umekemarket.com; 1001 Bishop St; mains $4-10; ☺7am-3pm Mon-Fri; ☞) Fresh, organic island produce, natural-foods groceries and a vegetarian- and vegan-friendly takeout deli counter for healthy pick-me-ups such as kale and quinoa salads, hummus sandwiches, hoisin turkey meatloaf and iced kombucha (effervescent tea).

Chinatown

Chinese restaurants are plentiful, but the cavalcade doesn't stop there – dishes from all across Asia and around the Pacific Rim are cooked in this historic downtown

65

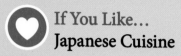

If You Like...
Japanese Cuisine

Connoisseurs might want to go out of their way to visit these in-the-know kitchens.

1 SUSHI SASABUNE
(Map p70; ☏ 947-3800; 1417 S King St; chef's tasting menu $125-150; ⏱noon-2pm Tue-Fri, 5:30-10pm Mon-Sat) Omakase (chef's tasting menus) are Honolulu's pick for die-hard sushi aficionados only.

2 INABA
(Map p70; ☏ 953-2070; http://inabahonolulu.com; 1610 S King St; mains $11-26; ⏱11:30am-2pm & 5:30-9pm Thu-Tue; P) Handmade soba noodles and lighter-than-air tempura.

3 ICHIRIKI
(Map p70; ☏ 589-2299; http://ichirikinabe.com; 510 Pi'ikoi St; dinner mains $22-48; ⏱11am-2pm daily, 5-11pm Sun-Thu, 5pm-midnight Fri & Sat) Sumo wrestler–sized nabemono, shabushabu and sukiyaki hot pots.

4 SHIROKIYA
(Map p70; www.shirokiya.com; Ala Moana Center, 1450 Ala Moana Blvd; most dishes $2-12; ⏱9:30am-8pm Mon-Sat, to 6pm Sun; P) A bazaar of hot and cold takeout bites.

5 GOMAICHI
(Map p70; www.rikautsumi.com/demo/gomaichi; 631 Ke'eaumoku St; mains $7-10; ⏱11am-2pm & 5:30-9pm Mon-Sat; P) Squeaky-clean ramen (egg noodles) shop with lots of fans for its 'No 1 Sesame' broth.

neighborhood, packed with hole-in-the-wall kitchens, dim-sum palaces and trendy fusion eateries for art scenesters.

TOP CHOICE DUC'S BISTRO   Fusion $$
(Map p46; ☏ 531-6325; www.ducsbistro.com; 1188 Maunakea St; mains $15-24; ⏱11am-2pm Mon-Fri, 5-10pm daily) Honolulu's bigwigs hang out after work at this swank French-Vietnamese bistro with a tiny bar. Ignore the surrounding seedy streets and step inside this culinary oasis for buttery escargot, bánh xèo (Vietnamese crepes), pan-fried fish with green mango relish, and fire-roasted eggplant. A small jazz combo serenades diners some evenings. Reservations recommended.

GREEN DOOR   Southeast Asian $$
(Map p46; 1110 Nu'uanu Ave; mains $8-14; ⏱11:30am-2:30pm Mon-Fri, 6-8pm or 9pm Wed-Sat) Betty Pang has moved her Malaysian and Singaporean-flavored kitchen from ritzy Kahala back to Chinatown. Behind the lime-green-painted doors, service is infamously slow and brusque. But the food is worth sticking around for, especially Nyonya (Straits Chinese-Malaysian) classics such as coconut-chicken curry. With just four tables squeezed inside, waits to sit can be long.

TO CHAU   Vietnamese $
(Map p46; 1007 River St; mains $7-9; ⏱8:30am-2:30pm) Always packed, this Vietnamese restaurant holds fast to its hard-earned reputation for serving Honolulu's best pho (Vietnamese noodle soup). With beef, broth and vegetables the dish is a complete meal in itself, but the menu includes other Vietnamese standards too. It's so popular that even as early as 10am you may have to queue underneath the battered-looking sign outside to score one of a dozen or so rickety wooden tables.

BANGKOK CHEF   Thai $
(Map p46; www.bangkokchefexpress.com; 1626 Nu'uanu Ave; mains $6-9; ⏱10:30am-9pm Mon-Sat, noon-8pm Sun; P 🚻) In this open-air kitchen it feels strangely like you're eating out of someone's garage. But who cares when the Thai curries, noodle dishes and savory salads taste exactly like those from a Bangkok street cart? Dessert is either mango ice cream over warm sticky rice topped with salty peanuts, or tapioca pudding cups in a rainbow of flavors – try the Thai tea, Okinawan sweet potato or banana.

LITTLE VILLAGE NOODLE HOUSE
Chinese $$

(Map p46; ☎545-3008; http://littlevillagehawaii.com; 1113 Smith St; mains $10-22; ☉10:30am-10:30pm Sun-Thu, to midnight Fri & Sat; P♿) Forget about chop suey. If you live for anything fishy in black-bean sauce, this is Honolulu's gold standard. On the eclectic pan-Chinese menu, regional dishes are served up garlicky, fiery or with just the right dose of saltiness. For a cross-cultural combo, fork into sizzling butterfish or roasted pork with island-grown taro. Bonuses: air-con and free parking in back. Reservations recommended.

SOUL DE CUBA
Cuban $$

(Map p46; ☎545-2822; www.souldecuba.com; 1121 Bethel St; sandwiches $9-14, mains $16-22; ☉11am-10pm Mon-Thu, to 11pm Fri & Sat, to 8:30pm Sun) Nowhere else in Honolulu can you sate your craving for Afro-Cuban food and out-of-this-world *mojitos* except at this hip resto-lounge near Chinatown's art galleries. Stick with family-recipe classics like *ropa vieja* (shredded beef in tomato sauce), *bocadillos* (sandwiches, served until 5pm) and black-bean soup. Reservations recommended.

INDIGO
Asian, Fusion $$

(Map p46; ☎521-2900; www.indigo-hawaii.com; 1121 Nu'uanu Ave; lunch buffet $16, dinner mains $20-35; ☉11:30am-2pm Tue-Fri, 6-9pm Tue-Thu, 6-10pm Fri & Sat) Once a standard-bearer for a revitalized Chinatown, this eatery lets you hobnob with the theater crowd over creative dim-sum appetizers like *'ahi* tempura rolls and goat-cheese wontons. Although lunch has slid to the buffet level, dinner stays strong with Pacific Rim and Asian classics and fusion fare such as cocoa-bean seafood curry and Malaysian beef *rendang*.

MEI SUM DIM SUM
Chinese $

(Map p46; 1170 Nu'uanu Ave; dim-sum dishes $2-4, mains $6-12; ☉7am-8:45pm) Where else can you go to satisfy that crazy craving for dim sum in the afternoon or evening (though maybe not as fresh as it is in the morning)? For over a decade, this no-nonsense corner stop has been cranking out a multitude of cheap little plates and a full spread of Chinese mains – ask for the secret garlic eggplant that's not on the menu.

ROYAL KITCHEN
Chinese $

(Map p46; http://royalkitchenhawaii.com; Chinatown Cultural Plaza, near cnr of Kukui & River Sts; steamed buns $1-2, plate lunches $6-8; ☉5:30am-4:30pm Mon-Fri, 6:30am-4:30pm Sat, 6:30am-2:30pm Sun) This is a humble shop alongside Nu'uanu Stream. It is worth fighting Chinatown's snarled traffic just for its famous *manapua* (steamed or baked buns) with tantalizing sweet and savory fillings: *char siu* (Chinese barbecue pork), chicken curry, sweet potato, *kalua* pig, black sugar and more.

Coconut and orchid lei
LINDA CHING/LONELY PLANET IMAGES ©

SUN CHONG
Bakery $

(Map p46; 127 N Hotel St; snacks $1-3; ⏰7am-5pm; ♿) You'd better show up early to buy Chinese baked goods such as almond cookies and other pastries at bargain prices. Sun Chong's shop is also the place to buy dried, sugared and spiced crack seed, from candied ginger and pineapple to dried squash and lotus root. It's like an experimental museum for the senses.

KEN FONG
Chinese $

(Map p46; 1030 Smith St; mains $5-12; ⏰11:30am-3pm & 5-9pm Mon-Sat) Blithely ignore new Chinatown's fashionably chic scene at this old-school storefront. Feast on home-style savory roast duck or ginger chicken atop a mountain of jasmine rice, or tuck into a spicy lamb hot-pot casserole. The family that cooks here, eats here – now that's a real vote of confidence.

DOWNBEAT DINER
Diner $$

(Map p46; www.downbeatdiner.com; 42 N Hotel St; mains $7-15; ⏰11am-3am Mon-Thu, 11am-4am Fri & Sat, 10am-10pm Sun; ✏♿) Shiny late-night diner with lipstick-red booths posts a vegetarian- and vegan-friendly menu of salads, sandwiches, grilled burgers and heaping island-style breakfasts such as *loco moco* (rice, fried egg and hamburger patty) and Portuguese sweet-bread French toast. Otto's cheesecake is unbelievably addictive.

MABUHAY CAFE & RESTAURANT
Filipino $

(Map p46; 1049 River St; mains $6-13; ⏰10am-9pm Mon-Sat) The red-and-white checked tablecloths, well-worn counter stools and jukebox should clue you in that this is a mom-and-pop joint. They've been cooking pots of succulent, garlic-laden pork *adobo* (meat marinated in vinegar and garlic) and *kare-kare* (oxtail stew) on this corner by the river since the 1960s.

LEGEND VEGETARIAN RESTAURANT
Chinese, Vegetarian $

(Map p46; Chinatown Cultural Plaza, 100 N Beretania St; dim-sum dishes from $2.50, mains $8-13; ⏰10:30am-2pm Thu-Tue; ✏) This

Left: Market scene in Chinatown **Below:** Seared 'ahi (tuna) pupu (appetizers)

100% vegetarian Buddhist-Chinese dining spot offers savory, imaginative dishes (vegetarian butterfish, sweet-and-sour vegetarian pork) made with vegan-friendly tofu and wheat gluten. The menu is extensive, if somewhat bland.

MAUNAKEA MARKETPLACE   Fast Food $
(Map p46; 1120 Maunakea St; meals from around $6; ☺7am-3pm; 🚶) In the food court of this open-air marketplace, you'll find about 20 stalls dishing out authentic Chinese, Filipino, Thai, Vietnamese and Korean fare. Chow down at tiny wooden tables crowded into the walkway. Cash only.

BA LE   Vietnamese $
(Map p46; www.ba-le.com; 150 N King St; mains $3-9; ☺7am-5pm Mon-Sat, to 4pm Sun) This fluorescent-lit bakery-cafe is part of a Hawaii-wide chain established by a Vietnamese immigrant. Best known for its chewy baguette sandwiches, it crafts equally chewy coffee, either hot or iced,

served with loads of sugar and milk. Also at 1154 Fort St Mall.

JJ DOLAN'S PIZZA PUB   Pizzeria $
(Map p46; www.jjdolans.com; 1147 Bethel St; pizzas from $16; ☺11am-2am Mon-Sat) Two guys from the mainland run this sociable Irish pub, firing up NYC-style pizza and pouring cold beer while sports games play on big-screen TVs.

Ala Moana & Around

Shopping-mall food courts are ground zero for this neighborhood, but surprisingly many star chef's kitchens are spread out along trafficked thoroughfares or on dumpy-looking side streets.

TOP CHOICE **ALAN WONG'S**   Hawaii Regional $$$
(Map p70; ☎949-2526; www.alanwongs.com; 1857 S King St; mains $30-50; ☺5-10pm; 🅿)

HONOLULU EATING

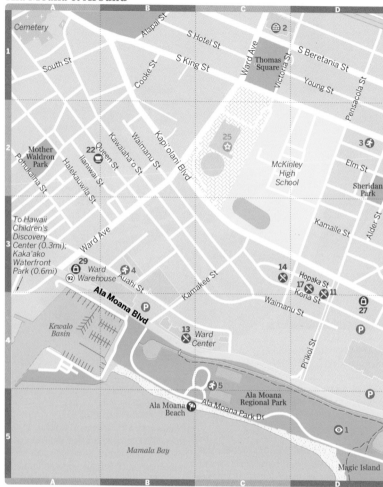

One of O'ahu's big-gun chefs, Alan Wong (p75) offers his creative interpretations of Hawaii Regional Cuisine inside an office building with, sadly, no view. Extra emphasis goes on fresh seafood and local produce, especially at the chef's bimonthly O'ahu Farmer Series Dinners. Skip the daily tasting menus. Instead order Wong's time-tested signature dishes such as ginger-crusted *onaga* (red snapper), Kona lobster seafood stew and twice-cooked *kalbi* (short ribs). Make reservations for in-demand tables weeks in advance. Valet parking $5.

NANZAN GIROGIRO Japanese $$$
(Map p70; ☑524-0141; 560 Pensacola St; chef's tasting menu from $50; ☺from 6pm Thu-Mon)
Like a culinary alchemist, Japanese chef Matsumoto imports his hometown of Kyoto's traditional *kaiseki ryōri* (seasonal small-course) cuisine and infuses it with Hawaii-grown fruits and vegetables, fresh seafood and, frankly, magic. Inside an art gallery, bar seats ring the open kitchen.

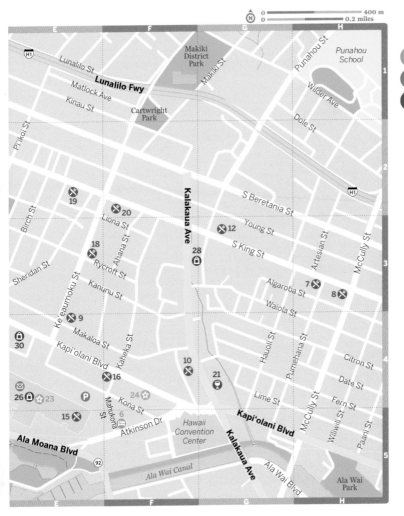

Ceramic turtles hide savory custard in their shells and pottery bowls harbor tea-soaked rice topped with delicately poached fish. Reservations essential (preferred seating times 6pm and 8:30pm).

SIDE STREET INN Local $$
(Map p70; ☎591-0253; http://sidestreetinn.com; 1225 Hopaka St; plate lunches $6-8, shared plates $7-20; ☺2pm-2am daily, takeout only 10am-2pm Mon-Fri) The outside looks like hell, and the sports-bar atmosphere wouldn't rate on a Zagat's survey, but this late-night mecca

is where you'll find Honolulu's top chefs hanging out after their own kitchens close, along with partyin' locals who come for hearty portions of *kalbi* and pan-fried pork chops. Make reservations and bring friends, or join the construction-worker crews ordering plate lunches at the takeout counter.

SUSHI IZAKAYA GAKU Japanese $$$
(Map p70; ☎589-1329; 1329 S King St; most shared plates $6-35; ☺5-11pm Mon-Sat; P) Known mostly by word of mouth, this

Ala Moana & Around

insiders' *izakaya* (Japanese gastropub) beats the competition with adherence to tradition and supremely fresh sushi and sashimi – no fusion novelty rolls named after caterpillars or California here. A spread of savory and sweet, hot and cold dishes include hard-to-find specialties such as *chazuke* (tea-soaked rice porridge) and *natto* (fermented soybeans). Reservations recommended, but accepted only for seatings from 5pm to 7pm (after that, it's all first come, first served).

CHEF MAVRO Fusion $$$
(Map p70; ☎944-4714; www.chefmavro.com; 1969 S King St; 4-course dinner without/with wine pairings from $75/125; ⏱6-9:30pm Tue-Sun; ✎) At Honolulu's most avant-garde restaurant, maverick chef George Mavrothalassitis creates conceptual dishes such as *kabocha* (Japanese squash) coconut custard and spiny lobster with coconut

froth and tamarind, all paired with Old and New World wines. Unfortunately the cutting-edge experimental cuisine, like the half-empty atmosphere, sometimes falls flat, although some will swear they've had the meal of a lifetime. Reservations essential. Dress code for men is long slacks and a collared shirt.

PINEAPPLE ROOM Hawaii Regional $$
(Map p70; ☎945-6573; www.alanwongs. com; 3rd fl, Macy's, Ala Moana Center, 1450 Ala Moana Blvd; prix-fixe 'express lunch' $26, dinner mains $25-35; ⏱11am-8:30pm Mon-Fri, 8am-8:30pm Sat, 9am-3pm Sun; P) All of star chef Alan Wong's classics are made inside this department-store kitchen. The casual menu shows off haute twists on island comfort food such as a *kalua* pig BLT sandwich and *loco moco* made with kiawe-grilled North Shore beef and veal jus. Desserts are killer, especially

HONOLULU EATING

the *haupia* (coconut pudding) with *halo halo* (mixed tropical fruit sweetened with condensed milk).

SHOKUDŌ
Japanese $$

(Map p70; 📞941-3701; www.shokudojapanese.com; 1585 Kapiʻolani Blvd; most shared plates $4-25; ⏰11:30am-1am Sun-Thu, 11:30am-2am Fri & Sat, last order 1hr before closing; 🅿) Knock back lychee sake-tinis at this sleek, modern Japanese restaurant (*shokudō* means 'dining room') that's always filled to the rafters. A mixed-plate traditional Japanese and island-fusion menu depicts dizzying dozens of dishes, from *mochi* (rice cake) cheese gratin to lobster dynamite rolls, more traditional noodles and sushi, and silky house-made tofu. Reservations recommended. Validated parking off Kona St, behind the restaurant.

HONOLULU MUSEUM OF ARTS CAFE
Modern American $$

(Map p70; 📞532-8734; www.honoluluacademy.org; Honolulu Museum of Arts, 900 S Beretania St; mains $11-22; ⏰seatings 11:30am-1:30pm Tue-Sat) Market-fresh salads and sandwiches made with Oʻahu-grown ingredients, a decent selection of wines by the glass and tropically infused desserts make this an indulgent way to support the arts. Romantic tables facing the sculpture courtyard fountain and underneath a monkeypod tree are equally well suited to dates or power-broker lunches. Reservations are recommended.

SORABOL
Korean $$

(Map p70; 📞947-3113; www.sorabolhawaii.com; 805 Keʻeaumoku St; shared plates $10-45; ⏰24hr; 🅿) Sorabol feeds lunching Korean ladies by day and bleary-eyed clubbers before dawn. Detractors often sniff that its reputation is undeserved, but the rest of the city has undying gratitude for this around-the-clock joint, often visited after midnight in a drunken stupor. Marinated *kalbi* and steamed butterfish are specialties. Watch out for a late-night service charge (20%).

HOME BAR & GRILL
Local $$

(Map p70; 1683 Kalakaua Ave; shared dishes $6-15; ⏰2pm-2am; 🅿) Run by hip young chefs

who graduated from the kitchens of Alan Wong's legendary Honolulu restaurants, this sports bar with a karaoke machine and dartboards also dishes up kickass pub grub that'll make you a believer in island-style fusion. Pull up a stool for *pau hana* (happy hour) and dig into tater-tot nachos, kimchi, *ʻahi poke* or garlicky chicken with chips. Parking lot $5.

HONOLULU FARMER MARKET
Market $

(Map p70; http://hfbf.org/markets; Neal S Blaisdell Center, 777 Ward Ave; ⏰4-7pm Wed; 🍴👶) Pick up anything from aquacultured seafood and Oʻahu honey to fresh fruit and tropical flowers, all trucked into the city by Hawaii Farm Bureau Federation members. Graze food stalls set up by island chefs, food artisans and Kona coffee roasters too.

KAKAʻAKO KITCHEN
Fast Food $

(Map p70; http://kakaakokitchen.com; Ward Center, 1200 Ala Moana Blvd; meals $7-12; ⏰8am-9pm Mon-Thu, to 10pm Fri & Sat, to 5pm Sun; 🅿👶) Though not as *ʻono* (delicious) as it once was, this counter joint still dishes up healthy-minded plate lunches with brown rice and organic greens. For a local deli twist, get the tempura mahimahi sandwich on a homemade taro bun.

MAKAI MARKET
Fast Food $

(Map p70; www.alamoanacenter.com; ground level, Ala Moana Center, 1450 Ala Moana Blvd; mains $6-12; ⏰9:30am-9pm Mon-Sat, 10am-7pm Sun; Ⓟ🚼) Let your preconceptions about mall food courts fly out the window at these Asian fusion–flavored indoor food stalls. Dig into Yummy Korean BBQ, Donburi Don-Don for Japanese rice bowls or the island-flavored Lahaina Chicken Company and Ala Moana Poi Bowl.

KUA 'AINA
Fast Food $

(Map p70; www.kua-aina.com; Ward Center, 1200 Ala Moana Blvd; burgers & sandwiches $5-10; ⏰10:30am-9pm Mon-Sat, to 8pm Sun; Ⓟ🚼) Shopping-mall outpost of Hale'iwa's gourmet burger joint serves crispy matchstick fries, pineapple and avocado beef burgers, and grilled 'ahi and veggie sandwiches for hungry young crowds.

University Area

Internationally flavored restaurants that'll go easy on your wallet cluster south of the UH Manoa campus near the three-way intersection of University Ave and S King and Beretania Sts. It's just a short bus ride from Waikiki.

TOP CHOICE IMANAS TEI
Japanese $$$

(Map p51; ☎941-2626; 2626 S King St; most shared plates $5-30; ⏰5-11:30pm Mon-Sat) Tucked behind Puck's Alley, look for the orange sign outside this long-standing *izakaya,* where staff shout their welcome ('*Irrashaimase!*') as you make your way to a low-slung tatami-mat booth. Sake fans come here for the liquid version of rice, then graze their way through a seemingly endless menu of sushi and epicurean and country-style Japanese fare, including crowd-pleasing *nabemono* meat and vegetable stews. Reserve days, if not weeks, in advance or stand in line for open seating after 7pm.

SPICES
Southeast Asian $$

(Map p51; ☎949-2679; http://spiceshawaii.com; 2671 S King St; mains $10-16; ⏰lunch 11:30am-2pm Tue-Fri, dinner 5:30-9:30pm Tue-Sun; Ⓟ) Setting a neighborhood-friendly table free of suffocating kitsch, this modern southeast Asian kitchen charges more than the competition, but the variety of homemade Vietnamese spring rolls, Thai curries, Lao soups and Burmese noodles is worth it. Look for wild, fresh ice-cream flavors like durian, pineapple-basil, banana-cinnamon and Okinawan sweet potato. Free parking in back.

SWEET HOME CAFÉ
Taiwanese $$

(Map p51; 2334 S King St; shared plates $3-12; ⏰4-11pm; Ⓟ) You won't believe the lines snaking outside this strip-mall eatery's door. On 10 long wooden family-style tables squat heavily laden, steaming-hot pots filled with lemongrass beef, sour cabbage, mixed tofu or Asian pumpkin squash, plus spicy dipping sauces and extra lamb, chicken or tender beef tongue as side dishes. Pick up your DIY ingredients from the refrigerators at the back. Bonus: complimentary shave ice for dessert!

DA SPOT
Fusion $

(Map p51; ☎941-1313; 2469 S King St; smoothies $3-5, plate lunches $6-10; ⏰11am-9:30pm Mon-Sat) An enterprising duo of chef-owners set up kiosks at farmers markets and on the UH Manoa campus, but this converted auto mechanic's garage is home base for their world fusion and island-flavored plate lunches, plus more than three dozen smoothie combinations. Egyptian chicken, southeast Asian curries and homemade baklava will leave you as stuffed as a dolma.

DA KITCHEN
Local $$

(Map p51; www.da-kitchen.com; 925 Isenberg St; meals $9-17; ⏰11am-9pm Mon-Sat; Ⓟ🚼) A crowded neighborhood storefront cooks Hawaiian food just so dang '*ono* that they've even been asked by President Barack Obama to cook at the White House. *Kalua* pork, chicken *katsu* (deep-fried cutlets) and steaming *laulau* (meat or fish wrapped in leaves and steamed) plate lunches are so huge you'll have to work hard to also make room for deep-fried Spam *musubi* (Japanese rice balls) or 'gorilla' pie.

KIAWE GRILL BBQ & BURGERS
Barbecue $$

(Map p51; www.kiawegrill.com; 2334 S King St; meals $8-14; ⊙10am-9pm Mon-Sat, to 8pm Sun; P 🛉) Enter a 1950s time warp inside this takeout joint, where green Formica tables heave with plastic plates of exotic venison, ostrich, buffalo and Kobe beef burgers piled high with heaping steak fries or spicy Korean vegetables. After chowing down here, you'll smell like barbecue smoke for the rest of the day.

PEACE CAFE
Health Food $

(Map p51; http://peacecafehawaii.com; 2239 S King St; mains $8-10; ⊙11am-9pm Mon-Sat, to 3pm Sun; P 🖉 🛉) Vegan home cooking is the theme at this strip-mall kitchen, where daily dishes get handwritten on the chalkboard. Pick a Popeye spinach or cilantro hummus sandwich to go, or a substantial lunch box with Moroccan stew. *Mochi* (Japanese pounded-rice cakes) and soy ice creams are dairy-free delights.

YAMA'S FISH MARKET
Seafood, Fast Food $

(Map p51; www.yamasfishmarket.com; 2332 Young St; meals $5-10; ⊙9am-7pm Mon-Sat, to 5pm Sun; P) Swing by this side-street seafood market for heaping island-style plate lunches (eg *kalua* pig, mochiko chicken, *lomilomi* salmon) and freshly mixed *poke* by the pound with sour poi (fermented taro paste) and sweet *haupia* pudding on the side.

🍃 DOWN TO EARTH NATURAL FOODS
Supermarket, Deli $

(Map p51; www.downtoearth.org; 2525 S King St; ⊙7:30am-10pm; P 🖉 🛉) Emphasizing organic and natural foods, this always-busy grocery store has a vegetarian- and vegan-friendly salad bar, a deli for made-to-order sandwiches, a juice and smoothie bar, and a few sidewalk tables for chowing down. Free garage parking on the 2nd floor.

🍃 KOKUA MARKET
Supermarket, Deli $

(Map p51; www.kokua.coop; 2643 S King St; ⊙8am-9pm; P 🖉) Hawaii's only natural-food co-op has an organic hot-and-cold

> ### Local Knowledge

NAME: ALAN WONG

OCCUPATION: CHEF-OWNER OF ALAN WONG'S RESTAURANTS

RESIDENCE: HONOLULU

How did you get started cooking? When I worked as a restaurant manager in Waikiki, I enrolled in a local culinary school... I found myself making salad dressing and bread, which I thought only came out of a bottle or package. After that, I never left the kitchen.

How has Hawaii's food scene evolved? When the food supply changes, the menu changes. Twenty years ago when Hawaii Regional Cuisine started, we didn't have as many farmers markets as today. We also talk more about sustainability now.

Where can visitors learn Hawaii's food culture? Hawaii's Plantation Village (p242). Three migrations of people came to Hawaii: Polynesians in canoes, tall ships of missionaries and whalers, and immigrant laborers who worked in the plantation fields. Those plantation immigrants were poor, but they brought with them their food, ingredients and culture. What they cooked was survival... They ate what they had. Today, it's our island soul food.

Any common misconceptions about Hawaii's food? A lot of people don't understand that there's an ethnic cuisine, a Native Hawaiian people. What is *laulau*? What is *kalua* pig? What is *poke*? These are traditional Hawaiian dishes, and they're not to be confused with local food, which is an ethnic melting pot.

How do visitors find great local food? Hole-in-the-wall kitchens. That's where you find the real essence of Hawaii. Every Saturday there's a farmers market at Kapi'olani Community College (p155). Look for restaurants that serve locally grown fruit and vegetables, or seafood... Attend the Hawaii Food & Wine Festival (p62), where chefs from all over the world work with local farm-to-table ingredients.

salad bar and a vegetarian- and vegan-friendly deli for takeout meals. Free parking off Kahuna Lane behind the tiny store.

BUBBIE'S
Ice Cream $

(Map p51; www.bubbiesicecream.com; Varsity Center, 1010 University Ave; items $2-6; ☺noon-midnight Mon-Thu, to 1am Fri & Sat, to 11:30pm Sun; P ♿) Homemade ice cream in tropical flavors such as papaya-ginger plus unique bite-sized frozen *mochi* treats.

Greater Honolulu

Kaimuki is making its mark on Honolulu's cuisine scene by sprouting trendy restaurants along Wai'alae Ave, east of the university area. More casual and classic homegrown joints worth going out of your way for are scattered between downtown and the airport.

TOP CHOICE HELENA'S HAWAIIAN FOOD
Hawaiian $$

(http://helenashawaiianfood.com; 1240 N School St; dishes $1-11, meals $9-19; ☺10:30am-7:30pm Tue-Fri; P) Walking through the door is like stepping into another era. Even though long-time owner Helena Chock has passed away, her grandson still commands the family kitchen, which opened in 1946. Most people order à la carte. Start with poi and rice, then add a couple of small plates of smoky *pipi kaula* (beef jerky), *kalua* pig, fried butterfish or squid cooked in coconut milk, and you've got a mini luau to go. It's just a few blocks southeast of the Bishop Museum.

12TH AVENUE GRILL
Modern American $$

(☎732-9469; http://12thavegrill.com; 1145 12th Ave; mains $18-35; ☺5:30-9pm Mon-Thu, to 10pm Fri & Sat) Hidden in a side alley, this Kaimuki neighborhood bistro with dark-wood booths and low lighting looks like it belongs more in San Francisco than Honolulu. Nouveau takes on comfort food include the grass-fed Maui Cattle Co flat-iron steak with 'Nalo corn hash and the Big Island *kabocha* pumpkin stuffed with pasta and pancetta. Not everything on the menu hits the mark, but take heart:

Left: Children dancing at the Prince Lot Hula Festival (p62)
Below: Hawaiian luau

(LEFT)PHOTO RESOURCE HAWAII/ALAMY©; (BELOW) DOUGLAS PEEBLES PHOTOGRAPHY/ALAMY©;

liliko'i (passion fruit) crème brûlée is what's for dessert.

SOUL   Southern $$

(http://pacificsoulhawaii.com; 3040 Wai'alae Ave; mains $9-20; ⏰11am-9pm Tue-Thu, 11am-10pm Fri, 9am-10pm Sat, 10:30am-8pm Sun; P) Authentic, rib-sticking Southern soul food with a Motown soundtrack in Kaimuki? Chef Sean Priester is all smiles as he delivers island-grown cabbage coleslaw, buttermilk-fried chicken, BBQ spare ribs and sassy vegetarian chili straight to your table. Gumbo, grits and Carolina pulled-pork *adobo* also will fill your belly. Wednesday's special – fried chicken and waffles – sells out superfast, so get there early.

TOWN   Modern American $$

(☎735-5900; www.townkaimuki.com; 3435 Wai'alae Ave; mains breakfast & lunch $5-16, dinner $16-26; ⏰7am-2:30pm daily, 5:30-9:30pm Mon-Thu, 5:30-10pm Fri & Sat) At this hip modern coffee shop and bistro hybrid in Kaimuki, filled with neighborhood yoga divas and muscle-bound surfers, the motto is 'local first, organic whenever possible, with aloha always.' On the daily-changing menu of boldly flavored cooking are burgers and steaks made from North Shore free-range cattle and salads that taste as if the ingredients were just plucked from a backyard garden.

SALT KITCHEN & TASTING BAR   Modern American $$

(http://salthonolulu.com; 3605 Wai'alae Ave; shared plates $5-21, mains $10-25; ⏰5pm-midnight Sun-Thu, 5pm-1am Fri & Sat, kitchen closes 1hr earlier) Mexican oxtail empanadas, Italian ravioli made with Hawaii-grown squash, and Indian naan with pickled eggplant fill the tapas-sized plates lined up all along the lacquered bar top. Bartenders shake up grapefruit daiquiris and tequila martinis for a chic crowd of urbane revelers during afternoon happy hours in the Kaimuki neighborhood.

If You Like...
Brewpubs

If you're searching for that perfect pint glass from the USA's westernmost state, you can round out your souvenir collection at the Big Island's **Kona Brewing Company** (p160) in Hawai'i Kai, or stop by these two Honolulu brewpubs.

1 SAM CHOY'S BIG ALOHA BREWERY
(http://samchoyhawaii.com; Sam Choy's Breakfast, Lunch & Crab, 580 N Nimitz Hwy; ⏱10:30am-9pm Sun-Thu, to 10pm Fri & Sat) West of downtown Honolulu, en route to the airport, sip Ehu Ale or a Big Aloha Blonde next to shiny metal brewing vats and sports TVs; skip the overpriced *pupu* (appetizers).

2 GORDON BIERSCH BREWERY RESTAURANT
(Map p46; www.gordonbiersch.com; 1st fl, Aloha Tower Marketplace, 1 Aloha Tower Dr; ⏱10am-midnight Sun-Thu, to 1am Fri & Sat) Down fresh lagers made according to Germany's centuries-old purity laws, often with live music by the waterfront.

LILIHA BAKERY   Diner $
(http://lilihabakeryhawaii.com; 515 N Kuakini St; snacks from $1.50, mains $6-10; ⏱24hr daily, except closed from 8pm Sun to 6am Tue; P 🚻) Not far northwest of Chinatown, this old-school island bakery and diner causes a neighborhood traffic jam for its coco-puff and green-tea cream pastries. Still hungry? Grab a counter seat and order a hamburger steak or other hearty lumberjack faves in Liliha's retro coffee shop.

NICO'S AT PIER 38   Local $
(http://nicospier38.com; 1133 N Nimitz Hwy; meals $6-10; ⏱6:30am-5pm Mon-Fri, to 2:30pm Sat; P 🚻) Chef Nico was inspired by the island-cuisine scene to merge his classical French training with Hawaii's humble plate lunch. French standards such as *steak frites* appear alongside market-fresh fish sandwiches and local belly-fillers such as *furikake*-crusted 'ahi and hoisin BBQ chicken. Tables with chairs are positioned near the waterfront and Honolulu's fish auction.

MITCH'S SUSHI   Seafood $$$
(📞837-7774; www.mitchsushi.com; 524 Ohohia St; small plates $5-35, set meals $25-40, chef's tasting menu $110; ⏱11:30am-8:30pm) A hole-in-the-wall sushi bar near the airport for cashed-up connoisseurs, who come for the chef's superbly fresh *omakase* tasting menu and rarely seen fishy delicacies shipped in from around the globe. Reservations essential; BYO.

CRACK SEED STORE   Candy Shop $
(1156 Koko Head Ave; ⏱usually 9am-6:30pm Mon-Sat; 🚻) Mom-and-pop candy store on a side street in Kaimuki vends overflowing glass jars of made-from-scratch crack seed, plus addictive frozen slushies spiked with *li hing mui* (salty dried plums).

🍷 Drinking & Entertainment

For what's going on after dark this week, from live-music and DJ gigs to theater, movies and cultural events, check the **Honolulu Star-Advertiser's TGIF** (www.honolulupulse.com) section, which comes out every Friday, and the free alternative tabloid **Honolulu Weekly** (http://honoluluweekly.com), published every Wednesday.

Cafes

TOP CHOICE MANIFEST   Cafe
(Map p46; http://manifesthawaii.com; 32 N Hotel St; ⏱8am-10pm Mon, 8am-2am Tue-Fri, 10am-2am Sat; 🛜) Smack in the middle of Chinatown's art scene, this lofty apartment-like space adorned with provocative photos and paintings doubles as a serene coffee shop by day and a cocktail bar by night, hosting movie and trivia nights and DJ sets (no cover). Foamy cappuccinos and spicy chais are daytime perfection.

🏖 BEACH BUM CAFÉ   Cafe
(Map p46; www.beachbumcafe.com; 1088 Bishop St; ⏱6:30am-6:30pm Mon-Thu, 6:30am-4pm Fri,

7am-1am Sat; 🛜) Setting up shop in downtown's high-rise financial district, this connoisseur's coffee bar serves 100% organic, grown-in-Hawaii beans, roasted in small batches and hand-brewed just one ideal cup at a time. Chat up the baristas while you sip the rich flavors of the Big Island, Maui, Kaua'i and even Moloka'i.

HONOLULU COFFEE COMPANY   Cafe
(Map p46; www.honolulucoffee.com; 1001 Bishop St; 🕑6am-5:30pm Mon-Fri, 7am-noon Sat; 🛜) Overlooking Tamarind Sq with city skyline views, here you can take a break from tramping around Honolulu's historical sites for a java jolt brewed from handpicked, hand-roasted 100% Kona estate-grown beans. Also at Ala Moana Center (Map p70).

GLAZERS COFFEE   Cafe
(Map p51; www.glazerscoffee.com; 2700 S King St; 🕑6:30am-11pm Mon-Thu, 6:30am-9pm Fri, 9am-11pm Sat & Sun; 🛜) They're serious about brewing strong espresso drinks and batch-roasted coffee at this university students' hangout, where you can kick back on comfy living-room sofas next to jazzy artwork and plentiful electrical outlets.

FRESH CAFE   Cafe
(Map p70; www.freshcafehi.com; 831 Queen St; 🕑8am-11pm Mon-Sat, 9am-6pm Sun; 🛜) At this alternative coffeehouse in an industrial warehouse area just west of Ala Moana Center, artists, bohemians and hipster hangers-on sip Vietnamese coffee, pikake iced tea, and Thai or *haupia*-flavored lattes. Evening special events vary.

WAI'OLI TEA ROOM   Teahouse
(Map p52; 📞988-5800; www.thewaiolitearoom. net; 2950 Manoa Rd; 🕑10:30am-3:30pm) If 19th-century author Robert Louis Stevenson were still hanging around Honolulu today, this is where you'd find him. Set in the verdant Manoa Valley, this open-air teahouse overlooks gardens of red ginger and birds-of-paradise. Afternoon high tea by reservation only.

Bars, Lounges & Nightclubs

Every self-respecting bar in Honolulu has a *pupu* menu to complement the liquid sustenance, and some bars are as famous for their appetizers as their good-times atmosphere. A key term to know is *pau hana* (literally 'stop work'), Hawaiian

La Mariana Sailing Club, a colorful tiki restaurant and bar (p80)

FRANCO SALMOIRAGHI/ALAMY ©

The Best...
Low-Key Locals' Hangouts

pidgin for 'happy hour.' Chinatown's edgy nightlife scene revolves around N Hotel St, which was the city's notorious red-light district not so long ago.

TOP CHOICE LA MARIANA SAILING CLUB   Tiki Bar
(www.lamarianasailingclub.com; 50 Sand Island Access Rd; ⏱11am-9pm) Who says all the great tiki bars have gone to the dogs? Irreverent and kitschy, this 1950s joint by the lagoon is filled with yachties and long-suffering locals. Classic mai tais are as killer as the other signature tropical potions, complete with tiki-head swizzle sticks. Grab a waterfront table and dream of sailing to Tahiti.

THIRTYNINEHOTEL   Lounge
(Map p46; http://thirtyninehotel.com; 39 N Hotel St; ⏱5pm-2am Fri & Sat) More arty than clubby, this multimedia space is an art gallery by day and a low-key dance scene by night. DJs don aloha wear for weekend spins, while rock bands test the acoustics some nights. Narrow stairs lead up to the all-white mod lounge (watch your step if you're schnockered!) adjoining a breezy patio with umbrella-shaded tables.

NEXT DOOR   Club
(Map p46; http://nextdoorhnl.com; 43 N Hotel St; ⏱8pm-midnight Mon, 9pm-2am Wed-Sat) Situated on a skid-row block of N Hotel St where dive bars are still the order of the day, this svelte cocktail lounge is a brick-walled retreat with vivid red couches and flickering candles. DJs spin house, hip hop, funk, mash-ups and retro sounds, while on other nights loud, live local bands play just about anything. The club blows up with big-name club DJs from the mainland on First Friday nights.

MAI TAI BAR   Bar
(Map p70; www.maitaibar.com; Ho'okipa Terrace, 4th fl, Ala Moana Center, 1450 Ala Moana Blvd; ⏱11am-1am) A happening bar in the middle of a shopping center? We don't make the trends, we just report 'em. During sunset and late-night happy hours, this enormous circular tropical bar is packed with a see-and-flirt crowd. Island-style live music plays nightly.

BAR 35   Bar
(Map p46; http://bar35hawaii.com; 35 N Hotel St; ⏱4pm-2am Mon-Fri, 6pm-2am Sat) Filled with aloha, this indoor-outdoor watering hole has a dizzying 100 domestic and international bottled beers to choose from, plus addictive chef-made gourmet fusion pizzas to go with all the brews. There's live music or DJs some weekend nights.

SOHO   Club
(Map p46; www.sohomixedmediabar.com; 80 Pau'ahi St; ⏱9pm-2am Tue-Sat) Spread across two giant dance floors, DJs spin everything from reggae to house and hip hop, and it's thumpin' on First Friday nights. The joint gets jam-packed when local bands play weeknight shows. The college-aged crowd skews young.

INDIGO LOUNGE   Lounge
(Map p46; www.indigo-hawaii.com; 1121 Nu'uanu Ave; ⏱5pm-midnight Tue, to 1:30am Wed-Sat) A small army of tropical martinis are shaken inside Indigo Lounge. As it is on the edge of Chinatown and near the Hawaii

Theatre, a mixed crowd gravitates here, with live jazz on some weeknights and weekend old-school and electronica DJs.

VARSITY GRILL & BAR
Sports Bar

(Map p51; www.facebook.com/VarsityBar; 1019 University Ave; ⊙11am-2am) Even though Ma-goo's has changed its name, University of Hawai'i students still crowd this open-air sidewalk bar. With dozens of microbrews from Hawaii and the US mainland on tap, come here for a cheap pitcher of Blue Moon and to catch the big game on TV.

APARTMENT 3
Lounge

(Map p70; www.apartmentthree.com; Century Center, 1750 Kalakaua Ave; ⊙6pm-2am Mon-Sat) This under-the-radar petite lounge is the kind of place Johnny Depp likes to drink when he's in town. Order up the classic Honolulu No 2 cocktail. Tuesdays are all-night happy hour, live music happens most Thursdays, and radio DJs spin all weekend long.

Live Music
Live Music

If traditional and contemporary Hawaiian music is what you crave, don't look any further than Waikiki (p127). But if it's jazz, alt-rock and punk sounds you're after, venture outside the tourist zone into Honolulu's other neighborhoods.

TOP CHOICE CHAI'S ISLAND BISTRO
Live Music

(Map p46; ☎585-0011; http://chaisislandbistro.com; Aloha Tower Marketplace, 1 Aloha Tower Dr; ⊙live music from 7pm nightly) Nobody really comes here for the food. Every night when the sun sets over the harbor, locals gravitate toward this shopping-center restaurant's bar to hear some of the greatest contemporary Hawaiian musicians on O'ahu play unplugged. Show up on Friday and cross your fingers to see the Brothers Cazimero up on stage.

HANK'S CAFE HONOLULU
Live Music

(Map p46; ☎526-1411; www.hankscafehonolulu.com; 1038 Nu'uanu Ave; ⊙3pm-1am) You can't get more low-key than this neighborhood dive bar on the edge of Chinatown. Owner Hank Taufaasau is a jack-of-all-trades when it comes to the barfly business: the walls are decorated with Polynesian-themed art, live music rolls in some nights and regulars practically call it home.

VENUE
Live Music

(Map p46; ☎528-1144; www.bambutwo.com; 1146 Bethel St; ⊙schedule varies) At the edge of Chinatown's new-wave arts district, next to BambuTwo cafe and martini lounge, this come-as-you-are multi-purpose stage books anyone from indie singer-songwriter acts to old-school

Friday Nights in Chinatown

Chinatown's somewhat seedy Nu'uanu Ave and Hotel St have become surprisingly cool places for a dose of urban art and culture, socializing and bar-hopping during **First Friday Honolulu** (www.firstfridayhawaii.com), held from 5pm to 9pm on the first Friday of each month. What was once a low-key art walk has become almost too big for its britches, according to local naysayers. A giant block party now rocks out to live music and DJs, with food trucks and over-21 wristbands required for getting into Chinatown's most popular bars and clubs – be prepared to queue behind velvet ropes. Aiming to lure back more chilled crowds, some art galleries, shops, cafes and restaurants have banded together to jump-start a newer event called **Slow Art Friday** (www.artsdistricthonolulu.com), happening from 6pm to 9:30pm on the third Friday of every month, featuring more local food, live music and art.

hip-hop DJs. Look for alternative cultural events, such as stand-up comedy nights.

DRAGON UPSTAIRS   Jazz
(Map p46; ☎526-1411; http://thedragonupstairs. com; 2nd fl, 1038 Nu'uanu Ave; ⏰6pm-2am) Right above Hank's Cafe, this claustro-phobic hideaway with a sedate older vibe and lots of funky artwork and mirrors hosts a rotating lineup of jazz cats, blues strummers and folk singers, usually on Thursday, Friday and Saturday nights (there's no cover charge, but there is a two-drink minimum).

ANNA O'BRIEN'S   Live Music
(Map p51; ☎946-5190; 2440 S Beretania St; cover $5-10; ⏰usually until 2am daily) A col-lege dive bar, part roadhouse and part arthouse, the reincarnation of Anna Bannanas goes beyond its retro-1960s 'Summer of Love' atmosphere to book reggae, alt-rock, punk and metal bands. Now, if only they'd bring back those hookah pipes – sigh.

JAZZ MINDS ART & CAFÉ   Live Music
(Map p70; ☎945-0800; www.honolulujazzclub. com; 1661 Kapi'olani Blvd; cover $5-10; ⏰9pm-2am Mon-Sat) Don't let the nearby strip clubs turn you off this place. This tattered brick-walled lounge with an almost speak-easy ambience pulls in the top island talent – fusion jazz, funk, bebop, hip hop, surf rock and minimalist acts. However, you will need to be prepared for a stiff two-drink minimum.

Performing Arts

Hawaii's capital city is home to a sym-phony orchestra, an opera company, ballet troupes, chamber orchestras and more, while more than a dozen commu-nity theater groups perform everything from David Mamet satires to Hawaiian pidgin fairy tales.

TOP CHOICE HAWAII
THEATRE   Performing Arts
(Map p46; ☎528-0506; www.hawaiitheatre. com; 1130 Bethel St) Beautifully restored, this grande dame of O'ahu's theater scene is a major venue for dance, music and theater. Performances include top Hawaii musicians such as the Brothers Cazimero, contemporary plays, interna-tional touring acts and film festivals. The theater also hosts the annual Ka Himeni Ana competition of singers in the traditional na-henahe style, accompanied by ukuleles.

NEAL S BLAISDELL CENTER
Performing Arts
(Map p70; ☎768-5252; www.blaisdellcenter.com; 777 Ward Ave; P ♿) A cultural linchpin, this modern performing-arts complex stages symphony and chamber-music

Hawaii Theatre
LINDA CHING/LONELY PLANET IMAGES ©

concerts, opera performances and ballet recitals, prestigious hula competitions, Broadway shows and more. Occasionally big-name pop and rock touring acts play here instead of at Aloha Stadium (Map p146). Parking costs from $6.

ARTS AT MARKS GARAGE
Performing Arts

(Map p46; ☏521-2903; www.artsatmarks.com; 1159 Nu'uanu Ave) On the cutting edge of the Chinatown arts scene, this community gallery and performance space puts on a variety of live shows, from stand-up comedy, burlesque cabaret nights and conversations with island artists to live jazz and Hawaiian music.

◈ KUMU KAHUA THEATRE
Theater

(Map p46; ☏536-4441; www.kumukahua.org; 46 Merchant St) In the restored Kamehameha V Post Office building, this little 100-seat treasure is dedicated to premiering works by Hawaii's playwrights, with themes focusing on contemporary multicultural island life, often richly peppered with Hawaiian pidgin.

FREE ALA MOANA CENTERTAINMENT
Performing Arts

(Map p70; ☏955-9517; www.alamoanacenter. com; ground fl, Center Court, 1450 Ala Moana Blvd; P ☺) The mega shopping center's courtyard area is the venue for all sorts of island entertainment, including music by O'ahu musicians and the Royal Hawaiian Band, Japanese *taiko* drumming and Sunday-afternoon *keiki* (children's) hula shows also take place.

DORIS DUKE THEATRE
Performing Arts

(Map p70; ☏532-8768; www.honoluluacademy. org; 900 S Beretania St; P) International jazz and chamber-music concerts and art lectures happen downtown at the Honolulu Museum of Arts. Validated weekday parking $3 (evenings and weekends free).

♥ If You Like…
Art Galleries

Chinatown overflows with art galleries.

1 **ARTS AT MARKS GARAGE**
(Map p46; www.artsatmarks.com; 1159 Nu'uanu Ave; ☺11am-6pm Tue-Sat) Performance art and eclectic works by up-and-coming island artists.

2 **PEGGE HOPPER GALLERY**
(Map p46; www.peggehopper.com; 1164 Nu'uanu Ave; ☺11am-4pm Tue-Fri) Prints and paintings of voluptuous Hawaiian women.

3 **CHINATOWN BOARDROOM**
(Map p46; http://chinatownboardroom.com; 1160 Nu'uanu Ave; ☺11am-4pm Tue-Sat) For ubercool 'lowbrow' art and one-of-a-kind customized surfboards.

4 **BETHEL STREET GALLERY**
(Map p46; www.bethelstreetgallery.com; 1140 Bethel St; ☺11am-4pm Tue-Fri, 11am-3pm Sat) Artist-owned cooperative exhibits a mixed plate of artworks.

5 **THIRTYNINEHOTEL**
(Map p46; http://thirtyninehotel.com; 39 N Hotel St; ☺4-9pm Tue-Sat) Provocative multimedia art gallery where DJs spin inside a cocktail lounge (p80).

6 **LOUIS POHL GALLERY**
(Map p46; www.louispohlgallery.com; 1111 Nu'uanu Ave; ☺11am-5pm Mon & Wed-Sat, 11am-2pm Tue) Paintings by a former 'living treasure' of Hawaii, along with multimedia works by contemporary artists.

HAWAIISLAM
Spoken Word

(Map p70; www.hawaiislam.com; Fresh Cafe, 831 Queen St; admission $3-5; ☺8:30pm 1st Thu of the month) One of the USA's biggest poetry slams, here international wordsmiths, artists, musicians, MCs and DJs share the stage. For aspiring spoken-word stars, sign up starts at 7:30pm.

Cinemas

For more theater locations, show times and ticketing, check **Fandango** (800-326-3264; www.fandango.com).

DORIS DUKE THEATRE   Cinema
(Map p70; ☎532-8768; www.honoluluacademy.org; 900 S Beretania St; admission $10; P) Shows a mind-bending array of experimental, alternative, retro-classic and arthouse films, especially ground-breaking documentaries, inside the Honolulu Museum of Arts. For weekday matinees, validated parking costs $3 (evenings and weekends free).

MOVIE MUSEUM   Cinema
(☎735-8771; www.kaimukihawaii.com; 3566 Harding Ave; admission $5; ☺usually noon-8pm Thu-Sun) In the Kaimuki neighborhood, east of the UH Manoa campus, this sociable spot screens classic oldies, foreign flicks and indie films, including some Hawaii premieres, in a tiny theater equipped with digital sound and just 20 comfy Barca-loungers. Reservations recommended.

🛍 Shopping

Although not a brand-name mecca like Waikiki, Honolulu has unique shops and multiple malls offering plenty of local flavor, from traditional flower lei stands and ukulele factories to Hawaiiana souvenir shops, and from contempo island-style clothing boutiques to vintage and antiques stores.

TOP CHOICE NATIVE BOOKS/ NĀ MEA HAWAI'I
Hawaiiana, Books
(Map p70; ☎597-8967; www.nativebookshawaii.com; Ward Warehouse, 1050 Ala Moana Blvd; ☺10am-8:30pm Mon-Thu, to 9pm Fri & Sat, to 6pm Sun; P) So much more than just a bookstore stocking Hawaiiana tomes, CDs and DVDs, this cultural gathering spot also sells beautiful silk-screened

Left: Aloha Tower Marketplace at night (p41) **Below:** Lei, Chinatown

fabrics, koa-wood bowls, Hawaii-made quilts and fish-hook jewelry. Pack your bags with Hawaii-made gourmet foodstuffs – Big Island honey, Maui sea salts, lavosh flatbread crackers – for all your friends and family back home. Call or check online for special events, including author readings and cultural classes (see p61).

ALA MOANA CENTER · Mall
(Map p70; www.alamoanacenter.com; 1450 Ala Moana Blvd; ⏱9:30am-9pm Mon-Sat, 10am-7pm Sun; P) Holy fashion! This open-air shopping mall and its nearly 300 department stores and mostly chain stores could compete on an international runway with some of Asia's famous megamalls. A handful of Hawaii specialty shops such as Crazy Shirts for tees, Reyn's for aloha shirts, Maui Waterwear and Loco Boutique for swimsuits and board shorts, Local Motion surfwear and Na Hoku jewelry are thrown into the mix.

ISLAND SLIPPER · Shoes
(Map p70; www.islandslipper.com; Ward Warehouse, 1050 Ala Moana Blvd; ⏱10am-9pm Mon-Sat, to 8pm Sun; P) Across Honolulu and Waikiki, scores of stores sell flip-flops (aka 'rubbah slippah'), but nobody else carries such ultracomfy suede and leather styles – all made in Hawaii since 1946 – let alone such giant sizes (as one clerk told us, 'We fit *all* the island people.'). Try on as many pairs as you like until your feet really feel the aloha.

MANUHEALI'I · Clothing, Handbags
(Map p70; www.manuhealii.com; 930 Punahou St; ⏱9:30am-6pm Mon-Fri, 9am-4pm Sat, 10am-3pm Sun; P) Look to this island-born shop for original and modern designs. Hawaiian musicians often sport Manuheali'i's bold-print silk aloha shirts. Flowing synthetic print and knit dresses and wrap tops take inspiration from the traditional muumuu but are transformed into spritely contemporary looks. Also in Kailua (p192).

KAMAKA HAWAII   Musical Instruments

(off Map p46; ☎531-3165; www.kamakahawaii.com; 550 South St; ⏲8am-4pm Mon-Fri) Skip right by those tacky souvenir shops selling cheap plastic and wooden ukuleles. Kamaka specializes in handcrafted ukuleles made on O'ahu since 1916, with prices starting at around $500. Its signature is an oval-shaped 'pineapple' ukulele, which has a more mellow sound. Call ahead for free 30-minute factory tours, usually starting at 10:30am Tuesday through Friday.

TIN CAN MAILMAN   Antiques, Books

(Map p46; http://tincanmailman.net; 1026 Nu'uanu Ave; ⏲11am-5pm Mon-Thu, to 4pm Fri & Sat) If you're a big fan of vintage tiki wares and 20th-century Hawaiiana books, you'll fall in love with this little Chinatown antiques shop. Thoughtfully collected treasures include jewelry and ukuleles, silk aloha shirts, tropical-wood furnishings, vinyl records, rare prints and tourist brochures from the post-WWII tourism boom. No photos allowed, sorry.

FIGHTING EEL   Clothing

(Map p46; www.fightingeel.com; 1133 Bethel St; ⏲10am-6pm Mon-Sat) A one-stop made-in-Hawaii shop for blowsy, draped dresses in modern solids, resort flowered and geometric prints. They're perfect no matter if you're hitting the beach in girly flip-flops or strapping on heels for an island wedding. Further northeast at Blank Canvas, you can custom order T-shirts, tank tops and hoodies in thousands of different designs.

CINNAMON GIRL   Clothing, Shoes

(Map p70; http://cinnamongirl.com; Ala Moana Center, 1450 Ala Moana Blvd; ⏲9:30am-9pm Mon-Sat, 10am-7pm Sun; P) Designed with girlish whimsy by O'ahu fashionista Jonelle Fujita, flirty rayon dresses and tops that are cool, contemporary and island-made for both women and kids hang on the racks, while bejeweled necklaces and sweet floppy sunhats sit on shelves. Also at Ward Warehouse (Map p70).

NOHEA GALLERY   Arts & Crafts

(Map p70; www.noheagallery.com; Ward Warehouse, 1050 Ala Moana Blvd; ⏲10am-9pm Mon-Sat, to 6pm Sun; P) A meditative space amid the shopping-mall madness, this high-end gallery sells handcrafted jewelry, glassware, pottery and woodwork, much of it made in Hawaii. Local artisans occasionally give demonstrations of their crafts on the sidewalk outside. Also at Waikiki's Moana Surfrider hotel (Map p96).

TUTUVI SITOA   Clothing

(Map p51; www.tutuvi.com; 2636 King St; ⏲10am-5pm Tue-Sat) Near the UH Manoa campus, designer Colleen Kimura's tiki-esque storefront floats racks of T-shirts, dresses, pa'u skirts, beach wraps, aloha shirts and natural-fiber sandals, all handmade and

Hula dolls for sale

DOUGLAS PEEBLES PHOTOGRAPHY/ALAMY ©

screen-printed with designs drawn from nature such as banana leaves, hibiscus and forest ferns.

HULA SUPPLY CENTER   Hawaiiana
(Map p51; www.hulasupplycenter.com; 1481 S King St; ⏰10am-6pm Mon-Fri, to 5pm Sat; [P]) For more than 60 years, traditional Hawaiian musicians and dancers have come here to get their *kukui*-nut lei, calabash drum gourds, Tahitian-style hula skirts, nose flutes and the like. Even if you don't dance, you can swing by to pick up a *kapa*-print aloha shirt, hula DVD or musical CD.

CINDY'S LEI SHOP   Flowers
(Map p46; www.cindysleishoppe.com; 1034 Maunakea St; ⏰6am-7pm Mon-Sat, to 6pm Sun) At this inviting little corner shop, a Chinatown landmark, you can watch aunties craft flower lei made of orchids, plumeria, twining maile, lantern '*ilima* (flowering ground-cover) and ginger. Several other lei shops clustered nearby will also pack lei for you to carry back home on the plane.

LION COFFEE   Gifts, Souvenirs
(www.lioncoffee.com; 1555 Kalani St; ⏰6am-5pm Mon-Fri, 9am-3pm Sat; [P] [🛜]) In an out-of-the-way warehouse west of downtown en route to the airport, this discount grown-in-Hawaii coffee giant roasts myriad flavors from straight-up strong (100% Kona 24-Karat and Diamond Head espresso blend) to outlandishly wacky (chocolate mac-nut, toasted coconut). Friendly baristas pour free tastes.

T&L MUUMUU FACTORY   Clothing
(Map p70; www.muumuufactory.com; 1423 Kapi'olani Blvd; ⏰9am-6pm Mon-Sat, 10am-4pm Sun; [P]) So much flammable aloha wear in one space! It's worth a visit for the kitsch factor alone. This is a shop for *tutu* (grandmothers), to whom polyester still represents progress. Bold-print muumuus run in sizes from supermodel skinny to Polynesian island queen, and *pa'u* skirts are just funky enough to wedge into an urban outfit.

The Best...
Made-in-Hawaii
Shops

ANTIQUE ALLEY   Antiques
(Map p70; www.portaloha.com/antiquealley; 1347 Kapi'olani Blvd; ⏰11am-5pm; [P]) Unbelievably crammed with rare collectibles and other cast-off memorabilia from Hawaii through the decades, this co-op shop, which once cameoed on PBS' *Antiques Roadshow*, sells just about any Hawaiiana that you can imagine buying, from poi pounders and traditional fish hooks to vintage hula dolls and Matson cruise liner artifacts.

MONTSUKI   Clothing
(📞734-3457; 1132 Koko Head Ave; ⏰call for hours) In the low-key Kaimuki neighborhood, the mother-daughter design team of Janet and Patty Yamasaki refashion classic kimono and *obi* designs into modern wearable art. East-west wedding dresses, formal wear and sleek day fashions can all be tailored. Call ahead to make an appointment before stopping by.

ℹ️ Information

Dangers & Annoyances

Drug dealing and gang activity are prevalent on the north side of Chinatown, particularly along Nu'uanu Stream and the River St pedestrian mall, which should be avoided after dark. Chinatown's skid rows include blocks of Hotel St.

Emergency

Police, Fire & Ambulance (☎911) For all emergencies.

Police Headquarters (off Map p46; ☎529-3111; 810 S Beretania St) For nonemergencies (eg stolen property reports necessary for insurance claims).

Internet Access

Cheaper cybercafes on King St near the UH Manoa campus stay open late.

FedEx Office (www.fedex.com; @ ☎) Ala Moana (☎944-8500; 1500 Kapi'olani Blvd; ☉7:30am-9pm Mon-Fri, 10am-6pm Sat, noon-6pm Sun); Downtown (☎528-7171; 590 Queen St; ☉7am-11pm Mon-Fri, 9am-9pm Sat & Sun); University area (☎943-0005; 2575 S King St; ☉24hr) Self-serve computer terminals (20¢ to 30¢ per minute), pay-as-you-go digital photo-printing and CD-burning stations and free wi-fi.

Hawaii State Library (☎586-3500; www. librarieshawaii.org; 478 S King St; ☉10am-5pm Mon & Wed, 9am-5pm Tue, Fri & Sat, 9am-8pm Thu; @ ☎) Free wi-fi and internet terminals (temporary nonresident library card $10) downtown that may be reserved by calling ahead.

Media

NEWSPAPERS & MAGAZINES Honolulu Magazine (www.honolulumagazine.com) Glossy monthly magazine covering arts, culture, fashion, shopping, lifestyle and cuisine.

Honolulu Star-Advertiser (www.staradvertiser. com, www.honolulupulse.com) Honolulu's daily newspaper; look for 'TGIF,' Friday's special events and entertainment pull-out section.

Honolulu Weekly (http://honoluluweekly.com) Free weekly arts-and-entertainment tabloid has a local events calendar listing museum and gallery exhibits, cultural classes, outdoor activities, farmers markets, volunteering meet-ups and 'whatevas.'

RADIO & TV KHET (Oceanic cable channel 10) Hawaii public TV (PBS).

KHON (Oceanic cable channel 3) Evening news broadcast ends with slack key guitar music by Keola and Kapono Beamer and clips of people waving the *shaka* (Hawaii hand greeting) sign.

KHPR (88.1FM) Hawaii Public Radio (NPR); classical music and news.

KIKU (channel 9) Multicultural community TV programming.

KINE (105.1FM) Classic and contemporary Hawaiian music.

KIPO (89.3FM) Hawaii Public Radio; news, jazz and world music.

KQMQ (93.1FM) 'Da Pa'ina' island-style music and Hawaiian reggae.

KTUH (90.3FM) Quirky University of Hawai'i student-run radio.

Medical Services

Hyperbaric Medicine Center (☎851-7030/ 7032; www.hyperbaricmedicinecenter.com; 275 Pu'uhale Rd) For scuba divers with the bends.

Longs Drugs (www.cvs.com/longs) Downtown (☎536-5542; 1330 Pali Hwy; ☉24hr) University area (☎949-2651; 2220 S King St; ☉24hr) Convenient 24-hour drugstores with pharmacies.

Queen's Medical Center (☎538-9011; www. queensmedicalcenter.net; 1301 Punchbowl St; ☉24hr) O'ahu's biggest, best-equipped hospital has a 24-hour emergency room downtown.

Straub Clinic & Hospital (☎522-4000; www.straubhealth.org; 888 S King St; ☉24hr) Operates a 24-hour emergency room downtown and a nonemergency clinic open weekdays (call ahead to check hours).

❶ Getting There & Around

For information on flights into Honolulu International Airport (Map p38), see p326. For ground transportation to/from the airport, see p327. For taxis, see p331. For bicycle rentals, see p60.

Bus

Just northwest of Waikiki, the Ala Moana Center (Map p70) mall is the central transfer point for TheBus, O'ahu's public-transportation system. For details about bus routes, schedules, fares and passes, see p328.

To reach Honolulu's various neighborhoods from Waikiki, several direct bus routes don't require transferring at Ala Moana Center.

Useful Bus Routes

ROUTE	DESTINATION
2	Waikiki, Honolulu Museum of Arts, 'Iolani Palace, downtown Honolulu, Chinatown, Bishop Museum
4	Waikiki, University of Hawai'i, 'Iolani Palace, downtown Honolulu, Chinatown, Queen Emma Summer Palace
8	Waikiki, Ala Moana Center, Ward Centers, downtown Honolulu, Chinatown
13	Waikiki, Honolulu Convention Center, Honolulu Museum of Arts, 'Iolani Palace, downtown Honolulu, Chinatown
19 & 20	Waikiki, Ala Moana Center, Ward Centers, Restaurant Row, Aloha Tower Marketplace, downtown Honolulu, Chinatown, Honolulu International Airport*; also Pearl Harbor (route 20 only)
42	Waikiki, Ala Moana Center, Ward Centers, downtown Honolulu, Chinatown, Pearl Harbor
B (CityExpress!)	Waikiki, Honolulu Museum of Arts, 'Iolani Palace, downtown Honolulu, Chinatown, Bishop Museum
E (CountryExpress!)	Waikiki, Ala Moana Center, Restaurant Row, Aloha Tower Marketplace, downtown Honolulu

*One piece of hand-held carry-on baggage only per person; luggage prohibited (see p327).

Car

Major car-rental companies (see p330) are found at Honolulu International Airport and in Waikiki (see p137).

Traffic jams up during rush hours, roughly from 7am to 9am and 3pm to 6pm weekdays. Expect heavy traffic in both directions on the H-1 Fwy during this time, as well as on the Pali and Likelike Hwys headed into Honolulu in the morning and away from the city in the late afternoon.

Two major thoroughfares run the length of Honolulu: Ala Moana Blvd (Hwy 92) skirts the coast from the airport to Waikiki, while the H-1 Fwy runs east–west between the beach and the mountains. To/from Waikiki, King St (one-way heading southeast) and Beretania St (one-way heading northwest) are alternate surface streets into and out of downtown. Chinatown is full of confusing one-way streets, and N Hotel St is open to buses only.

PARKING Downtown and Chinatown have on-street metered parking; it's reasonably easy to find an empty space on weekends but nearly impossible on weekdays. Bring lots of quarters.

Pay parking is also available at several municipal garages and there is a lot scattered around Chinatown and downtown. On the outskirts of the downtown core, the private Neal S Blaisdell Center (Map p70) offers all-day parking from $6, depending on special events.

Most shopping centers, including the Ala Moana Center (Map p70), provide free parking for customers. The Aloha Tower Marketplace (Map p46) offers a pay self-parking lot (three hours for $3 before 4pm Monday to Friday, or $5 flat rate after 4pm weekdays and all day on weekends). Restaurant patrons get three hours of free parking with validation.

Waikiki

Once a Hawaiian royal retreat, Waikiki is riding high on a new wave of effortlessly chic style these days. No longer just a plasticky beach destination for package tourists, this famous strand of sand is flowering, starting with a renaissance of Hawaiian music at beachfront hotels and resorts. In this concrete jungle of modern high-rises, you can, surprisingly, still hear whispers of Hawaii's past, from the chanting of hula troupes at Kuhio Beach to the legacy of Olympic gold medalist Duke Kahanamoku. Take a surfing lesson from a bronzed beachboy, then spend a lazy afternoon lying on Waikiki's golden sands. Before the sun sinks below the horizon, hop aboard a catamaran and sail off toward Diamond Head. Sip a sunset mai tai and be hypnotized by the lilting harmonies of slack key guitar, then mingle with the locals, who come here to party after dark too.

Sans Souci Beach Park (p100)
ANN CECIL/LONELY PLANET IMAGES ©

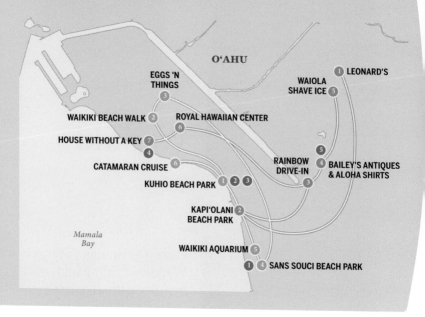

Waikiki Itineraries

O'AHU

LEONARD'S ①

WAIOLA SHAVE ICE ⑤

EGGS 'N THINGS ③

WAIKIKI BEACH WALK ②   ROYAL HAWAIIAN CENTER ⑥

HOUSE WITHOUT A KEY ⑦

④

CATAMARAN CRUISE ⑥

KUHIO BEACH PARK ① ② ③

RAINBOW DRIVE-IN

⑤

④ BAILEY'S ANTIQUES & ALOHA SHIRTS

③

KAPI'OLANI BEACH PARK ②

Mamala Bay

WAIKIKI AQUARIUM ⑤

① ④ SANS SOUCI BEACH PARK

Two Days

① **Kuhio Beach Park** (p95) Pay your respects to iconic surfer **Duke Kahanamoku's statue** before taking a morning surfing lesson from one of Waikiki's modern-day beachboys. Take the kids on an outrigger-canoe ride or just laze the hours away until the **torch lighting & hula show**.

② **Waikiki Beach Walk** (p133) After dark, Waikiki Beach Walk is the most buzzing place to be. Change out of your rubbah slippah and treat yourself to stellar Hawaii Regional cuisine at **Roy's Waikiki Beach**, a star island chef's bistro.

③ **Eggs 'n Things** (p121) Sometimes all the tourists really are headed in the right direction: dig into Portuguese sausage and fluffy pancakes topped with guava or coconut syrup at this always-busy diner early the next morning.

④ **Sans Souci Beach Park** (p100) Stroll, cycle or catch a bus down toward the Diamond Head side of Waikiki to this seldom-crowded strand. When morning waters are calm, snorkeling here is a joy.

⑤ **Waikiki Aquarium** (p100) Figure out exactly what all those fish you just snorkeled by actually are at this eco-conscious educational center. Don't miss the moon jellyfish and Palauan chambered nautiluses.

⑥ **Catamaran cruise** (p106) Amble back to Waikiki's main strip and climb aboard one of the party boats that pulls up right on the beach, catering sunset mai tais shaken by waves.

➡ THIS LEG: 4 MILES

Three Days

1 **Leonard's** (p125) Nothing says aloha like a sugary, sweet *malasada* (Portuguese-style doughnut), still warm and straight from the ovens of this 1950s vintage bakery.

2 **Kapi'olani Beach Park** (p99) Kick back with local families laying out picnic blankets on the grass shaded by palm trees at this friendly, sprawling stretch of sand. Runners and tennis players get their daily workouts here, while golfers book ahead for tee times at nearby **Ala Wai Golf Course**.

3 **Rainbow Drive-In** (p125) Join the local surfers and working folks on their lunch break at this authentic spot that dishes up mixed-plate lunches covered in good gravy.

4 **Bailey's Antiques & Aloha Shirts** (p133) Shrug off those heavy, sweaty clothes you brought from da mainland and get yourself a stylin' aloha shirt at this vintage clothing shop.

5 **Waiola Shave Ice** (p125) Detour further up Kapahulu Ave to this locals' after-school hangout to sample one of O'ahu's tastiest contenders for rainbow-colored icy goodness, layered with azuki beans or topped off with *liliko'i* (passion fruit) cream.

6 **Royal Hawaiian Center** (p134) At Waikiki's biggest, four-story shopping mall, browse for island-made surfwear and artisan crafts, or learn how to make a lei and dance the hula at free drop-in cultural classes, offered on many afternoons.

7 **House Without a Key** (p127) Sashay inside Waikiki's classiest resort and grab an ocean-view table outdoors by the century-old kiawe tree. Sip tropical cocktails while watching graceful hula dancers be serenaded by slack key guitar and ukulele muses.

THIS LEG: 5 MILES

Waikiki Highlights

1 **Best Beach: Sans Souci Beach Park** (p100) Here you can discover your own private little sandy hideaway.

2 **Best Activity: Surfing** (p103) *Malihini* (newcomers) learn to stand up on their boards at Kuhio Beach, while experts join the line-ups at Queens, Canoes and Populars.

3 **Best Free Entertainment: Kuhio Beach Torch Lighting & Hula Show** (p127) When the conch shell blows, hula dancers reach toward the sky.

4 **Best Bar: House Without a Key** (p127) Swizzle sunset cocktails while slack key guitars play island lullabies.

5 **Best Shop: Bailey's Antiques & Aloha Shirts** (p133) Almost a museum of aloha shirts that rock stars and celebrities swear by.

Statue of surfing legend Duke Kahanamoku (p100)
ANN CECIL/LONELY PLANET IMAGES ©

Discover Waikiki

History

Looking at Waikiki today, it's hard to imagine that less than 150 years ago this tourist mecca was almost entirely wetlands filled with fishponds and *kalo lo'i* (taro fields). Fed by mountain streams from the Manoa Valley, Waikiki (Spouting Water) was once one of O'ahu's most fertile farming areas. In 1795 Kamehameha I became the first *ali'i* (chief) to successfully unite the Hawaiian Islands under one sovereign's rule, bringing his royal court to Waikiki.

By the 1880s, Honolulu's more well-to-do citizens had started building gingerbread-trimmed cottages along the narrow beachfront. Tourism started booming in 1901 when Waikiki's first luxury hotel, the Moana, opened its doors on a former royal compound. Tiring quickly of the pesky mosquitoes that thrived in Waikiki's wetlands, early beachgoers petitioned to have the 'swamps' brought under control. In 1922 the Ala Wai Canal was dug to divert the streams that flowed into Waikiki and to dry out the wetlands. Tourists quickly replaced the water buffaloes.

In the 'Roaring '20s,' the Royal Hawaiian hotel opened to serve passengers arriving on luxury ocean liners from San Francisco. The Depression and WWII put a damper on tourism, but the Royal Hawaiian was turned into an R&R playground for sailors on shore leave. From 1935 to 1975, the classic radio show *Hawaii Calls,* performed live at the Moana hotel, broadcast dreams of a tropical paradise to the US mainland and the world. As late as 1950, surfers could still drive their cars right up to the beach and park on the sand – hard to imagine nowadays!

Swimming at Waikiki Beach
RICHARD L'ANSON/LONELY PLANET IMAGES ©

 Beaches

The 2-mile stretch of white sand that everyone calls Waikiki Beach runs from Hilton Hawaiian Village all the way to Kapi'olani Beach Park. Along the way, the beach keeps changing names and personalities. In the early morning, quiet seaside paths belong to walkers and runners, and strolling toward Diamond Head at dawn can be a meditative experience. By midmorning it looks like any resort beach – packed with water-sports concessionaires and lots of tourist bodies. By noon it's a challenge to walk along the packed beach without stepping on anyone.

Waikiki is good for swimming, bodyboarding, surfing, sailing and other water sports most of the year, and there are lifeguards, restrooms and outdoor showers scattered along the beachfront. Between May and September, summer swells make the water a little rough for swimming, but great for surfing. For snorkeling, head to Sans Souci Beach Park or Queen's Surf Beach.

The beaches are listed geographically from northwest to southeast.

KAHANAMOKU BEACH   Beach
Fronting the Hilton Hawaiian Village, Kahanamoku Beach is Waikiki's westernmost beach. It takes its name from Duke Kahanamoku (1890–1968), the legendary Waikiki beachboy whose family once owned the land where the resort now stands. Hawaii's champion surfer and Olympic gold medal winner learned to swim right here. Protected by a breakwater wall at one end and a pier at the other, with a coral reef running between the two, the beach offers calm swimming conditions and a gently sloping, if rocky bottom (wearing reef walkers will help protect your tender *malihini* feet). Public beach access is at the end of Paoa Pl, off Kalia Rd.

FORT DERUSSY BEACH   Beach
Seldom too crowded, this overlooked beauty extends along the shore of a military reservation. Like all beaches in Hawaii, it's free and open to the public. The only area off-limits to civvies is Hale Koa, a military hotel backing onto the beach, although the hotel's poolside snack bar sells to beachgoers. The water is usually calm and good for swimming, but it's shallow at low tide. When conditions are right, windsurfers, bodyboarders and board surfers all play here.

Usually open daily, beach-hut concessionaires here rent bodyboards, kayaks and snorkel sets. In addition to lifeguards, restrooms and outdoor showers, you'll find a grassy lawn with palm trees offering some sparse shade, an alternative to frying on the sand. A pay parking lot is available in front of the Hawai'i Army Museum.

GRAY'S BEACH   Beach
Nestled up against the Halekulani luxury resort, Gray's Beach has suffered some of the Waikiki strip's worst erosion. It was named after Gray's-by-the-Sea, a 1920s boarding house that stood here. Because the seawall in front of the Halekulani hotel is so close to the waterline, the beach sand fronting the hotel is often totally submerged by the surf, but the offshore waters are shallow and calm, offering decent swimming conditions. Public access is along a paved walkway.

KAHALOA & ULUKOU BEACHES   Beach
The generous stretch of beach between the Royal Hawaiian and Moana Surfrider hotels is Waikiki's busiest section of sand and surf, great for sunbathing, swimming and people watching. Most of the beach has a shallow bottom with a gradual slope. The only drawback for swimmers is the beach's popularity with beginning surfers, and the occasional catamaran landing hazard.

Queens and **Canoes**, Waikiki's best-known surf breaks, are just offshore, and on a good day there can be hundreds of surfers lined up on the horizon waiting to catch a wave. Paddle further offshore over a lagoon to **Populars** (aka 'Pops'), a favorite of long-boarders.

KUHIO BEACH PARK   Beach
If you're the kind of person who wants it all, this beach offers everything from protected swimming to outrigger-canoe rides, and even a free sunset-hula and Hawaiian-music show (see p127). You'll find restrooms, outdoor showers, a snack bar, surfboard lockers and beach-gear-rental stands at **Waikiki Beach Center**, near the friendly police substation.

The beach is marked on its opposite end by **Kapahulu Groin**, a walled storm drain with a walkway on top that juts out

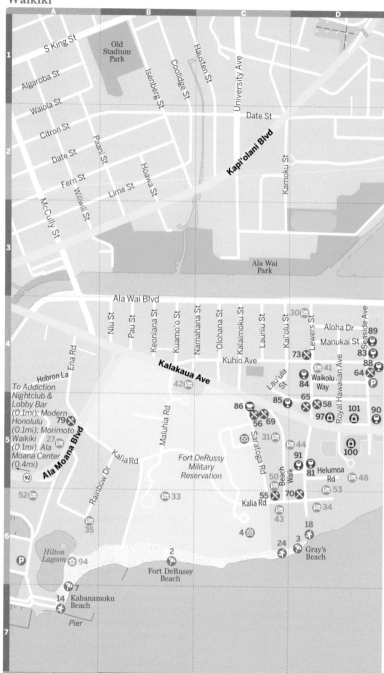

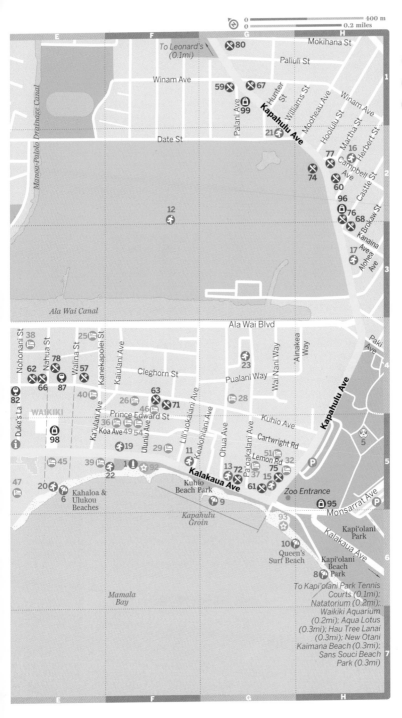

Waikiki

WAIKIKI BEACHES

into the ocean. A low stone breakwater, called the Wall, runs out from Kapahulu Groin, parallel to the beach. It was built to control sand erosion and, in the process, two nearly enclosed swimming pools were formed.

The pool closest to Kapahulu Groin is best for swimming, with the water near the breakwater reaching overhead depths. However, because circulation is limited, the water gets murky with a noticeable film of sunscreen oils, especially later in the day. The 'Watch Out Deep Holes' sign refers to holes in the pool's sandy bottom created by swirling currents, so waders should be cautious in the deeper part of the pool.

Kapahulu Groin is one of Waikiki's hottest bodyboarding spots. If the surf's right, you can find a few dozen bodyboarders, mostly teenagers, riding the waves. These experienced local kids ride straight for the groin's cement wall and then veer away at the last moment, thrilling the tourists watching them from the little pier above. Local kids also walk out on the Wall, but it can be dangerous due to a slippery surface and breaking surf.

KAPI'OLANI BEACH PARK   Beach
Where did all the tourists go? From Kapahulu Groin south to the Natatorium, this peaceful stretch of beach, backed by a green space of banyan trees and grassy lawns, offers a relaxing niche with none of

Island Insights

Near the police substation at Waikiki Beach Center, four ordinary-looking boulders are actually the legendary **Wizard Stones of Kapaemahu**, said to contain the secrets and healing powers of 16th-century Tahitian sorcerers. Just east is a **bronze statue of Duke Kahanamoku** standing with one of his long-boards, often with fresh flower lei hanging around his neck. Considered the father of modern surfing, Duke made his home in Waikiki. Many local surfers have taken issue with the placement of the statue – Duke is standing with his back to the sea, a position they say he never would've taken in real life. Stop to wave the *shaka* (Hawaiian hand greeting) sign to all the folks back home via the Duke's live-streaming webcam (www.honolulu.gov/multimed/waikiki.asp).

the frenzy found on the beaches fronting the Waikiki hotel strip. It's a popular weekend picnicking spot for local families, who unload the kids to splash in the ocean while adults fire up the BBQ. Facilities include restrooms and outdoor showers.

The widest northern end of Kapi'olani Beach is nicknamed **Queen's Surf Beach**. The stretch in front of the pavilion is popular with Waikiki's gay community. Its sandy bottom offers decent swimming. The beach between Queen's Surf Beach and The Wall is shallow and has broken coral. Long-boarders favor the offshore left-handed surf break **Publics**.

SANS SOUCI BEACH PARK   Beach

At the Diamond Head edge of Waikiki, Sans Souci is a prime sandy stretch of oceanfront that's even further away from the frenzied tourist scene. It's commonly called Kaimana Beach, as it's next door to the New Otani Kaimana Beach Hotel. Local residents often come here for their daily swims. A shallow reef close to shore makes for calm, protected waters and provides good snorkeling. Strong swimmers and snorkelers can follow the Kapua Channel that cuts through the reef. Be aware that currents can pick up in the channel, so play it safe and check conditions with the lifeguards before heading out. Limited beach facilities include outdoor showers.

 Sights

Let's be honest: you're probably just here for the beach. Honolulu's most important museums and historic sites are all outside Waikiki, but minor oceanfront diversions found here include two historical hotels, an eco-friendly aquarium, a military museum and a kiddie zoo. As you walk past public parks and landmarks, look for small interpretive signboards, part of the **Waikiki Historic Trail** (www.waikikihistorictrail.com), which points out tidbits of Waikiki's royal and modern history.

TOP CHOICE **WAIKIKI AQUARIUM**   Aquarium

(923-9741; www.waquarium.org; 2777 Kalakaua Ave; admission & self-guided audio tour adult/child 4-12yr/youth 13-17yr $9/2/4; 9am-5pm, last entry 4:30pm;) Located on Waikiki's shoreline, this modern university-run aquarium features a jaw-dropping shark gallery and dozens of tanks that recreate diverse tropical Pacific reef habitats. You'll see rare fish species from the Northwestern Hawaiian Islands, as well as hypnotic moon jellies and flashlight fish that host bioluminescent bacteria. Especially hypnotizing are the Palauan chambered nautiluses with their unique spiral shells – in fact, this is the world's first aquarium to breed these endangered creatures in captivity, a ground-breaking achievement. An outdoor tank out back is home to rare and endangered Hawaiian monk seals that can't be returned to the wild. Check the website or call ahead to make reservations for special family-friendly events and fun educational programs for kids such as 'Aquarium After Dark' adventures. Bus 2 Waikiki-Kapi'olani Park stops outside the aquarium, or it's about a 15-minute walk southeast of the main Waikiki beach strip.

FREE MOANA SURFRIDER
Historic Building

(☎922-3111; www.moana-surfrider.com; 2365 Kalakaua Ave; admission & tour free; ⏱1hr tours usually 11am Mon, Wed & Fri) Christened the Moana Hotel when it opened in 1901, this beaux-arts, plantation-style inn was once the haunt of Hollywood movie stars, aristocrats and business tycoons. The historic hotel embraces a seaside courtyard with a big banyan tree and a wraparound veranda, where island musicians and hula dancers perform in the evenings. Upstairs from the lobby, you'll find displays of memorabilia from the early days; everything from scripts of the famed *Hawaii*

Calls radio show broadcast live from the courtyard here between 1935 and 1975 to woolen bathing suits, historical period photographs and a short video of Waikiki back in the days when the Moana was the only hotel on the oceanfront horizon.

FREE ROYAL HAWAIIAN
Historic Building

(☎923-7311; www.royal-hawaiian.com; 2259 Kalakaua Ave; admission & tour free; ⏱1hr tours usually 2pm Tue, Thu & Sat) With its Moorish-style turrets and archways, this gorgeously restored 1927 art-deco landmark, dubbed the 'Pink Palace,' is a throwback to the era when Rudolph Valentino was *the* romantic idol and travel to Hawaii was by Matson Navigation luxury liner. Its guest list read like a who's-who of A-list celebrities, from royalty to Rockefellers, along with luminaries such as Charlie Chaplin and Babe Ruth. Today, historic tours explore the architecture and lore of this grande dame, including the gardens where Queen Ka'ahumanu's summer palace once stood. Ask the concierge for a self-guided walking-tour brochure.

Giant clam, Waikiki Aquarium

HAWAI'I ARMY MUSEUM   Museum

(✆955-9552; www.hiarmymuseumsoc.org; 2161 Kalia Rd; admission by donation, audio tour $5; ⏱9am-5pm Tue-Sun; P) At Fort DeRussy, this museum showcases an almost mind-numbing array of military paraphernalia as it relates to Hawaii's history, starting with shark-tooth clubs that Kamehameha the Great used to win control of the island more than two centuries ago. Concentrating on the US military presence in Hawaii, extensive exhibits include displays on the 442nd, the Japanese American regiment that became the most decorated regiment in WWII, and on Kaua'i-born Eric Shinseki, a retired four-star army general who spoke out against the US invasion of Iraq and has served as President Barack Obama's Secretary of Veterans Affairs, as well as a Cobra helicopter and military tanks and machinery. Validated parking costs from $2.

HONOLULU ZOO   Zoo

(✆971-7171; www.honoluluzoo.org; 151 Kapahulu Ave; adult/child 3-12yr $14/6; ⏱9am-4:30pm; P 🚻) Badly in need of renovations, this small zoo on the north side of Kapi'olani Park showcases some 300 species spread across 40-plus acres of tropical greenery, including a petting zoo for kids. Hawaii has no endemic land mammals, but in the aviary near the entrance you can see some native birds, including the *ae'o* (Hawaiian stilt), the *nene* (Hawaiian goose) and *'apapane,* a bright-red Hawaiian honeycreeper. Make reservations for family-oriented twilight tours, dinner safaris, zoo campouts and stargazing nights. Parking in the zoo's lot costs $1 per hour (bring quarters). You'll find free parking nearby at the Waikiki Shell off Monsarrat Ave.

Activities

Waikiki's beaches steal the spotlight, but landlubbers can also find plenty of fun in the sun. In the early mornings and late afternoons, runners pound the pavement next to Ala Wai Canal, where outrigger-canoe teams paddle. Just inland from the beach, Kapi'olani Park has tennis courts and sports fields for soccer and softball, even cricket. For an indoor

Surfboards lined up on Waikiki Beach (p94)

RICK STRANGE/ALAMY ©

Waikiki for Children

Start at the beach. In just an hour or so, the older kids can learn how to stand up on a board and surf, or they can rent a bodyboard and ride on their bellies. Another fun way to play is to take an outrigger-canoe ride and then paddle back into shore afterwards.

Want to see the world from beneath the waves? Don a snorkel and take a look at the colorful fish at Queen's Surf Beach or take a ride on the Atlantis Adventures submarine (p107) and see it all through a porthole.

At the beach at the north end of Kapi'olani Park, Waikiki Aquarium (p100), with its kaleidoscopic array of tropical fish and reef sharks, has lots of fun just for *nā keiki* (children). Check online for the schedule of family programs such as 'Marine Munchies' feedings for ages five and up, or wet-and-wild 'Exploring the Reef at Night' field trips for ages six and up (reservations required).

The small Honolulu Zoo has a petting zoo where children can get eye to eye with tamer creatures and weekend 'twilight tours' geared to children aged five and older. Buy special program tickets in advance, including for 'snooze in the zoo' campouts and 'breakfast with the animals.'

Families sprawl with beach mats on the grass to watch Kuhio Beach Park's free nightly torch lighting and hula show (p127). And then there are Waikiki's luau and dinner shows (p130), all with a lively drum beat and hip-shakin' hula and fire dancing. The Hilton Hawaiian Village puts on a kid-friendly poolside **Polynesian song and dance show** (per person $20) on Friday night, topped off with a grand fireworks display that's visible from the beach for free.

For Waikiki's best family-friendly hotels, resorts and condos, see p115.

---

workout, **24-Hour Fitness** (☎923-9090; www.24hourfitness.com; 2490 Kalakaua Ave; daily/weekly pass $25/70; ⏱24hr) is a modern gym with cardio and weight machines and group classes.

WAIKIKI OCEAN CLUB Water Sports
(☎927-9606; http://waikikioceanclub.com; adult/child under 4yr/youth 4-15yr $89/25/69; ⏱usually 9am-5pm) Zip on a shuttle over from the Hilton Hawaiian Village's pier or Ala Wai Yacht Harbor to this aquatic theme park moored offshore. Bounce on the ocean trampoline, swivel down the water slide or test the triple-level diving deck, then go snorkeling or swimming in the Pacific. Add-on activities such as sea kayaking, paddle boarding, jet skiing and parasailing all cost extra ($20 to $149 each). Reservations advised.

Surfing, Stand-up Paddling, Bodyboarding & Outrigger-Canoe Rides

Waikiki has good surfing year-round, with the largest waves rolling in during winter. Gentler summer surf breaks are best for beginners. Surfing lessons (from $75 for a two-hour group class) and surfboard, stand-up paddling (SUP) and bodyboard rentals (from $10 to $80 per day) can be arranged at the concession stands along the sand at Kuhio Beach Park, near the bodyboarding hot spot of Kapahulu Groin. Some surf outfits offer outrigger-canoe rides ($75 for two people) that take off from the beach and ride the tossin' waves home – kids especially love those thrills. **Girls Who Surf** (p58) in nearby Ala Moana offer women-only surf lessons.

Island Insights

Tourism at Waikiki Beach took off in the 1950s, after the age of jet travel arrived. As the beachfront developed, landowners haphazardly constructed seawalls and offshore barriers (called groins) to protect their properties, blocking the natural forces of sand accretion, which makes erosion a serious problem. Some of Waikiki's legendary white sands have had to be barged in from Papohaku Beach on the island of Moloka'i. In 2012, a massive hydraulic sand-pumping project was carried out off-shore in an attempt to restore Waikiki's shrinking beaches using an estimated 24,000 cubic yards of reclaimed sand.

TOP CHOICE HAWAIIAN FIRE
SURF SCHOOL Surfing

(☎888-955-7873; www.hawaiianfire.com; 3318 Campbell Ave; 👶) Small-group classes are expertly taught by real-life Honolulu firefighters at this safety-conscious surf school, which offers free transportation between Waikiki and a quiet beach on O'ahu's leeward coast.

HAWAIIAN
WATERSPORTS Surfing, Stand-up Paddling

(☎739-5483; www.hawaiianwatersports.com; 415 Kapahulu Ave; ⏰9am-5pm) Further inland, this shop offers surfing and SUP rentals and lessons away from the crowds at Diamond Head beaches (transportation to/from Waikiki included for lessons, $10 surcharge for rental delivery).

HANS HEDEMANN
SURF Surfing, Stand-up Paddling

(☎924-7778; http://hhsurf.com; Park Shore Waikiki, 2586 Kapahulu Ave; ⏰8am-5pm) You can take baby steps and learn to board or paddle surf at this local pro surfer's well-established school, which is conveniently opposite the main beach strip. Rentals are also available.

HAWAII SURFBOARD
RENTALS Surfing, Stand-up Paddling

(☎672-5055; www.hawaiisurfboardrentals.com) Free surfboard, SUP, bodyboard and car-rack delivery and pick-up with a two-day minimum rental; weekly rates are an especially good deal.

DCX SURF SCHOOL Surfing

(☎926-1414; http://surfingoahu.com) Personalized, relatively inexpensive small-group and individual surfing lessons at Waikiki Beach are given by a passionate, if quirky local surfer.

Snorkeling & Scuba Diving

Waikiki's crowded central beaches are not particularly good for snorkeling, so pick your spot carefully. Two top choices are Sans Souci Beach Park and Queen's Surf Beach, where you'll find some live coral and a decent variety of tropical fish. But to really see the gorgeous stuff – coral gardens, manta rays and more exotic tropical fish – head out on a boat. You can easily rent snorkel sets (from $10 to $20 per day) and scuba-diving equipment (from $35), or book ahead for boat trips (from $110) and PADI open-water certification courses (from $350).

AQUAZONE Scuba Diving, Snorkeling

(☎866-923-3483; http://scubaoahu.com; Outrigger Waikiki on the Beach, 2335 Kalakaua Ave; ⏰8am-5pm Mon-Sat) Dive shop and tour outfitter has a second location on Kalakaua Ave in front of the Waikiki Beach Marriott. Sign up for a beginner's scuba-diving pool lesson (no PADI certification required), a sea-turtle snorkeling tour or a morning deep-water boat dive, including out to WWII shipwrecks. Rental snorkel and diving gear available.

O'AHU DIVING — Scuba Diving

(☏ 721-4210; www.oahudiving.com) Specializes in first-time experiences for beginning divers without certification, as well as deep-water boat dives offshore and PADI refresher classes if you're already certified and have some experience under your diving belt.

SNORKEL BOB'S — Snorkeling

(☏ 737-2421, 800-262-7725; www.snorkelbob .com; 702 Kapahulu Ave; ⊙8am-5pm) Rates vary depending on the quality of the snorkeling gear and accessories packages, but excellent weekly discounts are available and online reservations taken. You can even rent gear on O'ahu, then return it on another island.

Kayaking & Windsurfing

Fort DeRussy Beach has fewer swimmers and catamarans to share the water with than Waikiki's central beaches, although most local windsurfers sail near Diamond Head (see p154).

HAWAIIAN WATERSPORTS — Windsurfing, Kayaking

(☏ 739-5483; www.hawaiianwatersports.com; 415 Kapahulu Ave; ⊙9am-5pm) Inland from the beach, this pro shop offers windsurfing and kayak rentals and lessons at Kailua Beach (p179) on the Windward Coast, a short drive over the Pali Hwy from Honolulu. Transportation to/from Waikiki is complimentary if you're taking lessons.

Golf

Ala Wai Golf Course — Golf

(☏ 733-7387, reservations 296-2000; www1 .honolulu.gov/des/golf /alawai.htm; 404 Kapahulu Ave; green fees $25-50, cart rental $20) With views of Diamond Head and the Ko'olau Range, this flat 18-hole, par-70 layout scores a Guinness World Record for being the world's busiest golf course. Local golfers are allowed to book earlier in the week and grab all the starting times, leaving none for visitors (who may call to reserve up to three days in advance). If you get there early in the day and put yourself on the waiting list – and as long as your entire party waits at the course – you'll probably get to play. Driving range and club rentals available.

Running

If you're into running, you're in good company: statistics estimate that Honolulu has more joggers per capita than any other city on the planet. Two of the best places to break out your running shoes in the early morning or late afternoon are along the Ala Wai Canal and around Kapi'olani Park.

FREE Honolulu Marathon Clinic — Running

(http://honolulumarathonclinic.org; Kapi'olani Park, 3833 Paki Ave; ⊙7:30am Sun mid-Mar–early

WAIKIKI ACTIVITIES

Kayaking, Waikiki
DOUGLAS PEEBLES PHOTOGRAPHY/ALAMY ©

Dec, except on 3-day holiday weekends) Free community volunteer-led training runs are open to everyone, with runners joining groups of their own speed.

Tennis

If you've brought your own rackets, the Diamond Head Tennis Center, at the Diamond Head end of Kapi'olani Park, has 10 courts. For night play, go to the Kapi'olani Park Tennis Courts, opposite the aquarium; all four courts are lit. All of these public courts are free and first-come, first-served. A few Waikiki condos and hotels offer tennis courts and equipment rentals for guests.

 Courses

 WAIKIKI COMMUNITY CENTER Hawaiiana
(☎ 923-1802; www.waikikicommunitycenter.org; 310 Pa'oakalani Ave; classes per person usually $5-15;) Try your hand at mah-jongg, the ukulele, hula, tai chi or a variety of island arts and crafts. Instructors at this

homespun community center are brimming with aloha. Although most students are locals, visitors are welcome too. Pre-registration may be required.

FREE **ROYAL HAWAIIAN CENTER** Hawaiiana
(☎ 922-2299; www.royalhawaiiancenter.com; 2201 Kalakaua Ave) Gargantuan shopping mall that offers free cultural classes and demonstrations in Hawaiian arts and crafts, such as quilting and flower lei-making, plus hula dancing, ukulele playing and even lomilomi traditional body massage.

 Tours

Several catamaran cruises leave right from Waikiki Beach – just walk down to the sand, step into the surf and hop aboard. A 90-minute, all-you-can-drink 'booze cruise' will typically cost you $25 to $40 per adult. Reservations are especially recommended for sunset sails, which sell out fast.

Catamaran, Waikiki Beach (p94)

MAITA'I CATAMARAN   Boat

(☎ 922-5665, 800-462-7975; www.leahi
.com; 👪) Ahoy! Pulling up on the beach
between the Halekulani and Sheraton
hotels, this white catamaran with green
sails offers the biggest variety of boat
trips. Reserve ahead for a 90-minute
daytime or sunset booze cruise (children
allowed) or a moonlight sail to take in the
Hilton's Friday fireworks show. Looking
for something a bit different? On weekdays, family-friendly reef-snorkeling tours
include an onboard picnic lunch.

NA HOKU II   Boat

(☎ 554-5990; www.nahokuii.com) With its
unmistakable yellow-and-red striped
sails, this catamaran is so famous you'll
see a photo of it on the Waikiki edition of
the Monopoly board game. Popular with
frat boys and MTV spring-break bikini
girls, these hard-drinkin' tours set sail
five times between 9:30am and 5:30pm
daily, shoving off from in front of Duke's
Waikiki bar. The sunset sail usually sells
out, so book at least a day or two in
advance.

WAIKIKI RIGGER   Boat

(☎ 922-2210; http://waikikibeachsailing.
com) Sporting tall white sails and a sleek
silver-and-blue body, this ex-champion-
ship racing catamaran offers windy but
thrilling high-speed cruises, more relaxed
snorkel trips and of course, a sunset
booze cruise departing from Gray's Beach
between the Halekulani resort and Waikiki
Shore condo hotel. Reservations required.

ATLANTIS ADVENTURES   Boat

(☎ 800-548-6262; www.atlantisadventures
.com; 90min tour adult $119, child under 13yr &
taller than 36in $53; 👪) See the world from
a porthole aboard the sub that dives to a
depth of 100ft near a reef off Waikiki, offering views of sea life otherwise reserved
for divers – though honestly, it's not
nearly as exciting as it sounds. There are
several sailings daily; you should book
ahead online for discounts. Check-in is at
the Hilton Hawaiian Village's pier in front
of the Ali'i Tower.

Local Knowledge

NAME: JOHN PREGIL, JR

OCCUPATION: HONOLULU
FIRE DEPARTMENT CAPTAIN
& OWNER OF HAWAIIAN FIRE
SURF SCHOOL

PLACE OF RESIDENCE:
KANE'OHE

When did you learn to surf? In the 1970s,
my father would take us down to surf in
summer. I got the bug like a lot of Hawaii
boys do.

What makes surfing in Hawaii different?
Because we're on an island, we catch good
swells from every direction. The water is
warm and there's always somewhere you can
go. During summer, you get smaller, gentler
rollers at Waikiki. In winter, there are more
challenging breaks at Pipeline (p213) and
Sunset Beach (p213).

**How did Hawaiian Fire Surf School get
started?** We were lifetime surfers with
firefighter training in open-water rescue and
lifesaving techniques. The beaches at Waikiki
and Diamond Head didn't look the safest to
us, so we found another spot that's perfect for
beginners: reef and sand, no undertow, chest-
deep water and gentle rollers.

**Any other favorite spots for surfing on
O'ahu?** Back in the day, I'd trek out to the
North Shore to surf, eat lunch, cruise and
surf again. Now I'm a full-time Honolulu fire
captain. Ala Moana (p36), right off Magic
Island, is the first place I look for summer
swells. When it's happening, the whole city
is buzzing.

**What should visitors know before they
take a surfing lesson?** Most people aren't
prepared for the physical motion of laying
on a board and paddling. Jump on a rowing
machine, or do pull-down resistance
exercises before your trip. Other than that,
get a good night's rest, don't drink too
much alcohol and get ready to have fun!

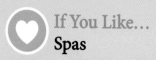

If You Like...
Spas

What's a beach vacation without a little pampering?

1 ABHASA SPA
(☎ 922-8200; www.abhasa.com; Royal Hawaiian, 2259 Kalakaua Ave; 50min massage from $135; ⏰ 9am-9pm) Locally inspired experiences include Hawaiian-style lomilomi ('loving hands') and *pohaku* (hot-stone) massage, sea-salt scrubs and *kukui*, coconut and coffee-oil body treatments.

2 NA HO'OLA SPA
(☎ 923-1234; http://waikiki.hyatt.com/hyatt/pure/spas/; Hyatt Regency Waikiki, 2424 Kalakaua Ave; 50min massage from $135; ⏰ 9am-9pm) At this bi-level award-winning spa, *limu* (seaweed) wraps detoxify, *kele-kele* (mud) wraps soothe sore muscles and *ti*-leaf wraps heal sun-ravaged skin, while macadamia-nut oil and fresh pineapple scrubs exfoliate. Ocean views are blissful.

3 SPA KHAKARA
(☎ 685-7600; www.khakara.com; 4th fl, Sheraton Waikiki, 2255 Kalakaua Ave; 50min massage from $120; ⏰ 9am-9pm) Petite spa specializing in organic, holistic and natural spa treatments. Afterward, unwind in the contempo relaxation lounge.

4 AQUASPA
(☎ 924-2782; www.aquaresorts.com; 50min massage from $95; ⏰ 9am-7pm) Offers deep discounts for delightfully personalized massage inside poolside cabanas at three of Waikiki's Aqua boutique hotels.

 Festivals & Events

Waikiki loves to party year-round. Every Friday night, usually starting around 7:45pm, the Hilton Hawaiian Village shoots off a big ol' **fireworks show**, visible from Kahanamoku Beach and sounding like thunder inside hotel rooms all across Waikiki.

DUKE KAHANAMOKU CHALLENGE Sports, Culture
(www.waikikicommunitycenter.com) Outrigger-canoe and stand-up paddling races, island-style local food, traditional Hawaiian games, arts-and-crafts vendors and live entertainment all happen on a Sunday in late January.

HONOLULU FESTIVAL Arts, Culture
(www.honolulufestival.com) Free Asian and Pacific arts and cultural performances are staged at Waikiki Beach Walk and Waikiki Shopping Plaza, with a festive parade along Kalakaua Ave followed by a fireworks show in mid-March.

WAIKIKI SPAM JAM Food, Music
(www.spamjamhawaii.com) On a Saturday in late April, join thousands of Spam aficionados celebrating at this street festival devoted to Hawaii's favorite tinned meat product.

TOP CHOICE PAN-PACIFIC FESTIVAL Arts, Culture
(www.pan-pacific-festival.com) In early June, this Asian and Polynesian cultural festival puts on a performing-arts showcase at the Royal Hawaiian Center, outdoor hula shows at Kuhio Beach Park, and a huge *ho'olaule'a* (celebration) block party and parade along Kalakaua Ave.

NA HULA FESTIVAL Arts, Culture
(www1.honolulu.gov/parks/programs/) Local hula *halau* (schools) gather for a full day of music and dance celebrations at Kapi'olani Park in early August.

HAWAIIAN SLACK KEY GUITAR FESTIVAL Music, Food
(www.slackkeyfestival.com) A day-long celebration of traditional Hawaiian slack key guitar and ukulele music with food vendors and an arts-and-crafts fair at Kapi'olani Park in mid-August.

ALOHA FESTIVALS Culture, Arts
(http://alohafestivals.com) During Hawaii's premier statewide cultural festival, Waikiki is famous for its royal court ceremonies

and also its *ho'olaule'a* evening block party and float parade along Kalakaua Ave, with food vendors, live music and hula dancers in mid-September.

NA WAHINE O KE KAI Sports, Culture
(www.nawahineokekai.com) Hawaii's major annual women's outrigger-canoe race is held near the end of September. It starts at sunrise on the island of Moloka'i and ends 42 miles later at Waikiki's Kahanamoku Beach.

MOLOKA'I HOE Sports, Culture
(www.molokaihoe.com) In mid-October, the men's outrigger-canoe world-championship race starts just after sunrise on Moloka'i and then finishes at Waikiki's Kahanamoku Beach less than five hours later.

HONOLULU MARATHON Sports
(www.honolulumarathon.org) From the starting line in downtown Honolulu, the USA's third-largest marathon races to Kapi'olani Park near Diamond Head on the second Sunday of December.

 Sleeping

Waikiki's main beachfront strip, along Kalakaua Ave, is lined with hotels and sprawling resorts. Some of them are true beauties with quiet gardens, seaside courtyards and either historic or boutique atmosphere, while others are generic high-rises, which cater to the package-tour crowd.

If stepping out of your room and digging your toes in the sand isn't a must, look for inviting small hotels on Waikiki's backstreets. Some hotels off Kuhio Ave and near Ala Wai Canal have rooms as lovely as many of the beachfront hotels, but at half the price. If you don't mind walking to the beach, you can save a bundle.

Be aware that 'ocean view' and its cousins 'ocean front' and 'partial ocean view' are all liberally used and may require a periscope to spot the waves. 'City', 'garden' or 'mountain' views may be euphemisms for rooms that overlook the

parking lot. When making a reservation, you should first check the hotel's property map online or call a reservations agent directly to find out about the different views. Generally, the higher the floor, the higher the price, and oceanfront rooms may cost over 50% more.

Book rooms as far in advance as possible for the best rates and availability; last-minute bookings are tough and generally expensive. Parking usually costs $15 to $30 per night, whether for valet or self-parking (the latter is sometimes off-site). Increasingly, Waikiki's bigger hotels are also charging mandatory 'resort fees,' which could tack another $20 or more per day onto your final bill. Resort fees may cover internet connections, local and toll-free phone calls and fitness-room entry, or no extra perks at all, but regardless, you're gonna have to pay.

All rates listed below are standard rates for high season (mid-December through late March or mid-April, depending on when Easter spring break falls). Substantial discounts are usually available online through the hotels' own websites, via travel booking and airline websites, or for flight and rental-car package deals, especially during the low season. For more tips and need-to-know facts about accommodations on O'ahu, see p318.

TOP
CHOICE **HALEKULANI** Resort $$$
(☏923-2311, 800-367-2343; www.halekulani .com; 2199 Kalia Rd; r $435-760; P ✳ @ ☎ ≋)
Evincing modern sophistication, this resort hotel lives up to its name, which means 'House Befitting Heaven.' It's an all-encompassing experience of gracious living, not merely a place to crash. Meditative calm washes over you immediately as you step onto the lobby's cool stone tiles. Peaceful rooms are equipped with all mod cons such as hi-tech entertainment centers, as well as deep soaking tubs and expansive lanai. Eclectic luxury suites include one personally designed by Vera Wang. Find ultimate relaxation in the Halekulani's pampering spa.

The historic Royal Hawaiian hotel

LINDA CHING/LONELY PLANET IMAGES ©

ROYAL HAWAIIAN   Historic Hotel $$$
(☏ 923-7311, 866-716-8110; www.royal-hawaiian
.com; 2259 Kalakaua Ave; r $420-695; P ❄ @
🛜 🏊 👪) Waikiki's original luxury hotel,
this pink Spanish-Moorish-style landmark
is loaded with charm, especially since
its splendid, multimillion-dollar renova-
tions were finished in 2009. The historic
section of the aristocratic 'Pink Palace'
maintains its classic appeal, although you
may prefer the modern high-rise tower for
its ocean views. Spa suites are adorned with
carved teak, bamboo and mosaic glass,
with cabana day beds on the lanai to help
you unwind. In-room wired internet and
limited wi-fi in public areas cost extra.

MOANA SURFRIDER   Historic Hotel $$$
(☏ 922-3111, 866-716-8109; www.moana
-surfrider.com; 2365 Kalakaua Ave; r $270-
785; P ❄ @ 🛜 🏊) Waikiki's most
historic beachfront hotel, this grand,
colonial-style establishment has been
painstakingly restored. A line of rocking
chairs beckons on the front porch and
Hawaiian artwork hangs on the walls,
while Japanese wedding parties sweep
through the bustling lobby every 10 minutes. Graceful yet compact guest rooms
no longer retain much of their period

look, having been upgraded with 21st-
century amenities and style. In-room
wired internet access and lobby and
poolside wi-fi cost extra. Self-parking is
inconveniently off-site.

SHERATON WAIKIKI   Resort $$$
(☏ 922-4422, 866-716-8109; www.sheraton
-waikiki.com; 2255 Kalakaua Ave; r $250-740;
P ❄ @ 🛜 🏊 👪) Looming over the
Royal Hawaiian, this chain high-rise has
plenty of room to accommodate families,
package-tour groups and conferences.
No-surprises rooms are clean and crisp,
with a well-equipped gym and drop-off
day-care center downstairs. By the beach,
an amphibious playground keeps kids
entertained with a 'superpool' and 70ft-
long waterslide, while adults retreat to the
infinity pool. In-room wired internet and
lobby wi-fi cost extra.

**MODERN
HONOLULU**   Boutique Hotel $$$
(☏ 943-5800, 866-970-4161; www.themodern
honolulu.com; 1775 Ala Moana Blvd; r $345-525;
P ❄ @ 🛜 🏊) Whimsical postmodernity
is hotel designer Ian Schrager's signature,
from a revolving bookcase in the lobby
that hides a sleek bar to the contempo-

rary video art in the hallways. Terraced oceanview rooms and suites are elementally chic, showing off teak doors, Frette linens and marble baths. The lanai deck pool overlooks Ala Wai Yacht Harbor, as does an Iron Chef's sushi bar, Morimoto Waikiki. The only downside to staying at this mod spa oasis is the 10-minute walk to a sandy beach.

Gay & Lesbian Waikiki

Waikiki's queer community is tightly knit, but it's full of aloha for visitors. Free monthly magazine *Odyssey* (www.odysseyhawaii.com) covers the admittedly small, but active scene. The magazine is available at the shop **80% Straight** (www.80percentstraight.com; Castle Waikiki Grand, 134 Kapahulu Ave; ⏰10am-11pm Mon-Thu, 10am-midnight Fri & Sat, noon-11pm Sun), which sells books, magazines, videos, beachwear and bedroom toys.

If you're new to Waikiki, make your first stop **Hula's Bar & Lei Stand** (www .hulas.com; 2nd fl, Castle Waikiki Grand, 134 Kapahulu Ave; ⏰10am-2am; @ 🛜). Upstairs from 80% Straight, this friendly, open-air bar, Waikiki's main gay venue, is a great place to make new friends, boogie and have a few drinks. Hunker down at the pool table, or gaze at the spectacular vista of Diamond Head.

On a side street, **Wang Chung's** (http://wangchungs.com; 2410 Koa Ave; ⏰5pm-2am) is a happy-go-lucky, living-room-sized karaoke bar, just a block inland from Kuhio Beach. Or drop by svelte **Bacchus** (www.facebook.com/bacchuswaikiki; 2nd fl, 408 Lewers St; ⏰noon-2am), an intimate wine bar and cocktail lounge, with happy-hour specials and a Sunday-afternoon beer bust.

Not far away, **Fusion Waikiki** (www.fusionwaikiki.com; 2nd fl, 2260 Kuhio Ave; ⏰10pm-4am Sun-Thu, 8pm-4am Fri & Sat) is a high-energy nightclub hosting weekend drag shows and go-go boys after midnight; women welcome. Next door **Lo Jax Waikiki** (www.lojaxwaikiki.com; 2256 Kuhio Ave; ⏰noon-2am; 🛜) is a raucous gay sports bar that ramps it up with pool tournaments and weekend DJs.

Tiki-themed **Tapa's Restaurant & Lanai Bar** (www.tapaswaikiki.com; 2nd fl, 407 Seaside Ave; ⏰noon-2am) is a more laid-back spot, with bear-y talkative bartenders, pool tables, a jukebox and a karaoke machine. **In Between** (http:// inbetweenwaikikionline.com; 2155 Lau'ula St; ⏰4pm-2am Mon-Thu, noon-2am Fri & Sat, 2pm-2am Sun), a rubbah-slippah neighborhood bar, attracts an older crowd with 'the happiest of happy hours.'

For daytime diversions, Queen's Surf Beach is the darling of the sun-worshipping gay crowd. Further afield near the lighthouse, Diamond Head Beach (p154) is another popular gay gathering spot, with some (technically illegal) clothing-optional sunbathing going on. Gay-oriented **Like Hike** (http://gayhawaii.com /likehike) organizes twice-monthly trips around O'ahu, but you must call or email the trip leader before joining up (check the website for details and schedules).

Where to sleep? The Castle Waikiki Grand, home to Hula's and 80% Straight, and the boutique Hotel Renew are not exclusively gay, but rank highly with LGBTQ visitors, as do Waikiki's **Aqua Hotels** (www.aquaresorts.com), especially the chic Modern Honolulu and tranquil Aqua Lotus branches.

For more about O'ahu's gay community, including helpful websites and local resources, annual special events, travel agencies and more, see p321.

Island Insights

When land is developed in Hawaii, more than earth and plants may be disturbed. Construction workers may dig up the *iwi* (bones) and *moepu* (funeral objects) of ancient Hawaiian burial sites. Locals tell 'chicken skin' (goose flesh) stories of machinery breaking down and refusing to operate until the bones are removed and prayers are said. It's common practice for a Hawaiian priest to bless ground-breaking at construction sites. A memorial in Kapi'olani Park contains the skeletal remains of around 200 Native Hawaiians unearthed over the years by construction projects in Waikiki. Some say that the foundations of all of Waikiki's resort hotels contain *iwi*, simply because the sand used to make the concrete also contained it.

TRUMP INTERNATIONAL
Luxury Hotel $$$

(☎683-7777, 877-683-7401; www.trump waikikihotel.com; 223 Saratoga Rd; studios $319-569, 1br/2br/3br apt from $579/979/1399; P ❄ @ 🛜 ♨ 🚻) With an enviable position right on Waikiki Beach Walk, this luxury high-rise lets you live the high life. The tower has stylish studio apartments and suites, each with a kitchenette, urbane furnishings and plenty of space to relax. A 6th-floor infinity pool and sun deck will ease the pain of not being right on the beach. Complimentary wi-fi throughout the hotel property. Valet parking only.

WAIKIKI PARC
Boutique Hotel $$$

(☎921-7272, 800-422-0450; www.waikikiparc .com; 2233 Helumoa Rd; r $285-415; P ❄ @ 🛜 ♨) Epitomizing new-wave Waikiki, this affordably hip hangout mixes nostalgic touches such as plantation-shuttered windows with minimalist contemporary furnishings. The staff are top-class, and although guest rooms are cool and modern, they're not nearly as spacious or as chic as Nobu Waikiki lounge and restaurant downstairs. For serenity, swim in the rooftop pool with oceanview cabanas. In-room wired internet, lobby wi-fi and valet parking (tip expected) are complimentary, as is admission to some of Honolulu's top museums and cultural attractions by showing your room key.

ASTON WAIKIKI BEACH TOWER
Condo Hotel $$$

(☎926-6400, 877-997-6667; www.astonho tels.com; 2470 Kalakaua Ave; 2br $500-735; P ❄ @ 🛜 ♨ 🚻) Full-service apartment-style hotel in the heart of Waikiki is a perfect fit for family reunions. Each contemporary condominium measures over 1000 sq ft and has a full kitchen, a washer/dryer and a private lanai with at least a partial ocean view. Rattan chairs and headboards, potted plants and palm-tree prints make it feel almost tropical. In-room wired internet and lobby and poolside wi-fi are free, as is valet parking (tip expected).

OUTRIGGER REGENCY ON BEACHWALK
Condo Hotel $$$

(☎922-3871, 866-956-4262; www.outrigger.com; 255 Beach Walk; 1br $199-385, 2br $269-445; P ❄ @ 🚻) This sleek, modern high-rise has more than respectable family-size rooms, with jewel and earth-toned furnishings, marble baths and bold, modern artwork. Spacious condo-style suites have full kitchens and some have private lanai with peek-a-boo ocean views. Step outside the downstairs lobby and you're right on Waikiki Beach Walk – then keep walking five minutes to the beach or the off-site swimming pool. Free in-room wired internet.

HOTEL RENEW   Boutique Hotel $$

(687-7700, 888-485-7639; www.hotelrenew
.com; 129 Pa'oakalani Ave; r incl breakfast $175-
260; P ❄ @ ☎) At this fabulous find, just
a half-block from the beach, attentive
concierge staff can be counted on to
provide all the little niceties, from chilled
drinks upon arrival to free beach mats
and bodyboards to borrow. Design-savvy,
eco-friendly accommodations come with
mod platform beds, projection-screen
TVs, spa robes, earth-toned furnishings
and Japanese-style *shōji* (sliding paper-
screen doors). It's romantic enough for
honeymooners, and also gay-friendly.
Complimentary wi-fi but no swimming
pool. Valet parking only.

OUTRIGGER REEF ON
THE BEACH   Resort $$$

(923-3111, 866-956-4262; www.outriggerreef
.com; 2169 Kalia Rd; r $199-435; P ❄ @
☎ ☒ ♿) Forget the hoity-toity attitudes
of the Outrigger's higher-priced beachfront neighbors. Nudging its way onto a
prime beachfront location, the renovated
Outrigger brings the aloha, starting with
live music at the Kani Ka Pila Grille and a
handmade Hawaiian outrigger canoe in
the Polynesian-style lobby, and flowing
through complimentary hula, ukulele and
lei-making classes for guests of all ages.
The modern, functional rooms are
good enough for the mostly suburban crowd here. Free in-room
wired internet and lobby and
poolside wi-fi.

AQUA LOTUS
    Boutique Hotel $$$

(922-1700, 866-971-2782;
www.aqualotus.com; 2885
Kalakaua Ave; r $179-580;
P ❄ @ ☎) Formerly the
hip W Diamond Head,
this Balinese-inspired
boutique hotel is a gently
worn sanctuary by Sans
Souci Beach, at the calm
southern edge of Waikiki.

Mingle with honeymooners looking for a
romantic escape at wine social hours in a
lobby that's more like a living room, with
flickering candles and overstuffed sofas.
In-room and lobby wi-fi cost extra, and so
does mandatory valet parking. No pool,
sorry.

OUTRIGGER WAIKIKI
ON THE BEACH   Resort $$$

(923-0711, 866-956-4262; www.outrigger
waikikihotel.com; 2335 Kalakaua Ave; r $189-389;
P ❄ @ ☎ ☒) While not the classiest
or the coolest place, this hotel caters to
those tourists who believe it is. Sprawled
on a prime stretch of sand, you can hit
the surf in the morning then join the
party crowd at Duke's Waikiki over sunset
cocktails. Generic hotel rooms look like
they could be anywhere in the world, but
at least they've been recently spruced up
with glassed-in lanai and better sound-
proofing. In-room wired internet, and
lobby and poolside wi-fi are complimentary for guests, as are Hawaiian hula and
lei-making classes. Valet parking only.

Drinks on the balcony of the Mai Tai
Bar (p127)

ANN CECIL/LONELY PLANET IMAGES ©

HILTON HAWAIIAN VILLAGE

Resort $$$

(☎949-4321, 800-445-8667; www.hiltonha waiianvillage.com; 2005 Kalia Rd; r $229-505; P❄@🛜🏊♿) On the Fort DeRussy side of Waikiki, the Hilton is Waikiki's largest resort hotel – practically a self-sufficient tourist fortress of towers, restaurants, bars and shops. It's geared almost entirely to families and package tourists, with standard-issue hotel rooms, swimming pools and a lagoon, and tons of kid-centric activities by the beach, including kayak and surfboard rentals. Expect check-in lines to move as slowly as TSA airport-security checkpoints.

ASTON AT THE WAIKIKI BANYAN

Condo Hotel $$

(☎922-0555, 877-997-6667; www.astonhotels .com; 201 Ohua Ave; 1br $180-250; P❄@🛜♿) Perfect for families, this all-suites high-rise hotel is a short walk from the aquarium, the zoo and of course, the beach. Roomy, if sometimes beat-up suites have a handy sofabed in the living room. Kids get a free souvenir sand pail filled with fun stuff at check-in, and the pool deck has a playground, a putting green and tennis and basketball courts. A mandatory nightly resort fee of $10 covers unlimited DVD kiosk rentals and in-room wired internet access. Currently, parking costs just $10 per night, less than half the going rate in Waikiki.

BEST WESTERN COCONUT WAIKIKI

Boutique Hotel $$

(☎923-8828, 866-782-5939; www.coconut waikikihotel.com; 450 Lewers St; r incl breakfast $159-289; P❄@🛜) Don't let the chain-gang name fool you: this Aqua-managed property delivers a splash of style for anyone doing Waikiki on a budget. The hotel has hip, mod decor: atomic starburst mirrors in the hallways, and cool mint-green paint. Quiet rooms have ergonomic work desks, microwaves and minifridges. Downstairs, there's a small cardio-workout room and a pool barely big enough to dip your toes in. Slow in-room wi-fi and faster lobby-level online computer access are free for guests.

AQUA BAMBOO & SPA

Boutique Hotel $$

(☎922-7777, 866-971-2782; www.aquabamboo .com; 2425 Kuhio Ave; incl breakfast r $149-289, ste $159-299, 1br apt $199-400; P❄@🛜♿)

Evening cocktails and music on Waikiki Beach

ANN CECIL/LONELY PLANET IMAGES ©

Looking for a meditative retreat in Waikiki's concrete jungle? Although there are hints of its less-glorious past as a budget crash pad, this recently refreshed boutique hotel with an intimate cabana spa has a small saltwater pool, should you tire of the ocean. Stylishly minimalist rooms include suites with kitchenettes or full kitchens. Free in-room wired internet, and lobby and poolside wi-fi.

NEW OTANI KAIMANABEACH
Boutique Hotel $$$

(923-1555, 800-356-8264; www.kaimana .com; 2863 Kalakaua Ave; r & ste $170-550; P ❄ @ 🛜) Location, location, location. Right? Incredibly small rooms will leave you wanting more space, but the soothing setting right on Sans Souci Beach makes this 1960s-era hotel special. There's no pool, but with a beach this gorgeous, who needs one? Book early because this low-key hotel is very popular with return visitors, especially those from Japan. Ask for a newly renovated room. Free in-room wired or wi-fi internet access.

ASTON WAIKIKI CIRCLE
Hotel $$

(923-1571, 877-997-6667; www.astonhotels .com; 2464 Kalakaua Ave; r $155-230; P ❄ @) Tired of square boxes? This circular building must have been *très chic* back in the playful era of postmodernism. Today this survivor is all about value, not fashion. About half of the contemporary redesigned rooms enjoy a full ocean view, but all have private lanai. The drawbacks: rooms aren't nearly big enough to practice your hula dancing in, and there's no pool. The cheapest city-view rooms aren't much worth bothering with. In-room wired internet costs extra.

OUTRIGGER LUANA WAIKIKI
Condo Hotel $$

(955-6000, 866-956-4262; www.outrigger .com; 2045 Kalakaua Ave; r/studios/1br from $129/149/189; P ❄ @ 🛜 ⛱) Well-kept studios equipped with kitchenettes and one-bedroom condos with kitchens are really the only digs worth booking at this high-rise hotel, which has a gorgeous swimming pool and sundeck. If you don't mind noise from the air-con units or pass-

The Best...
Family-Friendly Hotels

ing traffic below, some of these units have a surprisingly good view. In-room wired internet, and lobby and poolside wi-fi are complimentary, but valet parking isn't.

WAIKIKI MARINA RESORT AT THE ILIKAI
Condo Hotel $$

(955-7644, 866-451-3549; www.shellhospital ity.com; 1777 Ala Moana Blvd; studios $185-239; P ❄ @ 🛜 ⛱) On the far north side of Waikiki near the Ala Wai Yacht Harbor, this humble timeshare is just as close to the Ala Moana Center mall as it is to the beach, and both places are within walking distance. Recently renovated with island-style decor, these spacious high-rise studio apartments with full kitchens and private lanai are meticulously clean. Free in-room wired internet and lobby wi-fi. Valet parking only.

AQUA ALOHA SURF & SPA
Boutique Hotel $$

(923-0222, 866-971-2782; www.alohasurfho telwaikiki.com; 444 Kanekapolei St; incl breakfast r $129-225, ste $179-325; ❄ @ ⛱) If you don't mind a shoebox-size room, or being next to Ala Wai Canal, this youthful hotel can be a real bargain. The lobby is lively, with surf videos playing an endless-summer loop and hanging surfboards on the walls. Although bland-looking, contemporary

115

Below: View across to Waikiki Beach (p94) **Right:** Aerial view of Waikiki Beach at night

(LEFT) JON ARNOLD IMAGES LTD/ALAMY ©; (BELOW) JOHN ARNOLD IMAGES LTD /ALAMY ©

rooms are on the small side, they do have microwaves, minifridges and coffeemakers. Request an upper floor. Free in-room wired internet, and lobby and poolside wi-fi.

BREAKERS
Hotel $$

(☎923-3181, 800-426-0494; www.breakers-hawaii.com; 250 Beach Walk; r $130-195; P ❄ ☎ ☒) In a prohibitively priced neighborhood dominated by newer luxury high-rise hotels, this Polynesian-style place is a throwback to another era. You'll either love or hate the Breakers' old, creaky facilities and motel-style rooms, all with kitchenettes. Studios on the 2nd floor each have a private lanai and Japanese-style *shōji* (sliding-screen) doors. Parking is free but extremely limited and can't be reserved. Free lobby and poolside wi-fi internet access is erratic.

OHANA WAIKIKI MALIA
Hotel $$

(☎923-7621, 866-956-4262; www.outrigger.com; 2211 Kuhio Ave; r/ste from $110/130; P ❄ @ ☎) Tennis with a view? There's a rooftop court (rentals available) at this clean, convenient high-rise tower. Motel-style rooms sure show their age, but one-bedroom suites have kitchenettes and enough space for a couple of kids. If you want to take a dip in the plunge pool or whirlpool spa, expect lots of company – it's crowded here. Free in-room wired internet and lobby wi-fi. Limited self-parking available.

AQUA PALMS & SPA
Boutique Hotel $$

(☎947-7256, 866-971-2782; www.aquapalms.com; 1850 Ala Moana Blvd; r incl breakfast $129-300; P ❄ @ ☎ ☒) Poised for quick escapes from Waikiki, and within walking distance of the Ala Moana Center mall, the Palms feels more functional than fun. Delivering bang for your buck, tiny rooms don't have much tropical panache – think Tommy Bahama for the working class – yet you can't fault the bed, sofa or fluffy robes for comfort. There's a postage-stamp-sized swimming pool and workout

room too. Free in-room wired internet and lobby wi-fi.

HALE KOA
Hotel $$

(☏955-0555, 800-367-6027; www.halekoa.com; 2055 Kalia Rd; r $90-290; P ❄ @ 🛜 ⛵ 🚶)
One of the best oceanfront bargains in Waikiki, this high-rise hotel fronting Fort DeRussy Beach is reserved for active and retired US military personnel only. It's not exactly a happening spot, but for retired folks and families, the price is right. Ask for more recently renovated Ilima Tower rooms. In-room wired internet, and lobby and poolside wi-fi costs extra. Complimentary shuttle service available to off-site self-parking, which costs less than $10 per night.

OHANA WAIKIKI EAST
Hotel $$

(☏922-5353, 866-968-8744; www.outrigger.com; 150 Ka'iulani Ave; r & ste $110-269; P ❄ @ 🛜 ⛵) It lacks the historical charm and oceanfront setting of nearby iconic hotels, but in exchange for having a longer walk to the beach, you will prob-ably save money. The rooms and suites are excruciatingly small, although some of them have kitchenettes. Downstairs, locally owned Kimo Bean sells Hawaii-grown coffee and grab-and-go breakfast pastries and snacks. Wired or wireless in-room internet, as well as lobby and poolside wi-fi, are free. There is limited self-parking available.

STAY WAIKIKI
Hotel $$

(☏923-7829, 888-354-0803; www.stayhotelwaikiki.com; 2424 Koa Ave; r incl breakfast $105-135; P ❄ @ 🛜) More like a boutique backpacker hostel than an actual hotel, this mod property on a side street one block from the beach is cheery enough. Bare-bones, thin-walled rooms that look like an IKEA showroom have bunked twin, double or queen-size beds and come with tech amenities such as iPod docking stations, flat-screen TVs and DVD players. Upper-floor deluxe rooms with lanai are roomier. Coin-op laundry on-site. Limited self-parking ($15 per night).

117

CASTLE WAIKIKI GRAND
Condo Hotel $$

(923-1814, 800-367-5004; www.castleresorts.com; 134 Kapahulu Ave; r $165-220, studios $205-325; P ❄ @ ⛵) Small, gay-friendly condo hotel is best known as the home of Hula's Bar & Lei Stand (p111). Standard-issue rooms are compact, with limited kitchenette suites available. Each vacation-rental condo is individually owned, so they can vary quite shockingly in quality – view online photos with some skepticism. Free in-room wi-fi. Ask about weekly and low-season discounts. There is limited self-parking available on-site.

ILIMA
Condo Hotel $$

(923-1877, 800-684-2140; www.ilima.com; 445 Nohonani St; studios $190-270, 1br/2br from $250/320; P ❄ @ ⛵) Life feels less hurried at this older, island-style high-rise hotel, where the staff show true aloha spirit and Hawaiian paintings adorn the lobby. All studios and suites come equipped with kitchens, while those on the 10th floor or above have views of the Ko'olau Range and Ala Wai Canal. Book far ahead, as

this condo hotel regularly fills up. In-room wired internet and lobby wi-fi are free. Limited free self-parking available.

WAIKIKI PRINCE HOTEL
Hotel $

(922-1544; http://waikikiprince.com; 2431 Prince Edward St; r $70-95; P ❄ 🛜) Forget about ocean views and never mind the cramped check-in office at this six-story, 1970s-era apartment complex on an anonymous side street. Inside this standout budget option are two dozen compact yet cheery rooms with kitchenettes that feel fresh and reasonably modern. Free lobby wi-fi during office hours (9am to 6pm daily). Weekly rates available year-round.

HOSTELLING INTERNATIONAL (HI) WAIKIKI
Hostel $

(926-8313; www.hostelsaloha.com; 2417 Prince Edward St; dm $25-28, d $58-64, q $116-128; ⏱ reception 7am-3am; P @ 🛜) Occupying a converted low-rise, aqua-painted apartment building, this tidy hostel is just a few blocks from the beach. Inside are fan-cooled single-sex dormitories and simple private rooms, a self-catering kitchen, coin-op laundry and free bodyboards to borrow. No smoking or alcohol allowed, but no daytime lockout or curfew either. Reservations are strongly recommended (seven-night maximum stay). Limited self-parking ($5 per night).

ROYAL GROVE
Hotel $

(923-7691; www.royalgrovehotel.com; 151 Uluniu Ave; r $55-100; ❄ @ ⛵) No frills but plenty of aloha characterize this kitschy, candy-pink hotel that attracts so many returning snowbirds it's nearly impossible to get a room in winter without advance reservations. Retro motel-style rooms in the main wing are basic but do have lanai. Avoid rooms in the ancient-looking Mauka Wing, which are small,

Lobby at the Moana Surfrider (p110)
LINDA CHING/LONELY PLANET IMAGES ©

noisy and lack air-con. All rooms have kitchenettes. Inquire about discounted weekly off-season rates.

WAIKIKI BEACHSIDE HOSTEL Hostel $

(☎ 923-9566, 866-478-3888; www.waikikibeach sidehostel.com; 2556 Lemon Rd; dm $15-35, semi-private/private r from $66/127; P @ ⑦) This private hostel attracts an international party crowd and offers plenty of perks, from a 24-hour internet cafe to surfboard and moped rentals. Like most hostels on sketchy, back-alley Lemon Rd, this one occupies an older apartment complex. Each dorm (co-ed or women only) has its own kitchen, bathroom and telephone, but no air-con. Security, cleaning and hostel management are lax. Covered parking is available ($7 per night).

 # Eating

Warning for foodies: many of Waikiki's middle-of-the-road restaurants are overpriced and not worth eating at, no matter how enticing the ocean views look. For a more vibrant cuisine scene, check out downtown Honolulu, Chinatown and around the Ala Moana Center mall (p64).

By the Beach

Along Kalakaua Ave, suburban chains such as the Cheesecake Factory overflow with hungry tourists, while a few stellar beachfront hotel restaurants are overseen by Hawaii's top chefs. A block further inland, Kuhio Ave is great for cheap grazing, especially at multi-ethnic take-out joints.

TOP CHOICE ROY'S WAIKIKI BEACH Hawaii Regional $$$

(☎ 923-7697; www.royshawaii.com/waikiki .html; 226 Lewers St; mains $28-40, 3-course prix-fixe menu without/with wine pairings $45/60; ⊙11am-9:30pm Mon-Thu, to 10pm Fri-Sun) This contemporary oceanfront incarnation of Roy Yamaguchi's island-born chain is perfect for a flirty date or just celebrating the good life with friends. The ground-breaking

chef doesn't actually cook in the kitchen here, but his signature *misoyaki* butterfish, blackened 'ahi (tunafish), macadamia-nut-encrusted mahimahi and deconstructed sushi rolls are always on the menu (vegans and vegetarians have options too). Molten-chocolate soufflé for dessert is a must.

TOP CHOICE AZURE Seafood $$$

(☎ 921-4600; www.royal-hawaiian.com; Royal Hawaiian, 2259 Kalakaua Ave; mains $36-60, 5-course tasting menu without/with wine pairings $72/95; ⊙5:30-10pm, last seating 9pm) Chef Jon Mastubara, who apprenticed with Hawaii Regional cuisine star chefs Roy Yamaguchi and Alan Wong – helms this gold-medal kitchen. Seafood fresh from the pier, such as Kona abalone, red snapper and *ono* (white-fleshed mackerel), are all exquisitely prepared island-style, with finishing touches such as red Hawaiian sea salt and Moloka'i purple sweet potatoes on the side. Chic black-and-white tables and resort chairs, with pops of color in the lemon-yellow pillows and wrought-iron Moroccan lamps glowing above, add an exotic element to the already swoon-worthy ambience.

MORIMOTO WAIKIKI Asian Fusion $$$

(☎ 943-5900; www.morimotowaikiki.com; Modern Honolulu, 1775 Ala Moana Blvd; breakfast & lunch set meals $18-35, dinner mains $22-50; ⊙breakfast 6:30-10am daily, lunch 11am-2:30pm daily, dinner 5-10pm Sun-Thu, to 11pm Fri & Sat; P) Hidden upstairs in a chic boutique hotel, Iron Chef Morimoto's oceanfront dining room seduces with coconut cocktails and yacht-harbor views from a sunny poolside patio. Sink back against a mod sea-green pillow banquette and fork into cubic seafood *poke* (cubed rawfish) and sushi rolls, ginger-soy braised black cod, *wagyū* beef *loco moco* or curried whole roasted lobster. Complimentary valet parking with restaurant validation.

SANSEI SEAFOOD RESTAURANT & SUSHI BAR Asian Fusion $$

(☎ 931-6286; www.sanseihawaii.com; 3rd fl, Waikiki Beach Marriott, 2552 Kalakaua Ave;

The Best...
Breakfast & Brunch

shared plates $3-20, mains $16-35; ⏱5:15-10pm Sun-Thu, to 1am Fri & Sat) From the mind of one of Hawaii's hottest chefs, DK Kodama, this Pacific Rim menu rolls out everything from 'new look' fusion sushi and sashimi to Dungeness crab ramen with black-truffle broth. Tables on the torch-lit veranda equal prime sunset views. Queue for the early-bird special: 50% off all food ordered between 5:15pm and 6pm on Sunday and Monday nights. Night owls get the same deal after 10pm on Friday and Saturday.

BLT STEAK   Steakhouse, Seafood $$$
(☏683-7440; www.e2hospitality.com/blt -steak/; Trump International, 223 Saratoga Rd; mains $26-55; ⏱5:30-10pm Sun-Thu, to 11pm Fri & Sat) A trendy NYC import, chef Laurent Tourondel's steakhouse has fine chops broiled at 1700°F and finished off with herb butter and your pick of no fewer than nine sauces. The daily blackboard of specials shows fresh Pacific seafood, including Hawaiian lobster and a raw bar of oysters flown in from da mainland. With walnut floors, chocolate leather chairs and a breezy outdoor patio, the ambience is date-worthy.

LA MER   French $$$
(☏923-2311; www.halekulani.com; Halekulani, 2199 Kalia Rd; 2-/3-/4-course prix-fixe dinner menu $95/125/140; ⏱6-10pm) At the luxury Halekulani resort, La Mer is rated by traditionalists as Waikiki's ultimate gourmet dining destination, though it's old-fashioned. Some tables boast a spectacular view of Diamond Head through swaying palm trees. A neoclassical French menu puts the emphasis on Provençal cuisine with the addition of fresh Hawaii-grown ingredients, such as lobster gelée with sea urchin or big-eye tuna tartare. Wines are perfectly paired. Formal is the byword: men must wear either a jacket or a collared long-sleeved shirt.

NOBU WAIKIKI   Asian Fusion, Sushi $$$
(☏237-6999; www.noburestaurants.com /waikiki/; Waikiki Parc, 2233 Helumoa Rd; most shared plates $3-30, mains $30-40; ⏱restaurant 5:30-10pm Sun-Wed, to 11pm Thu-Sat, lounge 5pm-midnight daily) Globe-trotting chef Nobu Matsuhisa's first Japanese-fusion restaurant and sushi bar in Hawaii has made a big splash, and his elegant seafood tapas tastes right at home by the beach. Broiled black cod with miso sauce, new-style sashimi with spicy sauce drizzled on top and Japanese-Peruvian *tiradito* (ceviche) rank among Nobu's signature tastes. A low-lit cocktail lounge serves appetizing small (actually, microscopic!) bites and 'sake-tinis.'

MARUKAME UDON   Japanese $
(www.facebook.com/marukameudon; 2310 Kuhio Ave; menu items $2-8; ⏱11am-10pm, last order 9:30pm; 👶) Everybody loves this cafeteria-style Japanese noodle shop – off-duty military personnel, retirees babysitting their brood of grandkids, budget backpackers and hotel employees. Watch those thick udon noodles get rolled, cut and boiled fresh right in front of you, then stack mini plates of giant tempura and *musubi* (rice ball) stuffed with salmon or a sour plum on your cafeteria tray, washing it all down with iced barley or green tea.

ME BBQ
Local $

(151 Uluniu Ave; meals $4-12; ⏱7am-8:45pm Mon-Sat; 👪) The street-side takeout counter may have zero atmosphere, but there are plastic picnic tables sitting in the sunshine on the sidewalk where you can chow down. Korean standards such as kimchi and *kalbi* (marinated short ribs) are house specialties, but the wall-size picture menu offers a mind-boggling array of mixed-plate combos including chicken *katsu* (batter-fried chicken), Portuguese sausage and eggs for breakfast, and other only-in-Hawaii tastes.

EGGS 'N THINGS
Diner $

(http://eggsnthings.com; 343 Saratoga Rd; mains $8-13; ⏱6am-2pm & 5-10pm; 🖋👪) Never empty, this bustling, shiny-new diner dishes straight-up comfort food: banana-mac nut pancakes with tropical syrups (guava, honey or coconut), sugary crepes topped with fresh fruit, or fluffy omelets scrambled with Portuguese sausage. You'll fit right in with the early-morning crowd of jet-lagged tourists lined up outside the door – and sometimes around the block.

MENCHANKO-TEI
Japanese $

(www.menchankoteihawaii.com; Waikiki Trade Center, 2255 Kuhio Ave; mains $9-16; ⏱11am-midnight; P 👪) Japanese expats and locals alike squeeze into this modest kitchen for their fix of Hakata-style ramen soup with freshly made noodles, Hawaiian sea salt and a creamy broth. The cooks here also make a mean *tonkatsu* (deep-fried pork cutlet) and *chanko-nabe,* an everything-but-the-kitchen-sink stew that's a favorite of sumo wrestlers back in Japan. Free validated parking is available after 5pm.

SIAM SQUARE
Thai $$

(www.siamsquaredining.com; 2nd fl, 408 Lewers St; mains $11-16; ⏱11am-midnight Mon-Sat, 5-10pm Sun; 🖋) It's Waikiki's most authentic Thai restaurant, although that's not saying much. You want it spicy? You won't have to work too hard to convince your waitress that you can handle the heat when you order *larb* pork salad or fried fish with chili sauce. Service is standoffish, but the kitchen works so fast and furiously that you probably won't mind.

Asian fusion and sushi restaurant Nobu Waikiki

DOUGLAS PEEBLES PHOTOGRAPHY/ALAMY ©

WAIKIKI EATING

HULA GRILL
Breakfast, Seafood $$

(923-4852; www.hulagrillwaikiki.com; 2nd fl, Outrigger Waikiki on the Beach, 2335 Kalakaua Ave; mains breakfast $5-13, dinner $19-31; breakfast 6:30-10:45am Mon-Sat, brunch 9am-2pm Sun, dinner 4:45-10pm daily) Come early to score a table on the wraparound lanai overhanging Waikiki Beach and watch the sun set as slack key guitars play. Reward yourself with cheap mai tais, 'wrong island' ice teas and island-style *pupu*-like mango BBQ ribs, but don't get sucked into staying for a disappointingly blah dinner. Simple à la carte breakfasts bring out some refreshingly healthy options such as honeyed granola with tropical fruit and yogurt.

ORCHIDS
Buffet $$$

(923-2311; www.halekulani.com; Halekulani, 2199 Kalia Rd; Sun brunch buffet $65; 9:30am-2:30pm Sun) O'ahu's most elegant Sunday brunch spread covers all the bases, with a made-to-order omelet station; a buffet of *poke* (cubed raw fish mixed with *shōyu*, sesame oil, salt, chili pepper, *furikake*, *'inamona* or other condiments), sashimi, sushi and salads; and a decadent dessert bar with coconut pie and homemade Kona coffee ice cream. But don't come for the just-OK food – it's the smashing ocean view, tropical flowers and cheesy harp and flute music that set the honeymoon mood. Make reservations in advance. Resort attire required.

OKONOMIYAKI CHIBO
Japanese $$$

(922-9722; www.chibohawaii.com; 3rd fl, Bldg A, Royal Hawaiian Center, 2201 Kalakaua Ave; set lunch $12-40, dinner $30-78; 11:30am-10pm) Showing off a sleek, dark-wood interior, this high-end Japanese *teppanyaki* grill is a standout for its chef-made *okonomiyaki* (savory cabbage pancakes). Go traditional and order one made with *buta* (pork) or *ika* (squid), or splurge on steak, scallops and prawns. Lunch is a better deal; dinner is overpriced.

LULU'S SURF CLUB American $$

(926-5222; www.luluswaikiki.com; Park Shore Waikiki, 2586 Kalakaua Ave; mains breakfast $6-15, dinner $10-24; 7am-2am;) Surfboards on the wall and an awesome ocean view set the mood at this gregarious open-air restaurant, bar and nightclub. Lulu's filling breakfasts, complete with 'dawn patrol' omelets, eggs Benedict, stuffed French toast, *loco moco* and fruit bowls, are legendary, although most of what the kitchen churns out is mediocre.

RAMEN NAKAMURA Japanese $$

(2141 Kalakaua Ave; mains $9-14; 11am-11:30pm) Hit this urban connoisseur's noodle shop at lunchtime and you'll have to strategically elbow aside Japanese tourists toting Gucci and Chanel bags just to sit down. Then you're free to dig into hearty bowls of oxtail or *tonkatsu* (breaded and fried pork cutlets) or kimchi ramen soup with crunchy fried garlic slices on top. Cash only.

HAU TREE LANAI Breakfast, Seafood $$$

(921-7066; www.kaimana.com; New Otani Kaimana Beach, 2863 Kalakaua Ave; mains breakfast & lunch $14-20, dinner $30-55; breakfast 7-10:45am daily, lunch 11:45am-2pm Mon-Sat & noon-2pm Sun, dinner 5:30-9pm daily) A classic beachfront setting under an arbor of hibiscus trees brings retirees and Japanese tourists back to this pink-tablecloth restaurant on Sans Souci Beach. Perennially popular for the views, the overpriced, so-so menu adds local flavor with poi pancakes and *furikake*-spiced 'ahi burgers.

GYŪ-KAKU Japanese $$

(926-2989; www.gyu-kaku.com; 307 Lewers St; shared plates $3-24, set meals for 2 people $72-100; 11:30am-midnight) Who doesn't love a grill-it-yourself BBQ joint? Settle in with your entourage for Kobe rib-eye steak, *kalbi* short ribs, garlic shrimp and *enoki* mushrooms, served with plentiful sweet and spicy marinades and dips. Show up for happy-hour food and drink specials (before 6:30pm or after 10pm)

123

or better yet, all-you-can-eat lunch deals (from $25).

VEGGIE STAR NATURAL FOODS
Health Food $

(417 Nahua St; menu items $4-8; ⏲10am-8pm Mon-Sat; ✈) For organic, all-natural and health-conscious groceries, plus tropical smoothies and monster-sized vegetarian burritos, fake-meat burgers, salads and 'airplane ready' sandwiches wrapped to go, visit this little side-street shop. It's the vegan chili that makes the most people rave.

MUSUBI CAFE IYASUME
Japanese $

(www.tonsuke.com/eomusubiya.html; 2410 Koa Ave; menu items $2-8; ⏲6:30am-4pm) Hole-in-the-wall keeps busy making fresh *onigiri* (rice balls) stuffed with seaweed, salmon roe, sour plums and even Spam. Other specialties include salmon-roe rice bowls, bizarre Japanese curry and island-style *mochiko* fried chicken. In a hurry? Grab a *bentō* (boxed lunch) to go.

RUFFAGE NATURAL FOODS
Health Food $

(2443 Kuhio Ave; menu items $4-8; ⏲9am-6pm; ✈) This pint-sized health food store whips up taro burgers, veggie burritos, deli sandwiches with fresh avocado and real-fruit smoothies that will revitalize your whole body. At night, the grocery shop shares space with a tiny, backpacker-friendly sushi bar run by a Japanese expat chef.

WAILANA COFFEE HOUSE
Diner $

(1860 Ala Moana Blvd; mains $5-15; ⏲24hr, except closed midnight-6am Wed; 🚹) This retro all-night coffee shop is stuck in the 1970s (just like the karaoke howlers in the adjacent cocktail lounge). Wait staff know all the senior citizens and graveyard-shift workers sitting at counter stools by name. On a greasy-spoon menu, the best deal is all-you-can-eat pancakes with fried Spam on the side.

TEDDY'S BIGGER BURGERS
Fast Food $

(http://teddysbiggerburgers.com; Castle Waikiki Grand, 134 Kapahulu Ave; sandwiches $5-10; ⏲10am-9pm Mon-Thu, to 10pm Fri-Sun; 🚹) Although the 1950s-style black-and-white checkered decor looks a bit out of place by the beach, this Hawaii mini-chain's hand-formed burgers, garlicky fries and milkshakes fill up famished tourist crowds.

MOOSE MCGILLYCUDDY'S
American $

(http://moosemcgillicuddys.com; 310 Lewers St; mains $5-15; ⏲7:30am-10pm) This 1980s time-warped bar and dance club rakes in a cheapskate breakfast crowd with huge omelets, *loco moco* and fluffy banana muffins. You can clip a BOGO breakfast coupon from Waikiki's free tourist magazines. At night, a

Box of *malasadas* from Leonard's bakery
LINDA CHING/LONELY PLANET IMAGES ©

hard-drinkin' crowd swings by for cheap burgers and tacos.

ONO CHEESESTEAK   Fast Food **$**
(www.onocheesesteak.com; 2310 Kuhio Ave; sandwiches & fries $4-10; ⊙24hr; [⊞]) When you're soused and starving, slide by this 'round-the-clock shop for an almost authentic 'Philly cheesesteak in paradise,' covered in Cheez Whiz and with seasoned curly fries on the side.

FOOD PANTRY   Supermarket **$**
(2370 Kuhio Ave; ⊙6am-11:30pm) It's more expensive than chain supermarkets found elsewhere in Honolulu, but cheaper than buying groceries at Waikiki's convenience stores; look for a Coffee Bean & Tea Leaf coffee bar inside.

Inland

On the outskirts of Waikiki, Kapahulu Ave is always worth a detour for its standout neighborhood eateries, drive-ins and bakeries, cooking up anything from Hawaiian soul food to Japanese country fare. The strip malls of Monsarrat Ave are great spots to search out locals-only cafes.

[TOP CHOICE] LEONARD'S   Bakery **$**
(www.leonardshawaii.com; 933 Kapahulu Ave; items 75¢-$2; ⊙5:30am-9pm Sun-Thu, to 10pm Fri & Sat; [P][⊞]) It's almost impossible to drive by the Leonard's eye-catching vintage 1950s neon sign without stopping in. This bakery is famous on O'ahu for its *malasadas,* sweet fried dough rolled in sugar, Portuguese-style – like a doughnut without the hole. Order ones with *haupia* (coconut cream) or *liliko'i* (passion fruit) filling, and you'll be hooked for life. Pick up a souvenir 'got malasadas?' T-shirt for even sweeter island memories.

[TOP CHOICE] WAIOLA SHAVE ICE   Desserts **$**
(3113 Mokihana St; shave ice $2-5; ⊙7:30am-6:30pm; [P][⊞]) This clapboard corner shop has moved locations but still makes the same superfine shave ice as it did back in 1940, and we'd argue that it's got the formula exactly right. Get yours doused with 20-plus flavors of syrup and topped by azuki beans, *liliko'i* cream, condensed

milk, Hershey's chocolate syrup or spicy-sweet *li hing mui* (crack seed).

HALILI'S HAWAIIAN FOODS   Hawaiian **$$**
(http://hailishawaiianfood.com; 760 Palani Ave; meals $10-15; ⊙10am-7pm Tue-Thu, 10am-8pm Fri & Sat, 11am-3pm Sun; [⊞]) Halili's has been cooking up homegrown Hawaiian fare since the 1950s. Locals cheerfully shoehorn themselves into kid-friendly booths and tables, then dig into heaping plates of *kalua* pig, *lomilomi* salmon and *laulau* (meat wrapped in *ti* leaves and steamed) served with poi or rice. For a little variety, try the grilled *'ahi* plate lunches, bowls of tripe stew, poke bowls or fat tortilla wraps.

RAINBOW DRIVE-IN   Local **$**
(www.rainbowdrivein.com; 3308 Kanaina Ave; meals $4-8; ⊙7am-9pm; [P][⊞]) Started by an island-born US Army cook after WWII, this classic Hawaii drive-in wrapped in rainbow-colored neon is a throwback to another era. Construction workers, surfers and gangly teens order all their down-home favorites such as burgers, mixed-plate lunches, *loco moco* and Portuguese sweet-bread French toast from the takeout counter. The owners' family donates part of the profits to Hawaiian

The Best...
Local Grinds

1 Halili's Hawaiian Foods

2 Rainbow Drive-In

3 Side Street Inn on Da Strip (p126)

4 Me BBQ (p121)

5 Leonard's

6 Waiola Shave Ice

Typical Hawaiian food, including *kalua* (cooked in an underground pit) pork and butterfish

LINDA CHING/LONELY PLANET IMAGES ©

schools and local charities. Factoid: President Barack Obama eats here.

UNCLE BO'S   Asian Fusion $$
(735-8311; www.unclebosrestaurant.com; 559 Kapahulu Ave; shared plates $7-15, mains $16-27; 5pm-2am) Inside this chic storefront, boisterous groups of friends devour the inventive chef's encyclopedic list of fusion *pupu* (appetizers) crafted with island flair, such as *kalua* pig nachos with wonton chips and Maui onions or baby back ribs basted in pineapple BBQ sauce. For dinner, focus on market-fresh seafood such as baked *opah* (moonfish) with parmesan-panko crust or steamed *opakapaka* (pink snapper) with Thai chilies. Reservations recommended.

TOKKURI TEI   Japanese $$
(739-6480; 449 Kapahulu Ave; shared plates $3-15; lunch 11am-2pm Mon-Fri, dinner 5:30pm-midnight Mon-Sat, to 10:30pm Sun; P) An upbeat neighborhood *izakaya* (Japanese pub) offers contemporary versions of Japanese bar-food standards. Paper lanterns hang overhead and bookshelves behind the bar hoard customers' private bottles of sake and *shōchū* (potato liquor). Squid pancakes, crispy salmon-

skin salad and grilled yellowtail cheek sell out most quickly. Call ahead for reservations. Valet parking $5.

SIDE STREET INN ON
DA STRIP   Local $$
(739-3939; http://sidestreetinn.com; 614 Kapahulu Ave; shared plates $7-15, mains $12-25; 3pm-midnight; P) If you've been to the original sports bar over near the Ala Moana Center mall (see p71), you won't recognize this cleaned-up, shiny version of the Side Street Inn. All of the chef's famous recipes including pan-fried pork chops and kimchi fried rice are on the menu, but wait times can be ridiculous. Valet parking $5.

DIAMOND HEAD
MARKET & GRILL   Deli, Supermarket $
(www.diamondheadmarket.com; 3158 Monsarrat Ave; meals $5-15; market 6:30am-9pm, grill 7-10:30am & 11am-9pm; P) Step inside this neighborhood market for a gourmet deli packaging up the likes of roast pork loin and citrus jicama salad, perfect for a beach picnic. Outside at the takeout window, surfers and families order *char siu* (Chinese barbecued pork) plate lunches, portobello mushroom burgers and at breakfast, tropical-fruit pancakes.

IRIFUNE Japanese $$
(563 Kapahulu Ave; mains $12-18; ⊘11:30am-1:30pm & 5:30-9:30pm Tue-Sat) This bustling kitchen decorated with Japanese country kitsch may look very odd, especially when they turn off the lights so you can see those glow-in-the-dark stars on the ceiling. But it's locally beloved for garlic 'ahi and crab dinners. With bargain-priced bentō-box lunches and combo dinner plates, you'll never walk away hungry. BYOB (bring your own beer).

ONO SEAFOOD Seafood, Self-Catering $
(747 Kapahulu Ave; snacks & meals $4-14; ⊘usually 9am-6pm Mon & Wed-Sat, 10am-3pm Sun; P) At this addictive, made-to-order poke shop, get there early before they run out of fresh fish marinated in shōyu (soy sauce), house-smoked tako (octopus), spicy 'ahi rice bowls or boiled peanuts spiked with star anise. Limited free parking.

PEOPLE'S OPEN MARKET Market $
(www1.honolulu.gov/parks/programs/pom; Kapi'olani Park, cnr Monsarrat & Paki Aves; ⊘10-11am Wed;) City-sponsored farmers market in the park trades in fresh bounty from mauka (the mountains) to makai (the sea).

WAIKIKI FARMERS MARKET Market $
(www.waikikicommunitycenter.org; Waikiki Community Center, 310 Pa'oakalani Ave; ⊘7am-1pm Tue & Fri;) Fresh agricultural produce stands set up in the parking lot of this neighborhood gathering place.

🍷 Drinking & Entertainment

Whether you want to linger over one of those cool, frosty drinks with the little umbrellas or are craving live Hawaiian music and hula dancing, you're in the right place. For what's going on tonight, from DJ and live-music gigs to special events, check the Honolulu Star-Advertiser's TGIF (www.honolulupulse.com) section, which comes out every Friday, and the free alternative tabloid Honolulu Weekly (http://honoluluweekly.com), published every Wednesday.

Hawaiian Music & Hula

Traditional and contemporary Hawaiian music calls all up and down the beach in Waikiki, from the rhythmic drums and ipu (gourds) accompanying hula dancers to mellow duos or trios playing slack key guitars and ukuleles and singing with leo ki'eki'e (male) or ha'i (female) high falsetto voices. All performances are free, unless otherwise noted. For more insights into the island music scene, see p286.

TOP CHOICE KUHIO BEACH TORCH LIGHTING & HULA SHOW Live Music
(☎922-5331; www.honolulu.gov/moca; Kuhio Beach Park; ⊘usually 6-7pm Tue, Thu, Sat & Sun, weather permitting;) It all begins at the Duke Kahanamoku statue with the sounding of a conch shell and the lighting of torches after sunset. At the nearby hula mound, lay out your beach towel and enjoy the authentic Hawaiian music and dance show. It's full of aloha, and afterwards the performers often hang around the stage to chat and take photos with visitors.

TOP CHOICE HOUSE WITHOUT A KEY Live Music
(☎923-2311; www.halekulani.com; Halekulani, 2199 Kalia Rd; ⊘7am-9pm, live music 5:30-8:30pm) Named after a 1925 Charlie Chan novel set in Honolulu, this genteel open-air hotel lounge sprawled beneath a century-old kiawe tree simply has no doors to lock. A sophisticated crowd gathers here for sunset cocktails, Hawaiian music and solo hula dancing by former Miss Hawaii pageant winners. Panoramic ocean views are as intoxicating as the tropical cocktails, but skip the food.

MAI TAI BAR Live Music
(☎923-7311; www.royal-hawaiian.com; Royal Hawaiian, 2259 Kalakaua Ave; ⊘10am-11pm or midnight nightly, live music 6-10pm Tue-Sun) At the Royal Hawaiian's low-key bar (no preppy resort wear required), you can

The Best...
Sunset Drinks with Music & Ocean Views

catch some great acoustic island music acts and graceful solo hula dancers some nights. Even if you don't dig who's performing, the signature Royal Mai Tai still packs a punch and romantic views of the breaking surf extend down to Diamond Head.

BEACH BAR
Live Music

(☎ 922-3111; www.moana-surfrider.com; Banyan Courtyard, Moana Surfrider, 2365 Kalakaua Ave; ⏰10:30am-midnight, live music 6-9pm) Inside this historic beachfront hotel bar, soak up the sounds of classical and contemporary Hawaiian musicians playing underneath the old banyan tree where the *Hawaii Calls* radio program was broadcast nationwide during the mid-20th century. Live-music schedules vary, but hula soloists dance from 6pm to 8pm most nights.

DUKE'S WAIKIKI
Live Music

(☎ 922-2268; www.dukeswaikiki.com; Outrigger Waikiki on the Beach, 2335 Kalakaua Ave; ⏰7am-midnight, live music usually 4-6pm Fri-Sun & 9:30pm-midnight Sat) It's a crazy, tourist-filled scene, especially when weekend concerts by Henry Kapono, one of the biggest names in Hawaiian music, spill over onto the beach. Taking its name from Duke Kahanamoku, the surfing theme

prevails throughout. Drunken souvenir-photo taking and vacation-land camaraderie are encouraged. Upstairs, the tiki torch-lit veranda at the Hula Grill has a more soothing live Hawaiian soundtrack from 7pm to 9pm almost nightly.

TAPA BAR
Live Music

(☎ 949-4321; www.hiltonhawaiianvillage.com; ground fl, Tapa Tower, Hilton Hawaiian Village, 2005 Kalia Rd; ⏰3-11pm, live music 8-11pm) It's worth navigating through the gargantuan Hilton resort complex to this Polynesian-themed open-air bar just to see Jerry Santos and Olomana, one of the best traditional and contemporary Hawaiian groups performing on O'ahu today. The guys work their slack key guitar, ukulele and singing magic on Friday after the Hilton's fireworks show (p108) and Saturday nights starting around 8pm.

MOANA TERRACE
Live Music

(☎ 922-6611; www.marriottwaikiki.com; 2nd fl, Waikiki Beach Marriott, 2552 Kalakaua Ave; ⏰11am-11pm, live music 6:30-9:30pm) If you're in a mellow mood, come for sunset happy-hour drinks at this casual, poolside bar, just a lei's throw from Kuhio Beach. Slack key guitarists, ukulele players and *ha'i* falsetto singers make merry for a family-friendly crowd. Famous faces include George Kuo Martin Pahinui and Aaron Mahi on Sunday night and the *ohana* (extended family and friends) of the late, great 'Aunty Genoa' Keawe on Thursday.

KANI KA PILA GRILLE
Live Music

(☎ 924-4990; www.outriggerreef.com; lobby level, Outrigger Reef on the Beach, 2169 Kaila Rd; ⏰11am-10pm, live music 6-9pm) Once happy hour ends, the Outrigger's lobby bar sets the scene for some of the most laid-back live-music shows of any of Waikiki's beachfront hotels, with traditional and contemporary Hawaiian musicians playing their hearts out and cracking jokes. Show up on Wednesday night, when slack key guitar master Cyril Pahinui is in town. Tip: you can grab a seat in one of the hotel lobby chairs and eavesdrop on the music for free.

RUMFIRE
Live Music

(922-4422; www.rumfirewaikiki.com; Sheraton Waikiki, 2255 Kalakaua Ave; 11am-midnight, live music usually 5-8pm) The collection of vintage rum is mighty tempting at this lively hotel bar, with flirty fire pits looking out onto on the beach and live contemporary Hawaiian (or jazz) music, usually solo acts. Or wander over to the resort's cabana-like Edge of Waikiki Bar for knockout views, designer cocktails and more live Hawaiian and pop-rock music poolside, typically from 1:30pm to 3:30pm and 6:30pm to 8:30pm daily.

ROYAL GROVE
Live Music

(922-2299; www.royalhawaiiancenter.com; ground fl, Royal Hawaiian Center, 2201 Kalakaua Ave; live entertainment usually 6-7pm Tue-Sat) This shopping mall's open-air stage may lack oceanfront views, but Hawaiian music and hula performances by top island talent happen here almost every evening, along with twice-weekly lunchtime shows by performers from the Windward Coast's Polynesian Cultural Center and twice-monthly concerts by the Royal Hawaiian Band.

ROYAL HAWAIIAN BAND
Live Music

(922-5331; www.rhb-music.com; Kapi'olani Park; usually 2-3pm Sun) The tree-shaded Kapi'olani Bandstand is the perfect venue for this time-honored troupe that performs classics from the Hawaiian monarchy era on most Sunday afternoons, except during August, special events or festivals. Not many tourists find their way here. It's a quintessential island scene that caps off with the audience joining hands and singing Queen Lili'uokalani's 'Aloha 'Oe' in Hawaiian.

WAIKIKI SHELL
Live Music

(Kapi'olani Park) With Diamond Head as a backdrop, this outdoor amphitheater in Kapi'olani Park sporadically stages hula troupes and twilight shows by megastars such as ukulele-playin' rocker Jake Shimabukuro. Other concerts feature classical and contemporary Hawaiian musicians. Tickets are sold via the Neal S Blaisdell Center (p83) box office in downtown Honolulu.

Bars, Lounges & Nightclubs

Waikiki is tourist central with all the kitschy-fun telltale signs: fruity cocktails with paper umbrellas and coconut bikini bras. Almost all of the hip bars and nightclubs have migrated to Chinatown in downtown Honolulu. But if you crave spring-break-style dance clubs and tiki bars, hit Waikiki Beach Walk or rock on down Kuhio Ave after dark. For sunset 'booze cruises' on party boats that pull up right on the beach, see p106. For Waikiki's gay and lesbian scene, see p111.

Blue Hawaii cocktail
ANN CECIL/LONELY PLANET IMAGES ©

If You Like...
Luau & Dinner Shows

Choose from a hotel production right on the beach or a big bash outside town. Just don't expect anything too authentic – all of this fanfare is strictly for tourists.

1 'AHA 'AINA
(921-4600; www.royal-hawaiian.com/dining /ahaaina; Royal Hawaiian, 2259 Kalakaua Ave; adult/ child 5-12yr from $169/97; 5:30-9:30pm Mon) This sit-down dinner show is like a three-act musical play narrating the history of Hawaiian *mele* (songs) and hula. The food is top notch and there's an open bar.

2 PACIFIC SWING
(800-453-8020; www.pacificswinghawaii.com; Royal Hawaiian, 2259 Kalakaua Ave; adult/child under 12yr from $87/69; 7pm Tue-Thu) Starring Nathan Osmond (Donny and Marie's nephew) as the MC, this 1940s-style big-band show is a nostalgic, fun-loving romp through Hawaii's WWII days.

3 WAIKIKI STARLIGHT LUAU
(941-5828, 947-2607; www .hiltonhawaiianvillage.com/luau; Hilton Hawaiian Village, 2005 Kalia Rd; adult/child 4-11yr from $99/50; 5:30-8:30pm Sun-Thu, weather permitting; P) Enthusiastic pan-Polynesian show, with Samoan fire dancing and hapa haole (literally, 'half foreign') hula.

TOP CHOICE ADDICTION
NIGHTCLUB & LOBBY BAR   Club, Bar
(www.addictionnightclub.com; Modern Honolulu, 1775 Ala Moana Blvd; nightclub 10:30pm-3am Thu-Sun, beach club noon-4pm Sat, lobby bar 6pm-late daily) Superstar mainland DJs and island dynamos spin at this boutique hotel's chic nightspot with an upscale dress code (no shorts, flip-flops or hats). On special weekends, Addiction's daytime beach club lets you hang out on the pool deck with the sounds of electronica and techno grooves. For a more chill scene and artisanal cocktails, the hotel's svelte

Lobby Bar is craftily hidden behind a revolving bookcase.

LULU'S SURF CLUB   Bar, Club
(www.luluswaikiki.com; Park Shore Waikiki, 2586 Kalakaua Ave; 7am-2am) Brush off your sandy feet at Kuhio Beach, then step across Kalakaua Ave to this surf-themed bar and grill with 2nd-story lanai views of the Pacific Ocean and Diamond Head. Take your turn at shuffleboard or with the Wii sports controller during sunset happy hours (3pm to 5pm daily), then listen up for award-winning acoustic acts and local bands later most evenings. DJs crank up the beats after 10pm on Saturday for a beach-party crowd.

SHACK   Sports Bar
(www.shackwaikiki.com; Waikiki Trade Center, 2255 Kuhio Ave; 11am-4am) If you're wondering where Waikiki's resort-hotel bartenders go when they get off shift, check out this tiki-style sports bar, with huge TVs, a water-fall and live music most Tuesday to Saturday nights, mostly homegrown rock, Jawaiian or island sounds such as Kapena or Natural Vibrations.

5-0 BAR & LOUNGE   Bar, Club
(www.five-o-bar.com; 2nd level, Bldg B, Royal Hawaiian Center, 2233 Kalakaua Ave; noon-midnight Mon-Thu, noon-2am Fri & Sat, 11am-11pm Sun) You won't spot any *Hawaii 5-0* stars hiding out among the tropical lanai greenery inside this shopping-mall bar, but it's still loads of fun with friends. Boogie down on the dance floor or twirl the swizzle stick in your mai tai while listening to live bands, then belly up to the polished native-wood bar for *kalua* (underground pit-cooked) pork sliders.

YARD HOUSE   Sports Bar
(www.yardhouse.com; Waikiki Beach Walk, 226 Lewers St; 11am-1am or later) This garage-size chain restaurant pulls in raucous groups with its big-screen sports TVs and gigantic half-yard glasses of microbrewed draft beer from the US mainland, Europe and all around the Hawaiian Islands – Maui Brewing Coconut Porter or Kona Wailua

Wheat, anyone? It's pricey and loud, with a classic-rock soundtrack that never dies.

LEWERS LOUNGE
Cocktail Bar

(www.halekulani.com; Halekulani, 2199 Kalia Rd; ◷7:30pm-1am) The nostalgic dream of Waikiki as an aristocratic playground is kept alive at this hotel bar. Cocktails designed by Dale DeGroff of NYC's Rainbow Room are made from scratch using fresh (not canned) juices, including tropical lychee and ginger. Smooth jazz combos serenade after 8:30pm nightly.

GENIUS LOUNGE
Cocktail Bar

(http://geniusloungehawaii.com; 346 Lewers St; ◷6pm-2am) Like a Japanese speakeasy, this glowing candle-lit hideaway is a chill retreat for ultracool hipsters and lovebird couples. East-West tapas bites let you nibble on squid tempura, *loco moco* or banana cake while you sip made-in-Japan sake brews and retro jazz or cutting-edge electronica tickles your ears.

ARNOLD'S BEACH BAR & GRILL
Dive Bar

(339 Saratoga Rd; ◷usually noon-2am, hours vary) Just around the corner from Waikiki Beach Walk, this grass-shack dive bar with a smoky patio is where beach bums knock back cheap microbrews in the middle of a sunny afternoon. Down a stiff 'Tiki Tea' while pretending the bar's naked mannequins don't freak you out. It's down an alley next to Eggs 'n Things diner.

DA BIG KAHUNA
Tiki Bar

(2299 Kuhio Ave; ◷10:30am-4am) Do you dream of a kitschy tiki bar where fruity, Kool Aid–colored drinks are poured into ceramic mugs carved with the faces of Polynesian gods? To get soused fast, order Da Fish Bowl – just don't try picking up a pool cue or shimmying on the small dance floor once you've drained it. Full food menu served till 3am.

COCONUT WILLY'S
Bar, Club

(www.cwwaikiki.com; Waikiki Beach Walk, 227 Lewers St; ◷7pm-4am Mon-Thu, 11am-4am Fri, 5pm-4am Sat & Sun) A total tourist cliché, this tiki-bar-themed nightspot on Waikiki Beach Walk is the home of binge drinkin', beer pong, and wild spring-break dancing to cover bands and classic-rock, old-school, mash-up and electronica DJs who think they're comedians.

TOP OF WAIKIKI
Bar

(☏923-3877; www.topofwaikiki.com; 18th fl, Waikiki Business Plaza, 2270 Kalakaua Ave; ◷5-11pm) Rotating lazily at one revolution per hour, this decidedly retro tower-top restaurant takes in a 360-degree view. There's purportedly food involved, but the novelty is the slow-motion sit-and-spin with sunset cocktails at the bar.

NASHVILLE WAIKIKI
Bar, Club

(www.nashvillewaikiki.com; 2330 Kuhio Ave; ◷4pm-4am) Like Waikiki's own little

Sunset on the Beach

On some starry nights, most often on Saturdays, Queen's Surf Beach turns into a festive scene. Dubbed Sunset on the Beach, it's more fun than a gimmicky luau and almost everything is free – except for the food sold by local vendors, and even that's a bargain. Tables and chairs are set up on the sand and live Hawaiian music acts perform on a beachside stage for about two hours before show time. When darkness falls, a huge screen is unscrolled above the stage and a feature movie is shown, starting around 7pm. Sometimes it's a film with island connections, such as *Blue Hawaii* (the 1961 classic starring Elvis Presley), while other nights it's a Hollywood blockbuster. For more info, visit www.sunsetonthebeach.net.

Below: Children's ukuleles for sale in Waikiki
Right: Hawaiian music and dance at House Without a Key (p127)

honkytonk, this country-and-western dive bar can get as rowdy as a West Texas brawl. Homesick Southerners show up for sports TVs, billiards, darts, pool tournaments, and free line-dancing and two-steppin' lessons. Afternoon, evening and late-night happy hours seem endless.

Cafes

TOP CHOICE KIMO BEAN
Cafe

(http://kimobean.com; 2113 Kalakaua Ave; ⊙7am-6pm; 🛜) With multiple branches in Waikiki, this local roaster's shop is your best bet for a rich, fresh-brewed cup of Hawaii-grown coffee like hand-picked Kona peaberry, 'Maui Moka' or Ka'aui estate reserve. Fruit smoothies, banana waffles and Bubbie's *mochi* (Japanese pounded-rice cake) ice cream pop up on the simple menu. Also at the Ohana Waikiki East, Hyatt Regency and Courtyard Marriott hotels.

DIAMOND HEAD COVE HEALTH BAR
Cafe

(http://diamondheadcove.com; 3045 Monsarrat Ave; ⊙10am-8pm Mon, Fri & Sat, 10am-midnight Tue-Thu & Sun; P) Why rot your guts with the devil's brew when you can chill out with a coconut-husk dose of 'awa (kava), Polynesia's spicy, mildly intoxicating elixir made from the *Piper methysticum* plant? A relaxed vibe and a respect for the herb's roots in Hawaiian culture sets the tone on 'awa nights, when local musicians stop by to jam.

VERANDA
Cafe

(🕿921-4600; www.moana-surfrider.com; Moana Surfrider, 2365 Kalakaua Ave; afternoon tea $48; ⊙1-4pm; P) For colonial atmosphere that harks back to early-20th-century tourist traditions, traditional afternoon tea comes complete with finger sandwiches, scones with pillowy Devonshire cream and tropically flavored pastries. Portions are small, but the oceanfront setting and house-blended teas are memorable. Make reservations and come prepared

to shoo away those pesky beggar birds. Complimentary validated valet parking (tip expected).

Shopping

Hundreds of shops in Waikiki are vying for your tourist dollars. Catwalk designers such as Armani, Gucci and Pucci have boutiques inside the DFS Galleria at the northwest end of Kalakaua Ave. On beachfront Kalakaua Ave, Waikiki's shopping centers are mostly chock-full of the brand-label stores you'd find in any US mainland city. But a handful of only-in-Hawaii stores line Waikiki Beach Walk and round out the multistory Royal Hawaiian Center. For even more shopping, Ala Moana Center, Hawaii's largest mall, and the eclectic open-air Ward Centers strip malls are a short bus ride from Waikiki (see p84).

Not feeling flush? You'll never be far from Waikiki's ubiquitous ABC Stores, conveniently cheap places to pick up vacation essentials such as beach mats, sunblock, snacks and sundries, not to mention plastic flower and shell lei, 'I got lei'd in Hawaii' T-shirts and motorized, grass-skirted hula girls for the dashboard of your car back home. For offbeat, vintage and antique, and one-of-a-kind shops stocking island-style clothes and beachwear, handmade jewelry, arts and crafts, souvenirs and surfboards, walk inland along Kuhio Ave and locals' Kapahulu Ave.

TOP CHOICE BAILEY'S ANTIQUES & ALOHA SHIRTS
Clothing, Hawaiiana

(www.alohashirts.com; 517 Kapahulu Ave; ⊙10am-6pm) There's really no place like Bailey's, which has without a doubt the finest aloha-shirt collection on O'ahu. Racks are crammed with thousands of collector-worthy vintage aloha shirts in every conceivable color and style, from 1920s kimono-silk classics to 1970s polyester specials. Of the new generation of shirts, Bailey's only carries Hawaii-made labels such as Mamo and RJC. Prices dizzyingly vary from five bucks to several thousand dollars. 'Margaritaville' musician Jimmy Buffett is Bailey's biggest fan. Squeezed to the side are glass display cases full of assorted antiques, from early-20th-century Hawaii postcards to costume jewelry.

ROYAL HAWAIIAN CENTER   Mall
(www.royalhawaiiancenter.com; 2201 Kalakaua Ave; ⊙10am-10pm; P) Not to be confused with the Royal Hawaiian resort hotel next door, Waikiki's biggest shopping center has four levels and houses more than 80 breezily mixed stores. Beside designer-name brands such as Fendi, look for Hawaii-born labels such as Noa Noa for Polynesian-print sarongs, sundresses and shirts. Art galleries display high-quality koa carvings, while jewelers trade in Ni'ihau shell-lei necklaces and flower lei stands sell fresh, wearable art. Validated self-parking with purchase.

REYN SPOONER   Clothing
(www.reynspooner.com; ground fl, Sheraton Waikiki, 2259 Kalakaua Ave; ⊙8am-10:30pm) Since 1956, Reyn Spooner's subtly designed, reverse-print preppy aloha shirts have been the standard for Honolulu's businessmen, political power brokers and social movers-and-shakers. Reyn's Waikiki flagship is a bright, mod and clean-lined store, carrying colorful racks of men's shirts and board shorts, too. Ask about Reyn's Rack downtown for discounts on factory seconds.

HONOLUA SURF CO   Clothing
(www.honoluasurf.com; 2335 Kalakaua Ave; ⊙9am-11pm) Named after the bay of monster waves off Maui's northern shore where brave surfers prove their worth, this surfwear shop is split down the middle between styles for *kane* (men) and *wahine* (women). Board shorts, hoodies, T-shirts and knit cover-ups will last you just as long as an endless summer. Can't find what you need, ladies? Honolua Wahine boutique is just across the street.

LOCO BOUTIQUE   Clothing
(www.locoboutique.com; 150 Ka'iulani Ave; ⊙9am-11pm) After a day at the beach, you might realize with horror that your old swimsuit from da mainland just doesn't measure up to what island folks wear. Fix the sitch by combing the racks of this locally owned swimwear shop. Hundreds of mix-and-match bikinis, tankinis, board shorts, rash guards, rompers and more come in a rainbow of colors and retro, island-print, sexy and splashy styles.

MUSE   Clothing
(www.musebyrimo.com; 2310 Kuhio Ave; ⊙10am-11pm) Blowsy, breezy feminine fashions are what's sewn by this mainland designer from LA, whose Waikiki Beach shop is a

Shopping at the Royal Hawaiian Center
ANN CECIL/LONELY PLANET IMAGES ©

Detour:
Hawaiian Feather Lei

Aunty Mary Louise Kaleonahenahe Kekuewa and her daughter Paulette co-wrote Hawaii's celebrated handbook *Feather Lei as an Art*, which encouraged a revival of this indigenous art starting in the late 1970s. That was the heyday of the Hawaiian Renaissance, when indigenous arts, culture and language were being reborn. Although Aunty has since passed away, Paulette and her own daughter and grand-daughter keep alive the ancient Hawaiian craft of feather lei-making at **Na Lima Mili Hulu No'eau** (📞 732-0865; 762 Kapahulu Ave; 🕐 usually 9am-5pm Mon-Sat). This homespun little shop's name translates as 'the skilled hands that touch the feathers,' and it can take days to produce a single lei, prized by collectors. Call ahead to make an appointment for a personalized lei-making lesson.

serious addiction for jet-setting girls from Tokyo. Take your pick of cotton-candy tissue tanks, lighter-than-air sundresses, flowing maxi dresses, floppy hats or beaded sandals. Second location in Kailua.

MARTIN & MACARTHUR   Arts & Crafts
(www.martinandmacarthur.com; Sheraton Waikiki, 2255 Kalakaua Ave; 🕐 8am-10pm) With a motto like 'gracious Hawaiian living,' the nostalgia for Hawaii's plantation days just oozes here. Koa furniture takes up much of the shop, but there is also a standout selection of upmarket Hawaiiana, including carved boxes and tropical flower blown-glass bowls. Some of the handmade items are museum-quality – and they will cost you as much as at a fine-arts auction.

BOB'S UKULELE   Musical Instruments
(www.bobsukulele.com; Waikiki Beach Marriott, 2552 Kalakaua Ave; 🕐 9am-8pm) Avoid those cheap, flimsy imported ukuleles sold at so many shopping malls. Instead let the knowledgeable staff here teach you about island-made ukes handcrafted from native woods, including by Honolulu's own Kamaka Hawaii (p86). If you don't have enough space to pack it onto the plane, they ship worldwide.

NEWT AT THE ROYAL   Hats, Clothing
(www.newtattheroyal.com; Royal Hawaiian hotel, 2259 Kalakaua Ave; 🕐 10am-9pm) With stylish flair and panache, Newt specializes in Montecristi Panama hats – classic men's fedoras, plantation-style hats and women's *fino*. It also has fine reproductions of aloha shirts using 1940s and '50s designs. Everything's tropical, neat as a pin and top-drawer quality.

**INTERNATIONAL
MARKET PLACE**   Souvenirs
(www.internationalmarketplacewaikiki.com; 2330 Kalakaua Ave; 🕐 10am-9pm) At this kitschy 1950s outdoor market set under a sprawling banyan tree, more than 100 touristy stalls are crammed with lookalike seashell necklaces, beach sarongs, hibiscus-print handbags and more. Ride the waves into T&C Surf Shop for quality O'ahu-made surfboards, beachwear and rubbah slippahs. Hawaiian music, Polynesian dancing or steel drums are performed live almost nightly.

ART ON THE ZOO FENCE   Arts & Crafts
(www.artonthezoofence.com; Monsarrat Ave, opposite Kapi'olani Park; 🕐 9am-4pm Sat & Sun; 🅿) Dozens of artists hang their works along the fence on the south side of the Honolulu Zoo every weekend, weather permitting. Browse the contemporary watercolor, acrylic and oil paintings and colorful island photography as you chat with the artists themselves.

Information

Dangers & Annoyances

Never leave your valuables unattended on the beach. At night, it's risky to walk on the beach or along Ala Wai Canal. After dark, prostitutes stroll Kuhio Ave, preying on naïve-looking male tourists.

The hustlers who push time-shares and con deals on Waikiki's street corners are not totally gone either. Some have deceptively metamorphosed into 'activity centers' where time-share salespeople will offer you all sorts of deals, from a free luau and sunset cruises to $5-a-day car rentals, if you'll just come to hear their 'no obligation' pitch. *Caveat emptor*.

Emergency

Police, Fire & Ambulance (☎911) For all emergencies.

Police Substation (☎529-3801; www .honolulupd.org; Waikiki Beach Center, 2405 Kalakaua Ave; ☼24hr) If you need non-emergency help, or just friendly directions, stop here next to Kuhio Beach Park.

Internet Access

Most Waikiki hotels have wired internet connections in guest rooms (for which a surcharge may apply), with wi-fi only in the lobby or poolside. Cybercafes on Kuhio and Kalakaua Aves provide pay-as-you-go internet terminals, charging $6 to $12 per hour, but few places offer wi-fi.

Hula's Bar & Lei Stand (www.hulas.com; 2nd fl, Castle Waikiki Grand, 134 Kapahulu Ave; ☼10am-2am; @ ☞) Free wi-fi and two internet terminals inside the bar.

Waikiki Beachside Hostel (www .waikikibeachsidehostel.com; 2556 Lemon Rd; per hr $7; ☼24hr; @ ☞) Internet cafe terminals available to nonguests.

Waikiki-Kapahulu Public Library (☎733-8488; www.librarieshawaii.org; 400 Kapahulu Ave; ☼10am-5pm Tue-Wed & Fri & Sat, noon-7pm Thu; @ ☞) Free wi-fi and internet terminals (temporary nonresident library card $10) that may be reserved by calling ahead.

Laundry

Many accommodations have coin-operated laundry facilities for guests.

Campbell Highlander Laundry (3340 Campbell Ave; ☼6:30am-9pm) Self-serve washers and dryers; same-day laundry service available.

Waikiki Beach Marriott Resort (2nd fl, 2552 Kalakaua Ave; ☼24hr) There is a self-serve laundromat upstairs (guest-room key may be required for entry) with teak lounge chairs, magazines and air-con.

Medical Services

For 24-hour pharmacies and hospitals with 24-hour emergency rooms in Honolulu, see p88.

Straub Doctors on Call (www.straubhealth. org); North Waikiki (☎973-5250; 2nd fl, Rainbow Bazaar, Hilton Hawaiian Village, 2005 Kalia Rd; ☼8:30am-4:30pm Mon-Fri); South Waikiki (☎971-6000; Sheraton Princess Kaiulani, 120 Ka'iulani Ave; ☼24hr) Non-emergency walk-in medical clinics accept some travel health insurance policies.

Money

There are 24-hour ATMs all over Waikiki, including at these full-service banks near Waikiki Beach Walk.

Bank of Hawaii (www.boh.com; 2155 Kalakaua Ave; ☼8:30am-4pm Mon-Thu, 8:30am-6pm Fri, 9am-1pm Sat)

First Hawaiian Bank (www.fhb.com; 2181 Kalakaua Ave; ☼8:30am-4pm Mon-Thu, to 6pm Fri) Lobby displays Hawaii history murals by French artist Jean Charlot.

Tourist Information

Freebie tourist magazines containing discount coupons such as *This Week O'ahu* and *101 Things to Do* can be found in street-corner boxes and hotel lobbies and at Honolulu's airport.

Hawaii Visitors & Convention Bureau (HVCB; ☎923-1811, 800-464-2924; www.gohawaii.com; ste 801, Waikiki Business Plaza, 2270 Kalakaua Ave; ☼8am-4:30pm Mon-Fri) Business office hands out free tourist maps and brochures.

Getting There & Around

For information on flights into Honolulu International Airport, see p326. For driving directions and ground transportation to/from the airport, see p327.

Technically, Waikiki is a district of the city of Honolulu. It's bounded on two sides by Ala Wai Canal, on another by the ocean and on the fourth by Kapi'olani Park. Three parallel roads cross Waikiki: one-way Kalakaua Ave alongside the beach; Kuhio Ave, the main drag inland for pedestrians and buses; and Ala Wai Blvd, which borders Ala Wai Canal.

Bicycle

You can rent beach cruisers and commuter bikes all over Waikiki. For top-quality mountain and road bikes, visit downtown Honolulu's Bike Shop (p60).

Big Kahuna Motorcycle Tours & Rentals (www.bigkahunarentals.com; 407 Seaside Ave; per 4hr/9hr/24hr/week $10/15/20/100) Rents commuter-style mountain bikes only.

Hawaiian Style Rentals (www.hawaiibikes.com; Waikiki Beachside Hostel, 2556 Lemon Rd; per day $20-30) Multiday and monthly discounts on both beach cruiser and 'comfort bike' rentals.

Bus

Most public bus stops in Waikiki are found inland along Kuhio Ave. The Ala Moana Center mall, just northwest of Waikiki, is the island's main bus-transfer point. For more details about schedules, fares and passes, see p328.

Be careful to catch the bus that's going in your direction. Each route can have different destinations, and buses generally keep the same number whether inbound or outbound. For instance, bus 2 can take you either to the aquarium or downtown Honolulu, so take note of both the number and the written destination before you jump on – or you can just ask the driver.

It's hardly worth checking timetables for the routes in the box on p138, which run frequently throughout the day and evening, with most operating until around 9pm or 10pm daily.

Car

Major car-rental companies (see p330) have branches in Waikiki. If you're renting a car for the entire time you're on O'ahu, you may be better off picking up and dropping off at Honolulu's airport, where rates are usually cheaper, but then you'll also have to pay for parking at your hotel (averaging $15 to $30 per night).

Independent rental agencies in Waikiki include:

808 Smart Car Rentals (☎735-5000; http://smartcartours.com; 444 Niu St) Rents smart cars with convertible roofs that get over 40mpg on island highways; being smaller, they're also easier to park.

Green Car Hawaii (☎877-664-2748; www.greencarhawaii.com; Doubletree Alana, 1956 Ala Moana Blvd) Hourly and daily car-sharing rentals of hybrid sedans and SUVs; reserve ahead online, then check in with the hotel valet.

Paradise Rent-a-Car (☎946-7777; www.paradiserentacar.com; 1835 Ala Moana Blvd) Rents sedans, SUVs, jeeps and convertibles; drivers aged 18 to 24 accepted with a hefty cash deposit (no credit card required).

View of Waikiki Beach and Diamond Head at twilight (p94)
CHAD EHLERS/ALAMY ©

Useful Bus Routes

ROUTE	DESTINATION
2	Honolulu Museum of Arts, 'Iolani Palace, downtown Honolulu, Chinatown, Bishop Museum; also Waikiki Aquarium, Honolulu Zoo
4	University of Hawai'i, 'Iolani Palace, downtown Honolulu, Chinatown, Queen Emma Summer Palace; also Honolulu Zoo
8	Ala Moana Center, Ward Centers, downtown Honolulu, Chinatown; also Kapi'olani Park, Honolulu Zoo
13	Honolulu Convention Center, Honolulu Museum of Arts, 'Iolani Palace, downtown Honolulu, Chinatown; also Kapahulu Ave
19 & 20	Ala Moana Center, Ward Centers, Restaurant Row, Aloha Tower Marketplace, downtown Honolulu, Chinatown, Honolulu International Airport*
22	Honolulu Zoo, Kapi'olani Park, Diamond Head, Kahala Mall, Koko Marina Center, Hanauma Bay (no service Tuesday), Sea Life Park; also Ala Moana Center, Pearl Harbor
23	Honolulu Zoo, Kapi'olani Park, Diamond Head, Kahala Mall, Hawai'i Kai Towne Center, Sea Life Park; also Ala Moana Center
42	Ala Moana Center, Ward Centers, downtown Honolulu, Chinatown, Pearl Harbor; also Kapi'olani Park, Honolulu Zoo
B (CityExpress!)	Honolulu Museum of Arts, 'Iolani Palace, downtown Honolulu, Chinatown, Bishop Museum
E (CountryExpress!)	Ala Moana Center, Restaurant Row, Aloha Tower Marketplace, downtown Honolulu

*One piece of hand-held carry-on baggage only per person; luggage prohibited (see p327).

VIP Car Rental (☎922-4605; http://vipcarrentalhawaii.com; 234 Beach Walk) Rents compacts, sedans, jeeps, minivans and convertibles; drivers aged 18 to 24 accepted with a hefty cash deposit (no credit card required).

PARKING Most hotels charge $15 to $30 per night for either valet or self-parking. The **Waikiki Trade Center Parking Garage** (2255 Kuhio Ave, enter off Seaside Ave) and next-door **Waikiki Parking Garage** (333 Seaside Ave) usually offer Waikiki's cheapest flat-rate day, evening and overnight rates. At the less-trafficked southeast end of Waikiki, there's a free parking lot along Monsarrat Ave beside Kapi'olani Park with no time limit. Waikiki's cheapest metered lot (25¢ per hour, four-hour limit) is along Kapahulu Ave next to the zoo. But neither of these last two places are particularly safe for rental cars, which are marked with bar-code stickers that make them easy targets for smash-and-grab thieves.

Motorcycle & Moped

You can tool around on a motorcycle or moped, but don't expect to save any money that way –

Rainbow Tower and lagoon at the Hilton Hawaiian Village resort (p114)

ANN CECIL/LONELY PLANET IMAGES ©

two-wheeled vehicles can be more expensive to rent than a car. They're not necessarily safe – drivers should have some prior experience navigating in city traffic. For road rules and rental rates, see p331.

Big Kahuna Motorcycle Tours & Rentals (☎924-2736, 888-451-5544; www.bigkahunarentals.com; 407 Seaside Ave) Rents Harley-Davidson motorcycles and SYM scooters (over-21s with valid motorcycle license and credit card only) and Yamaha mopeds (over-18s only, major credit card required).

Chase Hawaii Rentals (☎942-4273; www.chasehawaiirentals.com; 355 Royal Hawaiian Ave) Rents Harley-Davidson, Kawasaki and Honda motorcycles and Vespa scooters (over-21s with valid motorcycle license and credit card only).

Cruzin Hawaii (☎945-9595, 877-945-9595; http://cruzinhawaii.com; 1980 Kalakaua Ave) Rents mostly Harley-Davidson motorcycles (over-21s with valid motorcycle license and credit card only).

Paradise Rent-a-Car (☎946-7777; www.paradiserentacar.com; 1835 Ala Moana Blvd) Rents scooters and mopeds; drivers aged 18 to 24 and hefty cash deposits accepted (no credit card required).

Taxi

Taxi stands are found at Waikiki's bigger resort hotels and shopping malls. Elsewhere, you'll probably need to call for a taxi (see p331).

Trolley

The motorized **Waikiki Trolley** (☎593-2822; www.waikikitrolley.com; adult/child 4-11yr/senior 4-day pass $52/30/31, 7-day pass $58/22/35; ☺schedules vary by route) runs three color-coded lines designed for tourists that connect Waikiki with the Ala Moana Center, downtown Honolulu, Chinatown, Diamond Head and Kahala Mall. Passes allow you to jump on and off the trolley as often as you like, but they don't offer much in the way of value compared with buses. Purchase trolley passes at **DFS Galleria** (330 Royal Hawaiian Ave) or **Royal Hawaiian Center** (2201 Kalakaua Ave), or buy them online in advance at a discount.

Pearl Harbor Area

The WWII-era rallying cry 'Remember Pearl Harbor!' that once mobilized an entire nation dramatically resonates on Oʻahu. It was here that the surprise Japanese attack on December 7, 1941, hurtled the US into war in the Pacific. Every year about 1.5 million tourists visit Pearl Harbor's unique collection of war memorials and museums, all clustered around a quiet bay where oysters were once farmed. Today Pearl Harbor is still home to an active and mind-bogglingly enormous US naval base. Anyone looking for a little soul-soothing peace, especially after a stirring visit to the USS *Arizona* Memorial, can head up into the misty Koʻolau mountains above the harbor, where an ancient Hawaiian medicinal temple and a forested hiking trail await. The island's largest flea market is another possible diversion. Note that there are no lodgings to speak of around Pearl Harbor, but Honolulu is less than 10 miles away.

Battleship *Missouri* Memorial (p147)
HOLGER LEUE/LONELY PLANET IMAGES ©

Pearl Harbor Itineraries

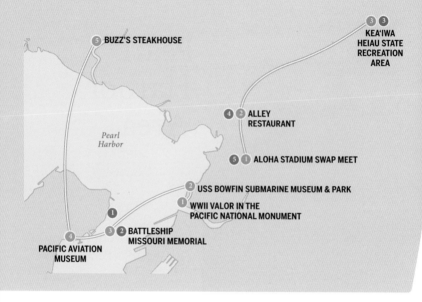

One Day

1 WWII Valor in the Pacific National Monument (p144) A full day is easily spent at the area's WWII-related sights; to go in depth, two days is not too much. Arrive early even if you've made advance reservations. Thousands of people per day come to take the tour that includes a moving theater presentation about the attack on Pearl Harbor and a boat ride to the USS *Arizona* Memorial, the watery grave for the sailors who fell here. Block out several hours for the tour, the monument's two museums, the gigantic bookstore and outdoor exhibits.

2 USS Bowfin Submarine Museum & Park (p145) Accessed through the monument are several other, paid, Pearl Harbor sights. Moored WWII-era submarine the *Bowfin* is worth exploring both above and below deck.

3 Battleship Missouri Memorial (p147) In the afternoon, take the shuttle bus from behind Bowfin Park to see the USS *Missouri*. This historic battleship not only served in two of WWII's final naval battles, Iwo Jima and Okinawa, but aboard its deck is where General MacArthur accepted the Japanese surrender.

4 Pacific Aviation Museum (p147) From there the shuttle bus continues out to the military aircraft museum that investigates the period from WWII through the US-Vietnam conflict.

5 Buzz's Steakhouse (p149) Sunset views over Pearl Harbor attract quite the crowd at this island steakhouse; make a reservation in advance so you can have dinner here.

➡ THIS LEG: 6 MILES

Two Days

1 **Aloha Stadium Swap Meet** (p149)
On day two, if you want to spend more time at any of the war sites, by all means do. Otherwise, you have some souvenir shopping to do. Kitschy carved signs, tropical-print muumuus and island-style quilts at this gigantic swap meet are all much more reasonable than in town. Note that it's open Wednesday, Saturday and Sunday only, and there's not much in the way of foodstuffs for sale.

2 **Alley Restaurant** (p149) Next, stop for a plate lunch or *furikake 'ahi* (seasoned tunafish) sandwich at this locally loved restaurant oddity that's attached to a bowling alley. The island-style eats are all good; don't pass up the lemon crunch cake.

3 **Kea'iwa Heiau State Recreation Area** (p148) If you didn't visit the memorials in the morning, you'll have plenty of time to hike in the afternoon. The site of an ancient heiau (stone temple), this park has a great trail that traverses lush vegetation and affords sweeping views over the mountains and coast.

THIS LEG: 4 MILES

Pearl Harbor Highlights

1 **Best History Lesson: USS Arizona Memorial** (p144) A solemn tribute to more than 1000 sailors who lost their lives shipboard during the Pearl Harbor attack.

2 **Best Tour: Battleship Missouri Memorial** (p147) A docent-guided, multideck tour of a legendary battleship.

3 **Best Hike: 'Aiea Loop Trail** (p148) Peace and quiet in the misty forest above Pearl Harbor.

4 **Best Food & Fun: Alley Restaurant** (p149) Should we eat dinner or go bowling? Both!

5 **Best Bargains: Aloha Stadium Swap Meet** (p149) Rows and rows of discounted island souvenirs and clothing.

USS *Arizona* Memorial
BILL BACHMANN/LONELY PLANET IMAGES ©

Discover Pearl Harbor Area

Pearl Harbor

December 7, 1941 – 'a date which will live in infamy,' President Franklin D Roosevelt later said – began at 7:55am with a wave of more than 350 Japanese planes swooping over the Ko'olau Range headed toward the un-suspecting US Pacific Fleet in Pearl Harbor. The battleship USS *Arizona* took a direct hit and sank in less than nine minutes, trapping most of its crew beneath the surface. The average age of the 1177 enlisted men who died in the attack on the ship was just 19 years. It wasn't until 15 minutes after the bombing started that American anti-aircraft guns began to shoot back at the Japanese warplanes. Twenty other US military ships were sunk or seriously damaged and 347 airplanes were destroyed during the two-hour attack.

The offshore shrine at the sunken USS *Arizona* alone doesn't tell the only story. Nearby are two other floating historical sites: the USS *Bowfin* submarine, aka the 'Pearl Harbor Avenger,' and the battleship USS *Missouri,* where General Douglas MacArthur accepted the Japanese surrender at the end of WWII. Together, for the US, these military sites represent the beginning, middle and end of the war. To visit all three, as well as the Pacific Aviation Museum, dedicate at least a day.

Sights

WWII VALOR IN THE PACIFIC NATIONAL MONUMENT Historic Site
(www.nps.gov/valr; Arizona Memorial Pl; ◷7am-5pm) One of the USA's most significant WWII sites, this National Park Service monument narrates the history of the Pearl Harbor attack and commemorates fallen service members. The monument is entirely wheelchair accessible. The main entrance also leads to Pearl Harbor's other parks and museums.

Offshore, the **USS Arizona Memorial** (◷tours 8am-3pm) was built over the midsection of the sunken ship, with deliberate geometry to represent initial defeat, ultimate victory and eternal serenity. In the furthest of three internal

USS *Missouri* WWII battleship
ANN CECIL/LONELY PLANET IMAGES ©

chambers the names of crewmen killed in the attack are engraved in marble. The central section has cutaways that allow you to see the remains of the ship. The US Navy servicemen who died inside the sunken vessel remain entombed in its hull, considered buried at sea. Visitors are asked to maintain respectful silence. A memorial visit is part of a 75-minute tour that begins with a 25-minute documentary film on the attack. Afterward, a boat takes you to the site. Free, timed, tour tickets are required for entry. Some are available on a first-come, first-served basis from the main ticket counter. However, up to 4500 people may visit the memorial on a sunny day, so it's best to pay the $1.50-per-ticket convenience fee and reserve ahead with www.recreation.gov.

The revamped monument grounds are much more than just a boat dock for the memorial. Be sure to stop at the two museums, where multimedia and interactive displays bring to life the **Road to War** and the **Attack & Aftermath** through historic photos, films, illustrated graphics and taped oral histories. Among the most interesting exhibit elements are the locals' testimonies about the unease before the attack (maybe it wasn't as much of a surprise to residents as to the military) and the frank look at the treatment of Japanese Americans during the war. A **shore-side walk** passes signs illustrating how the attack unfolded in the now-peaceful harbor. For $7 you can rent an **audio tour** with more personal accounts at stops throughout the memorial. Note that much of this is already covered thoroughly in the museums.

The giant **bookstore** sells just about every book and movie ever produced on the Pearl Harbor attack and WWII's Pacific theater, as well as informative illustrated maps of the battle. If you're lucky, the few remaining, 90-plus-year-old Pearl Harbor veterans who volunteer might be out front signing autographs and answering questions.

What questions do you think someone might take away from a Valor in the Pacific National Monument visit?
One leaves the monument with lingering questions about our military at that time. There were numerous warning signs that should have alerted the military to the impending attack.

What is the most important WWII-related island experience besides Pearl Harbor?
A visit to the National Memorial Cemetery of the Pacific (Punchbowl; p56) should be a mandatory spot to visit on O'ahu. There is a 200ft-long, 20ft-high panorama of all the Pacific theater battles during the war. It is in 3-D and in color with the names and dates of each battle. It is free to the public.

Any other lesser-known sites? There are numerous bunkers ['pillboxes'] all around O'ahu that housed large guns during and after the attack on Pearl Harbor [including at Lanikai, p183]. Perhaps the most visited are those on the peaks of Diamond Head. The Hawai'i Army Museum (p102) in Waikiki has a lot of information about the island before, during and after the attack. Some may want to visit the memorial at the Opama radar site near the entrance to the Turtle Bay Resort (p210) on the North Shore.

PEARL HARBOR
HISTORIC SITES   Historic Site
(www.pearlharborhistoricsites.org; Arizona Memorial Pl; 2-day pass adult/child $65/35) The park area around the **USS Bowfin Submarine Museum & Park** (park free, museum & submarine adult/child $10/4; ⏰7am-5pm, last entry 4:30pm) extends from the Valor in the Pacific monument grounds. As you stroll

Pearl Harbor

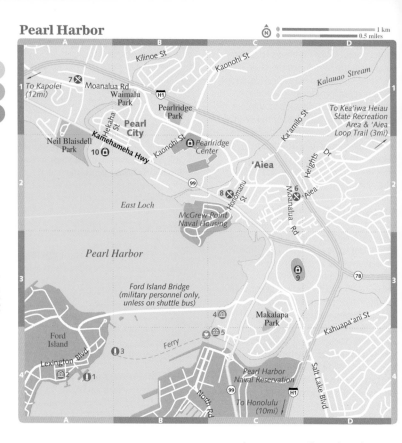

Pearl Harbor

◎ Sights
1 Battleship Missouri Memorial	A4
2 Pacific Aviation Museum	A4
3 USS Arizona Memorial	B4
4 USS Bowfin Submarine Museum & Park	C3
5 WWII Valor in the Pacific National Monument	C4

⊗ Eating
6 Alley Restaurant	C2
7 Buzz's Steakhouse	A1
8 Forty Niner Restaurant	C2

⊜ Shopping
9 Aloha Stadium Swap Meet	C3
10 Fabric Mart	A2

around, you can peer through periscopes and inspect a Japanese *kaiten* (suicide torpedo), the marine equivalent of a kamikaze pilot and his plane. Undoubtedly the highlight is clambering aboard and exploring what life was like for the crew on the WWII-era submarine USS Bowfin – watch your head below deck! (Children under age four are not allowed to board.) Launched one year after the Pearl Harbor attack, this sub sank 44 enemy ships in the Pacific. A slightly dated niche museum here traces the development of submarines and shows footage from sub patrols. No matter your age, we recommend the 'family' setting on the free audio tour; it's just as informative and much more entertaining.

To visit the **Battleship Missouri Memorial** (adult/child $20/10; ⏰8am-5pm Jun-Aug, to 4pm Sep-May), take the free shuttle from behind Bowfin Park to Ford Island. The last US battleship built during WWII, the 'Mighty Mo' saw action during the decisive battles of Iwo Jima and Okinawa. With the free self-guided audio tour, you can poke about the officers' quarters, browse exhibits on the ship's history and walk the deck where General Douglas MacArthur accepted the Japanese surrender on September 2, 1945. Taking a 90-minute **Battle Stations Tour** (adult/child $25/12) with a knowledgeable guide, many of whom have served in the US military, is well worth the extra time and expense, as it gets you onto decks not covered by general admission.

The next shuttle-bus stop is the **Pacific Aviation Museum** (adult/child $20/10, incl tour $30/20; ⏰9am-5pm). Though still a work in progress, this military aircraft museum has excellent, hi-tech exhibits focusing on the period from WWII through to the US conflicts in Korea and Vietnam. WWII subjects include the Pearl Harbor attack, the Doolittle Raid on mainland Japan in 1942 and the pivotal Battle of Midway.

Walk over to Hangar 79 to see planes such as a Japanese Zero and Russian Korean War MiGs. A guided Aviator's Tour allows access to the restoration workshop, great for airplane buffs.

Various ticket packages are available for the three attractions. The best deal is a two-day pass that includes admission to all, plus a Valor in the Pacific audio tour. Tickets are sold online, at the main monument ticket counter, and at each attraction. A free shuttle runs in a continuous loop from behind the *Bowfin* to the *Missouri* and on to the Pacific Aviation Museum. Note that the latter two are on Ford Island, an active military base that cannot otherwise be accessed by civilians. When the base is on high alert, an ID may be necessary to board the bus. The last tickets are sold at 4pm; the last shuttle leaves the museums at 5pm.

Tours

Private tours of Pearl Harbor from Waikiki don't add much, if anything, to the experience of visiting the memorials and museums. Besides, tourist boats

The USS *Arizona* Memorial (p144), erected on top of the sunken ship

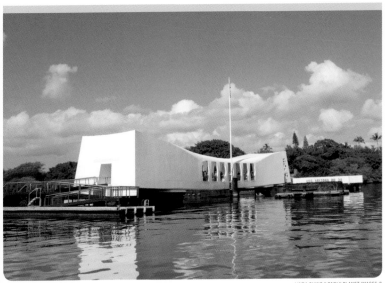

LINDA CHING/LONELY PLANET IMAGES ©

aren't allowed to disembark at the USS *Arizona* Memorial.

Festivals & Events

MEMORIAL DAY Commemoration
On the last Monday in May, this national public holiday honors military personnel killed in battle. The USS *Arizona* Memorial, dedicated on Memorial Day in 1962, has a special ceremony.

VETERANS DAY Commemoration
On November 11, this national public holiday honors US military veterans; the USS *Missouri* hosts a sunset ceremony and tribute.

PEARL HARBOR DAY Commemoration
On December 7, ceremonies at Pearl Harbor include a Hawaiian blessing and heartfelt accounts from survivors of the 1941 Japanese attack.

Eating

All four sights have concession stands or snack shops. The cafe at the Pacific Aviation Museum is the biggest, with the best selection; the hot dogs at Bowfin Park are the cheapest. For a full meal, detour to nearby 'Aiea or go a little further to the Kapolei area on the Leeward Coast.

Information

Strict security measures are in place at Pearl Harbor. You are not allowed to bring in *any* items that allow concealment (eg purses, camera bags, fanny packs, backpacks, diaper bags). Personal-sized cameras and camcorders are allowed. Don't lock valuables in your car. Instead use the **storage facility** (per item $3; ⏱6:30am-5:30pm) outside the main park gate.

Getting There & Away

The entrance to the Valor in the Pacific Monument and the other Pearl Harbor historic sites is off the Kamehameha Hwy (Hwy 99), southwest of Aloha Stadium. From Honolulu or Waikiki, take H-1 west to exit 15A (Arizona Memorial/Stadium), then follow the highway signs for the monument, not the signs for Pearl Harbor (which lead onto the US Navy base). There's plenty of free parking.

From Waikiki, bus 42 ('Ewa Beach) is the most direct, running twice hourly between 6am and 3pm, taking just over an hour each way. The 'Arizona Memorial' stop is right outside the main memorial entrance.

'Aiea

POP 8830

Just north of Pearl Harbor lies the town of 'Aiea. Beyond Aloha Stadium and its famous flea market, the crowded old community climbs the hill to a historic heiau (stone temple).

Sights & Attractions

FREE **KEA'IWA HEIAU STATE RECREATION AREA** Historic Site
(www.hawaiistateparks.org; off 'Aiea Heights Dr; ⏱7am-7:45pm Apr-early Sep, to 6:45pm early Sep-Mar) In the mountains north of Pearl Harbor, this state park protects Kea'iwa Heiau, an ancient *ho'ola* (healing or medicinal) temple. Today people wishing to be cured may still place offerings here. The 4ft-high terraces are made of stacked rocks that enclose an approximately 16,000-sq-ft platform; the construction may date to the 16th century.

The scenic, 4.8-mile (2½-hour) '**Aiea Loop Trail** starts from the top of the park's paved loop road. There are some steep, sometimes muddy switchbacks, but you'll enjoy sweeping vistas of Pearl Harbor, Diamond Head and the Ko'olau Range. About two-thirds of the way, the wreckage of a plane that crashed in 1944 can be spotted through the foliage on the east ridge.

The park has picnic tables, covered pavilions with barbecue grills, restrooms, showers, a payphone and drinking water. The four tent sites at the **campground** (tent sites by permit $5; ⏱8am Fri-noon Wed) are well tended but don't have much privacy. Permits must be obtained in advance; for more see p312. Bring waterproof gear; rains are frequent at this elevation. There's a resident

Island Insights

In ancient times, *kahuna lapa'au* (herbalist healers) used hundreds of medicinal plants that grew on the grounds surrounding a Hawaiian heiau. Among the plants were *noni,* whose pungent yellow fruits were used to treat heart disease; *kukui,* the nuts of which are an effective laxative; and *ti* leaves, which were wrapped around a sick person to break a fever. Not only did the herbs have curative value but the heiau was believed to possess life-giving energy that could be channeled by the kahuna.

caretaker by the front gate, which is locked at night.

To get here from Honolulu, take exit 13A 'Aiea off Hwy 78 onto Moanalua Rd. Turn right onto 'Aiea Heights Dr at the third traffic light. The road winds up through a residential area for over 2.5 miles to the park. From downtown Honolulu, bus 11 ('Aiea Heights; 35 minutes, hourly) stops about 1.3 miles downhill from the park entrance.

 Eating

Locally Kamehameha Hwy has numerous hole-in-the-wall and ethnic eateries.

TOP CHOICE **ALLEY RESTAURANT** Local $$
(99-115 'Aiea Heights Dr; breakfast $5-10, mains $9-17; ⏱7am-9:30pm Sun-Wed, to 10pm Thu-Sat) A bowling-alley-attached restaurant seems an unlikely place to get great food, but that's what makes it so fun. You can dig into a scrumptious *furikake 'ahi* sandwich with supercrispy fries, or Asian braised pork with brown rice, and then bowl a few rounds. Tuesday nights the two local *braddahs* (brothers) that own the place – one a classically trained chef – offer a tasting menu, believe it or not. Save room for lemon crunch cake. There is a full bar available.

FORTY NINER RESTAURANT Diner $
(98-110 Honomanu St; dishes $4-9; ⏱7am-2pm & 4-8pm Mon-Thu, to 9pm Fri & Sat) This little

1940s diner may look abandoned, but its old-fashioned *saimin* (local-style noodle soup) is made with a secret-recipe broth. The garlic chicken and hamburgers aren't half bad either.

BUZZ'S STEAKHOUSE Steakhouse $$$
(☎487-6465; 98-751 Kuahoa Pl, Pearl City; mains $20-40; ⏱5-9pm) Just west of 'Aiea, Buzz's classic island surf-and-turf steakhouse sits atop a bluff off Moanalua Rd, with sunset views of Pearl Harbor. You will need to make reservations.

 **Shopping**

ALOHA STADIUM SWAP MEET Market
(www.alohastadiumswapmeet.net; 99-500 Salt Lake Blvd; adult/child $1/free; ⏱8am-3pm Wed, Sat & Sun) Aloha Stadium's parking lot contains the island's biggest flea market. Don't expect to find any antiques or vintage goods, but there are endless stalls of cheap island-style souvenirs, including Hawaiian-style quilts. By car, take the H-1 west to Stadium/Halawa exit 1E. **VipTrans** (☎836-0317; www.viptrans.com; round-trip $14) runs shuttle buses from Waikiki hotels by reservation, every 30 minutes on meet days.

FABRIC MART Arts & Crafts
(98-023 Hekaha St; ⏱9am-5pm) Pick up all the fun and tropical prints you could need to sew your own quilts or aloha wear at this fabric megamart.

Southeast O'ahu

Cue the *Hawaii 5-0* theme music and pretend to be the star of your own TV show or Hollywood blockbuster on O'ahu's most glamorous stretch of coastline. It looks a lot like Beverly Hills by the beach, with cherry-red convertibles cruising past private mansions with drop-dead ocean views. But you'll also find more natural thrills that are open to the public on these scenic shores: the snorkeling hot spot of Hanauma Bay, hiking trails to the top of Diamond Head and the wind-blown lighthouse at Makapu'u Point, and O'ahu's most famous bodysurfing and bodyboarding beaches are all just a short ride east of Waikiki. Save time for this coast's more hidden delights, such as Doris Duke's former estate, filled with Islamic art; a fragrant botanical garden sheltering inside a volcanic crater; and O'ahu's biggest farmers market every Saturday morning.

Southeast Oʻahu Itineraries

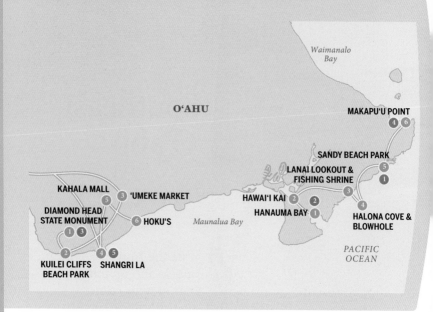

One Day

❶ Hanauma Bay (p162) It's worth getting out of bed early to beat the hordes of day trippers to this gorgeous crescent-shaped bay with its tropical fishbowl waters and coral kingdoms. Scuba divers have the bay's least-trammeled nooks practically all to themselves.

❷ Hawaiʻi Kai (p160) After you've taken off your snorkel mask and sunned yourself on the beach, head inland for lunch with views of Hawaiʻi Kai's marina from waterfront restaurant decks.

❸ Lanai Lookout & Fishing Shrine (p164) In the afternoon, cruise west along the Kalanianaʻole Hwy (Hwy 72), stopping at photo-worthy roadside lookouts for wide-open vistas of offshore islands.

❹ Halona Cove & Blowhole (p165) When the surf is blasting, you're almost guaranteed a good show at this lava-rock blowhole. The short cliffside trek down to Halona Cove is worth the scramble: this gorgeous pocket of sand cameoed in the steamy love scene from the classic flick *From Here to Eternity*.

❺ Sandy Beach Park (p166) Even if you're not an expert bodyboarder, you can still get your thrills vicariously as local bodysurfing and bodyboarding experts test their skills against skull-crushing waves.

❻ Makapuʻu Point (p167) Trek up toward the lighthouse to capture those panoramic photos that everyone back home will ooh and ah over. In winter, you might spot migrating whales way down below the trail's summit.

⊙ THIS LEG: 6 MILES

Two Days

1 **Diamond Head State Monument**
(p155) You don't have to sacrifice sleeping in late to tackle Diamond Head's summit, but it does help to get to the trailhead early for fewer crowds and cooler temperatures. Kids and grandparents alike can manage the hike to the top of this extinct volcanic crater, an O'ahu landmark.

2 **Kuilei Cliffs Beach Park** (p154) When the surf's up, join the locals getting in a few waves before work at this rocky beach park in the shadow of Diamond Head. Or come when the cooling tradewinds are blowing and do a little windsurfing.

3 **'Umeke Market** (p158) Keep it local with a healthy made-to-order lunch from this natural-foods store, which stocks island-made munchies and cooks with organic grown-in-Hawaii produce and locally ranched meats – and lots of aloha too.

4 **Shangri La** (p156) Backtrack west to downtown's Honolulu Museum of Arts, the departure point for an afternoon tour (you've made advance reservations, right?) of Doris Duke's private mansion Shangri La, scenically set on Black Rock.

5 **Kahala Mall** (p159) Not just another shopping mall, this eclectic center packs in boutique shops with authentic island flavor, whether you're searching for an aloha shirt or a sundress splashed with a tropical print.

6 **Hoku's** (p158) Aspire to the lifestyles of the rich and famous with a feast of Hawaii Regional cuisine at Kahala's most romantic restaurant, perfect for special occasions – of course, your trip to Hawaii qualifies!

THIS LEG: 28 MILES

Southeast O'ahu Highlights

1 **Best Beach: Sandy Beach** (p166)
O'ahu's wildest waves for pro bodyboarders and bodysurfers – and admiring crowds of awestruck onlookers.

2 **Best Snorkeling: Hanauma Bay** (p162)
Unbeatable spot for getting an up-close look at Hawaiian sea life.

3 **Best Hike: Diamond Head** (p155) Even families with kids in tow can tackle this military-built trail up an ancient volcanic crater.

4 **Best View: Makapu'u Point** (p167)
Walk up the lighthouse road for wind-whipped views of the deep blue ocean and uninhabited islands.

5 **Best Hidden Gem: Shangri La** (p156)
Tour the dazzling oceanfront hideaway once owned by billionaire heiress and art collector Doris Duke.

View of Honolulu from Diamond Head
ANN CECIL/LONELY PLANET IMAGES ©

153

Discover Southeast O'ahu

Diamond Head

A dramatic backdrop for Waikiki Beach, Diamond Head is one of the best-known landmarks in Hawaii. The mountain is actually a tuff cone and crater formed by a violent steam explosion long after most of O'ahu's other volcanic activity stopped. Ancient Hawaiians called it Le'ahi and at its summit they built a *luakini* heiau, a temple dedicated to the war god Ku and used for human sacrifices.

Ever since 1825, when British sailors found calcite crystals sparkling in the sun and mistakenly thought they'd struck it rich, the sacred peak has been called Diamond Head. In the early 1900s the US Army began building Fort Ruger at the crater's edge. They also constructed a network of tunnels and topped the rim with cannon emplacements, bunkers and observation posts. Reinforced during WWII, the fort today is a silent sentinel whose guns have never been fired.

Beaches

From Waikiki, bus 14 stops nearby the following beaches once or twice every hour.

TOP CHOICE KUILEI CLIFFS BEACH PARK
Beach

(3451 Diamond Head Rd) In the shadow of Diamond Head, this rocky beach draws experienced windsurfers when the tradewinds are blowing. When the swells are up, surfers take over the waves. The little beach has outdoor showers but no other facilities. You'll find paved parking lots off Diamond Head Rd, just east of the lighthouse. To find the paved trail down to the beach, just follow the surfers carrying their boards beyond the east end of the parking lot.

DIAMOND HEAD BEACH PARK
Beach

(3300 Diamond Head Rd) Bordering the lighthouse, this rocky beach occasionally draws surfers, snorkelers and tide-poolers, plus a few picnickers. The narrow strand nicknamed Lighthouse Beach is popular with gay men, who pull off Diamond Head Rd onto short, dead-end Beach Rd, then walk

Diamond Head, an extinct volcano
LYNN GAIL/LONELY PLANET IMAGES ©

east along the shore to find a little seclusion and (illegally) sunbathe au naturel.

 Sights & Activities

 DIAMOND HEAD STATE MONUMENT *Hiking*

(www.hawaiistateparks.org; off Diamond Head Rd btwn Makapu'u & 18th Aves; pedestrian/vehicle $1/5; ☺6am-6pm, last trail entry 4:30pm; P🚻) The extinct crater of Diamond Head is now a state monument, with picnic tables and a hiking trail up to the 760ft-high summit. The trail was built in 1908 to service military observation stations located along the crater rim. Although a fairly steep trail, it's partly paved and only 0.8 miles to the top, taking about an hour round-trip. Plenty of people of all ages make the hike. The trail, which passes through several tunnels and up head-spinning staircases, is mostly open and hot, so wear a hat and sunscreen and bring plenty of water. The windy summit affords fantastic 360-degree views of the southeast coast to Koko Head and the Leeward Coast to the Wai'anae Range. The Diamond Head lighthouse, coral reefs and surfers waiting to catch a wave are visible below. In winter, keep an eye out for migrating humpback whales passing by the headlands.

The state park has restrooms, drinking fountains, vending machines and a picnic area. From Waikiki, catch bus 22, 23 or 24; from the closest bus stop, it's about a 20-minute walk to the trailhead. By car, take Monsarrat Ave to Diamond Head Rd and turn right immediately after passing Kapi'olani Community College (KCC).

Eating

 SATURDAY FARMERS MARKET AT KCC *Market $*

(www.hfbf.org; parking lot C, Kapi'olani Community College, 4303 Diamond Head Rd; ☺7:30-11am Sat; ✈) At O'ahu's premier gathering of farmers and their fans, everything sold is locally made or grown and has

a loyal following, from Nalo greens to Kahuku shrimp and corn. Restaurants and vendors sell all kinds of tasty takeout meals, too, with Hawaii coffee brewed fresh and cold coconuts cracked open on demand. You might want to stuff some of the artisanal foods such as guava jam and Hawaiian sea salt into your suitcase to take back home on the plane.

Kahala

The affluent seaside suburb of Kahala is home to many of Honolulu's wealthiest residents, the island's most exclusive resort hotel and the Waialae Country Club, a PGA tournament golf course. The coastal road, Kahala Ave, is lined with expensive waterfront homes that block out virtually any ocean views. In between the mansions, a few shoreline access points provide public rights-of-way to the beach, but swimming here ain't grand – it's mostly shallow and rocky.

 Beaches

KA'ALAWAI BEACH *Beach*

(end of Kulamanu Pl) Swim in the lap of luxury at this jewel-like beach between Diamond Head and Black Point. It's in the same ritzy neighborhood as Doris Duke's Shangri La estate. From the intersection of Diamond Head Rd and Kahala Ave, turn *makai* (seaward) onto Kulamanu St; less than 0.2 miles later, Kulamanu Pl heads off right down toward the beach. There's limited free parking on Kulamanu St. From Waikiki, bus 14 stops nearby once or twice hourly.

WAI'ALAE BEACH PARK *Beach*

(4925 Kahala Ave) At this picturesque sandy beach, a gentle stream meets the sea. Local surfers challenge Razors, a break off the channel's west side. Swimming conditions are usually calm, thanks to the shallow reef, but there's no lifeguard. A favorite of wedding parties, the beach park has shady picnic tables, restrooms and outdoor showers. The parking lot is usually full; on-street parking near the bridge is often a squeeze.

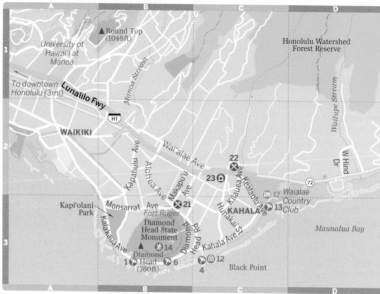

Sights

TOP CHOICE SHANGRI LA Museum

(☎866-385-3849; www.shangrilahawaii.org, www.honoluluacademy.org; 2½hr tour incl transportation $25; ☉tours usually 8:30am, 11am & 1:30pm Wed-Sat, closed Sep) Celebrity Doris Duke had a lifelong passion for Islamic art and architecture, inspired by a visit to the Taj Mahal during her honeymoon voyage to India at the age of 23. During that same honeymoon in 1935, she stopped at O'ahu, fell in love with the island and decided to build Shangri La, her seasonal residence, on Black Point in the shadow of Diamond Head. Over the next 60 years she traveled the globe from Indonesia to Istanbul, collecting priceless Islamic art objects.

Duke appreciated the spirit more than the grand scale of the world wonders she had seen, and she made Shangri La into an intimate sanctuary rather than an ostentatious mansion. One of the true beauties of the place is the way it harmonizes with the natural environment. Finely crafted interiors open to embrace gardens and the ocean, and one glass wall of the living room looks out at Diamond Head. Throughout the estate, courtyard fountains spritz. Duke's extensive collection of Islamic art includes vivid gemstone-studded enamels, glazed ceramic paintings and silk *suzanis* (intricate needlework tapestries). Art often blends with architecture to represent a theme or region, as in the Damascus Room, the restored interior of an 18th-century Syrian merchant's house.

Shangri La can only be visited on a guided tour departing from downtown's Honolulu Museum of Arts (p49), where you'll watch a brief background video first, then travel as a group by minibus to the estate. Tours often sell out weeks ahead of time, so make reservations as far ahead as possible. Children under 12 are not allowed. The house isn't air-conditioned, but free souvenir paper fans are handed out by your tour guide.

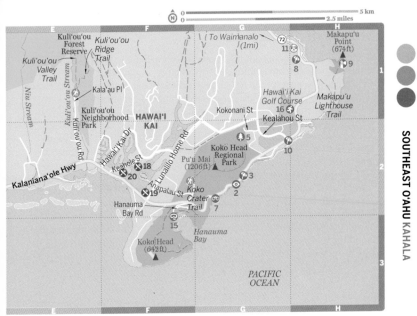

Southeast Oʻahu

Secrets of Shangri La

Shangri La is captivating not just for its collection but also for the unique glimpse it provides into the life of tobacco heiress Doris Duke (1912–93), once nicknamed 'the richest little girl in the world.' Like her contemporary Howard Hughes, she was eccentric, reclusive and absolutely fascinating.

Duke's immense fortune, which she inherited after her father died in 1925, when she was just 12 years old, granted her freedom to do as she pleased. Among other things, that meant two very public divorces and a scandalous marriage to an international playboy. While living in Hawaii, she became the first white woman to surf competitively and, naturally, she learned from the best: Olympic gold medalist Duke Kahanamoku and his brothers.

Curious to know more? Watch the HBO movie *Bernard and Doris,* starring Susan Sarandon as Doris Duke and Ralph Fiennes as her butler Bernard Lafferty. Upon her death, Doris appointed her butler as the sole executor of her fortune. She directed it to be used to further her philanthropic projects, including in support of the arts and against cruelty to children and animals.

 ## Sleeping

TOP CHOICE KAHALA HOTEL — Resort $$$

(☎739-8888, 800-367-2525; www.kahalaresort.com; 5000 Kahala Ave; r $425-1200; P ❄ @ 🛜 ♨ 🚼) Facing a private beach, this luxury resort is a favorite of celebs, royalty and other rich-and-famous types who crave Kahala's paparazzi-free seclusion. The grande dame still maintains an appealing island-style casualness: staff who have been working here for decades and guests who return every year know each other by name, and it's that intimacy that really separates it from the Waikiki pack. That said, some of the cheapest rooms are excruciatingly small and lack any views. A lei greeting at check-in, Hawaiian cultural classes, rental bicycles and stand-up paddling lessons are all complimentary, but overnight parking costs $25.

 ## Eating

TOP CHOICE HOKU'S — Hawaii Regional $$$

(☎739-8760; Kahala Hotel, 5000 Kahala Ave; dinner mains $35-70, brunch adult/child 4-12yr $60/30; �9 10am-2pm Sun, 5:30-10pm Wed-Sun) Chef Wayne Hirabayashi is revered for his elegant East-West creations such as braised short ribs with avocado tempura and wok-fried market-fresh fish paired with a world-ranging wine list. Sunday brunch buffet stars a seafood raw bar piled high with all-you-can-eat king-crab legs and a chocolate dessert fountain. Make reservations and inquire about the dress code.

'UMEKE MARKET — Supermarket, Deli $

(www.umekemarket.com; 4400 Kalaniana'ole Hwy; mains $5-15; �9 9am-7pm Mon-Fri, to 6pm Sat, to 5pm Sun; 🖉 🚼) With the slogan 'Healthy Living, Local Style,' this natural-foods store is a community hub. Stock up on homegrown snacks, order an acai (palm fruit) smoothie for breakfast before surfing or chow down on island-style fish tacos after hiking. The signature 'Buffalo Soul Jah' burger is topped off with Maui onions and garlicky hoisin sauce.

WHOLE FOODS — Supermarket, Deli $

(www.wholefoodsmarket.com; Kahala Mall, 4211 Wai'alae Ave; �9 7am-10pm; 🖉 🚼) Fill your picnic basket with organic produce and locally made specialty foods, hot and cold deli items, takeout sushi and salads, made-to-order hot pizzas and imported wines.

Entertainment

KAHALA MALL Cinema
(☎ movie infoline 593-3000; www.kahalamallcenter.com; 4211 Wai'alae Ave) Eight-screen multiplex frequently screens independent arthouse and foreign films.

Shopping

KAHALA MALL Mall
(www.kahalamallcenter.com; 4211 Wai'alae Ave; ⏰ 10am-9pm Mon-Sat, to 5pm Sun; 🛜) It's no competition for the Ala Moana Center, but this neighborhood mall has a noteworthy mix of only-in-Hawaii shops, including Cinnamon Girl and Kahala Kids clothing boutiques, Reyn's and Rix Island Wear for aloha shirts, and Sanrio Surprises selling collectible, hard-to-find imported Hello Kitty toys and logo gear.

Hawai'i Kai

Claiming a yacht-filled marina and breezy canals surrounded by mountains, bays and gentle beach parks, this meticulously planned suburb designed by the late steel tycoon Henry J Kaiser (he's the Kai in Hawai'i Kai) is a nouveau-riche scene. All the action revolves around the three shopping centers off Kalaniana'ole Hwy (Hwy 72) and Keahole St. If you're driving around southeast O'ahu, Hawai'i Kai is mostly just a convenient stop for a bite to eat or sunset drinks.

 Activities

The marina is flush with tour operators and water-sports outfitters that can hook you up with jet skis, banana and bumper boats, parasailing trips, wakeboarding, scuba dives, speed sailing – whatever will get your adrenaline pumping, they can hook you up, but it'll cost you plenty. Up in the mountains of the Ko'olau Range, which makes a cinematic backdrop for Hawai'i Kai, some wonderful, and often overlooked, hiking trails await for you to get your boots on.

KULI'OU'OU RIDGE TRAIL Hiking, Mountain Biking
West of town, this 5-mile round-trip route is open to both hikers and mountain bikers. The trail winds up forest switchbacks before making a stiff, but ultimately satisfying climb along a ridgeline to a windy summit offering 360-degree views of Koko Head, Makapu'u Point, the Windward Coast, Diamond Head and downtown Honolulu. The trail is not always well

Shangri La

The Best...
For Kids

1 Hanauma Bay (p162)

2 Diamond Head State Monument (p155)

3 Bubbie's (p161)

4 Halona Blowhole Lookout (p165)

5 Makapu'u Lighthouse (p167)

maintained and may be partly overgrown with vegetation. Start from the Na Ala Hele trailhead sign at the end of Kala'au Pl, which branches right off Kuli'ou'ou Rd, just over 1 mile north of the Kalaniana'ole Hwy (Hwy 72).

ISLAND DIVERS Diving, Snorkeling
(☎ 423-8222, 888-844-3483; www.oahus cubadiving.com; Hawai'i Kai Shopping Center, 377 Keahole St; boat dives $75-175) Five-star PADI operation offers boat dives for all levels, including expert-level wreck dives. If you're a novice, staff can show you the ropes and take you to calm, relatively shallow waters. Snorkelers can ride along on the dive boats ($40 per person, including equipment rental), which visit all sides of the island.

HAWAI'I KAI GOLF COURSE Golf
(☎ 395-2358; www.hawaiikaigolf.com; 8902 Kalaniana'ole Hwy; green fees incl cart rental $40-110) About 4 miles east of town, this aging 18-hole championship course sports Koko Head views, with a smaller par-3 executive course designed by Robert Trent Jones Sr in the 1960s. Beginners are welcome and club rentals are available. Experts will want to skip these less-than-pristine greens. Call ahead for tee-time reservations. Buses 22 and 23 stop nearby.

KOKO CRATER TRAIL Hiking
This nerve-rattling trail is not for anyone with a fear of heights! The somewhat risky, fully exposed route leads for almost a mile along an abandoned wooden-tie rail bed and across a heart-stopping wooden bridge suspended over a ravine to reach the summit of Pu'u Mai (1206ft). There's no shade, but don't worry: the panoramic views from atop the extinct crater's rim are worth your sweat. Turn north off the Kalaniana'ole Hwy (Hwy 72) onto Lunalilo Home Rd, which borders the east side of Koko Marina Center, then turn right onto Anapalau St, which leads into the community park where you'll find the trailhead.

Eating & Drinking

ROY'S – HAWAI'I KAI Hawaii Regional $$$
(☎ 396-7697; www.royshawaii.com; Hawai'i Kai Towne Center, 6600 Kalaniana'ole Hwy; mains $30-60, 3-course prix-fixe menu $45; ⏲5:30-9pm Mon-Thu, 5:30-9:30pm Fri, 5-9:30pm Sat, 5-9pm Sun) Roy Yamaguchi is one of the driving forces behind Hawaii Regional cuisine, emphasizing fresh local ingredients with artfully blended European, Asian and Pacific Rim influences. A pilgrimage to the chef's original outpost in Hawai'i Kai rarely disappoints – classics such as braised short ribs and chocolate soufflé star on the prix-fixe menu – but it's not as glitzy as Roy's Waikiki Beach (see p119). When making reservations, request a sunset-view table.

KONA BREWING COMPANY Brewpub $$
(☎ 394-5662; http://konabrewingco.com; Koko Marina Center, 7192 Kalaniana'ole Hwy; appetizers $5-16, mains $12-28; ⏲11am-10pm; 👶) With tiki-torch-lit tables hanging over the marina, this Big Island import is known for its microbrewed beers, especially the Longboard Lager and Pipeline Porter. Live Hawaiian music some nights occasionally brings out big-name musicians such as slack key guitar and ukulele master

Ledward Ka'apana. The brewpub's island-style *pupu* (appetizers), wood-fired pizzas, burgers, seafood and salads are filling but forgettable.

BLUWATER GRILL Seafood $$
(☎ 395-6224; www.bluwatergrill.com; Hawai'i Kai Shopping Center, 377 Keahole St; mains brunch $10-16, dinner $16-20; ⏰10am-11pm Mon-Thu, 11am-11pm Fri & Sat, 10am-10pm Sun) Perfect for chilling out with a cocktail, this breezy open-air restaurant lanai lets you gaze out to sea. Kiawe-grilled fare such as seafood kebabs don't rate highly, but Sunday brunch brings out delish bites such as spicy 'ahi (tuna fish) eggs Benedict and a tropical pancake bar.

KALE'S NATURAL FOODS Supermarket, Deli $
(http://kalesnaturalfoods.com; Hawai'i Kai Shopping Center, 377 Keahole St; ⏰8am-8pm Mon-Fri, to 5pm Sat & Sun; 🖊🚼) Healthy, organic and alternative-minded grocery store should be your first stop for take-out sandwiches, salads and smoothies, all made from scratch. Vegans and vegetarians won't go hungry here.

BUBBIE'S Ice Cream $
(www.bubbiesicecream.com; Koko Marina Center, 7192 Kalaniana'ole Hwy; items $2-6; ⏰10am-11pm Sun-Thu, to midnight Fri & Sat; 🚼) Bubbie's scoops homemade tropical-flavored and *mochi* (Japanese pounded-rice cake) ice cream and mixes mountainous sundaes.

Shopping

ISLAND TREASURES AT THE MARINA Arts & Crafts
(http://islandtreasuresatthemarina.com; Koko Marina Center, 7192 Kalaniana'ole Hwy; ⏰10am-6pm Mon-Sat, 11am-5pm Sun) Near the waterfront, this locally owned shop displays high-quality artisan handiwork such as koa wood carvings, etched glass, pottery and island paintings. Handmade soaps and lotions, jewelry and Hawaiian music CDs make memorable gifts.

Information

Bank of Hawaii (www.boh.com; Koko Marina Center, 7192 Kalaniana'ole Hwy; ⏰8:30am-4pm Mon-Thu, to 6pm Fri) A 24-hour ATM is available.

Makapu'u Beach (p167) with views of Kaohikaipu and Manana Islands

KARL LEHMANN/LONELY PLANET IMAGES ©

Straub Hawai'i Kai Family Health Center
(☎396-6321; www.straubhealth.org; Koko Marina Center, 7192 Kalaniana'ole Hwy; ⏰8am-5pm Mon-Fri, to noon Sat) Walk-in clinic for non-emergency medical services.

ℹ Getting There & Away

From Waikiki, bus 22 stops at Koko Marina Center (30 minutes, every 30 to 60 minutes) en route to Hanauma Bay (no service Tuesday). Running daily, bus 23 from Waikiki turns inland at Keahole St, stopping near the Hawai'i Kai Towne Center and Hawai'i Kai Shopping Center (35 minutes, every 30 to 60 minutes).

Hanauma Bay

A wide, curved bay of sapphire and turquoise waters protected by a rugged volcanic ring, Hanauma is a gem. You come here for the scenery, you come here for the beach, but above all you come here to snorkel – and if you've never been snorkeling before, it's a perfect place to start.

From the overlook, you can peer into crystal waters and view the 7000-year-old coral reef that stretches across the width of the bay. You're bound to see schools of glittering silver fish, the bright-blue flash of parrotfish and perhaps sea turtles so used to snorkelers they're ready to go eyeball-to-mask with you. Feeding the fish is strictly prohibited, to preserve the delicate ecological balance of the bay. Despite its protected status as a marine life conservation district, this beloved bay is still a threatened ecosystem, constantly in danger of being loved to death.

Past the entrance ticket windows is an award-winning educational center run by the University of Hawai'i. Interactive, family-friendly displays teach visitors about the unique geology and ecology of the bay. Everyone should watch the 12-minute video, intended to stagger the crowds and inform you about environmental precautions before snorkeling. Down below at beach level are snorkel and beach gear rental concessions, lockers, lifeguards and restrooms.

 Activities

The bay is well protected from the vast ocean by various reefs and the inlet's natural curve, making conditions favorable for **snorkeling** year-round. The fringing reef closest to shore has a large, sandy opening known as the Keyhole Lagoon, which is the best place for novice snorkelers. It's also the most crowded part of the bay and later in the day visibility can be poor. The deepest water is 10ft, though it's very shallow over the coral. Be careful not to step on the coral or to accidentally knock it with your fins. Feeding the fish is strictly prohibited.

For confident snorkelers and strong swimmers, it's better on

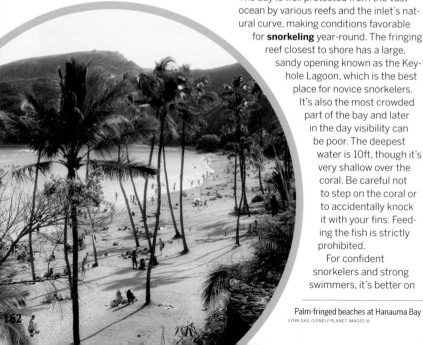

Palm-fringed beaches at Hanauma Bay
LYNN GAIL/LONELY PLANET IMAGES ©

the outside of the reef, where there are large coral heads, bigger fish and fewer people; to get there follow the directions on the signboards or ask the lifeguard at the southern end of the beach. Because of the channel currents on either side of the bay, it's generally easier getting outside the reef than it is getting back in. Don't attempt to swim outside the reef when the water is rough or choppy. Not only are the channel currents too strong, but the sand will be stirred up and visibility poor.

If you're **scuba diving**, you'll have the whole bay to play in, with crystal-clear water, coral gardens and sea turtles. Beware of currents when the surf's up, especially those surges near the shark-infested Witches Brew, on the bay's right-hand side, and the amusingly named Moloka'i Express, a treacherous current on the left-hand side of the bay's mouth.

ℹ️ Information

Hanauma Bay is both a county beach park and a **nature preserve** (📞396-4229; www.honolulu. gov/parks/facility/hanaumabay, http://hbep. seagrant.soest.hawaii.edu; adult/child under 13yr $7.50/free; ⏰6am-6pm Wed-Mon Nov-Mar, to 7pm Wed-Mon Apr-Oct; ♿). To beat the crowds, arrive as soon as the park opens, and avoid Monday and Wednesday, both very popular days because the park is closed every Tuesday.

ℹ️ Getting There & Away

CAR Hanauma Bay is about 10 miles east of Waikiki via the Kalaniana'ole Hwy (Hwy 72). Self-parking costs $1. As soon as the parking lot fills (sometimes before noon), drivers will simply be turned away, so get there early or take the bus. **BUS** Bus 22 (the 'Beach Bus') runs between Waikiki and Hanauma Bay (50 minutes, every 30 to 60 minutes) daily except Tuesday, when the park is closed. Buses leave Waikiki between approximately 8am and 4pm (4:45pm on weekends and holidays); the corner of Kuhio Ave and Namahana St is the first stop, and the bus fills up quickly. Buses back to Waikiki pick up at Hanauma Bay roughly from 10:45am until 5:20pm (5:50pm on weekends and holidays).

Local Knowledge

NAME: MATTHEW ZIMMERMAN

OCCUPATION: OWNER OF ISLAND DIVERS, HAWAI'I KAI

PLACE OF RESIDENCE: HAWAI'I KAI

What drew you to scuba diving in Hawaii? I became a dive master in San Diego, then traveled around the world, ran out of money and ended up in Hawaii. My first job was with a sailing club, and as a part of their crew, I sailed to all of the Hawaiian Islands except Ni'ihau.

What makes diving in Hawaii stand out? More than anything else, an abundance of green sea turtles. Your chances of seeing a sea turtle while diving are about 85%. Because Hawaii is the most isolated island chain on earth, it's a unique ecosystem. For example, one third of the endemic fish are found nowhere else in the world.

Anything divers should be aware of? The water here is almost always clear, with an average visibility of 80ft to 100ft, but it's a misconception that it's warm. A lot of people find 76°F surprisingly chilly after being immersed underwater for 45 minutes. You'll want to wear a 3mm-thick wetsuit.

Advice for someone who has never tried scuba diving before? If you're nervous, find a dive operation that gives you a swimming-pool session first – that's the safest way to learn.

What are some great dive sites on O'ahu? Hanauma Bay is an excellent dive, but it's logistically challenging. For first-timers, try a shallower reef dive. For experts, O'ahu is famous for its shipwrecks and also the Corsair, a WWII plane sunk over 100ft below the ocean's surface.

Koko Head Regional Park

With mountains on one side and a sea edged by bays and beaches on the other, the drive along this coast rates among O'ahu's best. The highway rises and falls as it winds around the eastern tip of the Ko'olau Range, looking down on stratified rocks, lava sea cliffs and other fascinating geological formations. Ah, yes – you've definitely left the city behind at last.

 Sights & Activities

FREE **LANA'I LOOKOUT**   Lookout
(Kalaniana'ole Hwy; **P**) Less than a mile east of Hanauma Bay, roadside Lana'i Lookout offers a panorama on clear days of several Hawaiian islands: Lana'i to the right, Maui in the middle and Moloka'i to the left. It's also a good vantage point for getting a look at lava-rock formations that form the sea cliffs along this coast.

FREE **FISHING SHRINE**   Shrine
(Kalaniana'ole Hwy) As you drive east, make sure to keep your eyes toward the ocean. At the highest point, on a sea cliff known locally as Bamboo Ridge, you should spot a templelike mound of rocks. The rocks surround a statue of Jizō, who is a Japanese Buddhist deity and a guardian of fishers. The fishing shrine is often decked out in flower lei and surrounded by sake cups. There is a little roadside pull-off in front of the shrine, about half-mile east of the Lana'i Lookout.

Left: Hanauma Bay (p162) **Below:** Koko Crater Botanical Garden (p166)

(LEFT) LYNN GAIL/LONELY PLANET IMAGES ©; (BELOW) ANN CECIL/LONELY PLANET IMAGES ©

FREE **HALONA BLOWHOLE LOOKOUT** Lookout

(Kalaniana'ole Hwy; P) Just watch where all the tour buses are turning off to find this one. Here, ocean waves surge through a submerged tunnel in the rock and spout up through a hole in the ledge. It's preceded by a gushing sound, created by the air that's being forced out of the tunnel by rushing water. The action depends on water conditions – sometimes it's barely discernible, while at other times it's a real showstopper. Don't ignore the warning signs and walk down onto the ledge, as more than a few unsuspecting people have been fatally swept off the ledge by rogue waves here.

FREE **HALONA COVE** Beach

(Kalaniana'ole Hwy) Take your lover down for a roll in the sand at this sweet pocket cove made famous in the steamy love scene between Burt Lancaster and Deborah Kerr in the 1953 movie *From Here to Eternity*. You can peer down at the cove from the Halona Blowhole parking lot, from where you'll just be able to make out a faint path leading down to the beach. Beginning at the south end of the parking lot, the path is steep but passable with caution. Warning! There is no lifeguard on duty at this beach and when the surf is up, violent waves earn it the nickname Pounders. With strong offshore currents, it's best to stay out of the water.

Island Insights

Once a favorite Hawaiian fishing spot, Hanauma Bay saw its fish populations nearly depleted by the time it was designated a marine life conservation district in 1967. After they were protected instead of being hunted, fish swarmed back by the thousands – and the bay's ecological balance went topsy-turvy. Compounding the problem, as many as 10,000 snorkelers started arriving at Hanauma Bay each day, many trampling on the coral and leaving human waste in the bay. Snorkelers feeding the fish led to a burst in fish populations beyond naturally sustainable levels and radically altered the variety of species. Now here's the good news: since 1990, scientific ecology management programs have begun to bring the bay's natural balance back.

TOP CHOICE SANDY BEACH PARK | Beach

(8801 Kalaniana'ole Hwy) Here the ocean heaves and thrashes like a furious beast. This is one of O'ahu's most dangerous beaches, with a punishing shorebreak, powerful backwash and strong rip currents. Expert bodysurfers and bodyboarders spend hours trying to mount the skull-crushing waves, as crowds gather to watch the daredevils being tossed around.

Sandy Beach is wide, very long and, yes, sandy, but this is no place to frolic. Dozens of people are injured every year, some with just broken arms and dislocated shoulders, but others with serious spinal injuries. Red flags flown on the beach indicate hazardous water conditions. Even if you don't see flags, always check with the lifeguards before entering the water.

Not all the action is in the water. The grassy strip on the inland side of the parking lot is used by people looking skyward for their thrills – it's both a hang-glider landing site and a favorite place for locals to fly kites. On weekends you can usually find a food truck selling plate lunches and drinks in the parking lot. The beach park has lifeguards, picnic tables, restrooms, outdoor showers and sparse shade trees.

From Waikiki, bus 22 stops here approximately hourly on weekdays (no service Tuesday) and every 30 minutes on weekends; the trip takes less than an hour each way.

KOKO CRATER BOTANICAL GARDEN | Garden

(www1.honolulu.gov/parks/hbg/kcbg.htm; end of Kokonani St; admission free; ☼sunrise-sunset, closed Dec 25 & Jan 1; P) According to Hawaiian legend, Koko Crater is the imprint left by the magical flying vagina of Kapo, sent from the Big Island to lure the pig-god Kamapua'a away from her sister Pele, the Hawaiian goddess of fire and volcanoes. Inside the crater today is a quiet, county-run botanical garden abloom with flowering aloe plants and *wiliwili* trees, fragrant plumeria, spiny cacti and other native and exotic dryland species. Connecting loop trails lead through the lonely garden.

To get here, turn inland on Kealahou St off the Kalaniana'ole Hwy (Hwy 72), opposite Sandy Beach. After about 0.5 miles, turn left onto Kokonani St, then continue on a rough, partly unpaved but short road past the equestrian center. From Waikiki, bus 23 stops every hour or so near the intersection of Kealahou and Kokonani Sts, just over 0.3 miles from the garden entrance.

Makapu'u Point

Makapu'u Point and its coastal lighthouse mark the easternmost point of O'ahu. On the north side of the point, a roadside **lookout** gives you an exhilarating view down onto Makapu'u Beach Park, its aqua-blue waters outlined by diamond-white sand and jet-black lava. It's an even more spectacular sight when hang gliders take off from the cliffs above.

From the lookout you can see two offshore islands, the larger of which is **Manana Island** (aka Rabbit Island). Once populated by feral rabbits, this aging volcanic crater now harbors burrowing wedge-tailed shearwaters. Curiously, it looks vaguely like the head of a rabbit with its ears folded back. In front is smaller, flat **Kaohikaipu Island**, another seabird sanctuary.

 Sights & Activities

MAKAPU'U LIGHTHOUSE TRAIL   Hiking
(www.hawaiistateparks.org; end of Makapu'u Lighthouse Rd; ☺7am-6:45pm early Sep-Mar, 7am-7:45pm Apr-early Sep; P) South of the lookout on the *makai* side of the road, a mile-long paved service road climbs toward the red-roofed Makapu'u Lighthouse. The gate at the beginning of the access road is locked to keep out private vehicles, but you can park in the lot just before the gate. Although not difficult, the uphill walk can be hot and extremely windy – hang onto your hat! Along the way stop to take in the stellar coastal views of Koko Head and Hanauma Bay and, in winter, migrating whales who might just happen to be swimming by below. Avoid the temptation to climb down the rocks to the lighthouse, as that's illegally trespassing on federal property.

The trail itself is part of the Ka Iwi State Scenic Shoreline.

MAKAPU'U BEACH PARK   Beach
(41-095 Kalaniana'ole Hwy; P) Opposite Sea Life Park and just barely within view of the lighthouse, Makapu'u Beach is one of O'ahu's top winter bodyboarding and bodysurfing spots, with waves reaching 12ft and higher. It also has the island's best shorebreak. As with Sandy Beach Park, Makapu'u is strictly the domain of experts who can handle rough water and dangerous currents. In summer, when the wave action disappears, calmer waters allow swimming. The beach park has restrooms, outdoor showers, drinking water and lifeguards. From Waikiki, catch bus 22 or 23; the ride takes under an hour. From Kailua or Waimanalo, catch bus 57.

SEA LIFE PARK   Amusement Park
(☎259-2500; www.sealifeparkhawaii.com; 41-202 Kalaniana'ole Hwy; adult/child 3-11yr $30/20; ☺10:30am-5pm; P) More like a circus than an aquarium, Hawaii's only marine-life park offers a small mixed bag of run-down attractions that, frankly, aren't worth your time. The theme-park entertainment includes choreographed shows and pool encounters with imported Atlantic bottle-nose dolphins, a controversial activity (see p299). Although the star attractions feature animals that aren't found in Hawaiian waters, the outdoor park also maintains a breeding colony of green sea turtles, releasing young hatchlings back into the wild every year. Still, if you want to learn about Hawaii's marine life, you're better off visiting the Waikiki Aquarium (p100) instead. Parking in the lot costs $5. From Waikiki, catch bus 22 or 23; the ride takes under an hour. From Kailua or Waimanalo, catch bus 57.

Windward Coast

Welcome to O'ahu's lushest, most verdant coast, where turquoise waters and light-sand beaches share the dramatic backdrop of misty cliffs in the Ko'olau Range. Cruise over the *pali* (mountains) from Honolulu and you first reach Kailua, aka adventure central. Many repeat visitors make this laid-back community their island base, whether they intend to kayak, stand-up paddle, snorkel, dive, drive around the island or just laze on the sand. To the south, more beautiful beaches await in Waimanalo. North up the coast, Kamehameha Hwy narrows into a winding two-lane road with a dramatic oceanfront on one side and small rural farms and towns on the other. Along the way there are good local eats, hiking diversions and a couple of major sights. So never mind the frequent tropical rain showers that guarantee everything stays green. Get going; the Windward Coast is only a half hour from Waikiki, but a world apart.

Kahana Valley (p199)

MARK A JOHNSON / CORBIS©

Windward Coast Itineraries

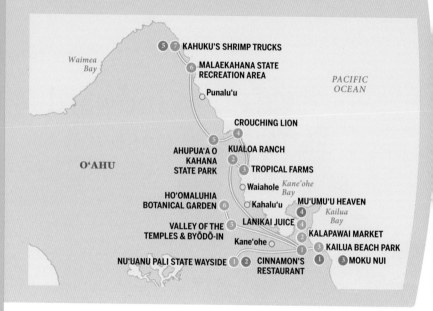

One Day

1 Nu'uanu Pali State Wayside (p172) As you drive over the mountains from Honolulu, stop at this windy viewpoint and walk a little ways down the Old Pali Hwy for panoramas of the Windward Coast. If you're inspired by the view, you can keep going along the Maunawili Trail, which winds in and out of lush, stream-fed gulches.

2 Kalapawai Market (p188) Belly up to the espresso bar as you wait for sandwiches made for your picnic at the beach. While there, you might want to look at the local foodstuffs and gifts inside this beloved 1930s general store and deli.

3 Kailua Beach Park (p179) Don't miss the Windward Coast's most beautiful white-sand beach, with gentle waves ideal for taking a dip. Swimmers, make sure you get here before afternoon breezes kick up (to the delight of windsurfers).

4 Lanikai Juice (p190) This healthy-minded juice bar is the best place to hang after surf and sun. The Pacific Passion smoothie – with pineapple, papaya, mango and passion fruit – is our favorite.

5 Valley of the Temples & Byōdō-In (p194) Although its location inside a cemetery is odd, this exquisite replica of an ancient Japanese temple backed by craggy *pali* (cliffs) is a rare beauty.

6 Ho'omaluhia Botanical Garden (p193) If you've got time to spare before sunset, take a wander through fragrant groves of tropical trees and around an artificial reservoir on soft, grassy paths.

· ·

➡ THIS LEG: 30 MILES

Two Days

1 **Cinnamon's Restaurant** (p188) Follow the one-day itinerary, then rise early for a drive through the 'country.' Before you hit the Kamehameha Hwy, though, stop at this local classic for breakfast.

2 **Kualoa Ranch** (p199) Ever wonder where the set designers for *Jurassic Park* and *Lost* found such incredible locations? Right here at this historic ranch, which offers several adventure tours; book ahead.

3 **Tropical Farms** (p198) Snack on free samples of freshly roasted macadamia nuts flavored with honey, dark chocolate or even garlic at this huge farm shop filled with made-in-Hawaii products.

4 **Crouching Lion** (p199) Everyone pulls off the highway to see this natural rock formation. Of course, ancient Hawaiians thought it looked like something very different from an African lion.

5 **Ahupua'a o Kahana State Park** (p200) Hike up the hill past an ancient fishing shrine to an overlook with knock-out views of Kahana Bay.

6 **Malaekahana State Recreation Area** (p204) Don't miss a stop at the northern Windward Coast's most inviting swimming and snorkeling beach. When the waters are calm and low, you can wade across to an offshore island.

6 **Kahuku's shrimp trucks** (p205) Few people drive around the island without stopping to devour a dozen crustaceans here. Dipped in garlic butter, doused in hot-and-spicy sauce or coconut fried – it's your choice. The picnic tables provide plenty of space to pig out.

• •

➡ **THIS LEG: 35 MILES**

Windward Coast Highlights

1 **Best Beach: Kailua Beach Park** (p179) Picture-perfect sand and surf, with colorful kitesurfing sails in the distance.

2 **Best View: Nu'uanu Pali State Wayside** (p172) Sweeping vistas of the corrugated Ko'olau Mountains, Kailua and Kane'ohe Bay.

3 **Best Activity: Kayaking to Moku Nui** (p181) Paddle out from Kailua or Lanikai to explore this offshore island with good sand and swimming.

4 **Best Shopping: Mu'umu'u Heaven** (p191) Stylish clothing and homewares crafted from recycled Hawaiian muumuus.

5 **Best Road-Trippin' Food: Kahuku's shrimp trucks** (p205) Classic food-truck fare made from shrimp from local ponds.

Byōdō-In Japanese temple (p194)
ANN CECIL / LONELY PLANET IMAGES ©

Discover Windward Coast

Pali Hwy

Slicing through the spectacular emerald Ko'olau Range, the Pali Hwy (Hwy 61) runs between Honolulu and Kailua. True, the H-3 Fwy is quicker, but the Pali wins hands down for beauty and scenic stops. If it's been raining heavily, every fold and crevice in the jagged cliffs will have a fairyland waterfall streaming down it.

Once upon a time, an ancient Hawaiian footpath wound its way perilously over these cliffs. In 1845 the path was widened into a horse trail and later into a cobblestone carriage road. In 1898 the Old Pali Hwy (as it's now called) was built along the same route but was abandoned in the 1950s after tunnels were blasted through the Ko'olau Range.

Sights & Activities

TOP CHOICE NU'UANU PALI STATE WAYSIDE
Lookout

(parking $3; ☉sunrise-sunset) About 5 miles northeast of Honolulu, turn south to the popular ridge-top lookout with a sweeping vista of Windward O'ahu from a height of 1200ft. Standing at the edge, Kane'ohe lies below straight ahead, Kailua to the right, Mokoli'i Island and the coastal fishpond at Kualoa Point to the far left. The winds that funnel through the *pali* here are so strong you can sometimes lean against them; it's usually so cool that you'll want a jacket.

A mile-long section of the abandoned Old Pali Hwy winds down from the right side of the lookout, past the car barricade, narrowing to an overgrown tangle of vegetation with a small pathway worn through to the Maunawili Falls Trail. Few people realize the road is here, let alone venture down it, thereby missing the magnificent views looking back up at the snaggle-toothed Ko'olau Range and out across the valley. It's worth walking even five minutes down the trail for the photo op.

When you return to the highway, instinct could send you in the wrong direction. Go to the left if you're heading toward Kailua, to the right if heading toward Honolulu. Buses

View of the Kualoa Mountains from Kualoa Regional Park (p198)
GREG WRIGHT /ALAMY ©

travel the Pali Hwy between Honolulu and Kailua but do not stop at the lookout.

TOP CHOICE MAUNAWILI TRAIL   Hiking
(Map p178) Winding down the coast, this scenic 10-mile one-way hiking and mountain-biking trail winds along the back side of Maunawili Valley, following the base of the lofty Ko'olau Range. It clambers up and down gulches, across streams, and along ridges, awarding panoramic views of mountains and the sea. Hiking the Maunawili Trail in an easterly direction is least strenuous, as you will be trekking from the mountains down to the coast at Waimanalo. Follow the entire route and you need to leave a second car in a remote, not so secure area. Instead, we recommend following the trail as long as you like and then backtracking to the trailhead. About 2 trail miles east of the Pali Hwy, a connector veers off downhill to the small, pooling Maunawili Falls.

Note that the Maunawili trailhead is on the southern side of the Pali Hwy and can only be accessed from the eastbound lane (coming from Kailua, you will have to pass it and turn around). About a mile northeast of the Nu'uanu Pali State Wayside, pull off right at the 'scenic point' turnout at the hairpin turn just before the 7-mile marker. Walk through the break in the guardrail where a footbridge takes you over a drainage ditch to the trail. The trail can also be picked up from the Nu'uanu Pali State Wayside by walking down a mile-long stretch of the Old Pali Hwy, but then your climb back out is harder.

MAUNAWILI FALLS TRAIL   Hiking
The most popular, and populated, trail on Windward O'ahu ascends and descends flights of wooden stairs and crosses a stream several times before reaching the small, pooling Maunawili Falls amid the tropical vegetation. When the trail forks, veer left; straight ahead is the connector to the Maunawili Trail. Even with the moderate elevation change, this 2.5-mile round-trip is kid-friendly and you'll see lots of families on the trail at weekends. Just be prepared, as the way can be muddy and mosquitoes are omnipresent.

To reach the trailhead, driving east on the Pali Hwy from Honolulu, take the *second* right-hand exit onto A'uloa Rd. (Again, from Kailua, you will have to pass it and turn around.) At the first fork, veer left onto Maunawili Rd, which ends in a residential subdivision; look for a gated trailhead-access road on the left. Note that this road is accessible only to pedestrians (and by residents' vehicles); nonresidents may not drive or park along this road. Instead, park along nearby residential streets that aren't gated. Respect residents by not loitering or being noisy while walking along the road.

OLD PALI HWY   Historic Site
If you're travelling westbound, from Kailua to Honolulu, you can make a scenic side trip along a remnant of the Old Pali Hwy, now called Nu'uanu Pali Dr. Turn right off the modern Pali Hwy (Hwy 61) across from the state wayside turn-out. The drive runs through a cathedral of trees draped with hanging vines and philodendrons. The lush vegetation along the detour includes bamboo groves, almond trees, banyan trees with hanging aerial roots, angel's trumpets and cup of gold, a tall climbing vine with large golden flowers. This short detour returns you to Hwy 61 heading southwest toward town, past Queen Emma's Summer Palace.

Waimanalo
POP 3660

Squeezed between the knife-edged Ko'olau Range and the crystal waters of Waimanalo Bay, this little bitty town has O'ahu's longest continuous stretch of beach. Five and a half miles of white sand spreads southeast all the way to Makapu'u Point in southeast O'ahu. A long coral reef protects much of the shore from big waves and the thick stands of ironwood pines can protect you from the sun. Though only 5 miles south of Kailua, you can definitely feel the rural vibe here. Small, hillside farms in 'Nalo, as it's called by locals, grow many of the fresh leafy greens served in Honolulu's top restaurants.

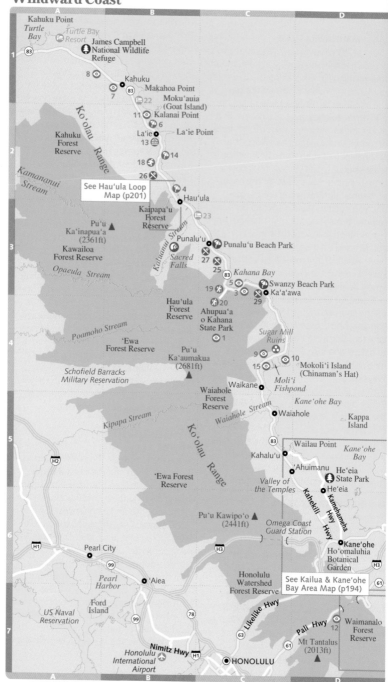

Kahuku Point

Turtle Bay

Turtle Bay Resort

James Campbell National Wildlife Refuge

8

7

Kahuku

22

Makahoa Point

Moku'auia (Goat Island)

11 Kalanai Point

6

La'ie

13 La'ie Point

18 14

26

See Hau'ula Loop Map (p201)

4 Hau'ula

Ko'olau Range

Kahuku Forest Reserve

Kamananui Stream

Kaipapa'u Forest Reserve

23

Pu'u Ka'inapua'a (2361ft)

Kawailoa Forest Reserve

Opaeula Stream

Kahawainui Stream

Punalu'u

27 Punalu'u Beach Park

25

Sacred Falls

Kahana Bay

19 5

3 Swanzy Beach Park

29 Ka'a'awa

Hau'ula Forest Reserve

20

Ahupua'a o Kahana State Park

1

Poamoho Stream

Sugar Mill Ruins

'Ewa Forest Reserve

Pu'u Ka'aumakua (2681ft)

9

15 10

Mokoli'i Island (Chinaman's Hat)

Moli'i Fishpond

Waikane

Waiahole Forest Reserve

Waiahole Stream

Kane'ohe Bay

Waiahole

Kappa Island

Kipapa Stream

Ko'olau Range

H2

Wailau Point

Kane'ohe Bay

Kahalu'u

'Ahuimanu

He'eia State Park

He'eia

'Ewa Forest Reserve

Valley of the Temples

Kahekili Hwy

Kamehameha Hwy

Pu'u Kawipo'o (2441ft)

Omega Coast Guard Station

H1

Pearl City

99

H3

Kane'ohe

Ho'omaluhia Botanical Garden

H3

Pearl Harbor

'Aiea

Honolulu Watershed Forest Reserve

See Kailua & Kane'ohe Bay Area Map (p194)

61

Ford Island

US Naval Reservation

99

78

63

Likelike Hwy

Pali Hwy

12

Waimanalo Forest Reserve

Nimitz Hwy

H1

Honolulu International Airport

HONOLULU

61

Mt Tantalus (2013ft)

174

Windward Coast

Beaches

As elsewhere at O'ahu's beaches, don't leave any valuables in your car; petty theft is not uncommon.

TOP CHOICE WAIMANALO BAY BEACH PARK Beach

(7am-7:45pm) A wide forest of ironwoods hides a broad sandy beach with little development in sight. This 75-acre county park has Waimanalo Bay's biggest waves and is popular with board surfers and bodyboarders. Even if you're not planning to hit the water, just take a walk along the cream-colored sand and try to imagine the feeling of old Hawaii. Lifeguards and restrooms are available onsite. One mile north of 'town'.

WAIMANALO BEACH PARK Beach

By the side of the roadway south of the main business area, this sloping strip of soft white sand has little puppy waves that are excellent for swimming. Manana Island and Makapu'u Point are visible to the south. The facilities include a huge grassy picnic area, restrooms, ball-sports courts, a playground and a rather unappealing campground. Lifeguards are on watch here too.

BELLOWS FIELD BEACH PARK Beach

(noon Fri-8am Mon) A long beach with fine sand and a natural setting backed by ironwood trees in places, this is another great beach. The only problem is that the park is only open to civilians on weekends (and national holidays) because it fronts Bellows Air Force Station. The small shorebreak waves are good for beginning bodyboarders and board surfers. There are several parking areas stretched out along the road to the base. Lifeguards, showers, restrooms, drinking water and camping are all available onsite. The park entrance is just north of Waimanalo Bay Beach Park.

 **Activities**

OLOMANA GOLF LINKS Golf

(www.olomanagolflinks.com; 41-1801 Kalaniana'ole Hwy; 18 holes $95) LPGA star Michelle Wie got her start here, and President Obama regularly swings through these two challenging nine-hole courses on his holidays. Played together they form a regulation 18-hole, par-72 course beneath the dramatic backdrop of the Ko'olau Range. The facilities include a driving range and a restaurant.

YOGA MOVES HAWAII Yoga

(www.yogamoveshawaii.com; 41-1025 Kalaniana'ole Hwy; classes $10; 5:30-6:45pm Tue, 8:30-9:45am Fri) Practise yoga with an India-trained Iyengar yogini, Laurie Freed. Laurie teaches classes in a peaceful, relaxing, open-air garden space behind Sweet Home Waimanalo.

 Sleeping

There are fewer private house and apartment-suite vacation rentals around Waimanalo than near Kailua; check with consolidators such as **VRBO** (www.vrbo.com) and **Home Away** (www.homeaway.com) and others (for more agencies see p318). All three Waimanalo beach parks have campsites; for information on getting the free-but-required Honolulu County advance permit, see p312.

TOP CHOICE BELLOW FIELD BEACH PARK Campground $

(tent sites by permit free; noon Fri-8am Mon) The nearby army base guard shack makes this the most secure of area campgrounds. Some of the 60 sites are beneath the ironwood trees, some by the beach. Barbecue grills, showers and restrooms available. Note that buses stop in front of the entrance road, about 1.5 miles from the beach itself.

BEACH HOUSE HAWAII
Vacation Rental $$

(☎ 259-7792, 866-625-6946; www.beach househawaii.com; apt $165) The beach is just across the street from the brightly tropical studio that this company rents out by the night. Cottages and larger places are available by the month.

WAIMANALO BAY BEACH PARK
Campground $

(tent sites by permit free; ⏰ 8am Fri-8am Wed) The 10 tree-shaded sites are a good choice if Bellows isn't open. It has BBQ grills and restrooms with showers.

 Eating

There isn't much to Waimanalo town, but a few food trucks usually hang out past the convenience store, on the *mauka* (inland) side of the road.

TOP CHOICE SWEET HOME WAIMANALO
Organic $

(41-1025 Kalaniana'ole Hwy; mains $8-13; ⏰ 9:30am-7pm; 🖉) Taste local Waimanalo's back-to-the-earth farm goodness from this family kitchen, where local chicken gets sauced with honey and citrus, and fresh corn tortillas wrap lime cream and grilled fish for tacos. Even the island standards get a twist: the *kalua* pork sandwich is topped with bok choy slaw. Take it to go for the beach or chow down in the colorful picnic area out front next to the highway.

KENEKE'S
Local $

(41-857 Kalaniana'ole Hwy; mains $4-8; ⏰ 9:30am-5:30pm) You can't miss this red-and-white checkered drive-in. From beneath the Christian scripture written on all the walls, they cook up good, basic island-style BBQ, triple-decker *loco moco* (dish of rice, fried egg and hamburger patty topped with gravy) and other plate lunches. Try the *mochiko* fried chicken or *laulau* pig. There's shave ice and ice cream, too.

 Shopping

NATURALLY HAWAIIAN GALLERY
Arts & Crafts

(41-1025 Kalaniana'ole Hwy; ⏰ 9:30am-5:30pm) Since it shares space inside a converted gas station with Sweet Home Waimanalo, you can browse island artists' paintings

The Battle of Nu'uanu

O'ahu was the lynchpin conquered by Kamehameha the Great during his campaign to unite the Hawaiian Islands under his rule. In 1795, on the quiet beaches of Waikiki, Kamehameha landed his fearsome fleet of canoes to battle Kalanikupule, the *mo'i* (king) of O'ahu.

Heavy fighting started around Puowaina ('Hill of Sacrifice,' now nicknamed Punchbowl), and continued up Nu'uanu Valley. O'ahu's spear-and-stone warriors were no match for Kamehameha's troops, which included a handful of Western sharpshooters. O'ahu's defenders made their last stand at the narrow ledge near the current-day Nu'uanu Pali lookout. Hundreds were driven over the top to their deaths. A century later, during the construction of the Old Pali Hwy, more than 500 skulls were found at the base of the cliffs.

Some O'ahu warriors, including their king, escaped into the forest. When Kalanikupule surfaced a few months later, he was sacrificed by Kamehameha to the war god Ku. Kamehameha's taking of O'ahu marked the last battle ever fought between Hawaiian warriors.

and handmade crafts while you wait for a kale smoothie. Naturalist Patrick Ching's prints are especially good.

**EAST HONOLULU
CLOTHING COMPANY** Clothing

(41-1537 Kalaniana'ole Hwy; ⊗9am-5pm) The striking, graphic one-color tropical prints on the clothing here are all designed and silk screened in-house. This company provides many local hula schools with their costumes.

🛈 Getting There & Away

Waimanalo is about a 35-minute drive (17 miles) from Waikiki via Hwy 61; it's 10 minutes (6 miles) down the coast from Kailua.

Bus 57 travels between Honolulu's Ala Moana Center and Waimanalo (one hour) via Kailua (25 minutes), running every 15 to 30 minutes. It makes stops along the Kalaniana'ole Hwy (Hwy 72) through town. A few continue on to Sea Life Park (five minutes).

Kailua

POP 38,635

A long, graceful bay protected by a coral reef is Kailua's claim to fame. The nearly 4-mile-long shoreline stretch of ivory sand is made for strolling, and the weather and wave conditions can be just about perfect for swimming, kayaking, windsurfing and kitesurfing. None of this has gone unnoticed. Decades ago expatriates from the mainland bought up cottages crowded into the little neighborly lanes; the ones near the beachfront were often replaced with megahouses. South along the shore lies the exclusive enclave of Lanikai, with million-dollar views – and mansions that may be valued at 10 times that much.

In ancient times Kailua (meaning 'two seas') was a home to Hawaiian chiefs, including briefly Kamehameha the Great after he conquered O'ahu. Today it's the Windward Coast's largest suburban town, where you'll find the vast majority of the coast's restaurants and retail. Eclectic boutiques and independent eateries predominate, but lately more chains have moved in. Many repeat travelers to O'ahu leapfrog over touristy Waikiki (only 15 miles and 30 minutes away) and stay in this laid-back, residential community. It's a great place to pretend you live.

 ## Beaches

TOP CHOICE **KAILUA BEACH PARK** Beach

A wide arc of sand drapes around the jewel-colored waters of Kailua Bay, with formidable volcanic headlands bookending either side and interesting little islands rising off shore. It's ideal for long, leisurely walks, family outings and all kinds of aquatic activities. The beach has a gently sloping sandy bottom with usually calm waters; it's good for swimming year-round, especially in the morning. The wind can blow any time but generally kicks up in the afternoon.

The southeastern end of the beach park, near the boat ramp and parking lot opposite Kaneapu Pl, has a local vibe. A food truck hangs out here, and you just may see three generations of women washing gourds in the ocean to make hula instruments. The main parking lot is southeast of Kaelepulu Stream, off Kawailoa Rd, opposite Buzz's steakhouse. This is

tourist and family central, and it has the biggest restroom. Many visitors only stop long enough to walk up past the picnic table and stand on top of the bluff staring at the water. Local outrigger-canoe teams work out in the large, grassy field, and stand-up paddlers and kayakers use the stream as a launching pad. We like parking further northwest, along Maklii Pl, where the crowds thin out and the kitesurfers launch in a colorful display of parachutes. To get here you will have to turn *makai* (seaward) on Kailua Rd at Kalapawai Market, and then veer right. All areas have restrooms and there are lifeguards nearby.

KALAMA BEACH PARK Beach

(Map p194) The sand itself doesn't stop at the Kailua Beach Park boundaries; it continues north for another 2 miles. If you're not staying in a rental with shared private access, Kalama Beach Park, 1 mile north on Kalaheo Ave, is the best place to park for a great walk. Climb over the grassy lawn to a much more residential stretch of sand. Weekdays there's hardly

Kailua Beach Park
DAVID L MOORE · HIO / ALAMY ©

Kailua

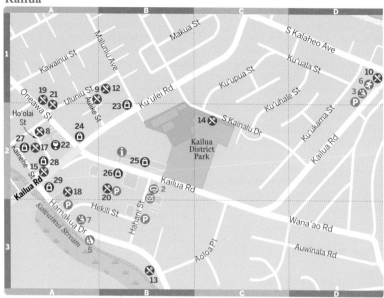

Kailua

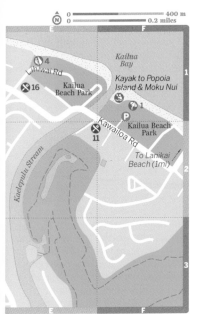

a soul besides tan, fit locals walking their dogs and the occasional group of moms with their infants. Restrooms and outdoor shower available. No lifeguards.

LANIKAI BEACH
Beach

(Map p194) Just southeast of Kailua, Lanikai is an exclusive residential neighborhood fronting a gorgeous stretch of powdery white sand overlooking two postcard-perfect islands, known locally as the Mokes. Today the beach is shrinking: nearly half the sand has washed away as a result of retaining walls built to protect the neighborhood's multimillion-dollar mansions. Still, it's a rare beauty, at its best during full-moon phases. Beyond Kailua Beach Park, the coastal road becomes one-way A'alapapa Dr, which loops back around as one-way Mokulua Dr. There are 11 narrow public beach-access walkways off Mokulua Dr. Avoid weekends as there's no designated parking and all the residential roadsides fill up. For the best stretches of sand, try the walkways furthest southeast, towards Wailea Point. No bathrooms, no lifeguards.

Sights

Note that sights in the nearby Kane'ohe Bay area are also easily accessible.

FREE ULUPO HEIAU STATE HISTORIC SITE
Archeological Site

(Map p194; www.hawaiistateparks.org; 1200 Kailua Rd; ☉sunrise-sunset) Rich in stream-fed agricultural land, abundant fishing grounds and protected canoe landings, Kailua was an ancient economic center that supported at least three temples. Ulupo, once bordered by 400 acres of cultivated fishponds and taro fields, is the only one left to visit. Construction of this imposing platform temple was traditionally attributed to *menehune*, the 'little people' who legend says created much of Hawaii's impressive stonework, finishing each project in one night. Fittingly, Ulupo means 'night inspiration.' It's thought the temple's final use may have been as a *luakini*, a place for human sacrifice dedicated to the war god Ku. Interpretive panels provide an artist's rendition of the site as it probably looked in the 18th century. Most years a *hoi'ke* (day-long celebration) of hula, music, traditional culture and food is held in July; you can check the events schedule online at www.kailuahawaiiancivicclub.com.

The heiau is a mile southwest of downtown Kailua, behind the YMCA at 1200 Kailua Rd. Coming over the Pali Hwy from Honolulu, take Uluoa St, the first left after passing the Hwy 72 junction, then turn right on Manu Aloha St and right again on Manu O'o St. The site is through the YMCA parking lot and beyond the rear of the building.

Activities

Water Sports

See those pretty little uninhabited islands off in Kailua Bay? Those are inside a protective reef, making this a great place to pick up a paddle. Kayak and stand-up paddle landings are allowed on Popoi'a

Island (Flat Island), off the southern end of Kailua Beach Park. Beginner paddle boarders practice on the Kaelepulu Stream, in the middle of the beach park, before heading out into the currents.

The magical twin Mokulua Islands, nicknamed 'the Mokes,' lie off Lanikai Beach. Landings are prohibited on the smaller, Moku Iki, a nature reserve. But it's fine to kayak over to Moku Nui, which has a beautiful beach for sunbathing and snorkeling. If you hike around to the back side of the island, there is an ideal 50ft-wide swimming hole the locals call Shark's Cove; just don't tell them that we told you about it.

The northwestern end of Kailua Beach Park is designated a kite- and windsurfing launch zone. Thanks to strong onshore winds, you can raise sail year-round here. Summer tradewinds average 10mph to 15mph, with stronger bursts in spring. Different parts of the bay have different water conditions, some good for jumps and wave riding, others for flat-water sails. Kitesurfing (also called kiteboarding), especially, requires a lot of muscle, stamina and coordination, but all you really need to start is the ability to swim.

Board surfers will find less love on this side of the island. Kalama Beach Park has one of the largest shorebreaks in the bay. When the waves are up, board surfers and bodyboarders can find decent conditions there.

Local outfitters suggest itineraries to match all skill levels for self-rental of kayaks ($49 to $65 per day), paddleboard set-ups ($45 to $60 per day) and surfboards ($30 per day), with beach delivery an option. Lodgings generally have snorkeling gear and bodyboards available free for guest use, but if not, you can rent those too ($15 to $20 per day). Two-hour, small-group stand-up paddle lessons average $100. Guided kayak tours (two/four hours $95/125) include a picnic, and give you time for snorkeling and swimming. Windsurfing lessons ($130) usually provide two hours of training, two hours of sailing. Three-hour private kitesurfing lessons run about $250. Discounts are often available if you book ahead online.

KAILUA SAILBOARDS & KAYAKS Water Sports
(☎262-2555, 888-457-5737; www.kailu asailboards.com; Kailua Beach Center, 130 Kailua Rd; ⏱8:30am-5pm) Good all-purpose outfitter with energetic staff and great kayak tours, near the beach. Can handle pretty much any of the options listed above.

NAISH HAWAII Water Sports
(☎262-6068, 800-767-6068; www.naish.com/les sons.html; 155 Hamakua Dr; ⏱9am-5:30pm) Owned by the family of one the sport's local pioneers, Robbie Naish, this is *the* place to go for windsurf-

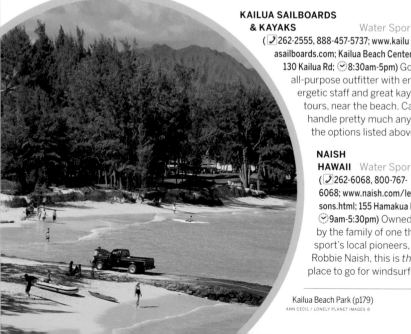

Kailua Beach Park (p179)

Detour:
Likeke Falls

Ready for a hidden waterfall, and maybe even being lucky enough to have it to yourself? The family-friendly **Likeke Falls Trail** (Map p194) winds through a forest of native and exotic trees into the lush Koʻolau Range. It starts out unspectacularly, uphill along a paved maintenance road. Veering left before a water tank, the trail enters the forest, ascending a set of steps alternating with moss-covered rocks and gnarled tree roots. This shady path eventually emerges briefly onto a cobblestone road (part of the Old Pali Hwy) that continues climbing. Keep a sharp eye out for the (often muddy) side trail leading to the right toward the waterfall. You'll do some more forest climbing before you reach the lacy 20ft-high cascade, where often the only sounds are of tumbling water and tropical bird song. The water is too shallow to take a dip, but you can get your feet wet. Be sure to continue up the short hill past the falls to see some great valley views. You can keep going for about another mile, but you'll have to turn around to return. The 2-mile round trip to the falls takes about an hour.

Do not attempt this hike if dark clouds are in the sky and rain is forecast; there is the danger of flash floods along the stream. Be aware that this trail accesses a frequently used but informal right of way on private land. While there were no 'Kapu' or 'No Trespassing' signs posted at the time of research, these could appear at any time. If so, then consider this trail closed to the public. It is illegal (not to mention unsafe) to trespass in Hawaii.

To get to the trail head, en route from Kailua to Kaneʻohe, turn off on Kionaole Rd, just west of Kamehameha Hwy (Hwy 83) near the H-3 Fwy junction. The trail starts past a chain-link gate at the uphill end of the Koʻolau Golf Club parking lot, in the furthest corner from the clubhouse.

ing. In addition to wind- and kitesurfing lessons, it also has the gear for rent ($45 to $55 per day).

AARON'S DIVE SHOP Diving
(☏262-2333, 888-847-2822; www.hawaii-scuba.com; 307 Hahani St; 2-tank dive $115-125, 3-day open-water certification $450; ⏱7am-7pm Mon-Fri, to 6pm Sat, to 5pm Sun) Sea caves, lava tubes, coral gardens and WWII-era shipwrecks can all be explored with this five-star PADI operation that has dives all over the island. Certification also offered.

TWOGOOD KAYAKS HAWAII Water Sports
(☏262-5656; www.twogoodkayaks.com; 134 B Hamakua Dr; ⏱9am-6pm Mon-Fri, 8am-6pm Sat & Sun) Focusing on kayaks: take a tour, rent your own or book an advanced lesson (four hours $55 to $70) and learn to surf the waves or race in the craft. Snorkel gear also available.

Hiking

LANIKAI PILLBOXES Hiking
(Map p194) Though officially named for Kaʻiwa Ridge, this 1.25-mile (one-way), half-hour trek is better known for the several WWII 'pillboxes', aka concrete bunkers, it passes. The barren trail is super steep and always slippery – when wet because of mud, when dry because of loose dirt. Make it to the top and you're rewarded with head-spinning views of the Mokulua Islands in Kailua Bay, Lanikai and the Koʻolau Range. The trailhead is in

Lanikai: turn right off Aʻalapapa Dr onto Kaʻelepulu Dr; park uphill just beyond the country club. On the side road across the street, you'll see a trail marker and a dirt track beginning next to a chain-link fence.

Bird Watching

The area historically was known for its marshes and you still may see rare water birds in their natural habitat, including the *koloa maoli* (Hawaiian duck), *aeʻo* (Hawaiian stilt), *ʻalae kea* (Hawaiian coot) and *kolea* (Pacific golden plover).

FREE **KAWAI NUI MARSH**   Park
(Map p194; www.kawainuimarsh.com; ☾sunrise-sunset) One of Hawaii's largest fresh-water marshes, Kawai Nui provides flood protection for the town. The inland water catchment is also one of the largest remaining fishponds used by ancient Hawaiians. Legend says the edible mud of the fishpond was once home to a *moʻo* (lizard spirit). Several local groups work to preserve and restore the marsh. To access the area, park in the lot at the end of Kaha St, off Oneawa St, just over a mile northwest of Kailua Rd. The paved, wheelchair-accessible recreational path leading around the marsh is shared with joggers.

Yoga & Spa Services

ALOHA YOGA KULA   Yoga
(☏772-3520; www.alohayogakula.com; classes $10); Aikahi (Map p194; 38 Kaneʻohe Bay Dr); Pali (Map p194; 1300 Kailua Rd) This yoga kula offers classes in a range of different yoga styles (vinyasa, flow, gentle, ashtanga) at two locations, several times a day Monday through Saturday.

LOMILOMI HANA LIMA HEALING CENTER & SPA   Spa
(☏253-0303; www.lomilomihanalima.com; Kailua Sq, 315 Uluniu St; 1hr massage $80; ☾9am-5pm Mon-Fri) Spoil yourself with a traditional Hawaiian lomilomi massage and an island-grown organic body wrap.

Left: Orchid flowers, Kailua **Below:** Windsurfing, Kailua (p181)

(LEFT) MARK A JOHNSON / ALAMY ©; (BELOW) ROBERT HOLMES / ALAMY ©

Tours

SEGWAY HAWAII-KAILUA   Segway
(262-5511; www.segwayofhawaii-kailua.com;
Kailua Beach Center, 130 Kailua Rd; tours $59-
129; 8:30am-5:30pm) Quiet and electric-
powered, Segway provides an ecofriendly
open-air ride. Take a tour along Kailua
Beach, into Lanikai, out to Ulupo Heiau or
through Kawanui Marsh.

Festivals & Events

'I LOVE KAILUA' TOWN PARTY   Culture
(www.lanikailuaoutdoorcircle.org/index/Kailua_
Town_Party; Kailua Rd) One Sunday in April
the whole community turns out for a giant
block party, with hula schools and bands
performing, local artists selling wares and
local restaurants feeding the masses.

'I LOVE HULA'   Culture
(www.castlefoundation.org; Kailua Rd) See a
rotating schedule of area hula schools

perform the second Sunday of every
month at 3pm, between Macy's and Pier
One downtown.

Sleeping

A soul-soothing alternative to hectic
Waikiki, Kailua has no hotels, but what it
does have is O'ahu's biggest selection of
vacation-rental houses, cottages, apartment suites and B&B-style rooms in private homes. Note that licensing stopped
in 1989 (even then no hot breakfast is allowed without a commercial kitchen), so
most of the places are unofficial, whether
listed at the local agencies below or with
national consolidators such as **Vacation
Rental By Owner** (VRBO; www.vrbo.com) and
others (see p318). What to expect locally:

○ 'Ohana (family), or mother-in-law suites,
are very common as Kailua rentals. These
will have private entrances but may share

185

walls with the main house. Noise can be an issue, as anywhere on O'ahu; people live close together here.

○ Licensed B&Bs will have off-street parking, other rentals may not (all those we recommend in Kailua do).

○ Unless otherwise noted all have a kitchenette or kitchen and beach chairs, snorkels and beach towels available for guest use.

TOP CHOICE MANU MELE BED & BREAKFAST
B&B $$

(☎ 262-0016; www.manumele.net; 153 Kailu-ana Pl; d incl breakfast $100-120; ❄ 🛜 🐾) Just 100 steps from the beach, Manu Mele enjoys a peaceful location a little ways from town. The simple, island-contemporary guest rooms have recently been redone and all feel light and bright. Creature comforts include private entrances, Hawaiian quilts, plush seven-layer beds, and a pool available for guest use – very rare. Complimentary baked goods and fruit are included.

KAILUA GUESTHOUSE
Guesthouse $$

(☎ 261-2637, 888-249-5848; www.kailuagu esthouse.com; d $129-159; ❄ 🛜) Not far from downtown, two large apartment studio-style suites let you pretend you live in Kailua. One opens out onto a large lanai overhung with plumeria, the other has a great balcony. Helpful amenities include flat-screen TVs with DVD players, digital in-room safes and shared washer and dryer access. The owner is an excellent source of local lore. It's a healthy walk to the beach, but it can be done. Japanese spoken; coffee only provided.

PARADISE PALMS BED & BREAKFAST
B&B $$

(☎ 254-4234; www.paradisepalmshawaii. com; 804 Mokapu Rd; d incl breakfast $110-120; ❄ 🛜) The welcoming hosts will make you feel like you're visiting newfound rela-tives at this suburban home on the far northwestern edge of town. Beds claim a lot of the room space, but the design is very high-end-resort looking. Private entrances with small lanai seating lead out onto a beautiful garden, and your

Traditional hula performance

MINAKO ISHII / PHOTO RESOURCE HAWAII / ALAMY ©

kitchenette's minifridge is stocked with fruit and bread.

SHEFFIELD HOUSE
B&B $$

(☎ 262-0721; www.hawaiisheffieldhouse. com; 131 Ku'ulei Rd; d incl breakfast $129-149; ✻ 🛜) Bring the family, the two private-entrance apartment-suites here welcome kids. The beach is an easy, 10-house walk down the road. And the suitably cottagey decor fits right in with the lush tropical gardens created by landscape designer and architect owners. Pastries and fruit for the first day included.

PAPAYA PARADISE BED & BREAKFAST
B&B $$

(☎ 261-0316; www.kailuaoahuhawaii.com; 395 Auwinala Rd; d incl breakfast $100-139; ✻ 🛜 ♨) The giant covered patio with comfortable sofas, reading nook and a dining table is more like a living room than a lanai – with views of Mt Olomana. The quiet atmosphere here is best suited to more mature travelers. Rooms are simple; kitchen facilities, shared.

Locally focused rental agencies:

TOP_{CHOICE} AWESOME O'AHU RENTALS
Vacation Rental $$

(☎ 281-6793; www.awesomeoahu.com; 1br apt $100-150, 2br apt $200-300, houses $250-950) Wide range of locations and sizes, super helpful staff.

AFFORDABLE PARADISE
Vacation Rental $$

(☎ 261-1693; http://affordable-paradise.com; apt $65-140) More reasonable, if basic, options.

LANIKAI BEACH RENTALS
Vacation Rental $$

(☎ 261-7895; www.lanikaibeachrentals.com; apt $150-225, houses $695-745) Lanikai specialist, with a couple of Kailua properties.

KAILUA BEACH VACATION ACCOMMODATIONS
Vacation Rental $$

(☎ 262-5409, 800-484-1036, ext 7912; www. beachrentalshawaii.com; apt $130-190) German, French and Spanish spoken.

Below: Buzz's lunch & dinner **Right:** Harvesting salad greens at 'Nalo Farms (p296), Waimanalo

(BELOW) ANN CECIL / LONELY PLANET IMAGES ©; (RIGHT) LINDA CHING / LONELY PLANET IMAGES ©

on the lanai or in the intimate candlelit dining room.

 Eating

In addition to what's recommended below, numerous hole-in-the-wall Asian food joints and BBQ drive-ins – heck, lots of restaurants in general – are scattered among the town's mini-strip malls. The grocery stores in town include Whole Foods and Foodland.

TOP CHOICE KALAPAWAI CAFÉ Local $$
(750 Kailua Rd; breakfast $4-7, lunch $7-12, dinner mains $20-40; ⏱6am-9pm Mon-Thu, 6am-9:30pm Fri, 7am-9:30pm Sat, 7am-9pm Sun) A gourmet, self-serve deli by day, after 5pm it transforms into an inviting, eclectic bistro. The eggplant bruschetta and other share dishes are excellent paired with a wine flight (a series of tasting-sized pours). But it's hard to resist the creative, ingredient-driven mains. Dine streetside

TOP CHOICE KALAPAWAI MARKET Deli $
(306 S Kalaheo Ave; breakfast $4-7, sandwiches $7-12; ⏱6am-9pm) A don't-miss 1930s landmark market near the beach stocks picnic supplies and serves the same fancy, made-to-order sandwiches and market-fresh salads as its in-town sister. Good coffee, too.

CINNAMON'S RESTAURANT Local $
(315 Uluniu St; mains $7-12; ⏱7am-2pm) Locals pack this family cafe decorated like Grandma's house for the airy chiffon pancakes drowning in guava syrup, Portuguese sweet-bread French toast, eggs Benedict mahimahi, curried-chicken-and-papaya salad, and Hawaiian plate lunches. Waits are long on weekends; only the breakfast menu is available Sunday.

BUZZ'S Steakhouse $$$
(☎261-4661; 413 Kawailoa Rd; lunch $9-16, dinner mains $20-40; ⏱11am-3pm & 4:30-9:30pm)

Classic mainlander expat territory; beachfront home-owning regulars here definitely get the best service. But the old-school kitschy island decor, surf-and-turf menu (complete with throwback salad bar) and proximity to the beach make it worth the stop. Book ahead, but still expect a wait.

FOOD COMPANY
Local $$

(Map p194; 1020 Keolu Dr; breakfast $5-9, original dishes $8-10, new mains $17-22; ⏱original 8am-8pm Tue-Sat, new 10am-8pm Tue-Sat) One side of this catering company's cafe (the 'original') serves filing plate lunches, including luaulike Hawaiian specialties on Friday. The other, upscale 'new' market-cafe side serves daily changing chef's specials made with some local ingredients. Consider taking yours to-go to your lanai; the cafe lighting is kinda bright and no alcohol is served.

RAI RAI RAMEN
Japanese $

(124 Oneawa St; mains $7-11; ⏱11am-8:30pm Wed-Mon) Look for the red-and-white banner written in kanji outside this brightly lit noodle shop. The menu of ramen styles ranges from Sapporo south to Hakata, all with rich broth and topped with tender pork, if you like. The gyōza (dumplings) are grilled or steamed bundles of heaven.

MOKE'S BREAD & BREAKFAST
Breakfast $

(27 Ho'olai St; breakfast & lunch $7-12; ⏱6am-3pm Wed-Mon) It's hard not to feel like a local sitting among neighbors reading the paper or petting their dogs at the blue-checkerclothed tables in this open-air cafe, a personal fave. Man, those liliko'i (passion fruit) pancakes and fresh veggie frittatas are good. Breakfast served until 1pm.

PRIMA
Tapas $$$

(☎888-8933; 108 Hekili St; lunch $11-16, dinner small dishes $8-15; ⏱11am-2pm & 5-10pm Tue-Sat) Sleek lines and stylishly black-clad servers are part of the attempt to cater to sophisticated diners. Italian-Mediterranean–inspired small dishes

189

The Best...
Picnic Food To Go

1 Sweet Home Waimanalo (p177)

2 Kalapawai Market (p188)

3 Waiahole Poi Factory (p197)

4 Thursday Farmers Markets (p190)

5 Tamura's Fine Wine & Liquors (p190)

aren't all a bull's-eye, but this *is* a new concept for Kailua's dining scene.

TOKUNAME SUSHI BAR & RESTAURANT   Japanese $$
(442 Uluniu St; lunch $10, sushi $5-10, dinner mains $10-16; 4-11pm Mon-Thu, 11am-11pm Fri-Sun) Surprisingly good sushi considering the suburban location. Daily early-bird and late-night sushi power hour (9pm to 10pm) specials help keep the costs down, too.

BACI'S   Italian $$
(30 Aulike St; mains lunch $10-15, dinner $15-25; 11:30am-2pm & 5:30-10pm Mon-Fri, 5:30-10pm Sat & Sun) Home-grown Italian cooking, where the owner knows most patrons by name. Don't miss the white chocolate mascarpone cheesecake.

DOWN TO EARTH NATURAL FOODS   Deli $
(www.downtoearth.org; 201 Hamakua Dr; dishes $4-7; 8am-10pm;) Huge natural-foods store with a delish take-out deli and hot-and-cold meal bar. There are some tables available outside.

AGNES PORTUGUESE BAKE SHOP   Local $
(46 Ho'olai St; snacks 75¢-$2, meals $5-7; 6am-6pm) Sweet breads, choco-mac

nut logs and *malasadas* (Portuguese fried doughnuts) made and served fresh. Daily hot meals (chicken and peppers, stew etc) sell out before midday.

THURSDAY FARMERS MARKET   Market $
(591 Kailua Rd; 5-7:30pm Thu) An incredible spread of vendors sell not only fruit and veggies but a bevy of hot meals to take out: organic pizza, Portuguese stew, BBQ, Filipino dishes, Thai curries – you name it. Located in the parking garage behind Longs Drugs.

KAILUA PEOPLE'S OPEN MARKET   Market $
(21 S Kainalu Dr; 9-10am) Get there early; locals line up for the freshest papayas, mangos and pink ginger flowers around.

TAMURA'S FINE WINE & LIQUORS   Seafood $
(Map p194; 25 Kane'ohe Bay Dr; per lb $7-15; 10:30am-7:45pm) Tucked into the back of a liquor store is a deli with a great *poke* selection (raw cubed fish with sauces, think Hawaiian sushi) – *opihi* (limpet), *tako* (octopus), 'ahi (tuna), shrimp, crab, etc – with a variety of flavorings.

BOB'S PIZZERIA   Pizzeria $
(263-7757; Kailua Beach Center, 130 Kailua Rd; slices $5-7; 11am-8pm Sun-Thu, to 9pm Fri & Sat) Gorgeous, ginormous, flat-crusted pizza pies baked near the beach. Buy a slice (enough for a meal) or a whole (enough for a party).

ISLAND SNOW   Desserts $
(Kailua Beach Center, 130 Kailua Rd; shave ice $2.50-5; 10am-6pm Mon-Fri, to 7pm Sat & Sun) Cool off with a Lanikai Lime or a Banzai Banana shave ice.

Drinking

Suburban Kailua does not have a hard-core nightlife. The places we list for drinking are also good for eating.

TOP CHOICE LANIKAI JUICE   Cafe
(Kailua Shopping Center, 600 Kailua Rd; 6am-8pm Mon-Fri, 7am-7pm Sat & Sun) With fresh

Hula skirts in rainbow colors

LINDA CHING / LONELY PLANET IMAGES ©

fruit gathered from local farmers, this addictive juice bar blends a tantalizing assortment of smoothies with names such as Ginger 'Ono or Kailua Monkey. Early in the morning, local yoga fanatics hang out at sunny sidewalk tables with overflowing bowls of granola topped with acai berries, bananas, blueberries and grated coconut.

MORNING BREW COFFEE HOUSE & BISTRO   Cafe
(Kailua Shopping Center, 600 Kailua Rd; ⏰6am-9pm Sun-Thu, to 10pm Fri & Sat; @ 🔊) Baristas at this pleasant cafe cup everything from chai to 'Funky Monkey' mochas with banana syrup. Swing by for an espresso or for bagel breakfasts, hot-pressed panini lunches and 'ahi tuna kebabs and wine at dinner.

KAILUA TOWN PUB   Pub
(26 Ho'olai St; ⏰10am-2am Mon-Sat, 7am-2am Sun) This casual Irish pub wannabe has tasty from-scratch Bloody Marys, sports on the TV and a friendly mixed-age crowd. Best burgers in town, too.

FORMAGGIO GRILL   Wine Bar
(305 Hahani St; ⏰4-11pm Mon-Thu, 4pm-1am Fri & Sat, 11:30am-2:30pm & 4-10pm Sun) Dozens of wines by the glass, convivially large, high dining tables with stools, and hearty dishes (think braised lamb) help ensure this place is always buzzing.

Shopping

Downtown Kailua has antiques, thrift and island gift stores aplenty, especially around the Macy's on Kailua Rd in the dead center of town. Various art galleries are best visited on the second Sunday afternoon of the month during the **Kailua Art Walk**.

TOP CHOICE MU'UMU'U HEAVEN   Clothing
(Davis Bldg, 767 Kailua Rd; ⏰10am-6pm Mon-Sat, 11am-4pm Sun) Recycling at its most fabulous: all the fun and funky, tropical-print dresses, skirts, tops and accessories are sewn using at least a little fabric from vintage muumuus. A second set of rooms contains equally colorful and eccentric homewares and original island art, some muumuu-inspired. It's just plain fun to shop among the repurposed flea-market and trash-bin furniture, with an 'ono (delicious) popsicle you bought there in hand.

191

BOOKENDS — Books
(Kailua Shopping Center, 600 Kailua Rd; ⏰9am-8pm Mon-Sat, to 5pm Sun) This independent book shop has a great selection of used and new Hawaiiana. Also a good place to pick up a light beach read.

LILY LOTUS — Clothing
(Suite 102, 609 Kailua Rd; ⏰10am-6pm Mon-Sat, 11am-4pm Sun) Outfit for the yoga lifestyle with breathable and organic clothing from a Honolulu-local designer. You can also buy mats, jewelry and accessories by her and other makers.

MANUHEALI'I — Clothing
(5 Ho'olai St; ⏰9:30am-6pm Mon-Fri, 9am-4pm Sat, 10am-3pm Sun) Looking for aloha-wear? Don't settle for less than one of the modern designs from this Honolulu artist.

UNDER A HULA MOON — Hawaiiana
(Kailua Shopping Center, 572 Kailua Rd; ⏰10am-6pm Mon-Sat) Bring a piece of Hawaii home in the form of island-made or inspired art, jewelry, stationery or home goods.

COCONUT MUSIC — Music
(418 Ku'ulei Rd; ⏰10am-6pm Mon-Sat) Small downtown guitar shop carries name-brand ukuleles – including Kamaka, handmade in Honolulu – and vintage ukes from the early 20th century. Adjacent, **Hungry Ear Records** stocks new, used and collectible Hawaiian music CDs and, yes, old-school vinyl records too.

ALI'I ANTIQUES II — Antiques
(Maluniu Ave; ⏰10:30am-4:30pm Mon-Sat) Search the stacks (and more stacks) and you may find a treasure among the mishmash of Hawaiiana and junk – a vintage postcard or print, a feather lei or tiki barware, maybe.

MADRE CHOCOLATES — Food & Drink
(20-A Kainehe St; ⏰9am-6pm Mon, Wed & Fri) Aficionados will be wowed by these Hawaiian-made boutique chocolates infused with island flavors – coconut and caramelized ginger, passion fruit, kiawe-smoked sea salt… Hours vary by whim.

ℹ Information

Kailua Information Center (☎261-2727; www.kailuachamber.com; Kailua Shopping Center, 600 Kailua Rd; ⏰10am-4pm Mon-Fri, to 2pm Sat) Retiree-run chamber of commerce center with limited info, good $1 maps. Open occasional Sundays 10am to 1pm.

Kailua Public Library (☎266-9911; www.librarieshawaii.org; 239 Ku'ulei Rd; ⏰10am-5pm Mon, Wed, Fri & Sat, 1-8pm Tue & Thu) Reservable internet terminals are available with three-month, nonresident library card ($10).

Morning Brew (Kailua Shopping Center, 600 Kailua Rd; rental per hr $6; ⏰6am-9pm Sun-Thu, to 10pm Fri & Sat; @ 🛜) Rent a laptop or use your own; free wi-fi with purchase.

Ho'omaluhia Botanical Garden
LINDA CHING / LONELY PLANET IMAGES ©

Getting There & Around

Outside the morning and evening commutes, it's normally a 30-minute drive between Waikiki and Kailua along the Pali Hwy (Hwy 61), about the same from the airport via the H-3 Fwy.

To/From the Airport

SpeediShuttle (☑877-242-5777; www. speedishuttle.com; 1 way $45) Shared-ride shuttle service from HNL.

Bicycle

Avoid parking headaches by cycling around town.

Bike Shop (☑261-1553; www.bikeshophawaii. com; 270 Ku'ulei Rd; per day/week from $20/100; ⊙10am-7pm Mon-Fri, 9am-5pm Sat, 10am-5pm Sun) Full-service sales, rental and repair shop. In addition to cruisers, it rents performance street and mountain bikes ($40 to $85 per day).

Hawaii B-cycle (http://hawaii.bcycle.com; day pass $5); Davis Building (767 Kailua Rd); Hahani Plaza (515 Kailua Rd) Kailua's bicycle exchange program was the first in the state. Pay for a pass online or at the kiosk, borrow the shiny-white cruiser bicycle with basket for a quick trip around town, and then return to any B-station.

Kailua Bicycle (☑261-1200; www.kailuabicycle. com; 18 Kainehe St; per day/week $20/100; ⊙9am-5pm) Rent regular, street cruiser bicycles or electric bikes ($25 per day).

Bus

Though having a car is most convenient, especially if you're visiting the rest of the Windward Coast, riding buses to, and around, Kailua is possible. Note that stop placement may require more walking than you're used to, and outlying vacation rentals may be difficult or impossible to access. Useful routes:

56 and 57 Honolulu's Ala Moana Center to downtown Kailua (corner Kailua Rd and Oneawa St, 45 to 60 minutes, every 15 minutes); all continue to Waimanalo (25 minutes), some go on to Sea Life Park (30 minutes).

70 Downtown Kailua to Kailua Beach Park (five minutes) and Lanikai (15 minutes), runs only every 90 minutes.

Kane'ohe Bay Area
POP 37,070

The state's largest bay and reef-sheltered lagoon, Kane'ohe Bay stretches from the Mokapu Peninsula north to Kualoa Point. It is largely silted and bad for swimming, although the near-constant tradewinds that sweep across the bay can offer some great sailing opportunities. The extended area has a couple of interesting sights that have day-trip potential. The town itself is a Marine-base suburb, populated by chain restaurants and stores. It just doesn't pack the eating and sleeping appeal of neighboring town Kailua, which is only 6 miles (15 minutes) south. For locations in this section, please see the map, p194.

Sights & Activities

FREE HO'OMALUHIA BOTANICAL GARDEN *Garden*
(www1.honolulu.gov/parks/hbg/hmbg.htm; 45-680 Luluku Rd; ⊙9am-4pm) Beneath the dramatic ridged cliffs of the Ko'olau Range, O'ahu's largest botanical garden encompasses 400 acres of trees and shrubs from around the world. Plants are arranged in six regionally themed areas accessible by car. Pick up a map, and an interpretive guide for the Hawaiian native section, at the small visitor center. The park was originally built to provide flood protection for the valley below, and one of the network of largely unmarked paths winds down from the visitor center to a reservoir. Don't miss the tropical-flower interpretive trail on the way. Even just the drive up to the end of the garden is lovely. The trails get muddy, so hiking shoes are recommended. Call ahead to register for free two-hour guided nature walks (10am Saturday and 1pm Sunday) and preschool nature hours (10:30am Tuesday). The visitor center is located at the far end of Luluku Rd, over 1 mile *mauka* from the Kamehameha Hwy.

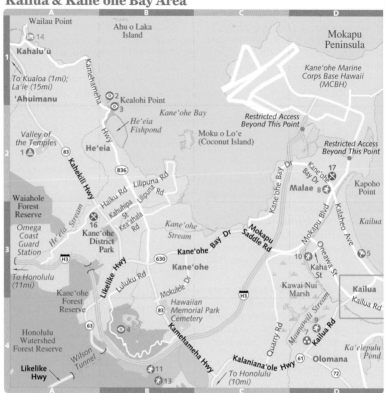

VALLEY OF THE TEMPLES & BYŌDŌ-IN
Religious

(47-200 Kahekili Hwy; valley free, temple adult/child $3/2; ☺9am-5pm) So peaceful and parklike, it might take you a minute to realize Valley of the Temples is an interdenominational cemetery. Up at the base of the Ko'olau mountain's verdant fluted cliffs sits Byōdō-In, a replica of a 900-year-old temple in Uji, Japan. The symmetry is a classic example of Japanese Heian architecture, with rich vermillion walls. The first rays of morning sunlight catch the 9ft, gold-leafed Lotus Buddha. Outside, wild peacocks roam beside a carp pond. Nearby, a 3-ton brass bell is said to bring peace and good fortune to anyone who rings it. Bus 65 stops near the cemetery on Kahekili Hwy,

but from there it's a winding 0.7-mile hike up to the temple.

HE'EIA STATE PARK
Park

(www.hawaiistateparks.org; 46-465 Kamehameha Hwy; ☺7am-7pm) Despite having little to offer, this park on Kealohi Point has picnic potential and views of He'eia Fishpond to the south. This location was sacred to the ancient Hawaiians as a place of final judgment at life's end. Some believe there is a still portal to the spirit world here, but the heiau on this site was destroyed in the 1800s and the park office and community hall were subsequently built over it. A small craft and fruit farmers market is held near the park's entrance from 9am to 3pm on Sunday, and there's a sometimes-used traditional Hawaiian

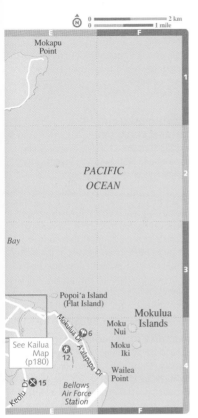

Kailua & Kane'ohe Bay Area

outrigger-canoe workshop just past the gate.

HOLOKAI KAYAK & SNORKEL ADVENTURE   Kayaking
(☎235-6905; www.heeiastatepark.org/kayaking; He'eia State Park, 46-465 Kamehameha Hwy; adult/child $80/60; ⏰8:30am Mon-Sat) Reserve ahead for a three-hour kayak tour on Kane'ohe Bay, including a visit to Moku o Lo'e (Coconut Island). Kayak rentals are also available.

HE'EIA PIER   Boating
Just north of, and run in conjunction with, the state park is one of the Windward Coast's only small boat harbors. It's fun just to watch the comings and goings of local boat owners. On weekends they head out to the 'sandbar', a raised spit in the bay that becomes a mooring party place for people to kick back and relax. **Captain Bob's Picnic Sails** (☎942-5077; www.captainbobpicnicsail.com; 4hr cruise $95) catamaran tour launches here and stops at the sandbar, as well as for reef snorkeling and lunch. But hang around long enough at the pier's-end **General Store & Deli** (breakfast & lunch $4-7; ⏰7am-4pm) and you might get a friendly invite aboard someone's private craft, for the price of some beer.

SUNSHINE ARTS GALLERY   Gallery
(www.sunshinearts.net; 47-653 Kamehameha Hwy; ⏰9am-5:30pm) Bold, tropical murals emblazon the exterior, but that's nothing compared to the riot of creativity inside. A rotating array of more than 60 island artists are represented at the coast's largest gallery. Most are works by

195

Island Insights

Offshore in Kane'ohe Bay, **Moku o Lo'e** (Coconut Island), southeast of He'eia State Park, was a royal playground, named for the coconut trees planted there in the mid-19th century by Princess Bernice Pauahi Bishop. During WWII, the US military used it for R&R. Today the Hawai'i Institute of Marine Biology occupies much of the island, which you might recognize from the opening scenes of the *Gilligan's Island* TV series.

modern and traditional painters, print-makers and photographers. But there's also some impressive blown glass, carved koa wood and jewelry. It's 5 miles north of the junction of the Kahekili and Kame-hameha Hwys.

SENATOR FONG'S PLANTATION & GARDENS Garden

(☎ 239-6775; www.fonggarden.net; 47-285 Pulama Rd, off Kamehameha Hwy; adult/child $14.50/9; ☺ tours 10:30am & 1pm) A labor of love by Hiram Fong (1907–2004), the first Asian American elected to the US Senate, these flowering gardens aim to preserve Hawaii's plant life for future generations. The lush 700-acre grounds are acces-sible only on the 1½-hour, 1-mile guided walking tours.

KO'OLAU GOLF CLUB Golf

(☎ 247-7088; www.koolaugolfclub.com; 45-550 Kionaole Rd; green fees $145) *The* toughest golf course on O'ahu. The par-73 tourna-ment course is scenically nestled beneath the Ko'olau Range. For practice, there's a driving range and both chipping and putting greens.

 Sleeping & Eating

Besides a few noted exceptions below, the nearby town of Kailua is by far a better place to sleep and eat – unless you crave big-name-chain fast food.

TOP CHOICE HO'OMALUHIA BOTANICAL GARDEN Campground $

(☎ 233-7323; www1.honolulu.gov/parks/hbg/hmbg.htm; 45-680 Luluku Rd; campsites $10; ☺ 4pm Fri-9am Mon) The grassy, botanical-garden-surrounded tent sites at the base of the Ko'olau Range are cool and green, fed by frequent mists. With an overnight guard and gates that close, it's among O'ahu's most petty-theft-free camp-grounds. Permits are issued at the visitor center during park hours; reserve ahead by phone. No alcohol. Bus 55 stops at the Windward City Shopping Center, opposite the start of Luluku Rd, from where the park visitor center is a 2-mile, uphill walk.

PARADISE BAY RESORT Resort $$

(☎ 800-735-5071; http://paradisebayresortha-waii.com; 47-039 Lihikai Dr; incl breakfast studio $149-229, apt $199-359; ✳ ☎) The Windward Coast's only resort property is a step above area rentals. Casual, earth-tone contemporary rooms with kitchenettes are just the beginning. Here, bayside breakfasts, a Wednesday Hawaiian-food happy hour, evening mai tais and Hawai-ian music, and a Saturday-morning bay cruise are all complimentary. Stand-up paddling lessons, kayaking, ecotours and spa services are available, but cost extra.

HALE'IWA JOE'S Local $$

(46-336 Haiku Rd; mains $18-33; ☺ happy hour 4-6pm, dinner 5-10pm) The view of the lushly green Haiku Gardens valley dropping off from the open-air dining room is a stunner worth travelling to see. You can munch coconut shrimp at the dining-room rail overlooking a lily pond beneath the Ko'olau Range. Alternatively, fill up on the more inventive cocktails and *pupu* that are discounted at the bar during happy hour – and the view's not much different. Reservations are not needed; arrive early.

ℹ️ Getting There & Around

Two highways run north–south through Kane'ohe. The slower but more scenic Kamehameha Hwy (Hwy 836) hugs the coast. Further inland, the Kahekili Hwy (Hwy 83) intersects the Likelike Hwy (Hwy 63) and continues north past the Valley of the Temples. Kane'ohe Marine Corps Base Hawaii (MCBH) occupies the entire Mokapu Peninsula; the H-3 Fwy terminates at its gate. Waikiki is 11 miles (25 minutes) over the *pali*, Kailua is 6 miles (15 minutes) south.

Sights are spread out in the Kane'ohe area, which makes using the bus a challenge, but it does run here.

Route 55 Honolulu's Ala Moana Center to downtown Kane'ohe (one hour, departs every 20 minutes), then continues along Kamehameha Hwy toward Turtle Bay on the North Shore.

Route 56 Connects Kailua and Kane'ohe (20 minutes) every 30 minutes or so.

Kahalu'ua & Waiahole

Driving north along the Kamehameha Hwy, you'll cross a bridge near Kahulu'u's Hygienic Store (it's not particularly clean, it just used to be part of Hygienic Dairy). There you'll make a physical and cultural departure from the gravitational pull of Honolulu. Now you've officially crossed into 'the country,' where the highway becomes a two-laner and the ocean shares the shoulder.

At the convergence of Kamehameha and Kahekili Hwys, a cluster of food trucks have taken up residence. **Mike's Huli Huli Chicken** (meals $7-8; ⏱11am-7pm) not only spit-roasts birds, it bakes *kalua* pork. If it's the weekend, we'd hold out for a meal a mile further north at **Waiahole Poi Factory** (48-140 Kamehameha Hwy; ⏱10am-3pm Thu-Sun); it not only sells *'ono* Hawaiian plate lunches, it actually pounds taro into poi at this roadside landmark.

Kualoa

Although nowadays there is not a lot of evidence, in ancient times Kualoa was one of the most sacred places on O'ahu. When a chief stood on Kualoa Point, passing canoes lowered their sails in respect. The children of chiefs were brought here to be raised, and it may have been a place of refuge where *kapu* (taboo) breakers and fallen warriors could seek reprieve from

Sunrise at Kualoa Beach, Kane'ohe Bay

the law. Because of its rich significance to Native Hawaiians, Kualoa is listed in the National Register of Historic Places.

What few sites remain are mostly on, or adjacent to, the omnipresent Kualoa Ranch which encompasses most of the area. Coastal He'eia Fishpond is an impressive survivor from the days when stone-walled ponds used for raising fish were common on Hawaiian shores. Boat tours, and other activities, are available both from the ranch and from a local macadamia nut farm.

◎ Sights & Activities

KUALOA REGIONAL PARK · Beach
(49-479 Kamehameha Hwy; ☺sunrise-sunset) Huge extended-family groups gather for weekend picnics on the wide, grassy field that fronts the narrow white-sand beach here. There's good swimming, with magnificent mountain scenery as a backdrop. Stroll south along the beach to **'Apua Pond**, a 3-acre brackish salt marsh on Kualoa Point that's a nesting area for the endangered *ae'o* (Hawaiian stilt). Continue southwest down the beach and you'll end up skirting the ancient **Moli'i**

Fishpond, its rock walls covered with mangroves. Tip: the pristine white-sand beach about a mile along is what Kualoa Ranch calls 'Secret Island', and charges a boatload to take you there – where you can walk for free. Just stay on the sand; all beaches are public on O'ahu. During low tide, you'll also see fisherfolk wading 1500ft (45 minutes) offshore toward **Mokoli'i Island** (Chinaman's Hat). If you go there, try to avoid disturbing the island's burrowing seabirds.

TROPICAL FARMS · Garden
(☏237-1960, 877-505-6887; 49-227 Kamehameha Hwy; shop free, tour $20; ☺9am-5pm, tours 11am Mon-Sat) Sure, it's a bit of a kitschy tourist trap, but everything for sale at this family-owned business is homegrown Hawaiian. The open-air store overflows with various flavored macadamia nuts, local jams and sauces, natural remedies and arts and crafts. Learn what guava trees and pineapple plants look like on the bus-and-boat tour that visits the farm's flowering gardens, fruit and coconut groves – and a couple of famous TV and movie locations out on the ancient Moli'i Fishpond.

Windward Coastal Drive

A day's leisurely drive up the coast to Kahuku – along rocky inlets, under overgrown monkey pod trees, past ancient fishponds and through valleys inhabited by small towns and farms – is a must-do on the Windward Coast. Turn north off the Likelike Hwy (Hwy 63) onto Kamehameha Hwy in Kane'ohe. You'll still be in the middle of civilization for a short while, but that way you won't miss sights such as the He'eia Pier and Sunshine Arts Gallery. As you head north from town, the scene quickly turns rural. We list the major sights in this chapter. But take your time, or else you'll miss the smaller treasures – an unattended roadside cart with tropical flowers and a honor jar for payment, a woodcarver's workshop where he turns trees into giant tikis with a chainsaw, tiny beach parks between road and sea, or an orchid nursery where you can stop and ship a gift home. Note that not all the places to eat along the way are worth the stop. We stand by our recommendations.

KUALOA RANCH Adventure Tour

(☎237-7321, 800-231-7321; www.kualoa.com; 49-560 Kamehameha Hwy; 1hr tour $25, 1hr rides $70; ⏲9am-3pm) In the 1800s, the Judd family purchased the roughly 4000 acres that make up today's Kualoa Ranch from Kamehameha III and Queen Kalama. It's still O'ahu's largest cattle ranch (with 1500 head), but the family's descendants expanded the business into a slick tourist sight to help support the land. If you want to see where Hurley built his *Lost* golf course, Godzilla left his footprints and the *Jurassic Park* kids hid from dinosaurs, take the movie tour that covers the many films and TV shows shot in the Ka'a'awa Valley. ATV and horseback rides also mosey along nose to tail, so to speak, in this busy area. Go a bit more off the beaten trail with the recommended 6WD jungle tour into Hakipu'u Valley's steep slopes covered with tropical vegetation. Hakipu'u is also where most of the ranch's ancient sites are located; you may have a bit more luck seeing some if you book a private Ali'i tour ($130, four hours). Other options include hula lessons, a guided Hakipu'u hike and a fishpond boat and garden tour. Give the short Legend & Legacy van tour a pass; if you're doing anything else, it's boringly repetitive. Book all tours at least a couple days in advance; they fill up. There's a cafe on-site.

 ## Sleeping

Camping is available at the popular (and sometimes noisy) regional park, but most look for vacation rental lodging south in Kailua or further north along the coast.

Ka'a'awa

POP 1325

Here the road tightly hugs the coast and the *pali* move right on in, with barely enough space to squeeze a few houses between the base of the cliffs and the highway. A narrow neighborhood beach used mainly by fishers has a grassy lawn fronted by a shore wall.

Stop just north of the 27-mile marker in the parking lot of the tourist bus

Island Insights

That eye-catching islet you see offshore from Kualoa Regional Park is called Mokoli'i (Little Lizard). In ancient Hawaiian legend, it's said to be the tail of a *mo'o* (lizard spirit) slain by the goddess Hi'iaka and thrown into the ocean. Following the immigration of Chinese laborers to Hawaii, this cone-shaped island also came to be called **Chinaman's Hat**, a nickname that predominates today, regardless of any political incorrectness.

favorite Crouching Lion Inn restaurant to look for the namesake **Crouching Lion** natural rock formation. According to legend, the rock is a demigod from Tahiti who was cemented to the mountain during a jealous struggle between Pele, the volcano goddess, and her sister Hi'iaka. When he tried to free himself by crouching, he was turned to stone. Stand at the restaurant sign with your back to the ocean and look straight up to the left of the coconut tree; the rock is smallish and midcliff.

Across from the beach at the center of 'town', such as it is, **Uncle Bobo's** (51-480 Kamehameha Hwy; dishes $6-12; ⏲11am-5pm Mon-Fri, to 6pm Sat & Sun) is a better place to eat. You don't usually find buns baked from scratch and organic carrot cake offered at a local Hawaiian BBQ joint. Bobo's has site-smoked brisket and ribs, grilled mahimahi and other homey faves done right. The cheery yellow dining room is small, but parks nearby have plenty of picnic tables.

Kahana Valley

In ancient times, the islands were divided into *ahupua'a* – pie-shaped land divisions that ran from the mountains to the sea – providing everything Hawaiians

DAVID SCHRICHTE / PHOTO RESOURCE HAWAII / ALAMY ©

needed for subsistence. Modern subdivisions and town boundaries have erased this traditional organization almost everywhere except here, O'ahu's last publicly owned *ahupua'a*.

Before Westerners arrived, the Kahana Valley was planted with wetland taro, which thrived in the rainy climate. Archaeologists have identified the remnants of more than 120 largely inaccessible sites: agricultural terraces and irrigation canals, the remains of a heiau, fishing shrines and numerous *hale* (houses). In the early 20th century the lower valley was planted with sugarcane, which was hauled north to Kahuku via a small railroad. The upper reaches were used during WWII to train soldiers in jungle warfare.

When the state purchased Kahana, it also acquired resident tenants, many of whom had lived in the valley for a long time – 31 families still do. In spite of more than 40 years of sporadic political controversy and failed plans for a living-history village, **Ahupua'a o Kahana State Park** (www.hawaiistateparks.org; Kamehameha Hwy; admission free; ☉sunrise-sunset) is currently still open to the public. As you turn south at the park signpost there are some picnic tables before you reach the closed visitor center. Hiking pamphlets are available outside that building and outside the Community Center across the road. Park by the latter to start the easy-to-moderate, 1.2-mile round-trip **Kapa'ele'ele Trail**, which runs along a former rail bed and past an ancient fishing shrine on the way to a bay-view lookout, then follows the highway back to the park entrance. Continue driving up the road and park *before* the neighborhood to access **Nakoa Trail**. You have to walk up half a mile on the road before you reach the 2.5-mile rainforest loop. Joggers and dog walkers only go up as far as the wide, level path lasts; after that the trail crisscrosses Kahana Stream through thick vegetation. The trail can be hard to follow, very slippery when wet, and hunters do use the adjacent area. Hiking alone is not recommended.

While most of the valley's archeological sites are hidden inaccessibly deep, **Huilua Fishpond** is readily visible from the main road and can be visited simply by walking down to the beach. Part of the state park, the beach is a locals' hangout that offers mostly safe swimming with a gently sloping sandy bottom. Watch out for the riptide near the reef break on the south end of the bay. The state park provides restrooms, outdoor showers, picnic tables and usually drinking water.

Punaluʻu

POP 880

This sleepy seaside community consists of a string of houses and businesses lining the highway. A long, narrow swimming beach has an offshore reef that protects the shallow waters in all but stormy weather. There are a couple of art galleries and places to eat around.

 Sleeping

Check **VRBO (www.vrbo.com)** and other online sites (see p318); this part of the coast has some good deals on beachfront vacation rentals.

PAT'S AT PUNALUʻU   Condo **$$**

(53-567 Kamehameha Hwy) An older, seven-story residential condominium complex, Pat's houses spacious, sometimes well-worn, units – all with ocean views. Rentals here are privately owned and listed; some are available through **Paul Comeau Condo Rentals** (293-2624, 800-467-6215; www.paulspunaluucondos.com; studio $90, 1br $110-250, 2br $250;) and **Oceanfront Condo & Our Getaway** (261-0316, 262-1008; http://kailuaoahuhawaii.com; studio & 1br $125-200;).

 Eating

KENEKE'S GRILL   Local **$**

(53-138 Kamehameha Hwy; dishes $4-10; 10am-8pm) A recently added adjunct of the Waimanalo drive-in classic, Keneke's comes complete with the trademark Christian sayings painted on the wall. Hawaiian plate lunches, such as *loco moco* and teriyaki steak, plus burgers and daily specials fill the menu. Don't miss having shave ice or Dave's ice cream for dessert.

SHRIMP SHACK   Food Truck **$$**

(53-352 Kamehameha Hwy; meals $10-16; 10am-5pm) The shrimp are imported from Kauaʻi then fried in garlic and dipped in butter, or you could order mussels or crab legs. You'll find this sunny, yellow-painted food truck parked outside Ching's c 1946 general store, which has great butter *mochi* (pounded-rice-cake sweets).

Hauʻula

POP 3470

A small coastal town sitting against a scenic backdrop of hills and majestic Norfolk pines, Hauʻula has a main drag with not much more than a general store, a modern strip mall and a 7-Eleven, but there are hiking possibilities in the area. It is a peaceful, central location on the northeastern coast, 21 miles (40 minutes) from Haleiwa on the North Shore and 24 miles (45 minutes) from Kailua. As you drive by Hauʻula Congregational Church, make sure you look up at the adjacent hill to see the stone ruins of Lanakila Church (c 1853).

Hauʻula Loop

Detour:
La'ie Point

Crashing surf, a lava arch and a slice of Hawaiian folk history await at the lookout at La'ie Point. The near-shore island with the hole in it is Kukuiho'olua (Puka Rock). In Hawaiian legend, this island was once part of a giant lizard chopped into pieces by a demigod to stop its deadly attack on O'ahu. From Kamehameha Hwy, head *makai* (seaward) on 'Anemoku St, opposite La'ie Shopping Center, then turn right onto Naupaka St.

 Sights & Activities

HAU'ULA BEACH PARK   Beach
Across the road from the middle of town, this ironwood-shaded beach has a shallow, rocky bottom that isn't too appealing for swimming but does attract snorkelers. It occasionally gets waves big enough for local kids to ride. The grassy lawn is popular for family picnics on weekends. The 15 roadside campsites here won't give you a good night's sleep.

HAU'ULA FOREST RESERVE   Hiking
(http://hawaiitrails.ehawaii.gov; Ma'akua Rd; ☉sunrise-sunset) Open to hikers and mountain bikers, the tranquil **Hau'ula Loop Trail** is a 2.5-mile loop (1½ hours) that clambers through Waipilopilo Gulch onto a ridge over Kaipapa'u Valley. The trail forks off to the right immediately after the road enters the forest reserve, and then rises quickly through a native forest of ohia and hala (screwpine) trees, as well as sweet-smelling guava and bizarre octopus trees. If you go straight past the Hau'ula trailhead, there is a left fork to **Ma'akua Ridge Trail** (2.5 miles). This is also a loop but it is a steeper climb. You can find the access path for both trails at a bend in Hau'ula Homestead Rd. But make sure you don't park there. Leave your car down at the highway-side beach parking. It will add a quarter-mile walk each way, but your vehicle will be less exposed to petty theft.

 Sleeping & Eating

TOP CHOICE / HALE KO'OLAU   Vacation Rental $$
(☎536-4263, 888-236-0799; www.halekoolau.com; 54-225 Kamehameha Hwy; studio $95-150, apt 1br $115-200, 2br $170-215, 3br $215-390; ❄☏) You're staying so close to the ocean here that during high tide the surf splashes one of the studio's windows. Beachfronts, lawns, hot tubs and washer-driers are all shared at this wonderfully comfy, slightly timeworn community of bungalows and residential buildings. Prices vary depending on unit size and location (not all have water views); there's even a five-bedroom house (from $370). Hawaiian-family owned and operated.

PAPA OLE'S   Local $
(Hau'ula Shopping Center, 54-316 Kamehameha Hwy; dishes $5-12; ☉7am-9pm Thu-Mon, to 3pm Tue) When billing itself as 'da original, with *'ono* grinds', Papa Ole's doesn't lie. Opt for sauteed veggies or a green salad instead of macaroni and you've made your Hawaiian plate lunch a tiny bit healthier. Dine inside the small cafe, outside at parking-lot picnic tables or take it to-go to the beach park.

La'ie
POP 4640

Bustling and up-to-date, La'ie is quite a contrast to its rural neighbors. This is the center of the Mormon community in Hawaii, so you are just as likely to see white-collared shirts as board shorts in town. Life here revolves around resident Brigham Young University (BYU) – Hawaii, where scholarship programs recruit students from islands throughout the Pacific. Many students help pay for their living expenses by working as guides at the local Polynesian Cultural Center (PCC), the tourist complex that draws gazillions of visitors each year (second only to Pearl Harbor among Oʻahu's attractions).

Laʻie is thought to have been the site of an ancient Hawaiian *puʻuhonua* – a place where *kapu* (taboo) breakers could escape being put to death. And it was a refuge for the Mormon missionaries as well; after an attempt to create a 'City of Joseph' on Lanai failed, the church purchased a 6000-acre plantation here in 1865. In 1919, construction began on a smaller version of the Salt Lake City, Utah, temple at the foot of the Koʻolau Range. This dazzling, formal white edifice – open only to practicing Latter Day Saint (LDS, also known as Mormon) church members – stands at the end of a wide boulevard and may be one of the most incongruous sights on Oʻahu.

 Beaches

POUNDERS BEACH   Beach
Half a mile south of the main entrance to the PCC, this is an excellent bodyboarding beach, but the shorebreak, as the name of the beach implies, can be brutal.

HUKILAU BEACH   Beach
North of Laʻie Shopping Center is a pocket of white sand that's a leisurely place for swimming when summer waters are calm. Just beware any time the surf's up.

 Sights & Activities

**POLYNESIAN
CULTURAL CENTER**   Cultural Building
(PCC; ☎293-3333, 800-367-7060; www.polynesia.com; 55-370 Kamehameha Hwy; park adult/child $50/36, incl dinner show from $90/62; ⏱villages noon-5pm; ♿) A nonprofit

Island Insights

A *hukilau* was a traditional Hawaiian method of group fishing with drag nets. In the late 1940s, this community celebration was revived for tourists as a local Mormon church fundraiser; this lasted until the early 1960s, when the state started imposing taxes.

cultural park owned by the Mormon Church, the PCC revolves around eight Polynesian-themed 'villages' representing Hawaii, Rapa Nui (Easter Island), Samoa, Aotearoa (New Zealand), Fiji, Tahiti and Tonga. The admission price is steep, but this includes frequent village shows and a park-wide boat parade showcasing native dances. BYUH students dressed in native garb demonstrate poi pounding, coconut-frond weaving, handicrafts, music and games. You'll learn a bit more if you add on the Ambassador option, which includes a personal guide. The evening **Aliʻi Luau** show and buffet, another add-on, is one of the island's biggest and best, with some authentic Hawaiian dances and foods. Afterwards you can see **Ha: Breath of Life**, a Polynesian song-and-dance revue that's partly authentic, partly Bollywood-style extravaganza. Check online for ticket packages; advance discounts are sometimes offered.

GUNSTOCK RANCH   Horseback Riding
(☎341-3995; http://gunstockranch.com; 56-250 Kamehameha Hwy; rides $89-159; ⏱by reservation Mon-Sat; ♿) Take a small-group horseback ride across a working ranch at the base of the Koʻolau Mountains. Options include scenic mosey-alongs, advanced giddy-ups, picnic and moonlight trail rides, plus there's a kiddie experience that includes a 25-minute guide-led ride (ages two to seven, $39).

Eating

HUKILAU CAFE   Local $

(55-662 Wahinepe'e St; mains $4-8; ⊙7am-3pm Mon-Sat, to 11am Sun) Tucked onto a backstreet in town, this small cafe is the kind of place locals would rather keep to themselves. (Sorry!) Local grinds – such as Portuguese-sweet-bread French toast and a teriyaki burger lunch – are right on. And it's always interesting to watch the mix of patrons: from the heavily tattooed in tank tops to the buttoned-down church set. Sunday is breakfast only. In case you're wondering, no, this isn't the restaurant featured in the movie *50 First Dates,* though it's said to be the inspiration for it.

Malaekahana State Recreation Area

You'll feel all sorts of intrepid pride when you discover this wild and rugged coastal area just north of La'ie. A long, narrow strip of sand stretches between Makahoa Point to the north and Kalanai Point to the south with a thick inland barrier of ironwoods.

A deep stand of pine trees forms the backdrop to the **recreation area** (⊙7am-7:45pm Apr-Aug, to 6:45pm Sep-Mar). The long, slightly steep, but relatively uncrowded beach is popular with families. Swimming is generally good here year-round, although there are occasionally strong currents in winter. Bodyboarding, board surfing and windsurfing are also possible. Kalanai Point, the main section of the park, is less than a mile north of La'ie. It has picnic tables, BBQ grills, restrooms, showers and good **public camping** (☎293-1736; www.hawaiistateparks.org; tent sites $18; ⊙8am Fri-8am Wed) – advance permits are required.

When the tide is low, you can wade over to **Moku'auia** (Goat Island), a state bird sanctuary about 400yd offshore. It has a small sandy cove with good swimming and snorkeling. But don't approach or disturb the nesting and burrowing seabirds, and be careful of the shallow coral (sharp) and sea urchins (sharper). When the water is deep, only strong

swimmers knowledgeable about rip currents should attempt a crossing; ask lifeguards about conditions.

Friends of Malaekahana (☎293-1736; www.malaekahana.net; 56-335 Kamehameha Hwy; tent sites per person $8.50, cabins $50-150; ⊙gates 7am-7pm, office 9am-5pm) maintains the Makahoa Point end of the park. Stay here in 'little grass shacks' (basically thatched-roof platforms), duplex cabins and eco-cabins and yurts. All very rustic, but the latter three have electricity. Twenty-four-hour security and outdoor hot showers are bonuses. Book as far in advance as possible; only tent sites are available (if there are openings) to walk-ups.

Kahuku

POP 1780

Kahuku is a former sugar-plantation town. Much of the old sugar mill that operated here until 1996 was knocked down, but the remnants of the smokestack and the old iron gears can be seen behind the post office. The rest of the former mill grounds have been transformed into a small shopping center containing the town's bank, post office, grocery store and eateries. Between here and the start of the North Shore at Turtle Bay Resort (4 miles north), look for roadside markets selling produce, an antique junk shop and craft stands.

 Sights & Activities

KAHUKU FARMS   Farm

(www.kahukufarms.com; 56-800 Kamehameha Hwy; tour adult/child $15/12; ⊙11am-5pm Fri-Sun) Take a tractor-pulled wagon tour through the taro patch and fruit orchards at this family farm – sampling included. Then stop at the gift shop for bath products and foodstuffs made from the farm's bounty.

KAHUKU LAND FARMS   Market

(Kamehameha Hwy; ⊙10am-7pm) Several local farm stands group together north of Kahuku. Stop here for a fresh-cold coconut water ($3) and to peruse the unexpected selection of fruits (rambutan, pomelo...).

Eating

Kahuku is a favorite eating stop on circle-island road trips. Shrimp ponds at the north side of town supply Oʻahu's top restaurants, while colorful food trucks that cook up the crustaceans are thick along the highway. Note that not all of these serve shrimp and prawns actually raised locally; some import the crustacean critters from elsewhere. Kahuku's food trucks line up *makai* along Kamehameha Hwy and are usually open from 10am to 6pm or 6:30pm daily (later in summer), depending upon supply and demand. Expect to pay at least $13 per dozen shrimp with two-scoop rice. Wait in line, order your shrimp or prawns the original way – drowning in delicious garlicky butter – or sweet-and-spicy, then chow down at outdoor picnic tables.

GIOVANNI'S Food Truck $$
(www.giovannisshrimptruck.com; 56-505 Kamehameha Hwy) The original, graffiti-covered shrimp truck that spawned an empire. No longer a lonely little vehicle, Giovanni's is flanked by a covered patio and surrounded by a bevy of other food trucks – serving different meals, smoothies, fro-yo and shave ice. Among the craft and souvenir stands toward the rear of the field, there's also a sweet Kahuku **corn stand**. Note that some of the vendors take Saturday or Sunday off.

KAHUKU GRILL Local $
(55-565 Kamehameha Hwy; mains $5-12; ☺8am-9pm Mon-Sat) Serving from a window in one of the old wooden mill buildings near the center of the small town, this outdoor

cafe has real aloha spirit. The pancakes are fluffy, the handmade beef burgers juicy and the island-style plates piled high. It's well worth the wait, especially for coconut and macadamia-crusted shrimp with organic Pupukea greens.

ROMY'S Food Truck $$
(www.romyskahukuprawns.org; 56-781 Kamehameha Hwy) Eat overlooking the aquaculture farm where your giant, and pricey, prawns are raised. Steamed shrimp and whole fish available too. Try the *pani popo* (Samoan coconut buns) for dessert.

FUMI'S Food Truck $$
(www.fumiskahukushrimp.com; 56-777 Kamehameha Hwy) Shrimp is sold from its original truck and just up the road from an added building; both have picnic tables. Alternative eating options include tempura shrimp, fried fish and burgers.

North Shore

Pipeline, Sunset, Waimea… You don't have to be a surfer to have heard of the North Shore; the epic breaks here are known worldwide. Sure, winter brings giant swells that can reach 15ft to 40ft in height. But there is more to this coast than monster waves. The beaches are gorgeous year-round, perfect for swimming in summer. And there are so many activities besides surfing. Try stand-up paddling or kayaking, take a snorkeling or whale-watching tour, go hiking or horseback riding – jump out of an airplane, even. The laid-back communities here are committed to keeping life low-key and rural. Atmospheric Hale'iwa, with its plantation-era buildings and eclectic shops and restaurants, is really the only 'town.' So slow down. Spend the day pedaling a cruiser from beach to beach, and don't forget to stop at Ted's Bakery for chocolate-*haupia* (coconut pudding) pie. North Shore country life can be awfully sweet.

Waimea Bay Beach Park (p218)

North Shore Itineraries

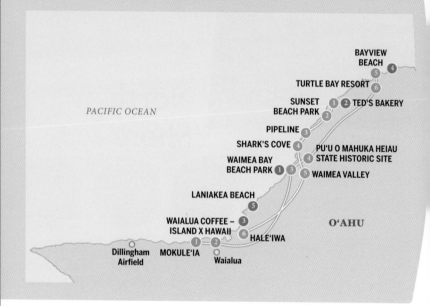

One Day

1 Ted's Bakery (p214) Grab a late breakfast at this classic North Shore eatery. The chocolate-covered glazer donuts are sinful, or you could fuel up with a full, hot meal of Spam and eggs.

2 Sunset Beach Park (p213) Cruise down the bike path under the shady trees to nearby Sunset Beach – great for lazing about, sun worshipping and ocean gazing.

3 Pipeline (p213) Keep heading west. If it's winter and the surf is up, you have to stop at 'Ehukai Beach Park and see if there are any pro surfers shooting through a barrel. If you know your way around a thruster, a gun or a fish, then you'll fit in just fine here.

4 Shark's Cove (p215) If the water is calm and the temperature warm, stop for some snorkeling instead. The reef at Shark's Cove is home to a beautiful array of marine life. Yes, that may include some not-very-aggressive, white-tipped sharks.

5 Waimea Valley (p219) In the afternoon, shake off the sand and head inland. Wander the trails through the lush tropical foliage of this impressive 1800-acre nature park, capping off the hike with a dip in the waterfall at the rear of the valley.

6 Hale'iwa (p220) Finish your day by heading to the only real town on the coast. Check out the shops and galleries before having a meal at one of the many restaurants, such as **Café Hale'iwa**.

⊙ THIS LEG: 8 MILES

Two Days

1 **Mokule'ia** (p230) Adrenaline junkies should get up early: morning is prime time for skydiving. If you'd prefer someone to actually be steering your flight, take a glider or a biplane ride from Dillingham Airfield instead.

2 **Waialua Coffee – Island X Hawaii** (p229) On your way back toward town, stop at the rambling warehouse, crammed full of Hawaiiana, that used to be part of the old sugar mill. The Waialua coffee and chocolate sold here were grown nearby.

3 **Waimea Bay Beach Park** (p218) If you haven't had enough shopping, you could stop again in Hale'iwa town. Otherwise continue on to beach time at Waimea Bay. The deep arc of light sand and dark-blue water is one of the prettiest on the island, but it's only safe to swim late spring through early fall. In winter the waves are epic.

4 **Pu'u o Mahuka Heiau State Historic Site** (p216) Not far up the hill from Waimea, a historic site offers insight into Hawaii's ancient past. The area around the temple's stone platforms also affords great views of the ocean.

5 **Bayview Beach** (p210) Moving along, the cove at Turtle Bay Resort is a perfect place for a swim. You can rent snorkel gear right on the beach, or hike from here 2 miles to the tip of the island.

6 **Turtle Bay Resort** (p211) By now you've worked up an appetite, so take your pick: appetizers at a beachfront restaurant, a five-course spread in a fine-dining establishment, or drinks and buffet food poolside – Turtle Bay Resort has numerous eating options.

THIS LEG: 18 MILES

North Shore Highlights

1 **Best Monster Waves: Waimea Bay Beach Park** (p218) The annual Eddie Aikau-memorial Quiksilver surfing competition is held here annually; need we say more?

2 **Best Island Eats: Ted's Bakery** (p214) Everything islandy – from tropical-fruit desserts to traditional plate lunches.

3 **Best Activity: Stand-up Paddling** (p221) The latest wave in water sports: paddle your surfboard while standing.

4 **Best Beach Hike: Bayview Beach to Kahuku Point** (p210) Stroll the water's edge, or under the ironwood trees, to the island's northeasternmost point.

5 **Best Animal Watching: Laniakea Beach** (p220) *Honu* (green sea turtles) are often found sunbathing here.

Bodyboarders at Sunset Beach Park (p213)
MERTEN SNIJDERS / LONELY PLANET IMAGES ©

Discover North Shore

Turtle Bay
POP 410

Idyllic coves and coastal rock beds define the island's northeastern tip, where the North Shore and the Windward Coast meet. Dominating the area is Turtle Bay Resort, with its low-key, view-perfect hotel and restaurants, golf course, condo village and public access to the nearby beaches. So far, it's the only large-scale tourist development on this side of the island, and locals have fought to keep it that way. Massive expansion plans have been scaled back to just 25% of original proposals, but whether even that will go through is still in question.

 Beaches

TURTLE BAY RESORT BEACHES Beach
The Turtle Bay resort hotel sits out on beautiful **Kuilima Point**. To the east of the building, sheltered **Bayview Beach** has swimming-pool-placid water and a wide arc of sand. There's an outer reef that not only knocks down the waves but creates good snorkeling. Rent snorkel sets, bodyboards and beach gear at the on-site **Sand Bar** (⊙9am-5pm).

An excellent beach hike heads east from Bayview. A mile's walk brings you to **Kaihalulu Beach**, a beautiful, curved stretch of sand backed by ironwoods. Except in one small spot, a rocky bottom makes for poor swimming, but the shoreline is good for morning beachcombers. Continue another mile east, with a detour up onto the bluff path near the golf course to avoid slippery rocks, to reach scenic **Kahuku Point**, where local fishers throw nets and pole fish from the rocks. From there you can see (or hike) another 0.75 miles south along **Hanika'ilo Beach** on the windward side.

West of Kuilima Point, and the hotel, is where the serious surfing begins. In winter, waves beyond the reef off **Turtle Bay Beach** provide some of the best close-in views of surfers on the island. For good swimming, and to visit an awesome thicket of banyan trees, walk west 1.5 miles on the shoreline trail that runs from the

Roadside sign, Hale'iwa (p220)
IAN DAGNALL / ALAMY ©

resort to **Kawela Bay Beach**. In winter you can sometimes see whales cavorting offshore to the north. After about a mile, you'll round **Protection Point**, named for the WWII bunker there, and you're at Kawela. Continue your hike to the middle of the beach, where you'll find the best conditions for swimming and snorkeling.

Note that all public-access beach parking on the Turtle Bay Resort grounds costs $5 per day.

 Activities

TURTLE BAY GOLF
Golf
(📞293-8594; www.turtlebaygolf.com; Turtle Bay Resort, 57-091 Kamehameha Hwy; 18 holes $115-175; ⏱by reservation) Turtle Bay's two top-rated, par-72 courses abound in water views. The more challenging Palmer Course is the site of the PGA Championship Tour. The Fazio Course is host of the LPGA Tour's SBS Open. You can get discounts for hotel guests and twilight play.

HELE HULI
ADVENTURE CENTER
Adventure Sports
(📞293-6024; www.turtlebayresort.com; Turtle Bay Resort, 57-091 Kamehameha Hwy) Swimming and snorkeling not exciting enough for you? Turtle Bay hotel's activity desk will arrange horseback rides, surfing lessons and moped rentals, plus kayaking, Segway and helicopter tours.

 Sleeping

A good number of the privately owned Turtle Bay area condos are available for vacation rental on websites such as **VRBO** (www.vrbo.com) and others (for more, see p318). Minimum stays may apply for all area lodging.

TURTLE BAY RESORT
Resort $$$
(📞293-6000, 800-203-3650; www.turtlebayresort.com; 57-091 Kamehameha Hwy; r $250-350) Situated on a dramatic point, Turtle Bay Resort boasts impressive 800-acre surrounds. Each of the slightly dated guest lodgings has an ocean view; deluxe rooms come with private lanai. Ocean villas ($550 to $1200) have high ceilings, deep soaking tubs and a villa-guest-only private pool, in addition to sharing the resort's many other amenities. Check for package discounts online.

TURTLE BAY
CONDOS
Vacation Rental $$
(📞293-2800, 888-266-3690; www.turtlebaycondos.com; 1br $110-165, 2br $165-275)

ESTATES AT
TURTLE BAY
Vacation Rental $$
(📞293-0600; www.turtlebay-rentals.com; 1br $120-200, 2br $195-275)

 Eating & Drinking

21 DEGREES
NORTH
Hawaii Regional $$$
(📞293-8811; Turtle Bay Resort, 57-091 Kamehameha Hwy; mains $27-50, 5-course tasting menu $75-105; ⏱6-10pm Tue-Sat) Panoramic windows with ocean views set the scene in this white-tablecloth dining room. From the organic menu, expect perfectly prepared, chef-driven seafood dishes with local flavor – braised Kona lobster or pepper-crusted 'ahi (tuna) with Kahuku corn fritters, for example. Discerning global wine list, too.

OLA
Local $$$
(📞293-0801; www.olaislife.com; Turtle Bay Resort, 57-091 Kamehameha Hwy; lunches $12-22, dinner mains $20-50; ⏱11am-10pm) Reserve in advance and you might get to dine by torchlight with your toes in the sand. This open-air cabana bar and restaurant stakes out an unparalleled position beachside. The menu is regular surf-and-turf; *pupu* (appetizers) such as *kalua* (cooked in an underground pit) pork nachos and 'ahi poke (cubed Hawaiian-style raw fish) are a bit more interesting. Live music on Sunday afternoons.

HANG TEN BAR
Bar
(Turtle Bay Resort, 57-091 Kamehameha Hwy; ⏱11am-9pm) Groove to live Hawaiian music every Monday, Wednesday and Friday

North Shore

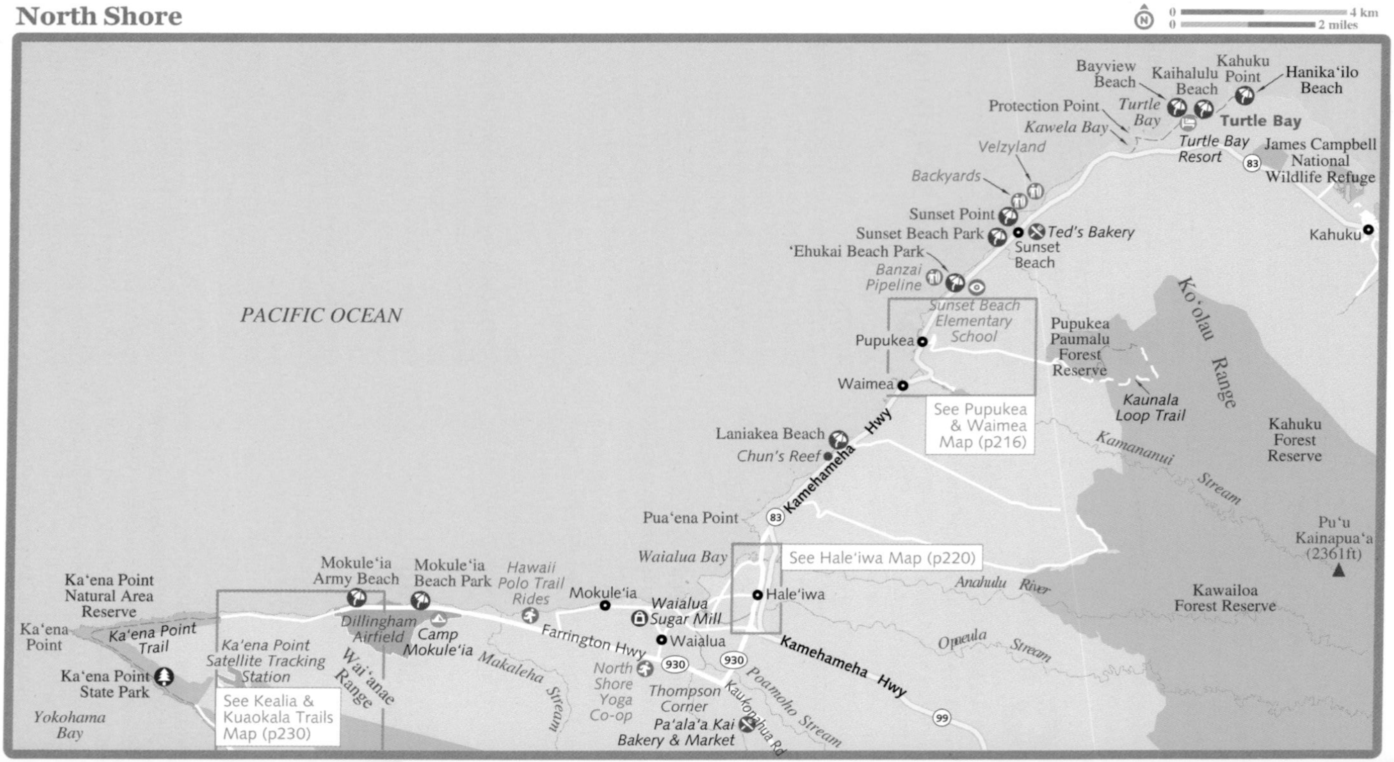

0 ___ 4 km
0 ___ 2 miles

TURTLE BAY

Kahuku

Hanika'ilo Beach
Kahuku Point
Kaihalulu Beach
Turtle Bay
James Campbell National Wildlife Refuge
Turtle Bay Resort
Bayview Beach
Protection Point
Turtle Bay
Kawela Bay
Velzyland
Ted's Bakery
Sunset Beach
Backyards
Sunset Point
Sunset Beach Park
'Ehukai Beach Park
Banzai Pipeline
Sunset Beach Elementary School
Pupukea Paumalu Forest Reserve
Pupukea
Waimea
See Pupukea & Waimea Map (p216)

Ko'olau Range

Kahuku Forest Reserve
Pu'u Kainapua'a (2361ft) ▲

Kamananui Stream
Kaunala Loop Trail

Kawailoa Forest Reserve

Anahulu River
Opae'ula Stream

Kamehameha Hwy

Laniakea Beach
Chun's Reef
See Hale'iwa Map (p220)
Hale'iwa

Pua'ena Point
Waialua Bay
Waialua Sugar Mill
Waialua
North Shore Yoga Co-op
Thompson Corner
Pa'ala'a Kai Bakery & Market
Poamoho Stream
Kaukonahua Rd

Mokule'ia Beach Park
Hawaii Polo Trail Rides
Mokule'ia
Makaleha Stream
Farrington Hwy

Mokule'ia Army Beach
Dillingham Camp
Mokule'ia Airfield
Wai'anae Range
See Kealia & Kuaokala Trails Map (p230)

Ka'ena Point Satellite Tracking Station

Ka'ena Point Natural Area Reserve
Ka'ena Point Trail
Ka'ena Point
Ka'ena Point State Park
Yokohama Bay

PACIFIC OCEAN

Detour:
James Campbell National Wildlife Refuge

At more than 250 acres, **James Campbell NWR** (📞637-6330; www.fws.gov/jamescampbell; tour free; 🕐late Oct-late Feb) preserves freshwater wetland habitat for four of Hawaii's six species of endangered water birds: the *'alae ke'oke'o* (Hawaiian coot), *ae'o* (Hawaiian black-necked stilt), *koloa maoli* (Hawaiian duck) and *'alae 'ula* (Hawaiian moorhen). During stilt-nesting season, normally from mid-February to mid-October, the refuge is off-limits to visitors. The rest of the year you can reserve ahead and join a naturalist-led walking tour, usually held Thursday afternoon and Saturday morning or afternoon. Ask for directions when you call; the entrance, off the Kamehameha Hwy between Turtle Bay and Kahuku, can be hard to find.

(5pm to 8pm) at this poolside bar with a view of Turtle Bay Beach.

Sunset Beach

Cruising southeast down the road from Turtle Bay you'll get a brief taste of what this rugged, rural coast was like before the surfers and superstars moved in. After about 4 miles, when an increasing number of homes appear through your windshield, you'll know you've hit the Sunset Beach area. Sure, the western orientation makes these beaches a great place to – guess what? – see the sun set. But way more people come to watch the surfers. The infamous Pipeline breaks here in winter, as do several world-class surfing competitions. The long stretch of golden sand is great for all ocean-lovers, and the laid-back residential community is a good location to rent a place and kick back island-style. A handy bike path leads from here almost to Waimea.

 Beaches

For every beach parking lot you see, there are at least four more pedestrian access paths tucked back into residential areas. Trick is there's limited to no parking. Going by bicycle is the best way to explore them all.

TOP CHOICE SUNSET BEACH PARK   Beach

Even from the road you can see the surf break off this popular beach. Like many on the North Shore, it has a split personality. In winter big swells come into this hot spot for pro wave riders and the posse of followers these rock stars of the sea attract. The second leg of the **Triple Crown of Surfing** (www.triplecrownofsurfing.com) takes place here in late November and early December.

In summer, Sunset is a prime place to log beach time. Waves calm down, there's a swimming channel before the reef and there are stands of trees for shade. Though the water is more inviting, be aware there are still some nasty currents about. From the beach park you can hike 1.25 miles north to **Sunset Point**. Along the way look for a lone picnic table in the tree line near the second residential access point. Some local surfers call this the 'table of knowledge,' as it's where they gather to survey the day's prospects.

This beach park has roadside parking, and it also has a lot across the street, where the restrooms and outdoor showers are located.

'EHUKAI BEACH PARK   Beach

Banzai Pipeline, aka Pipeline, aka Pipe – call it whatever you want, this place is known the world over as one of the biggest, heaviest and closest-to-perfect barrels in all of wave riding. When the strong

213

The Best...
Summer Swimming

1 Bayview Beach (p210)

2 Waimea Bay Beach Park (p218)

3 Hale'iwa Beach Park (p221)

4 Velzyland

westerly swells kick up in winter, the waves can reach over 15ft before breaking on the ultrashallow reef below. For board riders who know what they're doing (and no, a day surfing at Waikiki Beach doesn't count) this could be the holy grail. For the non-world-class surfer this is a great venue to watch the best do what they do. The final leg of the **Triple Crown of Surfing** (www.triplecrownofsurfing.com) is held here in early to mid-December. During summer, when everything is calm, there is even some decent snorkeling off the beach. The entrance to 'Ehukai Beach Park is opposite Sunset Beach Elementary School. You'll know if the surf is going off: there will be cars everywhere. The park has a lifeguard, restrooms and showers.

VELZYLAND
Beach

North of the University of Hawai'i Agricultural Station, Velzyland is a neighborhood fave, with a shorebreak on one end and a usually safe spot for swimming on the other. Always be cautious, year-round, when swimming on the North Shore. Access the tiny new parking lot off Waiale'e Beach Park Rd.

BACKYARDS
Beach

A smokin' surf break off Sunset Point, at the northern end of the beach near O'opuola St, under the right conditions Backyards draws top windsurfers. Note that there's a shallow reef and strong currents to contend with.

Activities

KE ALA PUPUKEA BIKE PATH
Cycling

A partly shaded bike path provides an excellent link between the beaches along this area of the North Shore. Pie-in-the-sky plans are to expand it from Turtle Bay to Waialua. In the meantime, the trail runs roughly 3 miles on the *makai* (seaward) side of Kamehameha Hwy, from O'opuola St in Sunset Beach to the guardrail at the northern end of Waimea Bay.

Sleeping

Rentals abound around Sunset Beach, check both the big online sights, such as **VRBO** (www.vrbo.com) and others (p318), plus local ones such as Team Real Estate in Hale'iwa.

O'AHU FAMILY RENTAL
Vacation Rental $$

(sunsetyards@mac.com; www.oahufamilyrentals.com; studios $90, 1br apt $150-165; ❄ 🛜) A local surfer family owns several rentals that are an easy bike ride from the beach (cruiser usage included). The smallest studio doesn't have much floor space but is fresh and cheery; a loftlike one bedroom has exposed-beam ceilings and original hula stained glass. Shared laundry facilities; insider beach advice included.

Eating

TOP CHOICE ▸ **TED'S BAKERY**
Cafe $

(59-024 Kamehameha Hwy; snacks $1-7, meals $7-16; ⏰7am-8pm Wed-Sun, to 6pm Mon & Tue) Quintessential North Shore, Ted's drive-in is the place surfers load up for breakfast, laid-back locals grab a quick snack, suntanned vacationers dig into plate lunches – and everybody goes for dessert. The chocolate-*haupia* (coconut) cream pie is legend all across the island. If that's not your thing, you have a dozen more choices, including guava cheesecake and *liliko'i* (passion fruit) mousse.

Full-meal favorites include the meat-filled fried rice with eggs at breakfast and melt-in-your-mouth, lightly pan-fried garlic shrimp any other time.

NORTH SHORE COUNTRY MARKET
Market $

(Sunset Beach Elementary School, 59-360 Kamehameha Hwy; ⊗8am-2pm Sat) Small local farmers market with some fresh-baked goods and handicrafts.

Pupukea

A largely residential area, Pupukea climbs from the coast further into the hills than you may think possible. There are a few services, including a big Foodland grocery store, along the highway. Higher up, hiking opportunities and an ancient Hawaiian site await.

Beaches

PUPUKEA BEACH PARK
Beach

With deep-blue waters, a varied coastline and a mix of lava and white sand, Pupukea, meaning 'white shell,' is a very scenic stretch. The long beach encompasses three areas: Shark's Cove to the north, Old Quarry in the center and Three Tables to the south. The waters off Pupukea Beach are all protected as a marine-life-conservation district.

Snorkelers take note: the reef formation at **Shark's Cove** provides an excellent habitat for marine life, including sea turtles. When seas are calm, this is a great area for water exploring, just make sure you always wear shoes to protect from sharp coral. And no, despite the cove's name, the white-tipped reef sharks aren't usually a problem; just keep your distance and don't provoke them. One of O'ahu's most popular cavern dives is also accessed here. Some of the caves are very deep and labyrinthine, and there have been a number of drownings, so divers should only venture into them with a local expert. This area is known for petty theft, so be sure to leave your belongings across the street in a rented locker ($5 per day) at **North Shore Surf Shop**; ☑638-0390; Kamehameha Hwy; ⊗8am-7pm). It also rents surfboards, snorkel sets and bicycles, as well as selling low-key beachwear.

Shark's Cove, Pupukea Beach Park

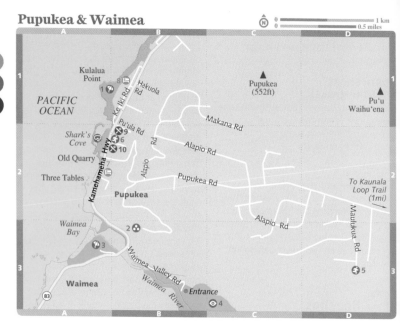

Pupukea & Waimea

The rock features at **Old Quarry** are sculpted as if they were cut by human hands, but rest assured that these features are natural. Coastal tide pools are interesting microhabitats, best explored at low tide during calm summer seas. Be careful, especially if you have kids in tow, because the rocks are razor sharp. There are showers and restrooms in front of Old Quarry; bus 52 stops out front.

The flat ledges rising above the water give **Three Tables** its name. In summer only, the area is good for snorkeling and diving. While it is possible to see some action around the tables, the best coral and fish, as well as some small caves, lava tubes and arches, are in deeper water further out. During the winter, the sandy bluff tucked near the tree line is a good place for an up-close-and-oceanfront picnic. Access to Three Tables is just beyond Old Quarry, where there are a few unmarked parking spots.

◉ Sights & Activities

FREE PU'U O MAHUKA HEIAU STATE
HISTORIC SITE   *Archeological Site*
A stellar view of the coast and a stroll around the grounds of one of O'ahu's largest temples reward those who venture up to this historical landmark. The terraced walls are each several feet of lava rock high. Collectively, the three

adjoining enclosures that form the main body of the heiau (stone temple) are more than 550ft in length. To avoid damaging and disturbing the ancient site, do not walk around inside the perimeter.

Pu'u o Mahuka means 'hill of escape,' and this was a *luakini* heiau, where human sacrifices took place. The original construction is attributed to the *menehune*, the 'little people' of legend who are said to have completed impressive works like this in just one night. It likely dates from the 16th century. Though the stone terraces leave a little to the imagination, this was a dramatic site for a temple, and it's well worth the drive to take in the commanding view, especially at sunset. To find it, turn *mauka* (inland) up Pupukea Rd at Foodland supermarket; the heiau turnoff is half a mile up, from where it's a roughshod 0.7 miles to the site.

KAUNALA LOOP TRAIL
Hiking

(http://hawaiitrails.ehawaii.gov; ⊙ sunrise-sunset Sat & Sun) A little-known, 4.5-mile loop hike (two hours) mixes an easy forest valley walk with a moderate ridge climb for sweeping views of Waimea Bay. After spying the beauty of the bay from viewpoints atop this trail, it's easy to see why Hawaiian royalty considered it sacred. The trail is officially open to the public only on weekends and state holidays. Hunting is allowed in the area, so wear bright colors and don't wander off the trail. To get here, travel 2.5 miles up Pupukea Rd from the Foodland. Park roadside before the Boy Scout Camp and follow the access path half a mile past the hiker sign-in to the trailhead.

HAPPY TRAILS HAWAII
Horseback Riding

(📞 638-7433; www.happytrailshawaii.com; Maulukua Rd; 1½/2hr ride $75/95) You can take to the mountainsides on horseback, over open pasture and near orchards, to reach panoramic views. Beginners are welcome, and all rides start with orientation and instruction. Reservations are required.

Island Insights

The large boulders standing at the end of Kulalua Point, which mark the northernmost end of Pupukea Beach, are said to be followers of Pele, the Hawaiian goddess of fire and volcanoes. To acknowledge their loyalty (or in alternative tellings of the legend, to punish their nosiness for observing the goddess's passage from onshore), Pele made her followers immortal by turning them to stone.

Sleeping

As with much of the North Shore, accommodation options here are mostly vacation rentals.

TOP CHOICE KE IKI BEACH BUNGALOWS
Vacation Rental $$

(📞 638-8829, 866-638-8229; www.keikibeach.com; 59-579 Ke Iki Rd; 1br apt $150-200, 2br apt $175-230; ❄ 🛜) Updated smartly, tropical decor adds to the retreat feel of this bungalow community on the white-sand beach just north of Pupukea Beach Park. Grassy lawns and a garden full of tropical trees complete the picture. Kick back on the shared beachfront lanai, nap in a hammock beneath the palm trees or head out for a swim. Though not all of the full-kitchen units have ocean views, none is more than a minute's walk from the water. The on-site manager is a font of area info.

BACKPACKERS VACATION INNS & PLANTATION VILLAGE
Hostel $

(📞 638-7838; http://backpackers-hawaii.com; 59-788 Kamehameha Hwy; dm $27-30, d $62-85, studios $120-145; 🛜) The only budget option on the North Shore. If you care more about money and location than about the odd bit of peeling paint or

217

modest-to-the-point-of-ramshackle furnishings, this friendly, backpacker-style village is for you. Hostel rooms are mostly located in the two large main buildings. Our preferred location is Plantation Village, a groovy collection of beach cabins, some private, some shared. You don't have to do much more than cross the street to get to the beach from either. Studio 'condos' directly overlook the ocean but are way too spartan for the price. Shared kitchens and laundry on-site.

 Eating

SHARKS COVE GRILL Local $
(712 Kamehameha Hwy; meals $7-16; ⏱8:30am-8:30pm) Order your taro burger or 'ahi skewers from the window, pull up a rickety covered patio seat and watch the waves as a chicken pecks the ground nearby. The food's OK; the experience is totally North Shore.

PUPUKEA GRILL Food Truck $
(59-680 Kamehameha Hwy; dishes $7-16; ⏱11am-9:30pm) Grilled-fish tacos, panini sandwiches and *poke* bowls aren't typical food-truck fare. Take yours to go; the parking-lot picnic tables aren't appetizing.

Waimea

An artist couldn't paint a better picture: white sand meets azure water at the mouth of a lushly green river valley. Black outcroppings of lava rock sit offshore a deep arc of beach. The bay is so stunning, in fact, that it's hard not to catch your breath when you round the highway curve and see it. Captain Cook's men, the first Westerners to sail into Waimea Bay, had the same reaction. An entry in the 1779 ship's log noted its uncommon beauty. Back then the valley was heavily settled; the lowlands terraced in taro, the valley walls dotted with house sites and the ridges topped with heiau. Just about every crop grown in Hawaii thrived in this valley, including a rare pink taro favored by *ali'i* (royalty). Back then Waimea River emptied into the bay and served as a passage for canoes traveling to upstream villages. Post contact, logging and plantation clearing resulted in a devastating 1894 flood, after which residents abandoned the settlement. Today, the beach park is an immensely popular stop on O'ahu itineraries, and you can hike up into the valley to see a few of the original sites.

 Beaches

WAIMEA BAY BEACH PARK Beach
It may be a beauty, but it's certainly a moody one. Waimea Bay changes dramatically with the seasons: it can be tranquil and flat as a lake in summer, then savage in winter,

Waimea Valley
KENNY WILLIAMS / ALAMY ©

Surf Movies 101

The North Shore's epic waves have starred, or at least had cameos, in some of the best surf movies ever made. Check these out:

- *Soul Surfer* (2011) A girl's journey back to competition surfing after a shark attack.
- *Riding Giants* (2004) This documentary surveys the history and lore of surfing.
- *The Ride* (2003) A hit on the head sends one wave-rider back to 1911, surfing with the Duke.
- *Blue Crush* (2002) Can love come between a surfer and the Banzai Pipeline?
- *North Shore* (1987) A big-wave wannabe braves a summer on the North Shore.
- *Five Summer Stories* (1972) Eddie Aikau co-stars as a legendary local surfer – himself.
- *Endless Summer* (1966) The original, existential, life-in-search-of-the-wave epic.

with the island's meanest rip currents. Typically, the only time it's calm enough for swimming and snorkeling is from June to September, maybe October. Winter water activities at this beach are *not* for novices. The waves at Waimea can get epically huge, and the beach plays host to the annual Eddie Aikau memorial surf competition **Quiksilver** (http://quiksilverlive.com) between December and February. Eddie Aikau was a legendary waterman and Waimea lifeguard who died trying to save compatriots from a double-hull outrigger-canoe accident en route from Hawaii to Tahiti.

This is the North Shore's most popular beach, so parking is often tight. On weekends, Waimea Valley across the street offers paid parking. Don't park along the highway; police are notorious for towing away dozens of cars at once. Note, too, that jumping off the big rock formation at the southern end of the cove is technically forbidden. Facilities include showers, restrooms and picnic tables, and a lifeguard on duty daily.

 Sights

WAIMEA VALLEY Garden
(✆ 638-7766; www.waimeavalley.net; 59-864 Kamehameha Hwy; adult/child $15/7; ⏰ 9am-5pm; 👪) Craving land instead of sea? This 1800-acre Hawaiian cultural and nature park, just inland from Waimea Bay, is a sanctuary of tropical tranquility. Among the junglelike foliage you'll find up to 5000 native and exotic plant species. Wander the numerous paths alongside Kamananui Stream and up to different cultural stations, which may have demonstrations of ancient Hawaiian games and practices. Don't miss the opportunity to take a dip at the base of 45ft-high Waimea Falls, 1 mile in.

The valley is home to numerous ancient sites, but few are on the paths. Equally interesting are the replicas of buildings ancient Hawaiians dwelled in and a restored heiau dedicated to Lono, the traditional god of fertility and agriculture. Guided hikes ($10 to $15) lead into otherwise inaccessible parts of the valley and are worth making time for; reservations required.

Laniakea Beach

The amazing *honu* (green sea turtles), weighing upwards of 200lb, that live here are not so different from other beachgoers that like to bask in the sun. The turtles like to hang out at Laniakea Beach, aka **Turtle Beach**. One of the more than 60 local **Malama na Honu** (Protect the Turtles; http://malamanahonu.org) volunteers is usually on hand during daylight hours, both to guard the precious creatures and to answer questions. Incidentally, the turtles are not permanent O'ahu residents – about once every four years they return to their ancestral nesting grounds in the remote French Frigate Shoals, 500 miles east of O'ahu, where they mate and nest. Look for the beach between the 3- and 4-mile markers along Kamehameha Hwy. This narrow spit of sand can get crowded with onlookers. Though it is a basking, not a nesting location, please be respectful of the threatened species. Loud noises and abrupt movements startle them. Approach slowly and keep a distance of at least 6ft, although further is recommended.

Hale'iwa

POP 2011

Originally a plantation-era supply town in the 1900s, Hale'iwa today is the de facto surf city of the North Shore. It's all about the waves here and everyone knows it. If the town is all hustle and bustle, chances are the ocean is flat. If the swells are breaking, it could take you an hour to travel the 8 miles through rubber-necking traffic to Sunset Beach. Despite being a tourist hub, there's a laid-back ambience to Hale'iwa town that's in perfect concert with the rest of the coast. Old false-front wooden buildings sell shave ice, and eclectic shops intermingle with modern amenities. As the biggest outpost around, this is the place to find a decent meal, pick up a new T-shirt, rent a long-board for the day and then hang around after sunset, wishing you could stay just a little bit longer.

Hale'iwa

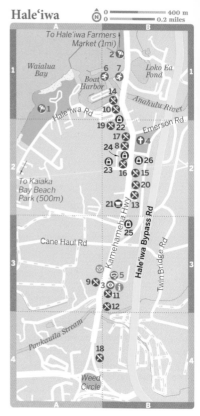

Beaches

HALE'IWA ALI'I BEACH PARK   Beach

Home to some of the best surf on the North Shore, waves here can be huge – with double or triple overhead tubes not uncommon. Not surprisingly, the beach is a popular spot for surf contests. In late November the **Triple Crown of Surfing** (www.triplecrownofsurfing.com) gets under way on this break. When it's relatively flat, the local kids rip it up with their bodyboards and mere mortals test their skills on the waves. The 20-acre beach park has restrooms, showers, a wide grassy area with picnic tables and lifeguards. The shallow areas on the southern side of the beach are generally the calmest places to swim.

Hale‘iwa

HALE‘IWA BEACH PARK　　Beach

On the northern side of the harbor, this park is protected by a shallow shoal and breakwater so is usually a good choice for swimming. There's little wave action, except for the occasional north swells that ripple into the bay. Although the beach isn't as pretty as others, the 13-acre park has basketball and volleyball courts, an exercise area, a softball field and a large parking lot. Note that Kahalewai Rd is often host to car-living residents.

KAIAKA BAY BEACH PARK　　Beach

Beachside trees a mile or so west of town offer shade, and turtles sometimes show up. But the swimming is better at the other local beaches, so look elsewhere if you're wanting to get wet.

 Sights

HISTORIC HALE‘IWA　　Walking Tour

(☎ 637-4558; www.gonorthshore.org; 66-434 Kamehameha Hwy; tour $10; ☺ 3pm Wed & 9:30am Sat) Reserve in advance for the 90-minute walking tours that take in the scattered historic buildings of town. The visitor center also sells illustrated tour maps ($2) that describe all the old

structures and can be followed at your own pace.

**LILI‘UOKALANI
PROTESTANT CHURCH**　　Church

(66-090 Kamehameha Hwy) Hale‘iwa's historic 1832 church takes its name from Queen Lili‘uokalani, who spent summers on the shores of the Anahulu River and attended services here. As late as the 1940s services were held entirely in Hawaiian.

 Activities

If you're a beginner board rider, the North Shore has a few tame breaks such as **Pua‘ena Point**, just north of Hale‘iwa Beach Park, and **Chun's Reef**, north of town. Even if you've caught a few waves in Waikiki, it's smart to take a lesson with one of the many freelancing surfers to get an introduction to local underwater hazards. Ask around the beach, where surf school vans rent gear and offer same-day instruction, or book ahead for surf or stand-up paddling lessons. Expect to pay from $75 to $90 for two-hour group lessons, $10 to $180 for a private lesson and $30 to $45 to rent a board for the day ($60 with paddle).

Whale-watching season is December through May, snorkeling season is June through September.

SURF 'N' SEA   Water Sports
(☎800-899-7873; www.surfnsea.com; 62-595 Kamehameha Hwy; ⏱9am-7pm) The big daddy of all surf shops, this colorful wooden building by the sea rents most any kind of water gear you can think of: surfboards, paddleboard set-ups, wetsuits, car racks, snorkel sets, kayaks, beach umbrellas and chairs... Lessons, tours and bicycle rental too.

RAINBOW WATERSPORTS   Water Sports
(☎372-9304, 800-470-4964; www.rainbow watersports.com) The local stand-up paddle specialist offers calm-water classes, lessons for braving the waves and four-hour coastal paddle tours ($200), with snorkeling and lunch included. Rentals available, too.

NORTH SHORE SURF GIRLS   Water Sports
(☎637-2977; www.northshoresurfgirls.com) Some of the instructors here were featured in the movie *Blue Crush*, and they're all especially great teaching kids and other women to bodyboard, surf and stand-up paddle. Packages include a sunset Hawaiian-BBQ dinner or a shrimp lunch.

SUNSET SURRATT SURF ACADEMY   Surfing
(☎783-8657; http://sunsetsurattsurfschool. com) ' Uncle Bryan,' born and raised on the North Shore, has been coaching pro surfers for decades. He and his staff teach all levels from beginner to advanced, and stand-up paddlers. Rentals offered.

DEEP ECOLOGY   Diving
(☎637-7946, 800-578-3992; www.oahuscu badive.com; 66-456 Kamehameha Hwy; shore/ boat dive from $109/145; ⏱8am-5pm) If you'd rather get under the waves than on top of them, the folks at Deep Ecology can help. Summer shore dives explore Shark's Cove and Three Tables, while offshore lava tubes, coral reefs, arches and cathedrals await boat divers. With a strong ecological bent, these divers are conscious about the ocean and create ecodive boat trips with that in mind. Summer snorkel trips and winter whale-watching cruises offered.

Surfing on Waimea Bay (p218)

NORTH SHORE
WELLNESS RETREAT   Health & Fitness
(☎638-8137; http://surfintoyoga.com; 59-142
Kamehameha Hwy; class $15, 1hr massage $120)
Pro surfer Rochelle Ballard founded this
wellness studio where you can take yoga
classes, indulge in lomilomi massage
or a facial scrub, book a surf lesson or
arrange an entire retreat, complete with
accommodation.

PLANET SURF N SHORE   Water Sports
(☎637-5002; 62-595 Kamehameha Hwy;
⏲11:30am-6pm) Snorkel, bodyboard,
surfboard and other rentals; full shop with
clothing and souvenirs.

NORTH SHORE
SHARK ADVENTURES   Shark Watching
(☎228-5900; http://sharktourshawaii.com;
Hale'iwa Small Boat Harbor; 2hr tour adult/child
$120/60) Submerge in a cage surrounded
by sharks 5ft to 15ft in length.

WATERCRAFT
CONNECTION   Water Sports
(www.thewatercraftconnection.com; Hale'iwa
Small Boat Harbor; per hour jet ski/kayak
$125/15; ⏲11am-5pm) Kayaks and jet skis
are first come, first served; rent from the
little booth at the harbor.

 Tours

Deep Ecology dive outfitters offer excellent boat tours as well.

NORTH SHORE ECOTOURS   Hiking
(☎877-521-4453; http://northshoreecotours.
com; hiking tour adult/child $90/60, driving tour
$65/45) Native Hawaiian guides lead three
different, easy-to-difficult hikes on private
land. All begin with a ride to the trailhead
in a Swiss military off-road vehicle; taking
a tour in the Pinzgauer is also possible.

O'AHU AGRI-TOURS   Van
(☎228-7585; www.oahuagritours.com; adult/
child $110/102; ⏲Sat & Sun; 👫) Get up close
and personal with Hawaiian traditional
farming practices. On one of five different
tours, you might visit a local farm, have
lunch in a taro patch, learn to pound poi,

**Stand-up paddling has really taken off,
why?** Stand-up paddling is a magic-carpet
ride. Everyone who has ever dreamed of
flying or walking on water loves it.

But what if I'm out of shape? With the
right equipment and proper instruction
anyone can stand-up paddle, regardless of
athletic ability. We have successfully taught
paddlers from seven to 70-plus years old.

**What are your favorite paddling sites
for starting out?** The Anahulu Stream and
Hale'iwa Beach Park are definitely prime
locations for starting out. Even when the
ocean waves are big, this area is protected,
smooth and calm. In the spring and summer,
my favorite is paddling down the coast from
either Sunset Beach or Waimea Bay to
Hale'iwa Beach Park. It's miles of vast ocean,
breathtaking coastlines, tropical fish, sea
turtles and spinner dolphins.

**Where do you recommend advanced
paddlers go?** North Shore waves are thicker
and more powerful than many surfers
are used to. Pua'ena Point in Hale'iwa is a
popular place to get introduced to Hawaiian
surf. It's more tame and forgiving than other
spots, and there are usually enough waves
for everyone.

**Do you have any personal paddling
spots around the rest of the island?**
Between you and me, I really don't. I love
the North Shore. It's the surf capital of the
world, the ocean is clean and the people
are friendly.

make crafts and taste locally grown and ground Waialua coffee. Transportation from Waikiki is included.

NORTH SHORE CATAMARAN CHARTERS Boat
(☎351-9371; www.sailingcat.com; Hale'iwa Small Boat Harbor; 3hr tour adult/child $80/60) Sunset cruises, whale-watching and snorkeling trips aboard a catamaran sailboat.

SURF BUS Bus
(☎226-7299; www.northshoresurfbus.com; adult/child $76/60) Although it's totally easy to do these things on your own, you could let the Surf Bus do the driving on a full day of North Shore sightseeing, town shopping and your choice of activity: bicycling, snorkeling, bodyboarding or hiking.

Festivals & Events

The Hale'iwa Farmers Market has special festival-like theme weekends throughout the year.

HALE'IWA ARTS FESTIVAL Arts
(www.haleiwaartsfestival.org) More than 100 artists gather at Hale'iwa one weekend in July to sell their wares. Music, food, cultural tours and hands-on demonstrations are also scheduled.

Sleeping

Hale'iwa has no hotels, but there are a number of vacation rentals in the area.

TEAM REAL ESTATE Vacation Rental $$
(☎637-3507, 800-982-8602; www.teamrealestate.com; 1br apt $95-165, houses $150-900) This local real-estate agency handles a dozen or so vacation rentals along the North Shore. Options run the gamut from studio apartments and condos to multibedroom beachfront luxury homes.

KAIAKA BAY BEACH PARK Campground $
(www1.honolulu.gov/parks/camping.htm; 66-449 Haleiwa Rd; tent sites with permit free; ⏰8am

Fri-8am Wed) Advance permits are required (see p302) for the seven tent sites at Hale'iwa's only campground. The park has restrooms, outdoor showers and picnic tables.

 Eating

TOP CHOICE CAFÉ HALE'IWA Local $$

(637-5516; 66-460 Kamehameha Hwy; breakfast & lunch $5-12, dinner mains $18-30; 7:30am-2pm Sun-Wed, 7:30am-2pm & 6-10pm Wed-Sat). Locals have been fueling up at this laid-back surf-style diner since the 1980s. Only recently has candlelight and creative food transformed the humble dining room after 6pm. A daily menu of fresh preparations focuses on local ingredients and may feature mains such as lamb or mahimahi. Here even the side-dish vegetables are stars. Grab a bottle of wine from Bonzers Wine Shop next door. For weekend breakfasts and dinners, out-door seating magically appears behind the buildings.

TOP CHOICE M MATSUMOTO STORE INC Desserts $

(www.matsumotoshaveice.com; 66-087 Kame-hameha Hwy; 9am-6pm;) O'ahu's clas-sic circle-island drive just isn't complete without stopping for shave ice at this tin-roofed 1920s general store, locally known as Matsumoto's. Prepare to stand in line here for a cone drenched with island flavors, including *liliko'i*, banana, mango and pineapple.

AOKI'S Desserts $

(www.aokisshaveice.com; 66-117 Kamehameha Hwy; 11am-6:30pm) Tourists flock to Mat-sumoto's, but some locals prefer Aoki's, which is also in an old building and has much shorter lines. The souvenir T-shirts aren't nearly as cool though.

Mobile Meals

Though we prefer the original Kahuku shrimp trucks, which are only 15 miles away on the Windward Coast, there are a number of food trucks around Hale'iwa town. Expect to pay between $8 and $14 a plate, between 10am and 6pm only. Look for **Blue Water Shrimp** by Gas Station 76 in the center of town; **Giovanni's** sits in a parking lot with several other food trucks across from the intersection with Pa'ala'a Rd; and **Macky's** is near the roundabout at the far southern end of town.

GRASS SKIRT GRILL   Local $

(66-214 Kamehameha Hwy; dishes $6-13; ⏰11am-6pm; 🍴) Retro surf decor covers every square inch of a very small space; think of it as a micro-tiki room. The names of the island-style plate lunches seem familiar – teriyaki chicken, *ono* (a type of mackerel) burgers...but the results are way above average, using brown rice, local greens and homemade sauces. These are great takeout meals when you're beach bound. Cash only.

LUIBUENO'S   Mexican $$

(📞637-7717; www.luibueno.com; 66-165 Kamehameha Hwy; mains $14-30; ⏰11am-midnight) If you've never tried a beer-battered mahimahi (firm pink-fleshed fish) taco or a big ol' grilled 'ahi burrito, here's your chance. In addition to modern Mexican, Luibueno's serves decent upmarket seafood and steaks. A local après-sea crowd hogs the bar while knocking back mango margaritas during twice-daily 'bueno' hours, before and after dinner.

OPAL THAI   Thai $

(66-165 Kamehameha Hwy; dishes $8-12; ⏰11am-3pm & 5-10pm Tue-Sun) What does a food truck want to be when it grows up? A great cafe, with reasonable prices and tasty Thai. Green-papaya salad, garlic crab noodles, Tom Yum soup...yummy, indeed.

BEET BOX   Health Food $

(66-443 Kamehameha Hwy; dishes $8-11; ⏰9am-5pm Mon-Sat, to 4pm Sun; 🍴) At the back of the town's karmically cool health-food store hides a popular vegetarian-friendly deli. Breakfast is served all day, lunch is hot plates, sandwiches or salads.

WAIALUA BAKERY   Bakery $

(66-200 Kamehameha Hwy; items $2-10; ⏰10am-5pm Mon-Sat) Many of the ingredients for the smoothies here come from the owners' farm in Waialua. Breads for the piled-high sandwiches, cookies and treats are all made from scratch.

HALE'IWA JOE'S   Seafood $$

(📞637-8005; 66-001 Kamehameha Hwy; lunches $9-18, dinner mains $16-30; ⏰11:30am-11pm) With a superb location overlooking the marina, Joe's is the place for romantic dinners. Lunches are just so-so; we much prefer the inventive *pupu*, discounted at happy hour.

BANZAI SUSHI BAR   Japanese $$

(North Shore Marketplace, 66-246 Kamehameha Hwy; mains $10-25; ⏰noon-9:30pm) It's all about the atmosphere at Banzai Sushi Bar. This open-air sushi bar has surf videos scrolling on the walls and live bands jamming on Saturday evenings.

KUA 'AINA   Burgers $

(66-160 Kamehameha Hwy; sandwiches $7-10; ⏰11am-8pm) We don't know that these are, as touted, the best hamburgers on the island, but they're juicy and do come with a variety of toppings.

🍷 Drinking

LANIKAI JUICE — Cafe

(66-215 Kamehameha Hwy; ⏲6am-8pm Mon-Fri, 7am-7pm Sat & Sun) Kailua's favorite smoothie and fresh-juice bar has branched out. You can expect the same commitment to fresh ingredients and creative combos.

COFFEE GALLERY — Cafe

(North Shore Marketplace, 66-250 Kamehameha Hwy; ⏲7am-8pm; @ 🛜) Coffee lovers rejoice over the house-roast beans and brews here.

🔒 Shopping

From trendy to quirky, you will find most of the North Shore's boutiques and galleries in Hale'iwa. The central shopping hub is in the North Shore Marketplace, which is across from Achui Lane in the center of town. There are T-shirt and surfwear shops everywhere.

TOP CHOICE / HALE'IWA FARMERS MARKET — Market

(www.haleiwafarmersmarket.com; ⏲9am-1pm Sun) So much more than produce; here 40 vendors sell artisan crafts and organic, seasonal edibles. At the time of research, the market was looking for a new location; check the website for updates.

HALE'IWA ART GALLERY — Arts & Crafts

(North Shore Marketplace, 66-252 Kamehameha Hwy; ⏲10am-6pm) Featuring works by 20-plus local and regional painters, photographers, sculptors and mixed-media artists.

GUAVA — Clothing

(66-165 Kamehameha Hwy; ⏲10am-6pm) A chic, upscale boutique for beachy women's apparel such as gauzy sundresses and strappy sandals.

KAI KU HALE — Homewares

(66-145 Kamehameha Hwy; ⏲10am-7pm) Bring island style home with Hawaiian art, wood wall carvings, homewares and jewelry.

GROWING KEIKI — Clothing

(66-051 Kamehameha Hwy; ⏲10am-6pm; 👪) This kids' shop has gear for junior surf grommets and budding beach bunnies, including mini aloha shirts, trunks and toys.

STRONG CURRENT SURF SHOP — Hawaiiana

(66-214 Kamehameha Hwy; ⏲10am-6pm) Cute Hawaiiana, sports clothing and custom surfboards. It has a good selection of surf movies, too.

NORTH SHORE SWIMWEAR — Clothing

(North Shore Marketplace, 66-250 Kamehameha Hwy; ⏲10am-6pm) Ground zero for fashionable women's wet-and-wild styles, all in

Shops at the North Shore Marketplace
ANN CECIL / LONELY PLANET IMAGES ©

mix and match sizes. Custom orders are handmade in Hawaii.

 Information

Coffee Gallery (North Shore Marketplace, 66-250 Kamehameha Hwy; per 30min $3; ⊙6:30am-8pm; @ 🛜) Pay-as-you-go internet terminals; free wi-fi.

First Hawaiian Bank (66-135 Kamehameha Hwy; ⊙8:30am-4pm Mon-Thu, to 6pm Fri)

Post Office (66-437 Kamehameha Hwy; ⊙8am-4pm Mon-Fri, 9am-noon Sat)

 Getting There & Around

From Honolulu International Airport to Hale'iwa is 27 miles, normally 40 minutes via the H-1, H-2 and Kamehameha Hwy. Because the North Shore basically only has one long road, it's time consuming, but possible to get around by bus. Route 52 (Circle Island Wahiawa) runs from the Ala Moana Center in Honolulu to Hale'iwa in 1¾ hours, making stops in town and at beaches all the way to Turtle Bay.

Bike 'n Boards (✏342-7815; http://biken boardshawaii.com; per day/week $20/90; ⊙by appointment) Free delivery and pick-up are included with cruiser bicycle rental. Surfboards, bodyboards and snorkel sets available too.

North Shore Airport Express (✏352-1818; www.northshoreairportshuttle.com; 1 way $80; ⊙office 9am-3pm) Book at least two days in advance for shuttle service from Honolulu International Airport.

Waialua

POP 2465

If you find the relatively slow pace of life on the North Shore just too hectic, head over to Waialua. This sugar-mill town ground to a halt in 1996, when production ended. Since then, creative locals have transformed the old mill into a crafty, island-born shopping complex. The surrounding area is filled with small-scale farms, nurseries and a few McMansions claiming ag-exempt tax status. Beach access is difficult here, but they aren't the North Shore's best anyway.

 Sights & Activities

WAIALUA SUGAR MILL　　　Historic Site
(67-106 Kealohanui St; www.sugarmillhawaii.com; ⊙9am-5pm Mon-Sat, 10am-5pm Sun)

Mokule'ia Beach Park

The now-defunct sugar mill that was the genesis of the town in the 1900s has been redeveloped to house a few shops and businesses. You can still see the old smoke stack and bits of the history revealed in the two main tourist shops. The rambling **Waialua Coffee – Island X Hawaii** warehouse is stuffed full of everything from vintage aloha shirts to wooden handicrafts and pieces of original art. In addition to buying its Waialua-local, estate-grown coffee as beans or grounds, you can pick up a hot cuppa Joe (or shave ice) from a little coffee stand in the corner. Be sure to look out back at the small interpretive history display.

The **North Shore Soap Factory** features sugar-mill history displays. While you're there, peek through the glass and watch the soap makers craft the all-natural bars they sell, made with local ingredients such as *kukui* (candlenut tree) nuts and coconut cream.

On Saturday, the **Waialua Farmers Market** (⊙8:30am-2pm Sat) sets up in the sugar-mill parking lot. Surfboard-makers and craft vendors keep this market lively.

**NORTH SHORE
YOGA CO-OP**   Health & Fitness
(☎349-3650; http://northshoreyoga.org; Weinberg Community Center, 67-174 Farrington Hwy; classes by donation; ⊙Mon-Sat) A consortium of local teachers offers numerous different yoga styles on a donation basis.

 Eating

**PA'ALA'A KAI
BAKERY & MARKET**   Bakery $
(66-945 Kaukonahua Rd; ⊙5:30am-8pm) Take a detour down a country road to find this family-run bakery, a pilgrimage for anyone craving a 'snow puffy' (flaky chocolate cream puff dusted with powdered sugar) or hot *malasadas* (Portuguese-style doughnuts).

Mokule'ia to Ka'ena Point
POP 1839

The further down the road you go, the fewer signs of habitation you'll see in this

desolate corner of the island. Farrington Hwy finally dead ends into a rocky, undeveloped patch short of the island's edge. Few visitors make it this far, but there are a string of striking beaches, and numerous aviation adventures from Dillingham Airfield, for those who do.

 Beaches

MOKULE'IA BEACH PARK   Beach
The beach itself is a nice sandy stretch, but the rocky seabed makes for poor swimming. When waters are calm and flat in summer, snorkelers swim out along the shallow reef. Keen windsurfers often congregate on this stretch of shore, taking advantage of the consistent winds. The park has a large grassy area with picnic tables, restrooms and outdoor showers; but there aren't any lifeguards. At the time of writing, camping had been suspended indefinitely.

MOKULE'IA ARMY BEACH   Beach
Opposite the western end of Dillingham Airfield, this is the widest stretch of sand on the Mokule'ia shore, although it's not maintained and there are no facilities. The beach also has very strong rip currents, especially during high winter surf.

229

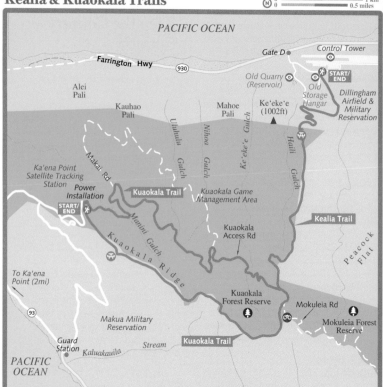

If the beach looks familiar, it might be because it appeared in the pilot of the hit TV drama *Lost*. When it was first being filmed, tourists driving along the highway could see the smoking wreckage of a crashed plane and would mistakenly report an emergency.

KA'ENA POINT STATE PARK   Beach
(☼ sunrise-sunset) From Army Beach you can drive another 1.6 miles down the road, passing still more white-sand beaches with aqua-blue waters. The bit of sand off the pull-out just beyond the first Ka'ena State Park sign has a small rock-free swimming area accessible in calm surf.

A mountain-bike-friendly hiking path leads from the end of Farrington Hwy along the remaining 2.5 miles out to

Ka'ena Point. The terrain is scrubland reaching up to the base of the Wai'anae Range, while the shoreline is wild and windswept. The large parking area is not only desolate but can also be a bit trashed. Graffiti, empty liquor bottles and car break-ins are all commonplace. December to May you may be able to spot whales from this area. But we recommend doing the full hike from the other side of the point, on the Wai'anae Coast.

🏃 Activities

Skydiving, hang gliding and biplane and glider rides all take off from **Dillingham Airfield** (68-760 Farrington Hwy). Call ahead, as flights are weather dependent.

HONOLULU SOARING
CLUB Scenic Flights

(☎637-0207; www.honolulusoaring.com; flights $80-305; ⏰10am-5:30pm) Take a scenic tour over the North Shore, go for an aerobatic thrill ride or have a minilesson in a glider plane.

PACIFIC SKYDIVING CENTER Skydiving

(☎637-7472; www.pacific-skydiving.com; tandem jumps $140-190; ⏰8am-3pm) Wanna get tossed out of a perfectly good airplane? A tandem jump attached to an instructor is a stomach-turning 14,000ft freefall, followed by a 15-minute float back to earth.

PARADISE AIR Scenic Flights

(☎497-6033; http://paradiseairhawaii.com; flights $135-370; ⏰by reservation) Soar like a bird in an ultralight powered hang glider, accompanied by an instructor who may even let you pilot.

STEARMAN BIPLANE
RIDES Scenic Flights

(☎637-4461; http://peacock.com/biplane/; flights $150-400; ⏰by reservation) Loop-de-loop on an aerobatic flight, take a short scenic tour (20 minutes) or retrace the route the Japanese took to Pearl Harbor (40 minutes) – all in a restored 1941 Boeing biplane.

FOREST RESERVE HIKES Hiking

(http://hawaiitrails.ehawaii.gov) Beyond the Gate D entrance above Dillingham Airfield, the 2.5-mile, one-way **Kealia Trail** switchbacks steeply up (1660ft elevation change) through exposed country with ocean views along the way. It connects to the 2.5-mile, one-way **Kuaokala Trail**,

which brings hikers to a justly celebrated ridge-top viewpoint over Makua Valley and the Wai'anae Range. Note that access to this trail is physically easier from the Wai'anae Coast but requires an advance permit to approach via the Ka'ena Point Satellite Tracking Station. Both trails are open to mountain bikes. Print out a topo map if you go; allow six hours for both.

HAWAII POLO
TRAIL RIDES Horseback Riding

(☎220-5153; http://hawaii-polo.org; 68-411 Farrington Hwy; 1½hr rides $95-125; ⏰by reservation Tue, Thu & Sat) When the polo ponies aren't playing, you can take a ride around their 100-acre stomping grounds at the polo club. Sunset beach rides recommended.

Sleeping

Surprisingly, even out here in the middle of nowhere there are vacation rentals. In addition to the usual agencies, **Solikai** (www.solikai.com) lists a few colorful, oceanfront beach cottages.

CAMP MOKULE'IA Campground $

(☎637-6241; www.campmokuleia.com; 68-729 Farrington Hwy; campsites per person $15, tent cabins $85; ☀) Looking for solace and solitude? This church-run seaside camp is open to travelers – by reservation only – as long as there isn't a prebooked group. Amenities are ultrabasic, with outdoor showers and chemical toilets. Give the well-worn lodge rooms, cabins and beach cottage a pass.

Central & Leeward O'ahu

The island's tallest mountains stand watch over the rugged rural highlands of central O'ahu. Squeezed between giant military reservations en route to the hip, laid-back North Shore, the region is much more of a thoroughfare than a destination unto itself. Few visitors make leeward O'ahu their first stop either. The land is dry and brown, and much of the region's population subsists at the lower end of the economic scale. Though the coast as a whole is a little rough around the edges, suburbanite Kapolei boasts a few family-friendly attractions and Disney's resort has caused a splash in Ko Olina. The intrepid traveler venturing further north will find undeveloped beaches and unvarnished communities. Cultural pride is alive here, as more Native Hawaiians live on the Wai'anae Coast than anyplace else island-wide. Near the island's tip at Ka'ena Point, habitation gives way to green-velvet-tufted mountains and rocky coastal ledges.

Ka'ena Point (p257) on the Waianae Coast
KARL LEHMANN / LONELY PLANET IMAGES ©

Central & Leeward O'ahu Itineraries

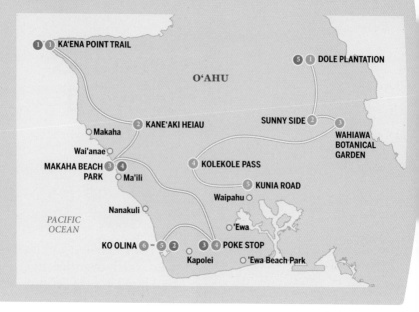

O'AHU

1 1 **KA'ENA POINT TRAIL**

5 1 **DOLE PLANTATION**

2 **KANE'AKI HEIAU**

SUNNY SIDE 2

3 **WAHIAWA BOTANICAL GARDEN**

○ **Makaha**

Wai'anae ○

MAKAHA BEACH PARK 3 4

○ **Ma'ili**

4 **KOLEKOLE PASS**

5 **KUNIA ROAD**

Waipahu ○

Nanakuli ○

PACIFIC OCEAN

○ **'Ewa**

KO OLINA 6 – 5 2

3 4 **POKE STOP**

Kapolei

○ **'Ewa Beach Park**

Half Day – Central

1 **Dole Plantation** (p237) Arrive early to enjoy the pineapple-shaped maze and gardens before the pavilion gets overrun with tourist-bus traffic in the afternoon. Kids love it and agriculturally inclined grown-ups are sure to find it interesting.

2 **Sunny Side** (p241) Hope you haven't filled yourself up on pineapple whip, because the next stop, Sunny Side diner, is home to wickedly delicious cream pies. Oh, and it has pretty good local food, too.

3 **Wahiawa Botanical Garden** (p239) Walk it all off with a wander through a free botanical garden; it's larger than you think and the chirping of the birds is a peaceful antidote to the pineapple craziness earlier in the day.

4 **Kolekole Pass** (p236) If you're in the mood for more hiking, detour onto the military reservation to see the picturesque main pass through the Wai'anae Range. Just don't touch Kolekole, the guardian spirit in the rock, or you may have bad luck.

5 **Kunia Road** (p236) A great way to finish the day, this drive heads down the region's most scenic road, providing good views. As you head toward the south coast the island opens up beneath you. Pineapple fields, blue sky and shimmering water fill your field of view – truly one of the best vistas on O'ahu.

➡ THIS LEG: 12 MILES

One Day – Leeward

1 Ka'ena Point Trail (p260) Avoid the unrelenting heat of the sun and hike along the dramatic northwestern point trail early in the day. You'll have fine views the entire way, with the blue ocean crashing against dark volcanic rocks on one side and the Wai'anae Range's craggy cliffs on the other. Bring a picnic breakfast.

2 Kane'aki Heiau (p256) Returning south, if you're not too tired, Kane'aki Heiau is a great detour in Makaha Valley. The reconstructed temple site provides real insight into what O'ahu was like before European settlement.

3 Makaha Beach Park (p255) Stop for a rest at this wide, sandy beach park. Summer swimming is good, and if you're a wave rider, the break here can be epic when the winter conditions are just right.

4 Poke Stop (p245) Need a snack after all that exertion? This Kapolei takeout has some of the island's freshest and most reasonable Hawaiian *poke* (bite-sized cubes of raw fish typically marinated in soy sauce, oil, chili peppers, green onions and seaweed).

5 Lagoons (p247) If you're staying at one of the Ko Olina resorts, check in. If not, head directly to the postcard-perfect Lagoons for a swim. The calm blue waters, palm-lined beaches and colorful fish along the rocks are everything paradise is meant to be.

6 Azul (p250) Cap off the day with a front-row seat to the sunset. Make sure you've booked ahead, or else you won't get one of the elegant outdoor tables at Azul, the Ihilani Resort's fine-dining restaurant. Linger over scrumptious paella while nature puts on a show.

● ●

➡ **THIS LEG: 21 MILES**

Central & Leeward O'ahu Highlights

1 Best Hike: Ka'ena Point Trail (p260) Explore the island's rugged coastline where seabirds frolic and monk seals sunbathe.

2 Best Vista: Lagoons at sunset (p247) A sunset perfectly framed by palm trees and reflected in the lagoon's glass-smooth water.

3 Best Seafood: Poke Stop (p245) Cubed raw fish never tasted as fresh as from this fisherman-owned deli.

4 Best Beach: Makaha Beach Park (p255) This beautifully arching beach is almost never crowded.

5 Best Family Activity: Pineapple Maze at Dole Plantation (p237) The world's largest maze is shaped like a pineapple at its core.

Pineapples for sale, O'ahu
RICHARD L'ANSON / LONELY PLANET IMAGES ©

Discover Central & Leeward O'ahu

CENTRAL O'AHU
Kunia Road (Hwy 750)

Three routes head north from the H-1 to Wahiawa, the region's central town. The H-2 Fwy is the fastest route. But if you're not in a hurry (and why would you be?), you should take the scenic, slightly longer Kunia Road through the center of the island. The drive starts in sprawling suburbia but soon breaks free into an expansive landscape with 360-degree views. As you gain altitude, views of Honolulu and Diamond Head emerge below you; be sure to pull off somewhere and look back at the landscape. Cornfields gradually give way to enormous pineapple plantations, all hemmed in by the mountains to the west.

If you want to see what a current-day plantation village looks like, turn west off Hwy 750 onto Kunia Dr, about 5.5 miles north of H-1. The little town of **Kunia**, in the midst of the pineapple fields, is home to the workers employed by Del Monte. Rows of gray-green wooden houses with corrugated-tin roofs stand on low stilts. Residents take pride in their little yards, with bougainvillea and birds of paradise adding a splash of brightness despite the wash of red dust that blows in from the surrounding pineapple farms.

The **Hawaii Country Club** (www.hawaiicc.com; 94-1211 Kunia Rd; 18 holes $80), a challenging par 72, is the longest-operating public golf course on the island – and one of the most reasonably priced.

The rural landscape continues until you pass Schofield Barracks Military Reservation. This massive army base is the largest on the island and is a hive of activity – it's not uncommon to be passed on the highway by camo-painted Humvees while Black Hawk choppers hover overhead. Onward from Wahiawa, two routes – rural Kaukonahua Rd (Hwy 803) and busy Kamehameha Hwy (Hwy 99) – lead through pineapple-plantation country to the North Shore.

Kolekole Pass

At 1724ft, Kolekole Pass occupies the main gap in the Wai'anae Range. Film buffs may recognize the landscape, as this is where

Hikers on the ridge of Kolekole Pass
JON OGATA / PHOTO RESOURCE HAWAII / ALAMY ©

WWII Japanese fighters passed through on their way to bomb Pearl Harbor in the classic war film *Tora! Tora! Tora!* (In reality, the planes flew along the inside, not through, the mountain range.)

The pass, on military property above Schofield Barracks, can be visited as long as the base isn't on military alert. Bring photo ID and your rental-car contract or proof of vehicle insurance. Access is granted by the security guards at Lyman Gate off Hwy 750, under a mile south of Hwy 750's intersection with Hwy 99. Follow Lyman Rd for 5 miles, passing a military infantry battle course, to reach the pass. Park on the left side of the road before reaching a security gate (without military ID, you can't keep driving over to the coast).

From a dirt parking pull-off, a short, steep hiking path with wooden steps leads for 10 minutes up to a fine view of the Wai'anae Coast. En route you'll pass a large, ribbed stone rumored to have been used by ancient Hawaiians for ritual sacrifices of fallen warrior *ali'i* (chiefs). In Hawaiian mythology, the stone is believed to be the embodiment of a woman named Kolekole, who took this form in order to become the perpetual guardian of the pass – keeping intruders from the coast from entering the sacred lands of Wahiawa. Local lore has it that if you touch the stone, bad luck may follow.

Wahiawa

POP 16,714

On first inspection Wahiawa, with its numerous fast-food joints and pawn shops, doesn't tend to inspire. It's just a residential town near Hawaii's largest army base. But the land around Wahiawa was long considered sacred; this was the summer home of royalty. The cooler temperatures made for serene living when the mercury climbed. Later the area was found to be well suited to agricultural purposes and plantations sprung up. Not much is left of the ancient temples and sites that once occupied the area, but you can pay tribute to the pineapple at Dole Plantation.

 Sights

DOLE PLANTATION   Gardens
(www.dole-plantation.com; 64-1550 Kamehameha Hwy; visitor center free; 🕙9am-5:30pm) Expect a sticky-sweet overdose of everything *ananas* (pineapples) when you walk into the plantation's visitor-center gift shop. After you've watched fruit-cutting

Tasty Tidbits

- In 1901 James Dole planted O'ahu's first pineapple patch in Wahiawa.
- Dole's original 12-acre Wahiawa plot has since grown to 8000 acres.
- Each acre of a pineapple field supports about 6500 plants.
- The commercial pineapple variety grown in Hawaii is smooth cayenne.
- It takes nearly two years for a pineapple plant to reach maturity.
- Each plant produces just two pineapples, one in its second year and one in its third year.
- Pineapples are harvested year-round, but the long, sunny days of summer produce the sweetest fruit.
- The average pineapple weighs 5lb.

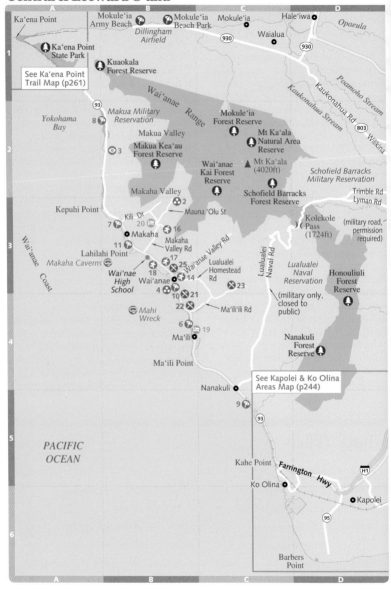

A map of Central & Leeward Oʻahu showing locations including Kaʻena Point, Mokuleʻia Army Beach, Mokuleʻia Beach Park, Mokuleʻia, Haleʻiwa, Dillingham Airfield, Waialua, Opaeula, Kaʻena Point State Park, Kuaokala Forest Reserve, Waiʻanae Range, Makua Military Reservation, Mokuleʻia Forest Reserve, Mt Kaʻala Natural Area Reserve, Kaukonahua Stream, Poamoho Stream, Wiliikina, Yokohama Bay, Makua Valley, Makua Keaʻau Forest Reserve, Waiʻanae Kai Forest Reserve, Mt Kaʻala (4020ft), Schofield Barracks Military Reservation, Trimble Rd, Lyman Rd, Makaha Valley, Schofield Barracks Forest Reserve, Kepuhi Point, Mauna ʻOlu St, Kolekole Pass (1724ft), military road permission required, Kili Dr, Makaha, Makaha Valley Rd, Lahilahi Point, Makaha Caverns, Lualualei Naval Rd, Lualualei Naval Reservation, Honouliuli Forest Reserve, Waiʻae Coast, Waiʻanae High School, Waiʻanae, Lualualei Homestead Rd, military only closed to public, Mahi Wreck, Maʻiliʻili Rd, Nanakuli Forest Reserve, Maʻili, Maʻili Point, Nanakuli, See Kapolei & Ko Olina Areas Map (p244), Kahe Point, Farrington Hwy, Ko Olina, Kapolei, Barbers Point, PACIFIC OCEAN. See Kaʻena Point Trail Map (p261).

demonstrations and bought your fill of pineapple potato chips and fruity trinkets, take your pineapple ice cream sundae outside for more educational fun. The small ornamental garden showcasing different species – including pink pineapple – is free; to see more, you'll have to pay to take the **Garden Tour** (adult/child $5/4.25). On the 20-minute **Pineapple Express** (adult/child $8/6) open-air train ride, you chug along through the upland scenery while more of Dole's story

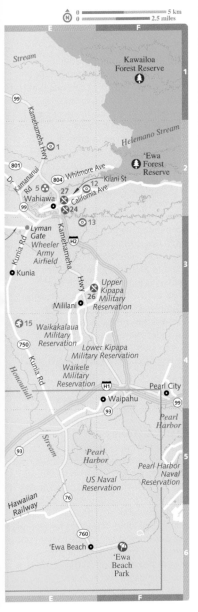

Central & Leeward O'ahu

the plantation's self-service grill restaurant, which is surprisingly well priced.

FREE WAHIAWA
BOTANICAL GARDEN Gardens
(1396 California Ave; ⊙9am-4pm) Started 80 years ago as an experiment by the local sugarcane farmers, the unstaffed 27-acre garden has evolved to showcase plants that thrive in a cool and moist climate. There's a mix of the manicured, with lawns and pruned ornamental plants, and the wild, with a gully of towering

is narrated. The **Pineapple Garden Maze** (adult/child $6/4) is meant purely as fun, as you find (or lose) your way among 14,000 Hawaiian plants on 1.5 miles of pathways. Guinness says it's the world's biggest. If you're hungry after that, you can stop at

Royal Birthstones

O'ahu's central uplands were once the domain of royalty, with the area so sacred that commoners were forbidden even to pass through. Kukaniloko, 0.75 miles north of Wahiawa, had unique importance as the *piko* (navel) or central point of the island, a portal to the spirit world. It was at this sacred spot that the divine welcomed chiefly offspring into the world. Consequently it was of great importance that a female *ali'i* (chief) reach the site in time for a ritual childbirth. Thirty-six chiefs were present to witness the event. The woman needed to lean properly against the backrest stone, named Kukaniloko, while giving birth for her child to be blessed by the gods. If all went according to plan, the child would be taken to a nearby temple and welcomed as a member of royalty. Those born here were of such a high lineage that chiefs from other islands would seek to enhance their prestige by marrying a Kukaniloko-born royal.

The freely accessible **Kukaniloko Birthstones State Historic Site** is not much to look at today, but it's one of only two documented birthing places in Hawaii (the other is on Kaua'i). The royal birth of Kapawa is thought to have been the first to take place here, but genealogical records are inexact, indicating only that his birth was sometime between 1100 and 1400. Experts estimate that the site dates to the 12th century. The stones were still in use during the time of Kamehameha I, who rushed up to Kukaniloko for the birth of his son Liholiho in 1797. Many of the petroglyphs you'll see on the rocks are of recent origin, but the eroded circular patterns are original. The original configuration would have been two rows of 18 stones for the 36 chiefs. Today more than 100 stones lie in a field 0.25 miles west of Kamehameha Hwy (Hwy 99), on the red dirt road opposite Whitmore Ave. Look for them past the pineapple field, among a stand of eucalyptus and coconut trees.

hardwoods, tropical ferns and forests of bamboo. Several paths, some wheelchair friendly, weave their way through the garden. It's located 1 mile east of Kamehameha Hwy (Hwy 99).

FREE **WAHIAWA FRESHWATER STATE RECREATION AREA** Park
(Walker St; ☺7am-6:45pm) Despite being just beyond Wahiawa center, this park has an unspoiled countryside feel, and the picnic tables with views of Lake Wilson are oh-so-inviting. Public fishing is allowed in the waters stocked with bass and other fish. Turn east off Kamehameha Hwy (Hwy 99) onto Avocado St at the south end of town and after 0.1 miles turn right onto Walker St.

HEALING STONES Spiritual
A powerful Hawaiian chief was buried in a field about a mile away from town. The stone thought to have marked the site was subsequently moved to the graveyard and in the 1920s people attributed healing powers to it. Thousands made pilgrimages there. A housing development and a Methodist church were later built, taking over the graveyard and leaving several stones sitting on the sidewalk. A small enclosure was constructed around them and a local Hindu group took over care of the objects, claiming a spiritual connection between Hawaiian and Indian beliefs. In 2010, the kahuna of the nearby Kukaniloko birthing stone site and his followers sought and received permission to move the stones to a more appropriate

and natively Hawaiian place. At present the stones are 'resting', with no word of when or if they will be made available to the public again.

Festivals & Events

WAHIAWA PINEAPPLE FESTIVAL Food
(www.wahiawatown.org) On a weekend in May everything pineapple is celebrated at this small-town community fair. A parade, music, food sales, games and demonstrations are all included.

Eating

Wahiawa is recommended as a day trip from, or a stopover en route to, the North Shore, which has better eating options. In town there are a number of small Asian eateries and fast-food joints.

SUNNY SIDE Local $
(1017 Kilani Ave; mains $4-9; ⏱7am-2pm) The last renovations may have been done a half-century ago (think plastic furniture and peeling paint), but all is forgotten when the local home-style breakfasts, such as the fried-rice special, arrive. Make sure you save some room for the wickedly delicious pies.

MAUI MIKE'S Fast Food $
(96 S Kamehameha Hwy; meals $5-9; ⏱11am-8:30pm) At Mike's you have the choice of chicken, chicken or chicken – all free range, fire roasted and super fresh. Even the Cajun-spiced fries are 100% natural and trans-fat free. There are a few tables inside, but most people grab and go.

 POKE STOP TOP CHOICE Seafood $
(95-814 Mehelua Pkwy, Mililani; dishes $4-10, meals $8-14; ⏱8am-8:30pm Mon-Sat, to 7pm Sun) The second location of this excellent fisherman-owned seafood outlet is 5 miles south of Wahiawa, off the H-2. Load up here for a picnic of incredible *poke* (bite-sized cubes of raw fish typically marinated in soy sauce, oil, chili peppers, green onions and seaweed) or a gourmet plate lunch of blackened fish and garlic shrimp. You can also eat in; this branch actually has seating.

LEEWARD O'AHU
Kapolei Area

Times they are a-changin' in the southwestern corner of O'ahu, once the stomping ground of sugarcane plantations and the US Navy. You'll still find a few run-down beach houses, but this is the fastest-growing residential area on the island today, with housing and super megamarts on the build. If you're looking

Pineapple Express Railway, Dole Plantation (p237)
GREG BALFOUR EVANS / ALAMY ©

for activities, scattered about are a water park, a go-kart track, a Sunday railroad and an old plantation living-history village. Plan ahead if you day-trip out or are stopping en route to the Ko Olina resorts; though it's less than a 10-mile drive from Honolulu, rush-hour traffic through established Waipahu, beachfront 'Ewa and suburban Kapolei is a real slow go.

 ## Beaches

'EWA BEACH PARK — Beach
(91-050 Fort Weaver Rd) A huge grassy lawn and sizable pavilion attract large Hawaiian families to this pleasant western beachfront on weekends. There's always a spare table or two for a picnic, and a good view of Honolulu from the spit of sand.

 ## Sights & Activities

HAWAII'S PLANTATION VILLAGE — Historic Site
(www.hawaiiplantationvillage.org; 94-695 Waipahu St, Waipahu; adult/child $13/5; ⊙ tours 10am-2pm Mon-Sat) Waipahu was one

Beach at Ko Olina (p246)

of O'ahu's last plantation towns, and its rusty sugar mill, which operated for almost a century until being shut down in 1995, looms on a knoll directly above this site. Though the village is definitely showing its age, you can still learn about the lives of plantation workers on the 90-minute tour. It starts on the hour and takes in buildings typical of an early-20th-century plantation: a Chinese cookhouse, a Japanese shrine and replicated homes of the seven ethnic groups – Hawaiian, Japanese, Chinese, Korean, Portuguese, Puerto Rican and Filipino – that worked the fields. There's also a small museum on-site. To get there by car from Honolulu, take the H-1 Fwy to exit 7, turn left onto Paiwa St, then right onto Waipahu St, continuing past the sugar mill and turning left into the complex.

HAWAIIAN RAILWAY — Historic Site
(www.hawaiianrailway.com; 91-1001 Renton Rd, 'Ewa; adult/child $12/8; ⊙1pm & 3pm Sun) For half a century from 1890 to 1940 a railroad carried sugarcane and passengers from Honolulu all the way around the coast through to Kahuku. The railway closed and the tracks were torn up after

DOUGLAS PEEBLES PHOTOGRAPHY / ALAMY ©

Homeless in Paradise

Living on the beach sounds like paradise, right? Even if you have no other choice? Estimates based on a late-2011 point-in-time survey by the government indicate that at least 4200 homeless people live on O'ahu. There are shelters and temporary encampments all over the island, but nearly 40% of that number reside on the Wai'anae Coast. Locals say this is because there are fewer rich residents and tourists here, and there's a not-in-my-backyard mentality on other parts of the island.

The homeless issue is a complex one. Though you might imagine many have traveled here from stateside to enjoy the warmth, the fact is that most of the disenfranchised are local. The skyrocketing housing prices during the real-estate bubble, and woefully inadequate public housing, forced many out into their cars or camps. But the homeless numbers remained relatively steady during the subsequent recession. Contrary to the lone-male stereotype, the homeless of the Wai'anae Coast overwhelmingly live in family groups. Many of those groups have at least one member who is employed. There are also some with drug-addiction problems, some with mental illness, and a few who choose this lifestyle, in the mix.

If citing a reason for the high number of homeless on the coast is challenging, coming up with a solution is even more problematic. In the past, periodic 'clean-ups' in both Waikiki and Wai'anae have forced the homeless to move from concentrations along beach parks and public rights-of-way. But adequate assistance has not always been provided during these actions and officials have been accused of caring more about appearances during international conferences than about the people.

In the past few years, several new homeless shelters have opened up on the Wai'anae Coast. The governor revealed an initiative that included a short-term, 90-day action plan and a longer-term goal of ending homelessness in Hawaii by 2021. To date numerous agencies are involved, but no new monies have been allocated for the project. Mismanagement of public housing, resulting in several class-action lawsuits, might threaten the future availability of federal funds. Only time will tell whether good intentions will lead to constructive solutions in this corner of paradise.

WWII and the automobile boom in Hawaii. Thanks to the historical society, trains run again, for pleasure, along a 6.5-mile segment of restored track between 'Ewa and Nanakuli. The 90-minute round-trip chugs along through sometimes pastoral, sometimes industrial scenery. Displayed in the abandoned-looking yard is the coal engine that pulled the first O'ahu Railway and Land Company (OR&L) train in 1889. To get here, take exit 5A off the H-1, drive south 2.5 miles on Fort Weaver Rd and turn right at the 7-Eleven onto Renton Rd.

WET 'N' WILD HAWAII Amusement Park
(http://hawaii.mywetnwild.com; 400 Farrington Hwy, Kapolei; adult/child $42/32; ☺10:30am-3:30pm Mon, Thu & Fri, to 4pm Sat & Sun) Every temperament from timid to thrill-seeking is served at this 25-acre water park. Float on a lazy river or brave a seven-story waterslide and the football-field-sized wave pool with bodysurfable rides. Such splashy fun doesn't come cheap; some activities and parking ($10) are extra. Bus 40 takes 1¼ hours to get here from the Ala

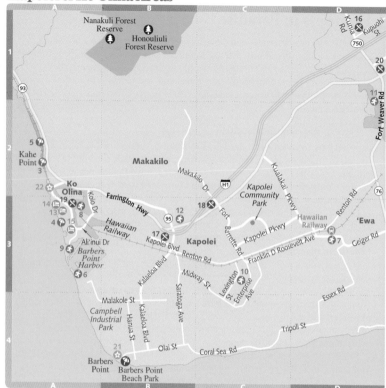

Moana Center in Honolulu; it runs every half hour between 8:30am and 6:30pm.

PODIUM RACEWAY Go-Kart Racing
(www.podiumraceway.com; 95-1085 Lexington St, Kapolei; per race adult/child $25/20; ⏱11am-9pm Sun-Thu, 10am-midnight Fri & Sat) Podium's adult go-karts reach speeds of up to 45mph, so this indoor track is good for adrenaline junkies as well as a rainy-day diversion.

WEST LOCH MUNICIPAL GOLF COURSE Golf
(☏675-6076; 91-1126 Okupe St, 'Ewa Beach; 18 holes $60) There are great ocean views throughout and nice wide fairways to keep the ball in play at this casual course. Club rental is not available.

HONOULIULI FOREST RESERVE Hiking
The land of this reserve once belonged to Hawaiian royalty and was named Honouliuli – meaning 'dark harbor' – for the dark, fertile lands that stretch from the waters of Pearl Harbor to the summit of the Wai'anae Range. More than 70 rare and endangered plant and animal species live here. An ownership change has closed trails indefinitely; check the Na Ala Hele website (http://hawaiitrails.ehawaii.gov) to see if any have since reopened.

Tours

HAWAII NAUTICAL Boat
(☏234-7245; www.hawaiinautical.com; Barbers Point Harbor, 91-607 Malakole St, Kapolei; tours adult $79-155, child $59-125) Set sail on a

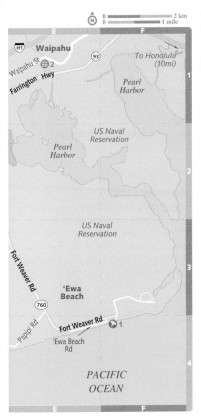

deluxe catamaran to look at marine life and go snorkeling on the southwest coast. You can either upgrade to snuba, or opt for a scuba dive trip, but don't expect to be frolicking with Flipper; this is a Dolphin Smart–certified boat that cares about all of the ocean's inhabitants. There are shuttle rides available from both Ko Olina and Waikiki.

Sleeping

The Kapolei area is best covered as a day trip from Honolulu, or from the Ko Olina resorts, 4 miles to the west. Large rental houses are available from **VRBO** (www.vrbo.com), **Home Away** (www.homeaway.com) and others. For more on island rentals, see p318.

Eating

Along Farrington Hwy there are numerous hole-in-the-wall Asian food eateries, strip-mall restaurants and supermarkets.

TOP CHOICE ⊘ **POKE STOP**   Seafood **$**
(Waipahu Town Center, 94-050 Farrington Hwy, Waipahu; dishes $5-11, meals $8-14; ⊘8am-7pm

The Best...
Family Activities

1 Ko Olina Lagoons (p252)

2 Poka'i Bay Beach Park (p252)

3 Dole Plantation (p237)

4 Wet 'n' Wild Hawaii (p243)

5 Hawaiian Railway (p242)

6 Makahiki character breakfast (p250)

Mon-Sat, 9am-4pm Sun) Tucked into a sleepy corner of a nondescript minimall, you'll find some of the freshest raw fish on O'ahu. We love the deconstructed sushi bowls and more than 20 kinds of poke – the sweet onion 'ahi tuna and furikake salmon will leave you salivating. It's also hard to pass up the spicy eggplant fries and tempura-dipped spicy tuna rolls. There are a couple of tables to sit at out front, but most people take the fish and run – you can't get a better picnic lunch.

AUNTIE PASTO'S　　　　　　Italian $$
(Kunia Shopping Center, 94-673 Kupuohi St, Waipahu; lunches $8-10, dinner mains $9-17; ⏱11am-9pm) Have a large family in tow? The lively atmosphere, cheery red-checkered tablecloths and large variety of made-from-scratch Italian food here is sure to satisfy. The shopping center is just off the H-1 Fwy, 5A exit.

DOWN TO EARTH　　　　Health Food $
(4460 Kapolei Blvd; meals $5-10; ⏱7:30am-10pm; 🖉) A giant outlet of the island's favorite health-food store. Choose from the hot vegetarian buffet or have a sandwich or smoothie made to order before you browse the aisles for healthy snacks.

KAPOLEI KOREAN BARBECUE　　　　　　Korean $$
(590 Farrington Hwy, Kapolei; dishes $10-15; ⏱10am-9pm) Good-sized portions of Korean standards like marinated galbi (short ribs) and beef barbecue draw kudos from readers.

 Entertainment

Transportation from Honolulu is available for both of these luau (Hawaiian feasts).

GERMAINE'S LUAU　　　　　　Luau
(📞949-6626, 800-367-5655; www.germaines-luau.com; 91-119 Olai St, Kapolei; adult/child $72/52; ⏱6-9pm) On the beach near industrial Barber's Point, Germaine's has the most local, backyard feel of all the island's luau. You still get a Hawaiian buffet, music and dance, but it's more kitschy than slick, and man, do the mai tais flow. Check www.hawaiidiscount.com for reduced-price tickets.

PARADISE COVE　　　　　　Luau
(📞842-5911, 800-775-2683; www.paradisecove.com; 92-1089 Ali'inui Dr, Kapolei; adult/child $88/66; ⏱5-9pm; 👶) Pre-buffet pig-out, activities include Hawaiian games and a hukilau (net-fishing party), adding an interactivity that kids love at this luau. The dinner show features dances from across Polynesia.

Ko Olina

Four perfect, sunset-facing coves with palm-lined sand and sea as calm as bathwater...is this too good to be true? Well, yes and no. Before this resort went under development, a key feature was missing – the beaches. After a bit of lateral thinking, a lot of construction and a couple of thousand tons of imported soft white sand – voilà, the lagoons were born. The JW Marriott Ihilani and luxury condominiums originally anchored the complex, but the recent addition of Disney's Aulani, its first Hawaiian resort, has made quite a splash. By law, the waterfront must be accessible to the public, and these human-made beaches are well worth a visit whether or not you're staying at the hotels. Water sports, golf, a marina and restaurants all add to the upscale attraction. Ko Olina is 25 miles (about 35 minutes) from downtown Honolulu, off the southern side of the Farrington Hwy near Kapolei.

 Beaches

LAGOONS
Beach

(off Ali'inui Dr) A wide, paved recreational path connects all four lagoons, inviting a lazy stroll from beach to beach. Extremely limited free public beach-access parking can be found at each. The largest and most elaborately landscaped and serviced lagoon fronts the Marriott Ihilani and Disney Aulani. In addition to the restaurant facilities, both resorts offer daytime beach-equipment rentals for snorkeling gear and such. The rocks that block the open sea from the lagoons are great places for spotting fish. Keep an eye on the kiddies, though – the current picks up near the opening. At dusk a Disney outrigger canoe enters the cove as a conch shell sounds the end to the day. The nearest free parking is north of the Ihilani. The hotels each charge $30 a day for valet parking but will validate if you spend at least an equivalent amount at one of their restaurants – easy to do.

The southern two lagoons are probably our favorite. Though they're smaller, the water and the sand are just as beautiful, and there are fewer people to contend with. The nearby free public parking is just before the marina at the end of the drive. Rent snorkels and beach gear at the lagoon adjacent to the Marriott Ko Olina Beach

Club. The rocks along the sides of the lagoons are the preferred location for spotting marine life.

 Activities

Though most facilities are reserved for guests, hotel grounds are open to the public during the daytime. Just wandering around the lush landscaping of Aulani or checking out the saltwater marine-life pools at Ihilani can be interesting. Both have incredible spas and activities desks that book boat tours and water sports.

KO OLINA MARINA
Water Sports

(☎ 853-4300; www.koolinamarina.com; 92-100 Ali'inui Dr; ⊙ 6am-6pm) The marina will hook you up with snorkeling tours, sunset cruises, whale watching (December through March) and sport-fishing charters. A five-hour boat tour ranges from $120 to $150 per person.

Lagoons, Ko Olina
CHRIS ROSE / ALAMY ©

MARRIOTT KO OLINA BEACH CLUB
ARTS & CRAFTS   Arts Center

(92-161 Waipehe Pl) The beach club hosts numerous art classes and craft shows that are open to the public. **Nalani Gourd** (www.hawaiianquilting.net; class $5, supplies $35; ☉10am-2pm Tue) teaches traditional Hawaiian quilting on an ongoing basis; for more see p249. **Donald Hall** (www. hawaiiartgallery.net; class $30; ☉noon-3:30pm Wed) helps you learn to capture the local beauty in paint. **Artfest** (www.hotcrafts.net; ☉9am-4pm Wed & Fri) hosts hand-crafters and artists selling their wares in a poolside courtyard. Note that valet parking at the resort is only $7.

KO OLINA GOLF CLUB   Golf

(📞676-5300; www.koolinagolf.com; 92-1220 Ali'inui Dr; 18 holes $189) Both the LPGA and the senior PGA tour have held tournaments at this highly acclaimed course and driving range. Mere golf mortals can also enjoy the landscaped oasis of green among the barren brown hills. Check online for special rates and packages; transportation from Waikiki available.

Tours

HAWAII NAUTICAL   Boat

(📞234-7245; www.hawaiinautical.com) In addition to offering cocktail cruises and snorkeling and snuba boat tours (see p244), Hawaii Nautical also has a catamaran trip reserved solely for Disney Aulani guests. The four-hour trip (adult/child $155/125) departs from the resort and takes in much of the coast, stopping for snorkeling and to view marine life. Also ask about the ferry service from Ko Olina to Waikiki.

Sleeping

Vacation rentals around Ko Olina are generally not small studios; they include villas, multibedroom beachfront condos, and golf-course homes. A two-bedroom place runs between $250 and $500, three bedrooms will set you back $400 to $800 a night. Check **VRBO** (www.vrbo.com) and other agencies (for more, see p318).

Aulani, Disney Resort & Spa, Ko Olina

DOUGLAS PEEBLES PHOTOGRAPHY / ALAMY

TOP CHOICE AULANI, DISNEY
RESORT & SPA
Resort $$$

(☎714-520-7001; http://resorts.disney.go.com/
aulani-hawaii-resort; 92-1185 Ali'inui Dr; r $450-
650; ✳ @ 🛜 🏊 👪) The daily activity list
at Aulani reads like a book. Tone up at
beach-body boot camp, take a Hawaiian
craft class or hula the day away. All the
while the little ones will be listening to
Hawaiian tales at Aunty's House kids club
and the older kids will be off on a treasure
hunt or tasting a healthy treat at the
teen spa. In the evening you can attend a
free Hawaiian dance and music revue, or
listen to Hawaiian music at a lounge, as
the teens and tweens karaoke. That's not
to mention the stingray interactive experi-
ence, character meet-and-greets, the
water-park-like pools – and oh, yeah, the
beach. Good thing there's so much to do.
Maybe you won't notice that the Hawaii-
inspired, casually luxe and characteristi-
cally understated (no giant Mickeys here)
accommodations are a full 35 minutes
from Honolulu – without traffic.

JW MARRIOTT
IHILANI RESORT & SPA
Resort $$$

(☎679-0079, 800-952-2027; www.ihilani.com;
92-1001 Olani St; r $350-600; ✳ @ 🛜 🏊)
Right on the beach, this glistening white
property is palatial, expansive and architecturally pleasing to the eye. It's popular
with those wanting to avoid the Waikiki
scene but still have all the trappings of
top-end luxury. If it looks a little familiar,
that's because Hollywood has even
checked in here – the Ihilani starred in the
surfer-girl movie *Blue Crush* as the hotel
in which the girls worked.

MARRIOTT KO OLINA
BEACH CLUB
Resort $$$

(☎679-4700, 888 236 2427; www.marriott.
com; 92-161 Waipahe Pl; 1br apt $220-370;
✳ @ 🛜 🏊) On one of the smaller
lagoons, this vacation-club property
is a relative bargain compared to its
neighbors. Plus you get a full kitchen in
every room, so you can cook your own
meals, and there are numerous free daily
activities for all ages.

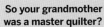

Local Knowledge

NAME: NALANI GOURD

OCCUPATION: QUILT
DESIGNER & ARTIST

RESIDENCE: PEARL CITY

So your grandmother was a master quilter?
Yes, my grandmother was late master
quilter Aunty Debbie Kakalia. She was
and still is well respected and known both
locally and internationally. I'm continuing
her legacy by teaching her techniques,
styles and beliefs.

What makes a quilt Hawaiian? Quilting
was introduced to the women of Hawaii in
the 1820s by visiting missionary women,
and from these teachings the women
adapted their own designs. What makes
a Hawaiian quilt Hawaiian are the designs
and the way the top is cut on a 1/8 fold like
a snowflake.

Is it possible to buy an island-made
quilt? Honestly, those of us that do quilt
very rarely sell our work. Instead, we choose
to share our art by educating people about
its history and teaching them to make their
own. Today, many Hawaiian quilts are hand-
sewn in the Philippines and China by expert
quilters so that the original designs can
be enjoyed and offered to the public at a
reasonable cost.

What if someone wants to take a class?
Well, I teach at the Ko Olina Beach Club
(p248) and other hotels offer classes. Also,
the Bishop Museum (p54), 'Iolani Palace
(p37) and Mission Houses Museum (p39)
sometimes sponsor classes.

Where is the best place on the island
to buy fabric? There used to be a lot
more fabric stores than there are now.
Fabric Mart has a good selection of
tropical colors and prints; I like the 'Aiea
store (p149) best for their service.

Eating

Though both the Ihilani and Aulani have dining outlets, don't expect cheap eats at a resort. There are a few more reasonable places in the **Ko Olina Station shopping center** (92-1047 Olani St), including a small market. Otherwise, to save costs drive a few miles east to Kapolei. A free shuttle scoots you between all places in Ko Olina proper.

AZUL
Seafood $$$

(679-3166; JW Marriott Ihilani Resort & Spa, 92-1001 Olani St; mains $28-42; 6-9pm Tue-Sat) Other resorts have upscale dining too, but Azul's eclectic mix of surf and turf and emphasis on organics put it in a class of its own. Sit at tables covered by crisp white linen in a palm-shaded courtyard or among the intimate luxury of dark wood and Hawaiian art inside. Be sure to reserve ahead and put on your best aloha shirt.

MAKAHIKI
Fusion $$$

(520-7001; Aulani, 92-1185 Ali'inui Dr; breakfast adult/child $27/14, dinner $43/21; 7-11am & 5-10pm;) A bountiful buffet indeed: at dinner you can try a comprehensive array of multicultural island dishes – *laulau* fish, *kalua* pork, fresh sushi and sashimi, Chinese noodles, Portuguese sausage and sweet rolls – and for breakfast you have all the Western and Asian favorites. Three mornings a week (Wednesday, Saturday and Sunday), tropically clad Disney characters join the fun. Though this costs $5 more per person, reservations are snapped up a month in advance.

KO OLINA HAWAIIAN BAR-B-QUE
Local $

(Ko Olina Station, 92-1047 Olina St; meals $8-15; 9am-9pm) Had too many $8 hot dogs? Opt instead for hearty plate lunches of *mochiko* (batter-fried) chicken, BBQ short ribs, teriyaki beef, pork *katsu* (deep-fried cutlets) and much more. All can be served with brown rice and green salad.

Left: Traditional Hawaiian *poke* with macadamia nuts and *limu* (seaweed); **Below:** Firedancer performing at a luau, Paradise Cove (p246)

(LEFT) ANN CECIL /LONELY PLANET IMAGES ©; (BELOW) LAWRENCE WORCESTER /LONELY PLANET IMAGES ©

ROY'S KO OLINA
Hawaii Regional **$$$**

(☎ 676-7697; Ko Olina Golf Club, 92-1220 Ali'inui Dr; lunches $14; dinner mains $18; ⏰ 11am-2pm & 5:30-9:30pm) Roy's serves at the casual '19th hole' of the area golf club. His famous Hawaii-regional food fusion is excellent, as always; don't miss the Ko Olina–specific items like *paniolo* (Hawaiian cowboy) pot roast.

TWO SCOOPS
ICE CREAM PARLOR
Desserts **$**

(Ko Olina Station, 92-1047 Olani St; items $5; ⏰ 11am-9pm) Pretty and pink, the decorations at this little ice cream and coffee shop are as sweet as the desserts. Try the locally made Hawaiian hot fudge.

 ## Entertainment

Live music is occasionally staged at the hotel bars of both Disney's Aulani and Marriott's Ihilani.

FIA FIA SHOW
Luau

(☎ 679-4728; www.fiafiashow.com; Ko Olina Beach Club, 92-161 Waipahe Pl; adult/child $90/45; ⏰ 5pm Tue; 👪) Though it's one of the least-known island luau, Fia Fia is among the most entertaining. The Polynesian performances lean heavily toward the Samoan, because that's where the hilarious Chief Sielu Avea, who MCs the evening, hails from. Kids love the preshow games and the fire and knife dances. Buffet's not bad either. Reserve in advance.

Kahe

If few nonislanders make it to southwest O'ahu, fewer still round the corner and follow the Farrington Hwy (Hwy 93) north up the Wai'anae Coast. Touring around here is best done by car and your first potential stop is Kahe. A hulking power plant complete with towering smoke stacks isn't the best neighbor for a beach – but, as they

251

say, you can't pick your neighbors. **Kahe Point Beach Park** (Map p244) is a rocky point that's popular with snorkelers and anglers. There are, however, great coastal views, as well as running water, picnic tables and restrooms. Just north, **Tracks Beach Park** (Map p244), also sometimes called Hawaiian Electric Beach, has sandy shores that are good for swimming in the summer and great for surfing in the winter. Its name stems from the train-transported beachgoers who frequented the beach prior to WWII.

Nanakuli

It's hard to find much that qualifies as aesthetic in this seaside town that's essentially a strip of fast-food joints along the highway. There's so little opportunity to experience the culture, you probably won't even realize there's a Hawaiian Homesteads settlement here with one of the largest native populations on O'ahu.

Nanakuli Beach Park lines the town in a broad, sandy stretch that offers swimming, snorkeling and diving during the summer. In winter, high surf can create rip currents and dangerous shorebreaks. The park has a playground, sports fields and beach facilities. To get to the beach park, turn *makai* (seaward) at the traffic lights on Nanakuli Ave.

Ma'ili

The town of Ma'ili doesn't have all that much to see beyond **Ma'ili Beach Park**. This attractive beach has the distinction of being one of the longest stretches of snow-white sand on the island. The grassy park that sits adjacent to the beach is popular with families having weekend barbecues and island-style parties. Like other places on the Wai'anae Coast, the water conditions are often treacherous in winter but usually calm enough for swimming in summer. The park has a lifeguard station, a playground, beach facilities and a few coconut palms that provide limited shade.

Walk out the patio door and right onto the beach if you stay at a one-bedroom **Ma'ili Cove** (📞 696-4186; www.mailicove.org; 87-561 Farrington Hwy; 1br per week $675; 🛜 ❄️)

condo. The two condos for rent are clean, comfortable and eclectically decorated. There are a barbecue available for your use. One-week minimum stays.

Wai'anae
POP 10,525

The coast's hub for everyday needs, Wai'anae has more grocery stores and eateries than anyplace else leeward. A nice family beach, a large harbor popular with nautical folks, and an ancient heiau (stone temple) make this a good stop. The town is a little rough around the edges, but new shops and more services keep emerging.

 Beaches

TOP CHOICE POKA'I BAY BEACH PARK   Beach
Protected by Kane'ilio Point and a long breakwater, the beach is a real beauty. Waves seldom break inside the bay, and the sandy beach slopes gently. Calm, year-round swimming conditions make it perfect for children, as evidenced by the number of Hawaiian families here on weekends. For fair snorkeling, paddle out to the breakwater, where fish gather around the rocks. The bay is also used by local canoe clubs, and you can watch them if you happen by on the right afternoon. The park has showers, restrooms and picnic tables, and a lifeguard is on duty daily. To get here, turn seaward off Farrington Hwy onto Lualualei Homestead Rd at the traffic light immediately north of the Wai'anae post office.

 Sights & Activities

FREE KU'ILIOLOA
HEIAU   Archeological Site
Along the south side of the bay, Kane'ilio Point is the site of a terraced-stone platform temple, partly destroyed by the army during WWII, then later reconstructed by local conservationists. The site was used in part as a teaching and blessing place for navigation and fishing. Wai'anae was one of the last places on

the island to accept Christianity, and the heiau continued to be used after the *kapu* (taboo) system was overthrown in 1819. Today the area around the terraces still affords superb coastal views all the way to Makaha in the north. If the waves aren't crashing, look for little tide pools harboring miniature marine life at the foot of the heiau. To get here start at the parking lot of Poka'i Bay Beach Park, walk straight across the lawn with the outrigger canoes at your right and take the path half a mile out to the point.

WILD SIDE SPECIALTY
TOURS Dolphin, Whale Watching

(306-7273; http://sailhawaii.com; Wai'anae Small Boat Harbor, 85-371 Farrington Hwy; 3hr tour $85-195) Recognized by the Hawaiian Ecotourism Association, Wild Side Tours caters to the naturalist in you. For respectful snorkeling, take a morning wildlife cruise and stay near the shore or go further to less-frequented sites with the Best of the West excursion for more dolphin and whale watching. The junior-explorer trip focuses on those aged seven years and up who want an oceanful of fun and learning.

OCEAN CONCEPTS Diving
(800-808-3483; www.oceanconcepts.com; Wai'anae Small Boat Harbor, 85-371 Farrington Hwy; trips from $135) Wai'anae's full-service diving outfitter runs excursions along the Leeward Coast. Sites include the Makaha Caverns and 29 Down, an airplane wreck turned artificial reef. There are lessons available, too.

PARADISE ISLE Water Sports
(695-8866; 84-1170 Farrington Hwy; rentals per day $15-50; 9am-5pm) Across from the beach, this island shop rents all things water-sport related: surfboards, stand-up paddling setups, kayaks, snorkels...plus it sells local crafts and dispenses free area information.

HALE NANU SURF
& BIKE Water Sports, Bicycle Rental

(www.halenalu.com; 85-876 Farrington Hwy; rentals per day $15-35; 10am-6pm Mon-Sat) This sports shop sells and rents mountain bikes, surfboards, snorkel sets and such.

DOLPHIN
EXCURSIONS Dolphin, Whale Watching

(239-5579; www.dolphinexcursions.com; Wai'anae Small Boat Harbor, 85-371 Farrington

Sunset on the Ko Olina coast (p246)

TIM MCDOW / ALAMY ©

Surfer at Makaha Beach Park

DAVID R FRAZIER PHOTOLIBRARY /ALAMY ©

Hwy; 3hr tour adult/child $110/85) Snorkeling and spinner-dolphin-watching cruises; whale watching seasonally.

 Eating

Wai'anae has numerous fast-food outlets, both chains and walk-up burger and barbecue joints. All are along Farrington Hwy.

KAHUMANA CAFE Health Food $$
(http://kahumanafarms.org; 86-660 Lualualei Homestead Rd; meals $10-14; ⏱11:30am-2pm & 6-7:30pm Tue-Sat; ✍) Way off the beaten track, this organic farm's cafe inhabits a cool, tranquil hardwood-floored dining room with green-field views. Fork into fresh daily specials, bountiful salads and sandwiches or macadamia-nut pesto pasta with fish or fowl. Don't forget the homemade *liliko'i* (passion fruit) and mango cheesecake. The cafe is about 2 miles inland from Farrington Hwy via Ma'ili'ili Rd.

HANNARA Local $
(86-078 Farrington Hwy; meals $5-12; ⏱6am-8pm Mon-Sat) Locals swear by the banana pancakes, hamburger steak, chicken *kalbi*

(grilled Korean-style) and other island faves. The interior is plain, but you could also take a *bentō* box to the beach park.

KA'AHA'AINA CAFÉ Local $
(82-260 Farrington Hwy; meals $4-9; ⏱6:30am-1:30pm Mon-Fri; 🕾) The oceanfront location on the grounds of a local health clinic has pluses and minuses. But the local-style plate lunches and seafood are sure priced right.

ONO POLYNESIAN MARKET Local $
(85-998 Farrington Hwy; dishes $3-9; ⏱7am-10pm) A ramshackle little market dishing up pan-Polynesian takeout treats such as Samoan *palusami* (corned beef wrapped in taro leaves and slow-cooked in coconut milk) as well as regular supplies.

WAI'ANAE ICE HOUSE American $
(85-371 Farrington Hwy; dishes $4-8; ⏱4am-2pm) Simple sandwiches and stews available at the Wai'anae Small Boat Harbor.

🛏 Sleeping

VRBO (www.vrbo.com) and other vacation-rental consolidators list few options in

Wai'anae. Most of the condo rentals on this coast are a few miles further north in Makaha. Otherwise the closest lodgings are the Ko Olina resorts, 10 miles (20 minutes) south.

Information

Wai'anae has several banks and ATMs along the main drag, Farrington Hwy.

Makaha
POP 7750

Big-wave surfing actually got its start here in the 1950s, when Makaha hosted Hawaii's first international surfing competition. Not that you would know it, as the oceanfront highway is blissfully free from the gawking tourists of the North Shore. It is worth a visit for the beautiful sandy beach alone – and the incredible sea views from the area condos. But be sure to turn inland toward the rugged interior for a look at O'ahu's best-restored heiau. Most services are 3 miles south in Wai'anae. As in other places along this coast, Makaha has its rugged edges. North out of town, the tree-lined beaches are home to a large homeless community.

 Beaches

MAKAHA BEACH PARK Beach

In December 1969 legendary surfer Greg Noll rode what was thought to be the biggest wave in surfing history (to that point) at Makaha. Speculation still rages as to exactly how big the monster wave was, but it is commonly accepted that it was at least a 30ft face – a mountain of water for the era. The long point break at Makaha still produces waves that inspire big-wave surfers. Winter brings big swells that preclude swimming – the golden sand, however, is a permanent feature. The beautifully arching beach invites you to spread out your towel and spend the day. Except for weekends and big surf days, you'll likely have the place to yourself. Snorkeling is good during the calmer summer months. There are showers and restrooms, and lifeguards on duty daily.

TURTLE BEACH Beach

Another beautiful, mostly deserted half-mile of sand sits behind the Hawaiian Princess and Makaha Beach Cabana condos. If you're lucky, you may see green sea turtles in the surf early mornings or late evenings. There are sea caves

Central & Leeward Farmers Markets

Farmers markets in central and leeward O'ahu are short-and-sweet affairs, sometimes lasting less than an hour. But they can be great, especially in areas where eating options are limited. Most are People's Open Markets; for more, log on to www.co.honolulu.hi.us/parks/programs/pom.

Wahiawa District Park (cnr N Cane & California Aves, Wahiawa; ⊙10-11am Tue)

'Ewa Beach Park (91-955 North Rd, 'Ewa Beach; ⊙9-10am Fri)

Kapolei Community Park (91-1049 Kama'aha Loop, Kapolei; ⊙7-8:30am Sun)

Wai'anae Farmers' Market (Wai'anae High School; 85-251 Farrington Highway; ⊙9:30-11am Sat)

Poka'i Bay Beach Park (85-037 Poka'i Bay Rd, Wai'anae; ⊙11-11:45am Fri)

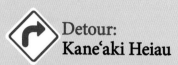

Detour:
Kane'aki Heiau

Turn inland from Farrington Hwy and the road skirts up along scalloped cliffs into Makaha Valley. Here, midway between the valley's wet, forested uplands and the dry, coastal lowlands, lies one of Hawaii's best-restored ancient sites. Despite the fact that the location today is within a gated community, few other places come close to **Kane'aki Heiau** (Mauna Olu Estates; admission free; ⏰10am-2pm Tue-Sun) in providing a glimpse into pre-Western-contact Hawaiian culture.

Constructed of stacked basalt rocks, the heiau has two terraced platforms and six enclosed courtyards. Its restoration, undertaken by Honolulu's Bishop Museum in the 1970s, took years to complete. The site was reconstructed using ohia logs hand hewn with adzes and thatch made from native *pili* grass gathered on the Big Island. Two prayer towers, a taboo house, a drum house, an altar and several deity images were built by Hawaiian craftspeople using traditional techniques and materials. Because it's on restricted land, very few tourists make it up this way, and that adds a quiet, untouched element to it all.

Kane'aki Heiau dates back to 1545 and was originally dedicated to Lono, the god of agriculture. As with many Hawaiian temples, over time it went through transformations in both its physical structure and its use. In the final phase it was rededicated as a *luakini* (a temple where human sacrifices occurred, dedicated to the war god Ku). It is thought that Kamehameha the Great used Kane'aki Heiau as a place of worship after he conquered O'ahu. The heiau remained in use until his death in 1819 however, the overthrow of traditional practices introduced by Kamehameha's successors resulted in the abandonment of this, and other temple sites. Although many of Hawaii's more accessible coastal heiau were dismantled and their stones used to build cattle fences and other structures, Kane'aki Heiau was protected by its remoteness and so survived largely intact.

To get to the heiau, turn inland from the Farrington Hwy onto Kili Dr. At the Makaha Valley Towers condominium complex turn right onto Huipu Dr. A half-mile down, make a left onto Mauna Olu St, which leads 1 mile to the Mauna Olu Estates community gate. You'll need to show your rental-vehicle contract or proof of insurance and driver's license at the gatehouse, so be sure to bring them. Note the limited access hours. The guard will provide a free pass and direct you to the heiau parking lot from there.

and rocks they use as a cleaning station offshore. Though the area is protected somewhat by Lahilahi Point to the south, be cautious if you have kids – the beach's sandy bottom has a quick and steep drop-off.

 **Activities**

DIVE SITES
Diving

Out where the waves break furthest offshore are the popular leeward diving spots. Mahaka Caverns has underwater caves at depths of 30ft to 50ft. Divers will delight in going down onto the wreck of the *Mahi,* a classic dive. And there are other underwater formations in the area. Ocean Concepts in Wai'anae (p253) leads dive trips.

MAKAHA VALLEY COUNTRY CLUB Golf (📞695-7111 www.makahavalleycc.com; 84-627 Makaha Valley Rd; 18 holes $85) A relaxed course tucked right up against the Wai'anae Range with great ocean views. The wide fairways and sand-encrusted greens get popular on the weekends. Driving range, club rental available.

Sleeping

Makaha has the majority of the vacation rentals available on the Wai'anae Coast; check out **VRBO** (www.vrbo.com), **Home Away** (www.homeaway.com), **Airbnb** (www.airbnb.com) and others (for more on rentals, see p318). Gated beachside condos are the most popular (one bedrooms run from $100 to $200, two bedrooms from $250 to $350). You should be wary of house rentals as they could be in sketchier neighborhoods. Three-night minimums are usually required.

MAKAHA RESORT & SPA Resort $$ (📞695-9544, www.makaharesort. net; 84-626 Makaha Valley Rd) At the time of research, Makaha Resort – a full-service, mid-valley golf resort – had closed indefinitely for renovation. Check to see about reopening.

AFFORDABLE OCEANFRONT CONDOS
Vacation Rental $$
(www.hawaiibeachcondos. com) Rents condos at both Makaha Cabanas

and Hawaiian Princess on Turtle Beach; 30-day bookings available at lower-lying Makaha Surfside.

DISCOUNT HAWAIIAN RENTALS Vacation Rental $$ (📞390-0085; www.discounthawaiicondos.com; ❄️✈️) Agency handling several units at the beachfront Hawaiian Princess condo high-rise.

INGA'S REALTY Vacation Rental $$ (📞696-1616; www.skrrentals.com) Has vacation rentals inland at Makaha Towers, in addition to beachfront.

Eating

Basic places to eat are 3 miles south in Wai'anae. Drive on to Ko Olina (13 miles, 25 minutes) for fine dining.

Makaha to Ka'ena Point
As you travel north of Makaha, you leave development behind. You won't find gas stations, restaurants – or even towns. A

Moonrise at Yokohama Bay (p259), Ka'ena Point
KARL LEHMANN / LONELY PLANET IMAGES ©

Below: Tropical fruit at a luau, Makua Valley **Right:** Makua Valley

(BELOW) LINDA CHING/LONELY PLANET IMAGES ©: (RIGHT) JON OGATA/PHOTO RESOURCE HAWAII/ALAMY ©

couple of beach parks have grassy strips or short stretches of sand, but there can be large numbers of homeless people camped permanently on the beach edge or in the surrounding trees. Though serious trouble is rarely reported, be mindful of petty theft such as car break-ins and bags disappearing while you swim.

Carved out by centuries of incessant waves, **Kaneana Cave** is a giant stone amphitheater and sacred site. The water has receded and now the highway sits between it and the seashore, 2 miles north of Kea'au Beach Park. Hawaiian kahuna once performed rituals inside the cave's inner chamber. Older Hawaiians consider it a sacred place and won't enter the cave for fear that it's haunted by the spirits of deceased chiefs. The entrance is blocked by barricades, but you can peer in.

Further north, scenic **Makua Valley** opens up wide and grassy, backed by a fan of sharply fluted mountains. It serves as the ammunition field of the Makua Military Reservation. The seaside road opposite the southern end of the reservation leads to a little graveyard that's shaded by yellow-flowered be-still trees. This site is all that remains of the valley community that was forced to evacuate during WWII when the US military took over the entire valley for war games. After several ground fires, and lawsuits charging that not enough environmental-impact studies had been done, live-fire exercises were discontinued in 2011.

Ka'ena Point State Park

You don't have to be well versed in Hawaiian legends to know that something mystical occurs at this dramatic convergence of land and sea in the far northwestern corner of the island. Powerful ocean currents altered by O'ahu's landmass have been battling against each other for

millennia here. The watery blows crash onto the long lava-bed fingers, sending frothy explosions skyward. All along this untamed coastal slice, nature is at its most furious and beautiful.

Running along both sides of the westernmost point of Oʻahu, Kaʻena Point State Park is a completely undeveloped 853-acre coastal strip with a few beaches. Until the mid-1940s the Oʻahu Railway ran up here from Honolulu and continued around the point, carrying passengers on to Haleʻiwa on the North Shore. Now the railbed serves as an excellent hiking trail.

Incidentally, those giant, white spheres that are perched on the hillsides above the park belong to the air force's Kaʻena Point Satellite Tracking Station. The satellite tracking station was originally built in the 1950s for use in the USA's first reconnaissance-satellite program, but now those giant white golf balls support weather, early-warning, navigation and communications systems.

 Beaches

MAKUA BEACH Beach
( 2pm Fri-8am Mon) Way back in the day, this beach was a canoe-landing site for interisland travelers. In the late '60s it was used as the backdrop for the movie *Hawaii*, which starred Julie Andrews. Today there is little here beyond a nice, gated stretch of sand and trees opposite the Makua Military Reservation.

YOKOHAMA BAY Beach
Some say this is the best sunset spot on the island. It certainly has the right west-facing orientation and a blissfully scenic mile-long sandy beach. Winter brings huge, pounding waves, making Yokohama a popular seasonal surfing and bodysurfing spot that's best left to the experts because of submerged rocks, strong rips and a dangerous shorebreak. Swimming is limited to the summer and then only when calm. When the water's

259

Island Insights

Ancient Hawaiians believed that when people went into a deep sleep or lost consciousness, their souls would wander. Souls that wandered too far were drawn west to Ka'ena Point. If they were lucky, they were met here by their *'aumakua* (guardian spirit), who led their souls back to their bodies. If unattended, their souls would be forced to leap from Ka'ena Point into the endless night, never to return.

flat, it's also possible to snorkel. The best spot with the easiest access is on the south side of the bay. You'll find restrooms, showers and a lifeguard station at the park's southern end.

Activities

TOP CHOICE **KA'ENA POINT TRAIL**   Hiking

A windy but mostly level 2.5-mile (one way) coastal trail runs from Yokohama Bay to Ka'ena Point, utilizing what remains of the old railroad bed. You can continue two more miles around the point to the North Shore, but we recommend parking at the end of the paved road at Yokohama Bay, hiking as far as the point, and then returning the same way you came (two to three hours round-trip).

This family-friendly trek has fine views the entire way, with the blue ocean crashing against dark volcanic rocks on one side and the Wai'anae Range's craggy cliffs on the other. Along the trail are tide pools, sea arches and lazy blowholes that occasionally come to life on high-surf days. A few sections where the railbed has collapsed require easy, uphill detours. The tip of the point itself is a freely accessible, fenced nature reserve (no dogs allowed); make sure to continue straight once you start slogging through sand (veering right takes you around the coast). As well as myriad native and migratory seabirds, you might spot Hawaiian monk seals sunbathing on the rocks – be careful to stay 150ft away so as not to disturb these beautiful, but endangered, creatures. The point itself is a fascinating convergence of two wave and water patterns. A few words of warning: the trail is nowhere-to-hide exposed, lacking any shade at all. Take sunscreen, a hat and plenty of water, and try to hike during cooler parts of the day. Be cautious near the shoreline, as there are strong currents and rogue waves can reach extreme heights in winter. Mountain bikers

Hawaiian monk seal, Ka'ena Point

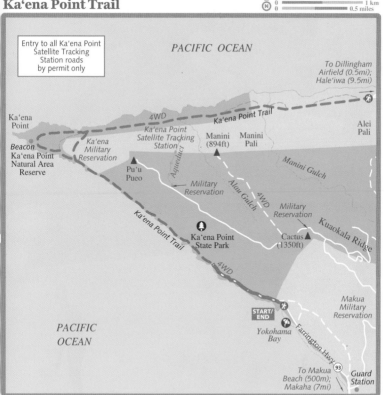

share trail access; the nearest bicycles for rent are in Wai'anae.

KUAOKALA TRAIL   Hiking

The Ka'ena Point Satellite Tracking Station is not open to the public, but the surrounding acreage is managed by **Hawaii's Division of Forestry & Wildlife** (http://hawaiitrails.ehawaii.gov), which issues the required advance permits for public hiking access to the trail system above the state park. Reserve your permit at least 10 days ahead, check in at the guard station near Yokohama Bay when you arrive,

and drive up to the dirt parking lot. The sometimes dusty 2.5-mile **Kuaokala Trail** follows a high ridge into Mokule'ia Forest Reserve. On a clear day you can see Mt Ka'ala (4025ft), O'ahu's highest peak and part of the Wai'anae Range. From there you can connect to the **Kealia Trail** (2.5 miles) and the North Shore at Dillingham Airfield, 1600ft below. Part of the land is also open to hunting, so hikers should wear brightly colored clothing for safety. Note that it's a much harder climb, but if you start on the North Shore (see p231), no permits are required.

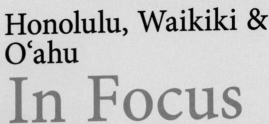

Honolulu, Waikiki & O'ahu

In Focus

Vintage postcard among brightly coloured lei
LINDA CHING / LONELY PLANET IMAGES ®

O'ahu Today

> O'ahu is a mosaic of cultures, both east and west, but underneath it all beats a Hawaiian heart

Kamehameha the Great statue at Ali'iolani Hale (p40), Honolulu

belief systems
(% of population)

51 None or unaffiliated
39 Christian
11 Other
9 Buddhist

if O'ahu were 100 people

44 would be Asian American
22 would be mixed race
21 would be Caucasian
10 would be Hawaiian
2 would be African American
1 would be other

population per sq km

USA   HAWAII   O'AHU

≈ 88 people

The Hawaiian Renaissance

In the 1970s, Hawaiian culture, battered by colonization, commodified and peddled to tourists, was ready for a revival; it just needed the spark. In 1976 a replica of the ancient Polynesian sailing canoe *Hokule'a* sailed to Tahiti using only the sun, stars, wind and waves for a compass, bringing a burst of cultural pride (see p268). That same year a group of Hawaiian activists occupied Kaho'olawe, which the US government had used for bombing practice since WWII. A Native Hawaiian rights movement soon emerged.

When the state of Hawaii held its landmark Constitutional Convention in 1978, it passed a number of amendments, such as making Hawaiian an official state language (along with English) and mandating that Hawaiian culture be taught in public schools. In the community, traditional arts such as *lauhala* (pandanus leaf weaving), *kapa* (bark cloth) making, wood carving, hula and *la'au lapa'au* (plant medicine) experienced a revival. Heiau

RAGA JOSE FUSTE / PRISMA BILDAGENTUR AG / ALAMY ©

(temples) and fishponds started being restored as well.

Today, O'ahu is a mosaic of cultures, both east and west, but underneath it all beats a Hawaiian heart. Traditional Hawaiian culture remains an important part of island life and identity, reflected in ways both large and small – in spontaneous hula dancing on an airplane, an *oli* (chant) sung before political ceremonies in Honolulu or a lomilomi massage at a healing spa.

Seeking a Sustainable Balance

Hawaii is almost wholly dependent on the outside world. The majority of the state's consumer goods, including 85% of its food, are imported. The state spends $6 billion a year on oil and coal, all of it imported. Despite a wealth of natural-energy sources, 95% of Hawaii's power still comes from carbon-based fuels. As the state's population swells to nearly

1.4 million – and 70% of those people reside on O'ahu – new housing developments sprawl, stressing water resources, transportation systems, public schools and landfills.

After losing sugar and pineapple to cheaper developing-world imports, Hawaii's economic eggs were left in one basket: tourism. When recession tanked the US economy in 2008, tourism to Hawaii went downhill with it. As state-revenue shortfalls soared to more than $725 million, then-governor Linda Lingle imposed severe budget cuts, but most politicians agree that diversifying Hawaii's economy is a longer-term solution. Current governor Neil Abercrombie is continuing Hawaii's push toward energy independence and agricultural self-sufficiency.

Tourism will likely be Hawaii's bread and butter for the foreseeable future, even though it comes at a price. It brings in seven million visitors annually – more than five times the state population – crowding roads, beaches and surf breaks, and driving up the price of real estate, not to mention fueling resistance to development. Some locals feel inundated by O'ahu's 'unofficial residents,' having mixed feelings about tourism and the US military, which controls vast tracts of land.

Many acknowledge that O'ahu's economic model is both unstable and unsustainable and that the island stands at a crossroads – Hawaii can either move toward securing a more homegrown future or it can suffer the worsening side effects of its addiction to tourism, imported goods and fossil fuels. Here's one reason for hope: both the modern sovereignty movement and antidevelopment activism are rooted in *aloha 'aina* (literally, 'respect for the land'), a traditional Hawaiian value that is deeply felt by almost everyone who lives here.

History

TRAVEL PICTURES / ALAM

More than 2000 miles from the US mainland, Hawaii can feel like another country – that's because it once was. Polynesians in canoes first colonized this tropical archipelago more than a millennium before Western explorers, whalers, missionaries and entrepreneurs arrived on ships. The tumultuous 19th century stirred a melting pot of immigrants from Asia, America and Europe even as it ended the Hawaiian kingdom founded by Kamehameha the Great.

Ancient Hawai'i

Almost nothing is known about the first wave of Polynesians (likely from the Marquesas Islands) who landed on this archipelago between AD 300 and 600. A second wave of Polynesians from the Tahitian Islands began arriving around AD 1000, and they conquered the first peoples and obliterated nearly all traces of their history and culture. Legends of the *menehune* – an ancient race of little people

10 million BC

Lava from an underwater volcano breaks the ocean's surface and O'ahu emerges as an island.

who built temples and great stoneworks overnight – may refer to these original inhabitants.

Although the discovery of Hawaii may have been accidental, subsequent journeys were not. Tahitians were highly skilled seafarers, navigating more than 2400 miles of open ocean without maps, and with only the sun, stars, wind and waves to guide them. In their double-hulled canoes, they imported to the islands their religious beliefs, social structures and over two dozen food plants and domestic animals. What they didn't possess is equally remarkable: no metals, no wheels, no alphabet or written language, and no clay to make pottery.

After trans-Pacific voyaging stopped completely around 1300 (for reasons unknown today), Hawaiian culture evolved in isolation. Nevertheless it retained a family resemblance to other Polynesian cultures. Ancient Hawaii's highly stratified society was run by chiefs (*ali'i*) whose right to rule was based on their hereditary lineage to the gods. Clan loyalties trumped expressions of individuality, elaborate traditions of gifting and feasting conferred prestige, and a humanlike pantheon of gods inhabited the natural world.

Several layers of *ali'i* ruled each island, and life was marked by warring battles as they jockeyed for power and status. The basic political subdivision was the *ahupua'a*, a wedge-shaped slice of land from the mountains to the sea that contained all the resources each chiefdom needed. Below the chiefs were the *kahuna* (experts or masters), who included both the priests and the guild masters – canoe makers, healers, navigators and so on. *Maka'ainana* (commoners) did most of the physical labor, and were obligated to support the *ali'i* through taxes. Below all was a small class of outcasts (*kaua*).

Ancient Hawaii's culture of mutuality and reciprocity infused what otherwise resembled a feudal agricultural society: chiefs were custodians of their people, and humans custodians of nature, all of which was sacred – the living expression (or *mana*, spiritual essence) of the universe's soul. Everyone played their part, through work and ritual, to maintain the health of the community and its relationship to the gods. In practice, a strict code of ritualized behavior – the *kapu* system – governed every

The Best...
Hawaiian Temples & Sacred Sites

AD 300–600
The first wave of Polynesians voyage by canoe to the Hawaiian Islands.

1000
Sailing from Tahiti, a second wave of Polynesian voyagers arrives in Hawaii.

1778–79
Captain Cook visits Hawaii twice, the first Westerner to arrive in Hawaii.

Polynesian Wayfaring

In 1976, a double-hulled canoe and her crew set off to recreate the journey of Hawaii's earliest settlers and also to do what no one had done in more than 600 years: sail 4800 miles round-trip to Tahiti without benefit of radar or compass, satellites or sextant.

Launched by the **Polynesian Voyaging Society** (http://pvs.kcc.hawaii.edu/), this modern-day reproduction of an ancient Hawaiian seafaring double-hulled canoe was named *Hokule'a* (Star of Gladness). The *Hokule'a* successfully sailed to Tahiti and back using only traditional Polynesian wayfaring navigational methods of observing stars, wave patterns, seabirds and clouds.

The *Hokule'a's* Micronesian navigator, Mau Piailug, wasn't without tools. He knew how to use horizon or zenith stars – those that always rose over known islands – as a guide, then evaluate currents, winds, landmarks and time in a complex system of dead reckoning to stay on course. In the mind's eye, the trick is to hold the canoe still in relation to the stars while the island sails toward you.

Academic skeptics had long questioned whether Hawaii's early settlers really were capable of journeying back and forth across such vast, empty ocean. After 33 days at sea, *Hokule'a* proved those so-called experts wrong by reaching its destination, where it was greeted by 20,000 Tahitians.

This historic achievement inspired a new appreciation for and interest in Polynesian and Hawaiian cultures. Today, the *Hokule'a* serves as a living classroom for schoolchildren to learn about indigenous Hawaiian and Polynesian traditions.

aspect of daily life; violating the *kapu* could mean death. Hawaiians also enjoyed life immensely, cultivating rich traditions in music, dance and athletic sports.

The First Westerners

British explorer Captain James Cook spent a decade traversing the Pacific Ocean over the course of three voyages. His ostensible goal was to locate a fabled 'northwest passage' between the Pacific and Atlantic Oceans. However, his were also self-conscious voyages of discovery, and he sailed with a full complement of scientists and artists to document the places, plants and peoples they found. In 1778, and quite by accident, Cook chanced upon the Hawaiian Islands. He dubbed the archipelago the Sandwich Islands in honor of his patron, the Earl of Sandwich.

1795

Kamehameha the Great conquers O'ahu, nearly completing the unification of the Hawaiian kingdom.

DAVID KLEYN/ ALAMY IMAGES ©

1819

Kamehameha II (Liholiho) abolishes the ancient *kapu* (taboo) system; heiau (temples) are destroyed.

Cook's arrival ended nearly 500 years of isolation, and it's impossible to overstate the impact of this, or even to appreciate now what his unexpected appearance meant to Hawaiians. Cook's arrival at Kealakekua Bay on the Big Island of Hawai'i happened to coincide with the *makahiki*, an annual harvest festival in honor of the god Lono. Cook's ships were greeted by a thousand canoes, and Hawaiian chiefs and priests honored Cook with feasting, religious rituals and deference suggesting they perhaps considered him to be an earthly manifestation of the god.

When Cook set sail some weeks later, he encountered storms that damaged his ships and forced him to return. Suddenly, the islanders' mood had changed: no canoes rowed out to meet the ships, and mistrust replaced welcome. A series of small conflicts escalated into an angry confrontation on the beach, and Cook, in an ill-advised fit of pique, shot to death a Hawaiian while surrounded by thousands of natives, who immediately descended on Cook, killing him in return.

Kamehameha the Great

In the years following Cook's death, a small, steady number of trading ships sought out Hawaii as a mid-Pacific supply point, and increasingly the thing that Hawaiian chiefs traded for most was firearms. Bolstered with muskets and cannons, Kamehameha, one of the chiefs on the Big Island, began a tremendous military campaign in 1790 to conquer all the Hawaiian Islands. Other chiefs had tried this and failed, but Kamehameha not only had guns, he was prophesied to succeed and possessed an unyielding, charismatic determination.

Within five bloody years Kamehameha had conquered all the main islands but Kaua'i (which eventually joined peacefully). The bloody campaign on O'ahu started with a fleet of war canoes landing on the shores of Waikiki in 1795. Kamehameha then led his warriors up Nu'uanu Valley to meet the entrenched O'auhuan defenders. The O'ahuans, who were prepared for spear-and-stone warfare, panicked when they realized Kamehameha had brought in a handful of Western sharpshooters with modern firearms. Fleeing up the cliffs in retreat, they were forced to make a doomed last stand (see the box, p177).

Kamehameha was a singular figure whose reign established the most peaceful era in Hawaiian history. A shrewd politician, he configured multi-island governance to mute competition among the *ali'i*. A savvy businessman, he created a highly profitable monopoly on the sandalwood trade in 1810 while trying to protect *'iliahi* trees from overharvest. Most of all, Kamehameha successfully absorbed growing foreign influences while fastidiously honoring ancient religious customs, despite creeping doubts among his people about Hawai'i's native gods.

Traders, Whalers & Soul Savers

After Cook's expedition sailed back to Britain, news of his 'discovery' of Hawaii soon spread throughout Europe and the Americas, opening the floodgates to Western

1820
The first Christian missionaries are permitted by the Hawaiian monarchy to land on O'ahu.

1826
Missionaries create an alphabet for the Hawaiian language and set up the first printing press.

1845
Kamehameha III, Hawaii's first Christian king, moves the capital of the kingdom from Maui to Honolulu.

The Best...
Honolulu Historical Buildings

explorers, traders and missionaries. By the 1820s, whaling ships began pulling into Honolulu for fresh water and food, supplies, liquor and women. To meet their needs, ever more shops, taverns and brothels sprang up around the harbor. By the 1840s, Hawaii had become the whaling capital of the Pacific.

To the ire of dirty-devil whalers, Hawaii's first Christian missionary ship sailed into Honolulu on April 14, 1820, carrying staunch Calvinists who were set on saving the Hawaiians from their 'heathen ways.' Their timing could not have been more opportune, as Hawaii's traditional religion had been abolished the year before following the death of Kamehameha the Great. Both missionaries and the whalers hailed from New England, but soon were at odds: missionaries were intent on saving souls, while to many sailors there was 'no God west of the Horn.'

The missionaries' zeal to save pagan souls was matched only by their disdain of nearly every aspect of Hawaiian culture. They worked tirelessly to stamp out public nakedness, 'lewd' hula dancing, polygamy, gambling, drunkenness and fornication with sailors. To them, all kahuna were witch doctors, and Hawaiians hopelessly lazy. Converts to Christianity came, since the missionaries' god was clearly powerful, but these conversions were not usually deeply felt. Hawaiians often quickly abandoned the church's teachings, reverting to their traditional lifestyle.

However, the missionaries gained enough influence with Hawaiian royalty to have laws enacted against drunkenness and prostitution. Most whaling boats then abandoned Honolulu, preferring to land at licentious Lahaina on Maui. By the mid-19th century, sons of O'ahu's original missionary families had become citizens of Hawaii and even more importantly, the island's new political and economic powerbrokers. Downtown Honolulu became the headquarters of their plantation-era corporations, whose board members today read much like a roster from the first mission ships.

Losing the Land

Born and raised in Hawaii after Western contact, Kamehameha III struggled to keep traditional Hawaiian society alive while evolving the political system to better suit foreign, and frequently American, tastes. In 1848 foreign missionaries convinced the king to pass a sweeping land-reform act called the Great Mahele. It permanently altered the

1848
King Kamehameha III institutes the Great Mahele, which allows commoners and foreigners to own land.

1866
The first group of patients with Hansen's disease (leprosy) are exiled from O'ahu to Moloka'i.

1885
Captain John Kidwell plants pineapples, today the state's biggest cash crop, in Honolulu's Manoa Valley.

Hawaiian concept of land rights: for the first time, land became a capitalist commodity that could be bought and sold.

The hope was that the Great Mahele would create a nation of small freeholder farmers, but instead it was an utter disaster – for Hawaiians, at least. Confusion reigned over boundaries and surveys. Unused to the concept of private land, and sometimes unable to pay the tax, many Hawaiians simply failed to follow through on the paperwork to claim their titles. Many of those who did – perhaps feeling that life as a taro farmer simply wasn't the attraction it once was – immediately cashed out, selling their land to eager and acquisitive foreigners.

Many missionaries ended up with sizable tracts of land, and more than a few left the church to devote themselves to their new estates. Honolulu's already prominent foreign community, composed largely of US and British expats, also opened businesses and schools, started newspapers and, most importantly, landed powerful government positions as ministry officials and consuls to the king, steadily wresting control over island affairs away from the Hawaiian monarchy.

'Iolani Palace (p37) decorated for King David Kalakaua's birthday, Honolulu

1893
Queen Lili'uokalani is overthrown. The son of an American missionary announces a new provisional government.

1901
Waikiki's first tourist hotel opens for Matson Navigation Company luxury-liner passengers.

1912
Champion Waikiki surfer Duke Kahanamoku wins his first gold medal for swimming at the Olympics.

King Sugar & the Plantation Era

Ko (sugarcane) arrived in Hawaii with the early Polynesian settlers. In 1835 Bostonian William Hooper saw a business opportunity to establish Hawaii's first sugar plantation. Hooper persuaded Honolulu investors to put up the money for his venture and then worked out a deal with Kamehameha III to lease agricultural land on Kaua'i. The next order of business was finding an abundant supply of low-cost labor, which was necessary to make sugar plantations profitable.

The natural first choice for plantation workers was Native Hawaiians, but even when willing, they were not enough. Due to introduced diseases such as typhoid, influenza, smallpox and syphilis, the Native Hawaiian population had steadily and precipitously declined. An estimated 800,000 indigenous people lived in the islands before Western contact, but by 1800, the Native Hawaiian population had dropped by two-thirds, to around 250,000. By 1860, Native Hawaiians numbered fewer than 70,000.

Wealthy plantation owners began to look overseas for a labor supply of immigrants accustomed to working long days in hot weather, and for whom the low wages would seem like an opportunity. In the 1850s, wealthy sugar-plantation owners began recruiting laborers from China, then Japan and Portugal. Many immigrants came intending to stay for a short time and return home rich, but ended up settling here instead and never leaving the islands, let alone getting rich.

During the US Civil War, sugar exports to Union states on the mainland soared, making plantation owners wealthier and more powerful. After annexing Hawaii in 1898, the US restricted Chinese and Japanese immigration, which made O'ahu's plantation owners turn to Puerto Rico, Korea and the Philippines for laborers. All of these different immigrant groups, along with the shared pidgin language they developed and the uniquely mixed culture of plantation life itself, transformed Hawaii into the multicultural, multiethnic society it is today.

Fall of the Monarchy

As much as any other monarch, King David Kalakaua, who reigned from 1874 to 1891, fought to restore Hawaiian culture and native pride. With robust joy, he resurrected hula and its attendant arts from near extinction – earning himself the nickname 'the Merrie Monarch' – much to the dismay of missionaries. He cared not a whit about placating the plantation oligarchy either. The king spent money lavishly and piled up massive debt. Wanting Hawaii's monarchy to be equal to any in the world, he built Honolulu's 'Iolani Palace, holding an extravagant coronation ceremony in 1883. Foreign businessmen considered these actions to be egotistical follies.

Kalakaua was a mercurial decision-maker given to summarily replacing his entire cabinet on a whim. A secret, antimonarchy group of mostly non–Native Hawaiian residents calling themselves the Hawaiian League formed, and in 1887 they forced Kalakaua to sign a new 'bayonet' constitution that stripped the monarchy of most of its powers, and changed the voting laws to include only those who met certain income

1936
Pan American airlines flies the first passenger planes from the US mainland to Hawaii.

1941
Japan stages a surprise attack on Pearl Harbor, catapulting the USA into WWII.

AP / CORBIS ©

and property requirements – effectively disenfranchising all but wealthy, mostly Caucasian business owners. To ensure economic profitability, the Hawaiian League was ready to sacrifice Hawaiian sovereignty.

When King Kalakaua died in 1891, his sister and heir, Princess Lili'uokalani, ascended the throne. The queen fought against foreign intervention and control as she secretly drafted a new constitution to restore Native Hawaiian voting rights and the monarchy's powers. In 1893, before Lili'uokalani could present this constitution to Hawaii's people, a hastily formed 'Committee of Safety' put into violent motion the Hawaiian League's long-brewing plans to overthrow the Hawaiian government. Without an army to defend her and opting to avoid bloodshed, the queen stepped down.

After the coup, the new provisional government immediately requested annexation by the US. However, much to their surprise, President Grover Cleveland reviewed the situation and refused: he condemned the coup as illegal, conducted under a false pretext and against the will of the Hawaiian people, and he requested Lili'uokalani be reinstated. Miffed but unbowed, the Committee of Safety instead established their own government, the Republic of Hawaii.

Annexation, War & Statehood

For five years, Queen Lili'uokalani pressed her case (for a time while under house arrest at 'Iolani Palace) – even collecting an antiannexation petition signed by the vast majority of Native Hawaiians – to no avail. In 1898, spurred by President McKinley, the US approved a resolution for annexing the Republic of Hawaii as a US territory.

In part, the US justified this colonialism because the ongoing Spanish-American War had highlighted the strategic importance of the islands as a Pacific military base. Indeed, some Americans feared that if the US didn't take Hawaii, another Pacific Rim power (such as Japan) just might. The US Navy quickly established its Pacific headquarters at Pearl Harbor and built Schofield Barracks, at that time the largest US army base in the world, in central O'ahu.

On December 7, 1941, a wave of Japanese bombers attacked Pearl Harbor (see p144), a devastating surprise attack that instantly propelled the USA into WWII. In Hawaii the US Army took control of the islands, martial law was declared, and civil rights were suspended. Japanese immigrants and Hawaii residents of Japanese ancestry suffered intense racial discrimination and deep suspicions over their loyalties, and around 1250 people were unjustly detained in internment camps on O'ahu.

The end of WWII brought Hawaii closer to the center stage of American culture and politics. Three decades had already passed since Prince Jonah Kuhio Kalaniana'ole, Hawaii's first delegate to the US Congress, introduced a Hawaii statehood bill in 1919, but it received a cool reception in Washington DC. Even after WWII, Hawaii was seen as too much of a racial melting pot for many US politicians to support statehood. Not until August 21, 1959, with more than 90% of the islanders voting for statehood, did Hawaii finally become the USA's 50th state.

1959
Hawaii becomes the 50th state; Japanese American WWII veteran Daniel Inouye elected to US Congress.

1993
President Clinton signs 'Apology Resolution,' recognizing the illegal overthrow of the Hawaiian kingdom in 1893.

2008
Barack Obama, who was born and grew up in Honolulu, becomes the 44th US President.

People of O'ahu

Local schoolchildren in Honolulu

Local schoolchildren in Honolulu

ERIC WHEATER / LONELY PLANET IMAGES ©

Everything you imagine when you hear the name Hawaii is probably true. Whatever your postcard idyll might be – a paradise of white sandy beaches, emerald cliffs and azure seas; of falsetto-voiced ukulele strummers, lithesome hula dancers and sun-bronzed surfers – it exists somewhere on the islands. But beyond the frame of that magical postcard is a startlingly different version of Hawaii, a real place where everyday people live.

Slow Down, This Ain't the Mainland

O'ahu is a Polynesian island, yes. But one with shopping malls, landfills, industrial parks, cookie-cutter housing developments, military bases and ramshackle small towns. In many ways, it's much like the rest of the US, and a first-time visitor stepping off the plane may be surprised to find a place where interstate highways and McDonald's look pretty much the same as back on 'da mainland.'

Underneath the veneer of an imported consumer culture is a different world, a world defined by – and proud of – its cultural separateness, its geographical isolation, its unique mix of Polynesian, Asian and Western traditions. While those cultures don't always blend seamlessly, there are very few places in the world today where so many different ethnicities, with no one group commanding a substantial majority, get along.

Perhaps it's because they live on a tiny island in the middle of an ocean that O'ahu residents strive to treat one another with aloha, act polite and respectful, and 'no make waves' (ie be cool). As Native Hawaiians say, 'We're all in the same canoe.' No matter their race or background, everyone shares the common awareness of living in one of the earth's most extraordinary spots.

The Best...
Local Cultural Experiences

1 Prince Lot Hula Festival (p62)

2 Nā Mea Hawai'i (p61)

3 Waikiki Community Center (p106)

4 Na Lima Mili Hulu No'eau (see the box, p135)

5 'I Love Kailua' Town Party (p185)

Island Identity

Honolulu is 'the city,' not only for those who live on O'ahu but for all of Hawaii. Far slower paced than New York City or Los Angeles, Hawaii's capital can still be surprisingly cosmopolitan, technologically savvy and fashion conscious. Right or wrong, Honoluluans see themselves at the center of everything; they deal with the traffic jams and high-rises because along with them come better-paying jobs, vibrant arts and cultural scenes, trendy shops and (relatively tame) nightlife. Ritzy suburbs sprawl along the coast east of Waikiki, while military bases are found around Pearl Harbor to 'Ewa in the west and Wahiawa in the island's center.

If it weren't for the occasional ride into the city to pick up supplies, the lifestyle of rural O'ahuans is as 'small town' as you'll find anywhere else in Hawaii. O'ahu's Windward Coast, North Shore and Leeward Coast are considered 'the country.' (Though in a landscape as compressed as this island, 'country' is relative: rural areas are not too far from the urban or suburban, and there are no vast swaths of uninterrupted wilderness like on the mainland.) Here status often isn't measured by a Lexus but by a monster truck.

'Ohana (extended family and friends) is important everywhere, but in small towns it's often the center of life. Even in Honolulu, when locals first meet, they don't ask 'What do you do?' but 'Where you wen' grad?' (Where did you go to high school?). Like ancient Hawaiians comparing genealogies, locals define themselves in part by the communities to which they belong: extended family, island, town, high school. And when two locals happen to meet outside Hawaii, there's an automatic bond, often based on mutual homesickness. But wherever they go, they're still part of Hawaii's extended 'ohana.

Multiculturalism

During the 2008 US presidential election, Barack Obama, who spent much of his boyhood in Honolulu, was lauded by locals because of his calm demeanor and his respect for diversity. He also displayed true devotion to his 'ohana by suspending his campaign and visiting his sick grandmother in Honolulu. She died days before the election. To locals, these are the things that count. What didn't matter to Hawaii is what the rest of the nation seemed fixated on: his race.

That Obama is mixed race was barely worth mentioning. Of course he's mixed race – who in Hawaii isn't? One legacy of the plantation era is Hawaii's unselfconscious and inclusive mixing of ethnicities; cultural differences are freely

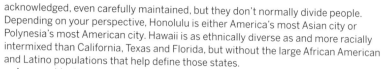

acknowledged, even carefully maintained, but they don't normally divide people. Depending on your perspective, Honolulu is either America's most Asian city or Polynesia's most American city. Hawaii is as ethnically diverse as and more racially intermixed than California, Texas and Florida, but without the large African American and Latino populations that help define those states.

Among older locals, plantation-era stereotypes still inform social hierarchies and interactions. During plantation days, whites were the wealthy plantation owners, and for years after people would half-seriously joke about the privileges that came with being a haole (Caucasian) 'boss.' Hawaii's youth often dismiss racial distinctions even as they continue to speak plantation-born pidgin. With intermarriage, it's not uncommon to meet locals who can rattle off several different ethnicities in their ancestry – for example, Native Hawaiian, Chinese, Portuguese and haole.

Lifestyle

The values of tolerance and acceptance extend beyond race – they apply also to religion and sexual orientation. While for many years Hawaii was politically behind the curve in its treatment of gay, lesbian and transgender people, especially in some tight-knit rural communities, today the right to same-sex civil unions is guaranteed by state law.

Politically, most voters are middle-of-the-road Democrats who vote along party, racial, ethnic, seniority and local/nonlocal lines. In everyday life, most people don't jump into a controversial topic just to argue the point. At community meetings and activist rallies, the most vocal liberals are often mainland transplants. Yet as more mainlanders settle on O'ahu, especially around Kailua and Kane'ohe on the Windward Coast, traditional stereotypes are fading.

Native Hawaiians still struggle with the colonial legacy that has marginalized them in their own homeland. Hawaiians constitute a disproportionate number of those homeless (about a third) and impoverished. Native Hawaiian schoolchildren, on average, are below state averages in reading and math and are more likely to drop out of school. Hawaiian charter schools were created in part to address this problem. However, many Native Hawaiians feel that some form of sovereignty is necessary to correct these deeply entrenched inequities.

Who Are You?

- **Haole** White person (except local Portuguese). Can be insulting or playful, depending on context.
- **Hapa** Person of mixed ancestry, usually hapa haole (literally, 'half white').
- **Hawaiian** Person of Native Hawaiian ancestry. Don't use the term 'Hawaiian' as a catchall for island residents; Native Hawaiians are the indigenous race.
- **Kama'aina** Person who is native to a particular place (literally, 'child of the land'). Commonly, 'kama'aina discounts' apply to any island resident (ie anyone with a state driver's license).
- **Local** Person who grew up in Hawaii. To call a transplant 'almost local' is a compliment, despite its emphasis on the insider/outsider mentality.
- **Transplant** Person who moves to Hawaii as an adult; can never be 'local.'

Honolulu's Chinatown still has its seedy edges, just like in the 19th-century whaling days, with skid rows of drug addicts, prostitutes and panhandlers. The use of 'ice' (methamphetamine, aka crystal meth) became rampant in the 1990s, in both urban and rural communities, where it's an ongoing social and law-enforcement challenge. Homelessness and a lack of affordable housing are also serious social and political issues, with hundreds of O'ahuans encamped semipermanently at public beaches, especially on the Wai'anae Coast (see p243).

Traditional Hawaiian dance performance at the Polynesian Cultural Center (p203), La'ie
HOLGER LEUE / LONELY PLANET IMAGES ©

Hawaii's Cuisine

Garlic shrimp at the Grass Skirt Grill (p226), Hale'iwa

CHRISTINA LEASE / LONELY PLANET IMAGES ©

Forget about pineapple upside-down cake and tiki-bar cocktails. 'Dis is seriously broke da mout!' That's the ultimate compliment you'll hear if you hang around locals long enough. It means something is so delicious it breaks the mouth. And that's no exaggeration. Here in the islands, people go crazy over food, especially in Honolulu. So, be brave and eat everything in sight. It's all 'ono grinds (good eats).

The Island 'Diet'

Before human contact, the only indigenous edibles in Hawaii were ferns and 'ohelo berries. The first Polynesians to journey to this archipelago from far across the Pacific brought with them *kalo* (taro), *'ulu* (breadfruit), *'uala* (sweet potato), *mai'a* (banana), *ko* (sugarcane) and *niu* (coconut), plus chickens, pigs and dogs for meat – and they enjoyed an abundance of seafood.

Western explorers dropped off cattle and horses, and later missionaries and settlers planted exotic fruits such as pineapple and guava. When the sugar industry peaked in the late 19th century, bringing waves of immigrant laborers from Asia and Europe, Hawaii's cuisine developed a taste and identity all its own. It took plantation imports, including rice, *shōyu* (soy sauce), ginger and chili pepper, but never abandoned Native Hawaiian staples like *kalua* pork and poi (pounded taro root).

Today, Hawaii's food traditions are multiethnic. Local *grinds* (food), like saimin noodle soup and Spam *musubi* (rice balls), are island renditions of comfort food from other countries, often Asia. This tasty culinary mishmash has turned locals into adventurous and passionate eaters who are always hungry for that next knockout mouthful of *'ono kine grinds* (good food), maybe from a food truck near you.

Hawaiian Traditions

With rich, earthy flavors and indigenous Polynesian ingredients, Hawaiian cooking is unique. *Kalua* pig (traditionally roasted in an underground pit layered with hot stones and banana and *ti* leaves) and starchy poi (a purplish paste pounded from taro, often fermented and sour-tasting) are Hawaii's endemic 'meat and potatoes'. Locals describe the consistency of poi as one-, two- or three-finger, indicating how many fingers are required to scoop it from bowl to mouth.

Poi is nutritious and easily digestible but tastes relatively bland – its purpose is to balance the stronger flavors of other dishes, such as *lomilomi* salmon (minced salted fish with diced tomato and green onion) or *laulau* (a bundle of pork, chicken or fish wrapped in taro and *ti* leaves and steamed). Other savory Hawaiian dishes include baked *'ulu, limu* (seaweed), *'opihi* (tiny limpet shells picked off reefs at low tide) and *pipi kaula* (beef jerky). Sweet *haupia* pudding is made of coconut cream traditionally thickened with arrowroot.

Local Food

Sticky white rice is more than a side dish in Hawaii. It's a culinary building block, an integral partner in everyday meals. Without rice, Spam *musubi* would just be a slice of canned meat. The *loco moco* would be nothing more than an egg-covered hamburger. Just FYI, rice almost always means sticky white rice. Not fluffy rice. Not wild rice. And *definitely* not instant rice.

Cheap, filling and tasty, a local 'mixed plate lunch' includes two-scoop rice, a scoop of mayonnaise-laden macaroni salad and a hot, hearty main dish, such as Korean–style *kalbi* short ribs, Filipino pork *adobo,* batter-fried *mochiko* (Japanese rice-flour) chicken or *furikake*-encrusted mahimahi. Islanders on a healthy kick will ask for brown rice and tossed salad greens instead of the usual sides.

Another local favorite is *poke,* which is bite-sized cubes of raw fish typically marinated in *shōyu*, oil, chili peppers, green onions and seaweed, though you'll find all kinds of flavor profiles. Saimin is an island-style soup of chewy egg noodles and Japanese broth, garnished with green onion, dried nori or perhaps *kamaboko* (pureed, steamed fish cake) or an egg. *Manapua,* the local version of Chinese *bao* (steamed or baked buns), have a variety of fillings, from *char siu* (barbecued pork) to black sugar.

On a hot day, nothing beats a mound of snowy shave ice, packed into a cup and drenched with sweet syrups in an eye-popping rainbow of hues. Purists stick with only ice but, for added decadence, ask for sweet azuki beans, *mochi* (sticky, sweet Japanese pounded-rice cakes) or ice cream underneath, or maybe *haupia* cream or a dusting of *li hing mui* (dried, salted plums) powder on top.

Hawaii Regional Cuisine & Locavarianism

In the early 1990s, island chefs including Alan Wong, Roy Yamaguchi and Sam Choy started partnering with local farmers, ranchers and fishers. Dubbed Hawaii Regional cuisine (HRC), this culinary movement was hallmarked by its Asian and Pacific Rim fusion tastes such as Peking duck in ginger-*liliko'i* (passion fruit) sauce or grilled butterfish glazed with Japanese miso (fermented soybean paste). But Hawaii Regional cuisine remained upscale, usually only found at destination beach-resort restaurants and celebrity chefs' kitchens.

Spam Capital of the USA

Hawaii may be the only place in the nation where you can eat canned Spam with pride. While US food maker Hormel's Spam, a pork-based luncheon meat, is the butt of jokes almost everywhere, there's little stigma in Hawaii. Here locals consume nearly seven million cans per year!

Of course, Spam looks and tastes different in Hawaii. It is always eaten cooked (typically sautéed to a light crispiness in sweetened *shōyu*), not straight from the can, and is served as a tasty breakfast dish – Spam and eggs, Spam and rice, etc.

Spam was first canned in 1937 and introduced to Hawaii during WWII, when the Hawaiian Islands were considered a war zone. During that period fresh meat imports were replaced by this standard GI ration. By the time the war ended, Hawaiians had developed an affinity for the fatty canned stuff.

The most-common preparation is Spam *musubi*: a block of rice with a slice of fried Spam on top (or in the middle), wrapped with a strip of black sushi nori. Created in the 1960s, it has become a classic, and thousands of *musubi* are sold daily at grocers, lunch counters and convenience stores.

For Spam trivia, recipes and games, go to www.spam.com. Or plan your trip around the **Waikiki Spam Jam** (p108), a huge street festival in late April.

Today, Hawaii's locavarian cuisine focuses on seasonally fresh, sustainable, often organic ingredients, such as Nalo greens or grass-fed beef from North Shore free-range cattle. It's as popular at food trucks and farmers' markets as gourmet dining rooms. Meanwhile, small-scale farmers are slowly shifting island agriculture away from corporate-scale, industrialized monocropping (eg pineapples) enabled by chemical fertilizers, pesticides and herbicides. With more than 85% of Hawaii's food having to be shipped in, the locavarian food movement is about not just taste but also economic self-sufficiency.

Island Drinks

Fruit trees thrive in Hawaii, so you'd expect to find fresh juices everywhere. Wrong. Only syrupy fruit drinks like POG (passion fruit, orange and guava) are readily found at supermarkets. For more pure, often organic and locally harvested juices, check out farmers' markets, natural-foods stores and **Lanikai Juice** (p190). Two traditional Hawaiian tonics made from island-grown plants are 'awa (kava), a mild sedative and intoxicant, and *noni* (Indian mulberry), which some consider a cure-all. Both are pungent in smell and taste.

Every beach-hotel bar mixes zany tropical cocktails topped with a fruit garnish and a little toothpick umbrella. The legendary mai tai is a mix of rum, grenadine, orange curaçao, orgeat syrup and orange, lemon, lime and/or pineapple juices. The state's best-known microbrewer is the **Kona Brewing Co** (http://konabrewingco.com), which has an outpost in Hawai'i Kai (p160). A few local brewpubs have also popped up in Honolulu (see p78).

Hawaii is the only state in the USA to grow coffee. The finest coffee beans come from the Big Island, where 100% Kona coffee has gourmet cachet. **Waialua Estate** (www.waialuaestate.com) coffee is grown on O'ahu's North Shore by the Dole Corporation, which also owns the pineapple fields of Wahiawa. **Waialua Soda Works** (www.waialuasodaworks.com) bottles old-fashioned soda pop that's naturally flavored by tropical fruit such as *liliko'i*.

Celebrating with Food

Throughout Hawaii, to celebrate is to feast. Whether a 300-guest wedding or a birthday party for *'ohana* (extended family and friends), a massive spread is mandatory. Most gatherings happen outdoors at parks, beaches and backyards, featuring a potluck buffet of homemade dishes. If you're invited to someone's home for a meal, show up on time, remove your shoes at the door and bring dessert (eg a local bakery cake).

In ancient Hawaii, a luau was held to commemorate auspicious occasions such as births and war victories. Luau are still commonplace in contemporary island life, for example, to celebrate a baby's first birthday or a wedding. Commercial luau offer the elaborate feast and hip-shaking, grass-skirted Polynesian dancing that many tourists expect, and an all-you-can-eat buffet with a typically mediocre sampling of traditional Hawaiian dishes.

Annual events such as the **Hawaii Food & Wine Festival** (p62) and **Wahiawa Pineapple Festival** (p241) showcase the island's bounty. Honolulu's **Pan-Pacific Festival** (p62) and **Aloha Festivals** (p108) also feature *ho'olaule'a* (block parties) with local chefs and food vendors. Weekly farmers' markets held all around O'ahu share the same festive atmosphere year-round.

Dining Out & Self-Catering

Informal dining is Hawaii's forte. For local food and rock-bottom prices, swing by retro drive-ins and diners with Formica tables, open from morning till night, or Japanese–style *okazuya* (takeout delicatessens), which are sold out by early afternoon. Portion sizes can be gigantic, so feel free to split a meal or take home leftovers, like locals do.

For gourmet cuisine by Hawaii's star chefs, explore Honolulu. Hawaii's cutting-edge foodie trends, such as *izakaya* (Japanese pubs serving food), all start in the capital city, too. Outside Honolulu and Waikiki, restaurants close early in the evening (for typical opening hours and prices, see p320). Open from *pau hana* (happy hour) until late, most bars serve tasty *pupu* (appetizers or small shared plates) like *poke,* shrimp tempura or edamame (fresh soybeans in the pod).

The casual Hawaii dress code means T-shirts and flip-flops are ubiquitous, except at Honolulu's most upscale restaurants and at Waikiki's luxury resort hotels. The older generation of locals tends toward neat, modest attire, which for men usually just means an aloha shirt and slacks. Smoking is not allowed inside restaurants. For tips on eating out with kids, see p292.

For groceries, head to farmers' markets and locally owned supermarkets. In Hawaii, most groceries are imported. The everyday price of food averages 30% more than on the US mainland, so you may not save much money by cooking your own meals.

The Best...
Local Plate Lunches

1 Poke Stop (p245)

2 Ted's Bakery (p214)

3 Da Kitchen (p74)

4 Me BBQ (p121)

5 Rainbow Drive-In (p125)

6 Waiahole Poi Factory (p197)

Food Glossary

If someone offers you a *broke da mout malasada* or *'ono kine poke,* would you try it? Don't miss out because you're stumped by the lingo. Visit www.lonelyplanet.com/hawaiian-language for our free downloadable language guide.

adobo – Filipino chicken or pork cooked in vinegar, *shōyu,* garlic and spices

'awa – kava, a Polynesian plant used to make an intoxicating drink

bentō – Japanese–style box lunch

broke da mout – delicious; literally 'broke the mouth'

char siu – Chinese barbecued pork

chirashizushi – assorted sushi and/or sashimi served over rice

crack seed – Chinese preserved fruit; a salty, sweet and/or sour snack

donburi – Japanese–style large bowl of rice topped with a protein (eg chicken cutlet)

furikake – Japanese seasoning or condiment, usually dry and sprinkled atop rice; in Hawaii, often mixed into *poke*

grind – to eat

grinds – food (usually local)

guava – green-yellow fruit with moist, pink flesh and lots of edible seeds

gyōza – Japanese grilled or steamed dumplings, usually containing minced pork or shrimp

haupia – coconut-cream pudding dessert

hijiki – Japanese seaweed

hulihuli chicken – rotisserie-cooked chicken with island-style barbecue sauce

Children eating shave ice
LINDA CHING / LONELY PLANET IMAGES ©

ikura – salmon roe

imu – underground earthen oven used to cook *kalua* pig and other luau food

'inamona – roasted ground *kukui* (candlenuts), used to flavor dishes such as *poke*

izakaya – Japanese pub serving food

kaiseki ryōri – formal Japanese cuisine consisting of a series of small, seasonally inspired dishes

kalbi – Korean–style grilled dishes, often marinated short ribs

kalo – taro, often pounded into poi

kalua – traditional Hawaiian method of cooking pork and other luau food in an underground pit

kamaboko – pureed, steamed fish cake

katsu – deep-fried cutlets, usually pork or chicken; see *tonkatsu*

kaukau – food

ko – sugarcane

laulau – a bundle made of pork or chicken and salted butterfish, wrapped in taro and *ti* leaves and steamed

li hing mui – sweet-salty preserved plum; also a flavor of crack seed

liliko'i – passion fruit

loco moco – dish of rice, fried egg and hamburger patty topped with gravy or other condiments

lomilomi salmon – minced, salted salmon with diced tomato and green onion

luau – Hawaiian feast

mai tai – tiki-bar drink typically containing rum and tropical fruit juices

The Best...
Island Sweets

Crack Seed

Forget candy bars. Hawaii's most popular snack is crack seed, sold prepackaged in supermarkets and convenience stores or by the pound at candy shops. It's an addictive, mouth-watering Chinese invention that can be sweet, sour, salty, spicy or some combination of all four (umm, *umami*). Like Coca-Cola or curry, the various flavors of crack seed are impossible to describe. Just one taste and you'll be hooked.

Crack seed is usually made from dried fruit such as plums, cherries, mangoes or lemons. The most popular flavor – which is also the most overwhelming to the uninitiated – is *li hing mui*. These days powdered *li hing mui* – sour enough to pucker the most stoic of faces – is used to spice up just about everything, from shave ice to fresh-fruit margaritas.

The Best...
Star Chefs' Kitchens

1 Alan Wong's (p69)

2 Roy's Waikiki Beach (p119)

3 Sansei Seafood Restaurant & Sushi Bar (p119)

4 Azure (p119)

5 Hiroshi Eurasian Tapas (p64)

6 Chef Mavro (p72)

malasada – sugar-coated Portuguese fried doughnut (no hole), often with a custard filling

manapua – island version of *bao* (Chinese–style steamed or baked bun) with sweet or savory filling

miso – Japanese fermented soybean paste, usually red or white

mochi – sticky, sweet Japanese pounded-rice cake

musubi – island version of Japanese *onigiri* (rice ball)

nabemono – Japanese clay-pot soup or stew made with meat and/or vegetables

nigiri – hand-molded Japanese sushi atop oval-shaped rice

niu – coconut

noni – Indian mulberry with smelly, yellow-green fruit, used medicinally in Hawaii

nori – Japanese seaweed, usually dried

ogo – crunchy, salty seaweed, often added to *poke; limu* in Hawaiian

okazuya – Japanese takeout deli, often specializing in home-style island cooking

'ono – delicious

'ono kine grinds – good food

'opihi – edible limpet

pau hana – happy hour; literally 'stop work'

pho – Vietnamese soup, typically beef broth, noodles and fresh herbs

pipi kaula – Hawaiian beef jerky

poha – cape gooseberry

poi – staple Hawaiian starch made of mashed taro, often fermented until sour

poke – cubed raw fish mixed with *shōyu,* sesame oil, salt, chili pepper, *furikake, 'inamona* or other condiments

ponzu – Japanese citrus sauce

pupu – bar snack or appetizer

saimin – local-style noodle soup, similar to Japanese *rāmen*

shave ice – cup of finely shaved ice, sweetened with colorful syrup

shōyu – Japanese soy sauce

soba – thin Japanese buckwheat-flour noodles

star fruit – translucent yellow-green fruit with five ribs like the points of a star and sweet, juicy pulp

taro – plant with edible starchy corm used to make poi; called *kalo* in Hawaiian

teppanyaki – Japanese style of cooking with an iron grill

tonkatsu – breaded and fried pork cutlets, also prepared as chicken *katsu*

tsukemono – Japanese pickled vegetables

don – thick Japanese wheat-flour noodles

ulu – breadfruit, a staple Hawaiian starch prepared much like a potato

ume – Japanese pickled plum

uni – sea urchin, often served as *nigiri* sushi

wagyū – Japanese marbled beef, usually served as steak

Name That Fish

In Hawaii, most fish go by Hawaiian and/or Japanese names. For sustainable seafood and sushi choices, download the free Hawaii pocket guide from **Monterey Bay Seafood Watch** (www.montereybayaquarium.org/cr/seafoodwatch.aspx).

ahi – yellowfin or bigeye tuna; red flesh, served raw or rare

aku – skipjack tuna; red flesh, strong flavor; *katsuo* in Japanese

ama'ama – mullet; delicate white flesh

awa – milkfish; tender white flesh

kajiki – Pacific blue marlin; *a'u* in Hawaiian

mahimahi – 'dolphin' fish; firm pink flesh

moi – threadfish; flaky white flesh, rich flavor; traditionally reserved for *ali'i* (Hawaiian royalty)

monchong – pomfret; mild flavor, firm pinkish-white flesh

o'io – bonefish; rarely eaten outside of Hawaii

onaga – ruby snapper; soft and moist; *'ula'ula* in Hawaiian

ono – a white-fleshed, flaky mackerel; also called wahoo

opah – moonfish; firm and rich

opakapaka – pink snapper; delicate flavor

opelu – mackerel scad; usually pan-fried

papio – jackfish; also called *ulua*

shutome – broadbill swordfish; succulent and meaty

tako – octopus; chewy texture; *he'e* in Hawaiian

tombo – albacore tuna; light flesh, mild flavor, silky texture

unagi – freshwater eel; usually grilled or served raw as sushi

IN FOCUS HAWAII'S CUISINE

Hawaii's Arts & Crafts

Musicians performing traditional Hawaiian music, Waikiki

LEE FOSTER / LONELY PLANET IMA

The islands' arts are all around you. Any night in Waikiki you might catch a slack key guitar great in concert. But you also may overhear an impromptu ukulele performance at a rural beach park or happen upon a hula hālau (school) performing at a farmers' market. Keep your eyes and ears open, the local music, hula, native crafts and storytelling are a great way to experience Hawaiian culture.

Music

Tune your rental-car radio to a Hawaiian station and you'll hear everything from contemporary Hawaiian folk rock to reggae-inspired 'Jawaiian' sounds. Traditional Hawaiian music is rooted in ancient chants and missionary hymns. As arriving immigrants introduced new melodies and instruments, those were then incorporated and adapted to create a unique local style. The sound usually includes *leo ki'eki'e* (falsetto, or high voice) vocals, sometimes just referred to as 'soprano' for women, that employs a *ha'i* (vocal break, or split-note) style, with a singer moving abruptly from one register to another. Traditional instruments used are the steel guitar, slack key guitar and ukulele.

Both the ukulele and the steel guitar contribute to the lighthearted hapa haole Hawaiian tunes with English lyrics that were popularized in Hawaii after the 1930s, of which 'My Little Grass Shack' is a classic example. The *Hawaii Calls* radio show was broadcast worldwide for 40 years from Waikiki's Moana Hotel, making this music instantly recognizable. Don Ho further popularized the genre. The modern slack key era was launched with legendary Gabby Pahinui's first recording, 'Hi'ilawe', in 1946.

The most famous traditional Hawaiian musician today is probably still the late Israel (IZ) Kamakawiwo'ole, whose *Facing Future* is Hawaii's all-time bestselling album. Among women, the unquestioned master was the late Aunty Genoa Keawe, whose impossibly long-held notes in the song 'Alika' set the standard (and set it high). Her O'ahu-born 'ohana (family) still performs as a group in Waikiki. Also look for albums by Keali'i Reichel, Amy Hanalali'i Gillom and Raiatea Helm. The slack key tradition lives on in Keola Beamer, Led Kaapana and Cyril and Martin Pahinui, among others. Dennis and David Kamakahi combine their talents on slack key guitar and ukulele, respectively.

In Honolulu, for classic and contemporary Hawaiian music tune into KINE Radio (105.1 FM). You can browse for recordings online at **Mountain Apple Company** (www.mountainapplecompany.com) or **Mele** (www.mele.com). Also check out recent winners of the **Na Hoku Hanohano Awards** (www.nahokuhanohano.org), Hawaii's version of the Grammies.

The Best...
Live Local Acts

1 Brothers Cazimero

2 Martin Pahinui

3 Jerry Santos & Friends

4 Kelly Boy De Lima with Kapena

5 Henry Kapono

6 Natural Vibrations

Hula

In ancient Hawaii hula was both a solemn ritual and entertainment. Dancers used hand gestures, facial expressions and synchronized movement, accompanied by rhythmic beats and *mele* (chants), as an offering to the gods or to celebrate the accomplishments of *ali'i* (chiefs). Hula contained the oral history for the ancient Hawaiians, who had no written language.

When Christian missionaries arrived, they viewed hula dancing as licentious and condemned the practice. The tradition might have been lost forever if King Kalakaua, the Merrie Monarch, had not revived it in the late-19th century. Today serious students still join a hula *halau*, where they study under a *kumu hula* (hula teacher). Schools teach both *kahiko* (ancient) and *'auana* (modern) hula styles. *Kahiko* performances are raw and elemental, accompanied only by chanting and thunderous gourd drums. Western-influenced *'auana* is the more mainstream contemporary style, using English lyrics, harmonious singing, stringed instruments, modern island-style clothing and sinuous arm movements. Big commercial productions with vigorously shaking hips and Vegas showgirl–style headdresses might be entertaining, but they're more related to Tahitian dance than hula. (Ancient dancers here wore pounded-bark cloth, or *kapa*, skirts or wraps – not grass skirts).

Waikiki is the best place to reliably catch hula performances. Bars, restaurants and hotels often include hula in their evening entertainment, and the daily Kuhio Beach Torch Lighting & Hula Show is free. Another way to experience hula is to attend a luau; the Polynesian Cultural Center on the Windward Coast has the most authentic performances. You never know, you may also be lucky enough to see a *halau* performing at a local festival; always check event calendars. For more on hula see p187.

287

Want to learn yourself? Island resorts often have an introductory hula lesson in their activity schedule, as does Waikiki Community College.

Hawaiian Art & Crafts

Ancient Hawaiian skills still contribute to many of the beautiful artisan products produced today. Some of the most prized items are native-wood bowls, often made of

The Art of the Lei

Lei making may be Hawaii's most transitory art form. Fragrant and ephemeral, lei embody the beauty of nature and the embrace of the community, freely given and freely shared. In the islands' ancient past, lei makers wound, braided or strung together feathers, nuts, shells, seeds, seaweed, vines, leaves and fruit, in addition to the fragrant tropical flowers more common today. Lei were part of sacred hula dances, given as special gifts to loved ones, used as healing medicine for the sick and as offerings to the gods. So powerful a symbol were they that on ancient Hawaii's battlefields, the right lei could bring peace to warring armies.

Today, locals continue to honor loved ones with lei at weddings, birthdays, anniversaries, graduations and public ceremonies. For visitors to Hawaii, the tradition of giving and receiving lei dates back to the 20th-century steamships; disembarking passengers were greeted by local vendors who would toss garlands around their necks.

In 1927, the poet Don Blanding called for making a holiday to celebrate lei. Leonard and Ruth Hawk later composed the popular tune 'May Day is Lei Day in Hawaii'. Today, May 1, Lei Day, is celebrated across the islands with Hawaiian music, hula dancing, parades, lei-making workshops and contests.

A typical Hawaiian lei costs anywhere from $10 for a single strand of orchids or frangipani to thousands of dollars for a 100% genuine Ni'ihau shell lei necklace. Be aware that most *kukui* (candlenut) lei are cheap imports, thus the low prices. Freshly made flower lei are available near the airport and in Chinatown among other places, including some supermarkets. For intricately crafted feather lei, drop by Na Lima Mili Hulu No'eau in Waikiki. Services such as **Lei Greeting** (www.leigreeting.com) can arrange to meet your party at the airport with a suitable floral welcome.

LEI ETIQUETTE

o Never refuse a lei or take one off in the presence of the giver. It's considered rude as the giving is a sign of affection or regard.

o Resist the temptation to wear a lei intended for someone else. It's thought to be bad luck.

o Don't give a closed lei to a pregnant woman, as many believe it can bring bad luck to the unborn child; choose an open (untied) lei or *haku* (head) lei instead.

o Ideally, you should not throw a lei in the trash, as it could be taken as a sign you are throwing the giver's love away. If possible instead, untie the string and return the lei's natural elements to the earth (eg scatter flowers in the sea, bury seeds or nuts).

beautifully grained tropical hardwoods such as koa and milo. Hawaiian bowls are not decorated or ornate, but are shaped to bring out the natural beauty of the wood. The thinner and lighter the bowl, the finer the artistry and the greater the value. Don't be fooled by cheap monkeypod bowls imported from the Philippines.

Protestant missionaries introduced quilting to Hawaii in the early-19th century, but the vibrant colors and natural patterns are based on indigenous *kapa* (pounded-bark cloth) designs. Traditional quilts typically have one solid colored fabric, which has been folded into fourths or eighths and cut into a repeating pattern (remember making snowflakes in school?). These are then appliquéd onto neutral foundation cloth. Each part of a traditional quilt has meaning and each design was once thought to contain the very spirit of the crafter. For example, an *'ulu* (breadfruit) design symbolizes abundance, pineapple represents the warmth and welcome of an aloha, and *kalo* (taro) embodies strength. If you want to buy a hand-sewn, island-made treasure, expect to pay thousands of dollars at galleries. If prices are low, such as at the Aloha Swap Meet in Pearl Harbor, the quilts were likely made in the Philippines. The Mission House at the Polynesian Cultural Center on the Windward Coast sells works made by Mormon volunteers.

Try your own hand at it by learning from experienced Hawaiian quilters during day classes often organized by island resorts. Area museums sometimes also have classes. Noted quilt makers and designers like Althea Poakalani Serrao and family (www.poakalani.net), Elizabeth Root (www.quiltshawaii.com), Nalani Gourd (http://hawaiianquilting.net) have websites that are excellent tools. For more on the latter see p248.

Many modern painters, printmakers, photographers and graphic and textile artists draw inspiration from Hawaii's cultural heritage, as showcased at the multimedia Hawai'i State Art Museum in downtown Honolulu. Also check out the contemporary island art galleries in nearby Chinatown. Arts and crafts fairs take place island wide throughout the year. The Honolulu **Made in Hawaii Festival**

Handicrafts on display in a Waikiki shop
LEE FOSTER / LONELY PLANET IMAGES ©

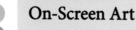

On-Screen Art

Academy Award–winning film *The Descendants,* based on Kaui Hart Hemmings' novel, caused quite the buzz on Oʻahu where it originated. The story is about Matt King (George Clooney), a man descended from Hawaiian royal and missionary ancestors who manages a family land trust on Kauaʻi.

He has to learn to be a father to his daughters after his wife is involved in a critical accident and he discovers she was having an affair. The movie producers spent a month preparing for the film by living in Lanikai and 11 weeks of filming there. Locals have noted how surprisingly accurate the portrayal of the island and its people is compared to other movies. Numerous scenes were shot locally on Waikiki Beach and around Honolulu. The gorgeous island-style homes featured actually increased interest in the local real-estate market. Look for Hemmings in a cameo as King's secretary, and with family members in the party scene at the Outrigger Canoe Club below Diamond Head.

For more island-based films, see p25.

(www.madeinhawaiifestival.com) happens during a weekend in August; check out the **Island Craft Bulletin** (www.icb-web.net/icb/shoppers.html) for other events.

Literature

Hawaii's early literary canon has long been dominated by foreign writers. Authors such as Mark Twain and Isabella Bird wrote the earliest travelogues about the islands. Later James Michener's historical saga *Hawaii* became a classic tome. More recently, Hawaii-based historical fiction has included *The Last Aloha* by Gaellen Quinn, *Honolulu* by Alan Brennert, and *Bird of Another Heaven* by James Houston.

Contemporary literature by local writers doesn't exoticize Hawaii as it examines the everyday complexities of island life – today and in the past. Honolulu-born Kiana Davenport's works are well recommended: *Song of Exile* follows two fictional families from WWII through US statehood. Kaui Hart Hemmings, also Oʻahu-born, made a splash when her first novel, *The Descendants,* was made into a movie. Lois-Ann Yamanaka, author of the award-winning anthology *Saturday Night at the Pahala Theatre,* caused controversy with the gritty depictions of local life in her novels and poetry. To read about up-and-coming authors, check out the biannual journal published by **Bamboo Ridge Press** (www.bambooridge.com), which has launched many local writers' careers. For more suggested reads, see p25.

Family Travel

Family kayaking at Kailua Beach Park (p179)

ANN CECIL / LONELY PLANET IMAGES ©

With so much surf and sand, O'ahu's coastline could be likened to a giant, free water park. But there are also plenty of outdoor activities and a few good museums and sights to keep kids of all ages occupied when they tire of swimming. Traveling families have been coming to the island for decades; local resorts, hotels and restaurants are well prepared. So stop for a shave ice and relax; keiki (children) are most welcome here.

Sights & Activities

Beaches line the entire island, so families really can't go wrong on O'ahu. All sides have opportunities to swim, snorkel, bodyboard and beachcomb at some time during the year.

Since the largest number of kid-catering resorts and restaurants are concentrated in the 20-block area of Waikiki, it's a top choice for families. At the beach teens and tweens can learn to surf – and everybody loves the outrigger-canoe rides. Nearby are the Waikiki Aquarium, with its learning-oriented fun, and the Honolulu Zoo. Whale watching and other boat excursions base locally. From Waikiki it's a short drive to greater Honolulu sights such as the interactive Bishop Museum, where the little ones get to walk through a 'volcano', and to Manoa Valley with its hikes and gardens.

If you like your family trip a little more low-key, Kailua on the Windward Coast is also a great base. Several good beaches are nearby and older kids and adults can learn to kayak or stand-up paddle at the town beach park. Hikes are possible in the area, and north up the coast is the Polynesian Cultural Center, one of the island's biggest attractions. Southeast O'ahu's highlights, including the fabulous and family-friendly snorkeling at Hanauma Bay and Makapu'u Lighthouse, are a short jaunt south. For that matter, Honolulu is less than 30 minutes over the *pali* (cliffs).

Discount admission to sights is usually available for children aged between four and 12; little ones under four are often free.

The surf is the main attraction at the North Shore, which has some treacherous winter waves. Swimming in summer is usually safe, but there's little beyond the beach to entertain kids.

Those staying out at Disney's Aulani resort in leeward O'ahu are a solid 40 minutes (without traffic) from Honolulu. The Lagoons (the coves at Ko Olina) offer some of the island's most child-friendly swimming. And the coast has a few other attractions – boat cruises, another swimming beach, a water park – but it *is* isolated.

For more sight and activity suggestions, see the Honolulu for Children (p65), Waikiki for Children (p103) and the Best for Kids (p160) boxed texts.

Children's Programs

Area botanical gardens host occasional children's programs, especially on weekends, as do the larger museums and animal parks.

Sleeping & Eating with Kids

Children under 18 often stay for free when sharing a hotel room with their parents, if they use existing bedding. Cribs (cots) and roll-away beds are usually available on request (sometimes for a surcharge) at hotels and resorts, but it's best to check in advance. Vacation rentals may have these, or an extra futon for the little ones to flop down on. The bigger the resort, the more likely it is to have extensive family-oriented services such as kids activities and clubs, game rooms or arcades, wading and other playful pool features. Hotel concierges are usually a good resource for finding babysitting services, or you can contact Nannies Hawaii (http://nannieshawaii.com).

Don't be scared away from dining out on O'ahu; even fancy places like Roy's or Alan Wong's welcome well-behaved little ones. Many restaurants have children's menus (eg grilled cheese sandwiches, chicken fingers) at significantly lower prices,

Need to Know

- **Changing facilities** Available in shopping malls, big hotels and at sights
- **Cribs (cots)** Usually available, check ahead with hotel
- **Diapers (nappies)** Sold island-wide at grocery, drug and convenience stores
- **Health** Doctors most accessible in Honolulu
- **Highchairs** Usually available
- **Kids' menus** Widely available
- **Strollers** Bring your own, or rent online and have delivered to your hotel
- **Transport** Reserve car seats with rental agencies in advance

and high chairs are usually available. Food trucks and other outdoor eateries are family faves, as they're super casual and the location may provide space for kids to roam. Many beach parks have picnic tables. Sandwiches and meals to-go are readily available at cafes, drive-ins and grocery stores. Look for baby food, infant formula, soy and cow's milk at any supermarket or convenience store. Note that most women choose to be discreet about breastfeeding in public.

Restaurants, lodgings and sights that especially cater to families, with good facilities for children, are marked with a family icon (👪) throughout this book.

Getting Around

Most car-hire companies rent child-safety seats from $10 per day. Online services such as Paradise Baby (www.paradisebabyco.com) and Baby's Away (www.babysaway.com) deliver rented car seats, strollers, playpens and cribs and more right to your door.

Many public women's restrooms have changing tables. Separate, gender-neutral 'family' facilities are sometimes available at airports, museums and other sights. For valuable tips on traveling, consult Lonely Planet's *Travel with Children,* which is also full of interesting anecdotes.

The Best...
Family Fun

1 Hanauma Bay (p162)

2 Waikiki Aquarium (p100)

3 Bishop Museum (p54)

4 Polynesian Cultural Center (p203)

5 Manoa Valley sights (p65)

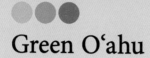

Green Oʻahu

Oʻahu is a Polynesian paradise possessing varied natural environments – from mountain to sea, lushly verdant to dismally dry. It's also a high-profile test case of whether humans can achieve a sustainable relationship with nature. Conservation efforts, both state-funded and grassroots, are gaining strength. From marine biologists and wildlife conservationists to Hawaiian artists and rural land-loving locals, aloha ʻaina (love or respect for the land) runs deep.

Environmental Issues

Though Oʻahu lags a little behind some of her sisters, environmental consciousness has taken root on this, the most densely populated and heavily touristed of the Hawaiian Islands. A wide coalition of scientists, activists and residents has made conservation efforts a slow, but steady success. For the latest environmental issues facing the island, check out **Environment Hawaii** (www.environment-hawaii.org).

Conservation

Hawaii's ecosystem is fragile – so fragile, in fact, that 25% of all the endangered species in the US are endemic to the Hawaiian Islands. Vast tracts of native forest were long ago cleared to make way for the monocrop industries of sugarcane and pineapple. In the 1960s the advent of mass tourism posed new challenges to the environment with the rampant development of land-hungry resorts and water-thirsty golf courses, which now number more than 40. Additionally, the large military presence has come into question for its environmental practices. Just the sheer number of visitors to the island puts immense pressure on the ecosystem.

That said, some notable progress has been made. There is a strong local belief in 'Keeping the Country, Country', a sentiment you may see on bumper stickers, T-shirts or homemade yard signs. Legal action has successfully been used to halt development in rural areas such as the Windward Coast and the North Shore.

The waters around the island have been made part of the Hawaiian Islands Humpback Whale National Marine Sanctuary; approaching within 100yd of a whale is illegal. Overfishing is still a problem, but the killing of sea turtles by the longline industry has been banned and there's an effort afoot to restrict the laying of gillnets.

Though invasive species still threaten endemic ones, a recently proposed bill contains measures meant to help quarantine any brown tree snakes that stowaway aboard aircraft. This species poses a severe threat to the island's bird populations. For more about O'ahu's wildlife, see p300.

Some local conservation groups have gotten together to work toward restoring habitats in their neighborhoods. For example, a Maunalua Bay project removed more than three million pounds of invasive algae by organizing community *huli* (pull) parties.

Recycle & Reuse

Recycling bins are not common on the street, but you'll find them at beaches, public parks and some museums and tourist attractions. Local hotels are lagging a bit behind in the recycling. Thankfully, a good number of local restaurants now provide compostable and biodegradable to-go containers. Some businesses even make recycling an art: Mu'umu'u Heaven, in Kailua on the Windward Coast, turns old Hawaiian dresses into chic new ensembles. And local surfboard makers are experimenting with soy- and sugar-based foam forms.

Transportation

Being on the dry and less-windy side of the island, Honolulu occasionally sees increased levels of vehicle-related smog. After decades of controversy, O'ahuans are set to break ground on a light-rail commuter transit system in 2012. The elevated train should connect Kapolei, via the airport, with Honolulu. Further development is intended to stretch through Waikiki to Manoa.

Honolulu's public transportation system, TheBus, has six hybrid vehicles in service at the time of writing, and plans to introduce 19 more shortly. Future proposals include the purchase of 'clean' biodiesel buses. Recycling has already been implemented system-wide, and only low volatile organic compound (VOC) paints and petroleum-free, part-cleaning solvents are used.

Pollution

O'ahu has no air-polluting heavy industry. However, corporate agribusiness has been guilty of violating Environmental Protection Agency (EPA) guidelines. It took almost 15 years after it was added to the EPA's Superfund national priority list before O'ahu's Del Monte Foods plantation was finally cleaned up. Environmental concern over water pollution caused by ag-runoff and debates over whether genetically modified organisms (GMO) should be outlawed continue.

Plastic pollution can be an issue on and offshore. Other Hawaiian islands have banned plastic store bags, but as yet, O'ahu has not. These and other plastic items can be mistaken as jellyfish and eaten by endangered sea turtles. Further out in the ocean around O'ahu, the density of floating debris is ever increasing. Some scientists estimate that the 'great Pacific garbage patch' may be larger than Texas and reach 90ft deep. A local Honolulu company is pioneering efforts to develop monitoring vessels and systems, which could protect the island's shores from the mass.

Sustainable Travel

More than 4.5 million visitors land on O'ahu's shores every year – outnumbering residents more than three to one – and tourism, either directly or indirectly, provides one out of every three jobs in Hawaii. Pressures from tourism can be intense, as corporations seek to build more condos and hotels, to irrigate golf courses and to, well, sprawl. Sustainable travel practices can help ensure the island stays a paradise in the years to come.

Hawai'i 2050 Initiative

Even the government has gotten into the green swing of things, creating the **Hawai'i 2050** (www.hawaii2050.org) sustainability plan. This evolving statewide program combines community input with a governmental task force to formulate economic, social and environmental policies that focus on renewable energy, living sustainably within the bounds of the islands' natural resources and striking a balance between profitable tourism and Hawaiian cultural preservation. A tall order, but as the plan itself states, this is 'not an academic or political exercise; it is a matter of the survival of Hawai'i as we know it.'

Eat Locally

Every food product not made on O'ahu has been imported. The great distances and amount of fuel used makes the 'locavore' or 'eat local' movement sound even more appetizing. More and more restaurant menus these days sound like agricultural report cards. Creative island chefs love featuring island-grown produce such as Nalo greens, North Shore grass-fed beef and locally caught seafood – and telling you so; for more, see p279.

Farmers' markets, too, are booming on O'ahu. Search for a comprehensive list of locations and times at www.hawaii.gov. Even farms themselves have gotten in on the trend. Waialua on the North Shore is known for its small orchards and taro patches. The organizers of noteworthy Hale'iwa Farmers Market have gotten several of these growers together to participate in **O'ahu Agri-Tours** (http://oahuagritours.com), which take you on a variety of farm and Hawaiian cultural practice tours from Waikiki. Around Kahuku on the Windward Coast, numerous fresh fruit and vegetable stands sit roadside, and one farm has opened its fields to visitors on weekends. Further south, planters in Waimanalo turn out incredible produce. **'Nalo Farms** (www.nalofarmfresh.com) is the granddaddy of all local agricultural outfits, unfortunately its reservation-only ecotours are for groups of 10 or more. **Slow Food O'ahu** (http://slowfoodoahu.org) also sponsors agro tours and organizes social events.

Support Ecofriendly Businesses

How ecofriendly a company really is can be hard to determine. Look for our sustainable icon throughout the text or contact local watch groups when in doubt.

Dolphin Smart (http://sanctuaries.noaa.gov/dolphinsmart/) NOAA certifies boat tour businesses that use prescribed dolphin-safe practices. For more on dolphin encounters, see p299.

Hawaii Ecotourism Association (www.hawaiiecotourism.org) Has an ecotour certificate program and honors noteworthy outfitters, hotels and other local businesses.

Green Hotels Association (www.hawaiiecotourism.org) So far only a few local hotels are listed, but the Aqua Bamboo and Hotel Renew in Waikiki are among them.

Alternative Hawaii (www.alternative-hawaii.com) Focuses on Hawaii's natural and cultural beauty, with hundreds of tourism listings – and some advertorial.

Tread Lightly

Every step we take has an impact, but we can minimize the effect by being aware of our surrounds. Staying on trails helps preserve the area plant life. Riding ATVs can cause erosion damage even when keeping to one track. Coral is a living creature: touching it, standing on it, bumping into it or stirring up sand that settles on top of it can kill the delicate polyps.

No plant nor animal would be living on this island if it hadn't been transported here by plan or accident. But there's no need to perpetuate the process! Seeds caught in the soles of shoes or bugs hiding out in the bottom of backpacks potentially pose a threat. Cleaning thoroughly before arrival helps fight the introduction of invasive species.

As mentioned, plastics are a problem. The tap water on the island is completely safe and drinkable. Buying a refillable bottle from a local business or sight can help reduce waste (and it's a cool souvenir). Local reusable grocery bags are also available at every drugstore and supermarket for just a dollar or two. Pick up one with a tropical design – or a funny illustrated diagram of a *poke* (cubed raw fish) bowl –and you'll get a minivacation every time you shop at home.

Offset Carbon

Waikiki and greater Honolulu have a comprehensive bus network; parking is such a hassle there that staying without a rental car elevates a lot of aggravation. Further afield, a car becomes more necessity than luxury. But it's still possible to keep it parked and cycle around the North Shore and Kailua on the Windward Coast. Kailua town has started B-Cycle, a low-cost bicycle-swap program with two station locations at present. Smart Cars and some hybrid vehicles are available as rentals in Waikiki; see p137. **Climate Care** (www.climatecare.org) runs an flight carbon-offset donation program; for more see www.lonelyplanet.com.

Volunteering on Vacation

Give something back during your trip by volunteering even a few spare hours. Whether pulling invasive plants, counting migratory whales, restoring ancient Hawaiian

Sustainable Icon

It seems like everyone's going green these days, but all ecotourism outfits are not created equal. Throughout the book, the sustainable icon (🌿) indicates listings that we are highlighting because they contribute to sustainable tourism. Many are involved in conservation, others support a locavore lifestyle, and some maintain and preserve Hawaiian identity and culture.

archaeological sites or rebuilding hiking trails, there's no better way to connect with locals and their *aloha 'aina* tradition. The free tabloid **Honolulu Weekly** (www.honolulu weekly.com/calendar) lists volunteering opportunities. Check out the following organizations for other possible projects.

Hawai'i Nature Center (www.hawaiinaturecenter.org) Volunteering-tourism opportunities in Honolulu to help the environment and encourage community development.

Hawaiian Islands Humpback Whale National Marine Sanctuary (http://hawaiihumpbackwhale.noaa.gov) Join in one of three annual whale counts.

Hui o Ko'olaupoko (http://huihawaii.org/) Restores the *'aina;* projects include replanting wetlands like He'eai Stream on the Windward Coast.

Kahea (www.kahea.org) This environmental alliance preserves sensitive shorelines and Native Hawaiian cultural sites.

Malama Hawai'i (www.malamahawaii.org) A volunteer-oriented network of community and environmental groups with volunteer listings and conservation projects for *keiki* (kids).

Malama Maunalua (http://malamamaunalua.org) Opportunities to help restore Maunalua Bay in southeast O'ahu.

Nature Conservancy (www.nature.org/hawaii) Protects Hawaii's rarest ecosystems by buying up tracts of land; it also sometimes has volunteer opportunities.

Preserve Hawai'i (www.preservehawaii.org) A local volunteer-opportunity clearing house that uses social media to post events.

Sierra Club (www.hi.sierraclub.org/oahu) Activities range from political activism to trail maintenance and environmental clean-up.

Surfrider Foundation (www.surfrider.org/oahu) Grassroots group dedicated to oceans and beaches; holds regular weekend beach clean-ups.

Panama flame flower at the Ho'omaluhia Botanical Garden (p193), Kane'ohe
MARK A JOHNSON / ALAMY ©

Land & Sea

With a total land area of 594 sq miles, O'ahu is the third-largest Hawaiian island. Though it accounts for less than 10% of Hawaii's total land mass, roughly 70% of state residents call 'the gathering place' home. The City and County of Honolulu incorporates the entire island, as well as the Northwestern Hawaiian Islands – dozens of small, unpopulated islands and atolls stretching more than 1200 miles across the Pacific.

Geography

The island of O'ahu is really two separate shield volcanoes that arose about two million years ago and formed two mountain ranges: Wai'anae in the northwest and Ko'olau in the southeast. O'ahu's last gasp of volcanic activity occurred between 10,000 and one million years ago, creating the tuff cone of Diamond Head, southeast O'ahu's most famous geographical landmark. The forces of erosion – wind, rain and waves – subsequently added more geologic character, cutting valleys, creating beaches and turning a mound of lava into paradise. O'ahu's highest point, Mt Ka'ala (4020ft), is in the central Wai'anae Range.

All of this oceanic plate tectonic activity can really shake things up. Small earthquakes are not uncommon here – several were reported between 2010 and 2012 – but Honolulu tends to be safely distant from the epicenter and feels only minor shocks. A tsunami could hit the island, although this has not happened recently; for more, see p324.

An Evolving Ecosystem

It has been said that if Darwin had arrived in Hawaii first, he would have developed his theory of evolution in a period of weeks instead of years. Almost all the plants and animals carried by wind and waves across the vast ocean adapted so uniquely to these remote volcanic islands that they evolved into new species endemic to Hawaii. For example, the 56 known species of the honeycreeper bird all descended from a single type of finch. Unfortunately, only 18 of those species survive, and six are on the endangered list. Having evolved with limited competition and few predators, native species fare poorly among more aggressive introduced flora and fauna and foreign-borne diseases.

Dolphin Swims

Signing up for a dolphin 'encounter' deserves careful consideration. According to many marine biologists, human interaction tires wild dolphins, potentially leaving them without critical energy to feed or defend themselves. Repeated contact has driven some dolphins out of their natural habitats into less-safe resting places.

In captivity, dolphins are trained to perform using techniques ranging from positive behavioral modification to food deprivation. Some have had to undergo surgery to repair damaged fins after participating in dolphin-swim programs; all can be exposed to human-borne illnesses and bacteria. The 2008 Oscar-winning documentary *The Cove* (www.thecovemovie.com), featuring an ex-dolphin trainer turned activist, looks at the 'dolphinarium' biz.

Prior to human contact, the Hawaiian Islands had no native mammals, save for monk seals and *'ope'ape'a* (hoary bats), which are rarely seen on O'ahu. When Polynesians arrived, they introduced pigs, chickens, rats, coconuts, bananas, taro and about two dozen other plants... not to mention people. The pace of alien-species introduction escalated with the arrival of Europeans, who brought cattle, goats, mongooses, mosquitoes, foreign song birds and more. Nearly every species introduced has been detrimental to the local environment. Today, Hawaii is the 'extinction capital of the USA', accounting for 75% of the nation's documented extinctions. Most environmentalists agree that the next big threat on O'ahu is from the brown tree snake, which has led to the extinction of all native birds on the Pacific island of Guam.

Animals

Marine Life

Up to 10,000 migrating North Pacific humpback whales come to Hawaiian waters for calving each winter; whale watching (p309) is a major highlight. The world's fifth-largest whale, the endangered humpback can reach lengths of 45ft and weigh up to 50 tons. Other whales (such as rarely seen blue and fin whales) also migrate through.

O'ahu waters are home to a number of dolphins, the most notable of which is the spinner dolphin that likes the western waters off leeward O'ahu. These acrobats are nocturnal feeders that come into sheltered bays during the day to rest. They are sensitive to human disturbance, and federal guidelines recommend that swimmers do not approach closer than within 50yd; for more on dolphin encounters, see p299.

One of the Pacific's most endangered marine creatures is the Hawaiian monk seal, named both for the monastic cowl-like fold of skin at its neck and for its solitary habits. The Hawaiian name for the animal is *'ilio holo kai,* meaning 'the dog that runs in the sea.' Adults are more than 7ft long and 500lb of toughness, some with the scars to prove they can withstand shark attacks. Once nearly driven to extinction, they now number around 1300. Although monk seals breed primarily in the remote Northwestern Hawaiian Islands, they have begun hauling out on the northwestern beaches and may be spotted at Ka'ena Point in leeward O'ahu. For their wellbeing, keep at least 150ft from these endangered creatures, limit your observation time to 30 minutes, and never get between a mother and her pup.

Native Hawaiians traditionally revere the green sea turtle, which they call *honu*. Often considered a personal *'aumakua* (protective deity), a *honu* frequently appears in petroglyphs (and today in tattoos). For ancient Hawaiians they were a prized source of food, caught in accordance with religious and traditional codes. Adults can grow more than 3ft long and weigh more than 200lb. Young turtles are omnivorous, but adults (unique among sea turtles) become strict vegetarians. This turns their fat green – hence their name. Green sea turtles can be seen along the North Shore. Note that they are endangered and protected by federal law. Keeping a distance of 50ft is advised.

O'ahu's near-shore waters also harbor hundreds of tropical fish, including rainbow-colored parrotfish, moray eels and ballooning puffer fish, to name just a few. For more on species, and responsible snorkeling and diving, see p310.

Feathered Friends

Most of the islets off O'ahu's Windward Coast are sanctuaries for seabirds, including terns, noddies, shearwaters, Laysan albatrosses and boobies. For more on native species and island bird watching, see p315.

Plants

Oʻahu blooms year-round. The classic hibiscus is native to Hawaii, but many of the hundreds of varieties growing here have been introduced. Other exotic tropical flowers commonly seen include blood-red anthurium, brilliant orange bird-of-paradise, showy bougainvillea and numerous varieties of heliconia. Strangely enough, while Hawaii's climate is ideal for orchids, there are only three native species. Most of the agricultural plants associated with the island, such as the pineapple, were introduced. Other endemic species you might see include:

ʻohia lehua A native shrub or tree with bright-red, tufted pompom flowers; thought to be sacred to the goddess Pele.

koa trees Tall, upland tree with flat, mature crescent-shaped leaves; wood is used to make canoes, ukuleles and exquisite bowls.

ʻilima The island's official flower, a native groundcover with delicate yellow blossoms often strung into lei.

naupaka A common shrub with oval green leaves and a small pinkish-white, five-petal flower. It's said that the mountain variety and beach variety were once a young male and female, separated and turned into plants because of Pele's jealousy of their love.

National, State & County Parks

Oʻahu has no national parks, but the federal government manages Valor in the Pacific National Monument at Pearl Harbor, as well as the James Campbell National Wildlife Refuge on the edge of the North Shore. About 25% of the island's land is protected, although some tension exists between the government and a few rural communities that want more land for affordable housing and farming. From Diamond Head near Waikiki to Kaʻena Point on the remote northwestern tip of the island, a rich system of state parks and forest reserves is loaded with outdoor opportunities, especially hiking. Dozens of county beach parks offer all kinds of aquatic adventures. For more on outdoor activities, see p302. The state's **Department of Land & Natural Resources** (www.hawaii.gov/dlnr) has useful online information about hiking, history and aquatic safety.

The Best...
Natural Preserves

1 Kaʻena Point State Park (p258)

2 Diamond Head State Monument (p155)

3 Waimea Valley (p219)

4 Hoʻomaluhia Botanical Garden (p193)

5 Lyon Arboretum (p52)

6 Hanauma Bay Nature Preserve (p163)

Outdoor Activities & Adventures

Children snorkel in the tidal pools at Shark's Cove (p215)

DAVID SCHRICHTE / ALAMY

O'ahu is a dream destination for those keen to get outside, whether you're searching for action and adventure or just a leisurely stroll. Here you can hike the sandy beachside, or climb up into the mountains for a forest trek. Go for a simple snorkel or an all-day scuba dive. Island-wide opportunities for swimming, kayaking, stand-up paddling and more abound. Oh, and did we mention there's some pretty decent surfing?

Water Sports

If you want to get wet, O'ahu is the place for you. The island is ringed with beautiful white-sand beaches, ranging from crowded resorts to quiet, hidden coves. All of the beaches on the island are public, though a few have park gates that close during specified hours. Most of the more than 50 beach parks have restrooms and showers; about half are patrolled by lifeguards.

Swimming

O'ahu has distinct coastal areas, each with its own peculiar seasonal water conditions. As a general rule, the best places to swim in winter are in the south, and in summer, to the north. The southern stretch from Barbers Point in leeward O'ahu to Kailua Beach in windward O'ahu encompasses some of the most popular beaches on the island. This includes the legendary Waikiki Beach. Small summer swells here pick up from May through to September, making it a tad rougher for swimming. A word of warning: approximately 10 days after a full moon, box jellyfish swim into the shallow waters, especially around Waikiki, and stay for a day or two; check www.808jellyfish.com for predicted arrivals.

The North Shore has epic waves in winter; swimming is not advisable from at least late October through to early May. During summer, the ocean can be as calm as a lake. The exception is Bayview Beach in Turtle Bay, which is well protected year-round. The Wai'anae Coast in leeward O'ahu typically has similar swimming conditions to those of the North Shore, with incredible surf in winter and more swimmable conditions in summer. But you'll find sheltered year-round swimming at Ko Olina and Poka'i Bay Beach Park.

Snorkeling

There really isn't much of an excuse to not go snorkeling on O'ahu. The water is warm, the currents are generally gentle and the underwater visibility is awesome. Shallow reefs and nearshore waters are awash with fish and colorful corals. You can expect to spy large rainbow-colored parrotfish munching coral on the sea floor, schools of silver needlefish glimmering near the surface, brilliant yellow tangs, odd-shaped filefish and ballooning puffer fish.

As activities go, this is about as cheap as it gets, with mask and snorkel rentals available nearly everywhere for around $15 a day. If you're staying at a vacation rental or condo, one or two sets are usually free for guest use.

The year-round snorkeling mecca is scenic Hanauma Bay Nature Preserve in southeast O'ahu, which has a protected bay. When summer waters are calm on the North Shore, Waimea Bay and Shark's Cove in Pupukea provide top-notch snorkeling in pristine conditions, and far less human activity than at Hanauma. Sans Souci Beach Park and Queen's Surf Beach are smaller snorkel sites in Waikiki.

Bodysurfing & Bodyboarding

Bodysurfing is a great way to catch some waves, sans equipment. There's a bit of a knack to it, but once you've found the groove, it's good times ahead. The ideal locations are sandy shorebreaks where the inevitable wipeouts aren't that painful.

If you're just getting started, Waimanalo Bay and Bellows Field Beach Parks in windward O'ahu have gentle shorebreaks. If you're someone who knows your way around the surf, head to Sandy and Makapu'u Beach Parks in southeast O'ahu. Other challenging shorebreaks are at Waimea Bay Beach Park on the North Shore, and at Kailua's Kalama Beach and La'ie's Pounders Beach on the Windward Coast.

Bodyboarding is the bridge between bodysurfing and surfing – with that in mind, you're spoilt for break choices. If you want to see and be seen, the island's most popular bodyboarding site is Kapahulu Groin in Waikiki. Otherwise, if you're keen for shorebreaks, try the aforementioned bodysurfing waves. If you want something a bit bigger, have a look at the surfing spots below.

Surfing

O'ahu is known the world over for surfing – and rightfully so. The island boasts 594 defined surfing sites, nearly twice as many as any other Hawaiian island. Whether you're a seasoned board rider or brand new to the sport, you'll find the appropriate break for your taste here. See p308, for more information on popular surf beaches.

Beginner surfing lessons are available in Waikiki, in Honolulu and in Kailua on the Windward Coast. On the North Shore, lessons are available out of Hale'iwa, but there

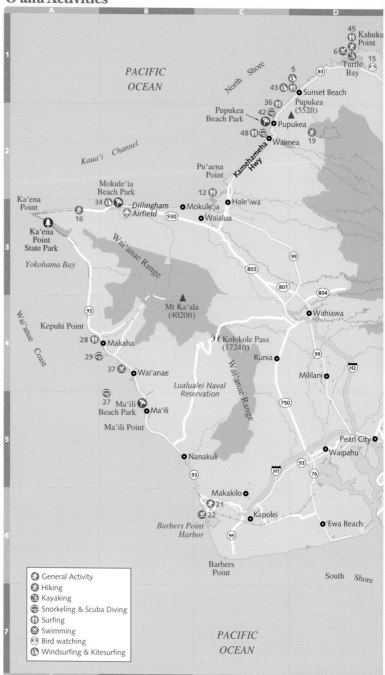

PACIFIC OCEAN

45
Kahuku Point
6
15
Turtle Bay
North Shore
5
83
43
Sunset Beach
36
Pupukea
42
Pupukea (552ft)
48
Pupukea
19
Waimea

PACIFIC OCEAN

Kaua'i Channel

Pu'aena Point
Kamehameha Hwy
12
Hale'iwa

Mokule'ia Beach Park
34
Dillingham Airfield
930
Mokule'ia
Waialua

Ka'ena Point
16
Ka'ena Point State Park

Yokohama Bay

Wai'anae Range

99
803
801
804

Mt Ka'ala (4020ft)

Wahiawa

Kepuhi Point
28
Makaha
29
37
Wai'anae

Kolekole Pass (1724ft)
Kunia

99
H2
Mililani

Lualualei Naval Reservation

750

27
Ma'ili Beach Park
Ma'ili

Wai'anae Range

Ma'ili Point

Pearl City
Waipahu

Nanakuli
93
H1
93
76

Makakilo
21
22
Kapolei
'Ewa Beach

Barbers Point Harbor
95

Barbers Point
South Shore

🛩 General Activity
🚶 Hiking
🛶 Kayaking
🤿 Snorkeling & Scuba Diving
🏄 Surfing
🏊 Swimming
🦅 Bird watching
🪁 Windsurfing & Kitesurfing

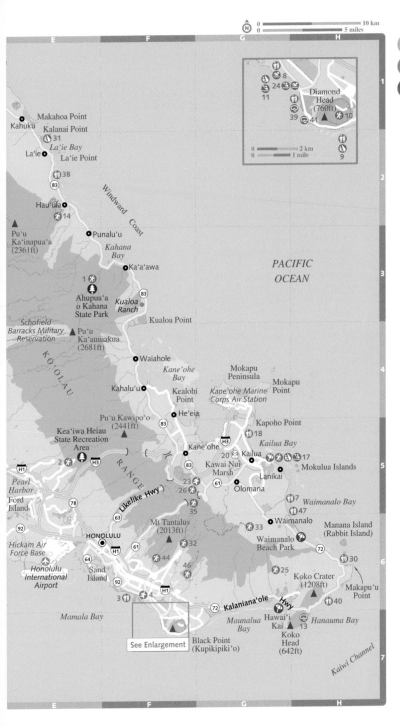

0 ———— 10 km
0 ———— 5 miles

Inset (top right):

Diamond Head (760ft)

8
24
11
39 41
10
9

0 ———— 2 km
0 ———— 1 mile

Main map:

Makahoa Point
Kahuku
Kalanai Point 31
La'ie Bay
La'ie
La'ie Point
38
83
Hau'ula
14
Windward Coast
Pu'u Ka'inapua'a (2361ft)
Punalu'u
Kahana Bay
Ka'a'awa
1
Ahupua'a o Kahana State Park
Kualoa Ranch
83
Kualoa Point
Schofield Barracks Military Reservation
Pu'u Ka'aumakua (2681ft)
Waiahole
Kane'ohe Bay
Mokapu Peninsula
Mokapu Point
Kahalu'u
Kealohi Point
Kane'ohe Marine Corps Air Station
He'eia
Kapoho Point
Kea'iwa Heiau State Recreation Area
Pu'u Kawipo'o (2441ft)
83
18
H3
Kane'ohe
20 Kailua 17
Kailua Bay
Pearl Harbor
Ford Island
H1
2
H3
KO'OLAU RANGE
Kawai Nui Marsh
61
23
Lanikai
Mokulua Islands
26
Olomana
35
78
Likelike Hwy
63
7
47
Waimanalo Bay
Mt Tantalus (2013ft)
33
Waimanalo
Manana Island (Rabbit Island)
HONOLULU
H1
61
32
44
Waimanalo Beach Park
72
Hickam Air Force Base
64
Sand Island
46
25
Koko Crater (1208ft)
Makapu'u Point
Honolulu International Airport
92
3
4
H1
30
40
Mamala Bay
72 *Kalaniana'ole Hwy*
See Enlargement
Black Point (Kupikipiki'o)
Maunalua Bay
Hawai'i Kai
13
Hanauma Bay
Koko Head (642ft)
Kaiwi Channel

PACIFIC OCEAN

Oʻahu Activities

are only two small, beginner breaks there. Most North Shore waves are pro-level advanced. Even if you're experienced, you should take a lesson from one of the local experts to learn about the conditions. Daily board rentals ($35 to $45) are available at surf shops in the above-mentioned areas, plus in Waiʻanae on the Leeward Coast. The colorful **Franko's Oʻahu Surf Map** (www.frankosmaps.com), available at souvenir and sport shops islandwide, lists every beach and break, with a short description.

Wahine (women) looking for a more intensive experience should sign up for one of the week-long surf camps (about $2200) that operate here. Along with daily lessons and accommodation, packages usually include meals, yoga or massage, and other activities. Check out: **Sunset Suzy's Surf Camp** (☏780-6963; www.sunsetsuzy.com), retreats at **Surf into Yoga** (☏638-8137; http://surfintoyoga.com), **Kelea Surf Spa** (☏949-492-7263; www.keleasurfspa.com) and Girls Who Surf (p58).

Stand-Up Paddling

The latest craze in board riding has taken the Oʻahu scene by storm. Stand-up paddling, or stand-up paddle boarding, is a derivative of surfing where the rider stands on the board and uses a long paddle instead of stroking with his or her arms. It can be done on flat water and, for those who know what they're doing, in the surf. Beginners love it as there is little risk (the water is calm), and it's easily learned by a variety of ages and athletic abilities – besides, it's just plain fun. For more about the sport see the box, p223.

You can take lessons in Waikiki, Honolulu, Kailua on the Windward Coast, and in Hale'iwa and Turtle Bay on the North Shore. Guided tours are sometimes also available. Equipment rentals (about $60 per day) are widely available from the island's water-sports outfitters.

Kayaking

Who says you need an engine to get around the sea? Kayaking is an enjoyable way to explore the turquoise waters. Rentals run from about $35 to $55 per day. The top kayaking destination is undoubtedly Kailua Beach on the Windward Coast, which has three uninhabited islands within the reef to which you can paddle. Landings are allowed on two of the islands: Moku Nui, which has a beautiful beach good for sunbathing and snorkeling; and Popoi'a Island (Flat Island), where there are some inviting walking trails. You can reserve ahead for rentals, or some may be available at the beach. At writing time, a law was under consideration which would ban on-beach rentals at least on Saturday afternoon and Sunday – maybe all week. Contact outfitters directly for rental.

Guided kayak tours (four hours, approximately $125) are available from Kailua and from the nearby Kane'ohe Bay area, plus up at Turtle Bay on the North Shore. Waikiki doesn't have the same *Robinson Crusoe* feel to it, but kayak rentals are also available at Fort DeRussy Beach, plus you can rent in Hale'iwa on the North Shore.

Kitesurfing & Windsurfing

Kite- and windsurfing action on O'ahu centers on Kailua along the Windward Coast, where you'll find the vast majority of rentals and lessons. Kailua Beach has persistent year-round tradewinds and superb conditions for all levels, from beginner to pro, in different sections of the bay. It's never a slacker, but the very best winds typically occur in summer, when east-to-northeast trades run at eight to 15 knots. And when high-pressure systems come in, they can easily double that, which makes for awesome speed.

Just a few years ago, nobody had heard of kitesurfing (also sometimes called kiteboarding). Fast-forward to today and, when it's windy, you'll see more kites over the water than over the land. Combine a wakeboard with a small parachute and add water, stir in the mentality of a windsurfer and the water knowledge of a surfer, and you have kitesurfing. It's amazing to watch and hard to master – if you're keen to learn on O'ahu, the place to try your hand is Kailua. The same top-notch outfitters there teach both kitesurfing and windsurfing, and have rental gear for both. Hawaiian Watersports in Waikiki will provide transport to Kailua free with a lesson. In general, kitesurfing lessons cost about $250 for three hours, windsurfing $130 for two. Rentals run $30 to $45 per day for a windsurfing rig or just a kite board; a full kitesurfing set up is about $260 for three hours and requires supervision.

In addition to Kailua, the speed and jumps at Diamond Head in southeast O'ahu are also popular with local kite- and windsurfers. If you have your own equipment, other recommended spots include Malaekahana State Recreation Area in windward O'ahu

The Best...
Beaches for
Keiki (Kids)

1 Ko Olina lagoons (p247)

2 Hanauma Bay (p162)

3 Kuhio Beach Park, Waikiki (p95)

4 Bayview Beach (p210)

5 Poka'i Bay Beach Park (p252)

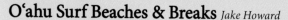

Oʻahu Surf Beaches & Breaks *Jake Howard*

Hawaiian for 'the gathering place', Oʻahu has become a hub for the islands' surf economy. Because Oʻahu has some of the most diverse surf breaks in the islands, boarders of all skill levels can find what they're looking for.

In Waikiki, slow and mellow combers (long, curling waves) provide the perfect training ground for beginners. Board rentals abound on central **Waikiki Beach** and local beachboys are always on hand for lessons at spots like mellow **Queens**, mushy left- and right-handed **Canoes**, gentle but often crowded **Populars** and ever-popular ,. In Honolulu proper, **Ala Moana** offers a heavy tubing wave – it's *not* a learning locale. Waves in this area are best during summer, when south swells arrive from New Zealand and Tahiti.

Reckon yourself a serious surfer? A pilgrimage to the famed North Shore is mandatory. In winter, when the waves can reach heights of more than 30ft, spots like **Waimea Bay**, **Pipeline** (at ʻEhukai Beach Park) and **Sunset Beach** beckon to the planet's best professional surfers.

While home to some great waves, the **Waiʻanae Coast** in leeward Oʻahu has turf issues; the locals who live and surf here cherish this area and are trying to hold onto its last vestiges of Hawaiian culture and community. In winter, large west swells can make for big surf at places like **Makaha Beach Park**, but tread lightly: the locals know each other here, so there will be no question that you're from out of town.

If you're looking for a multipurpose wave, **Diamond Head Beach** in Honolulu is friendly to short-boarders, long-boarders, windsurfers and kitesurfers. And for a good day of bodysurfing, **Sandy Beach Park** and **Makapuʻu**, in southeast Oʻahu, are ideal. If you go out here, do so with caution: the pounding waves and shallow bottom have caused some serious neck and back injuries.

For surf reports, call **Surf News Network** (☎ 596-7873; www.surfnewsnetwork.com), a recorded surf-condition telephone line that reports winds, wave heights and tide information, or check out **Wavewatch** (www.wavewatch.com) or **Surfline** (www.surfline.com) online.

JAKE HOWARD IS A WRITER FOR ESPN.COM AND THE SURFER'S JOURNAL, AND PREVIOUSLY WROTE FOR SURFER MAGAZINE.

for open-water cruising; Mokuleʻia Beach Park for consistent North Shore winds; and Backyards, off Sunset Beach on the North Shore, with the island's highest sailable waves. In Waikiki, Fort DeRussy Beach offers good conditions, but you have to contend with catamarans and crowds.

Outrigger Canoeing

There's not much in Hawaii that's more traditional then outrigger canoeing. First popularized by Native Hawaiians as a means to get around the Pacific, it has since become an activity popular with tourists, hard-core water sportspeople and recreational ocean goers. The best place to give it a crack is Kuhio Beach Park in Waikiki, where you can ride right from the sand and surf the waves back in. The round trip will cost around $25 and is very popular with kids.

Diving

Whether you're an old pro or a beginner, O'ahu has plenty to offer under the sea: lessons, boat dives, shore dives, night dives, reef dives, cave dives and wreck dives. The water temperatures are perfect for diving, with yearly averages from 72°F to 80°F. Even better than the bathwater temperatures is the visibility, which is usually perfect for seeing the plethora of fish, coral and other sea creatures. Because of its volcanic origins, the island also has some cool underwater caves and caverns.

Two-tank boat dives average about $120 to $150 and include all gear. Several dive operators offer a beginners' 'discover scuba' option, an introductory course that includes brief instruction, and possibly swimming-pool practice, followed by a shallow beach or boat dive. The cost is generally $130 to $180, depending on the operation and whether a boat is used. Full, open-water PADI certification courses can be completed in as little as three days and cost around $500.

O'ahu's top summer dive spots include the caves and ledges at Three Tables and Shark's Cove on the North Shore, and the Makaha Caverns off Makaha Beach in leeward O'ahu. For wreck diving, the sunken 165ft ship *Mahi,* also off Makaha Beach, is a prize. Numerous spots between Honolulu and Hanauma Bay on southeast O'ahu provide good winter diving. Diving outfitters operate out of Waikiki, Hawai'i Kai in southeast O'ahu, Kailua on the Windward Coast, Hale'iwa on the North Shore and Wai'anae and Kapolei/Ko Olina in leeward O'ahu. In Kapolei, snuba (modified scuba diving where you remain attached via oxygen line to the boat) is also available.

Franko's O'ahu Dive Map (www.frankosmaps.com), a full-color illustrated map available around the island, lists dive sites and descriptions. **Divers Alert Network** (www.diversalertnetwork.org) provides advice on diving insurance, emergencies, decompression services, illness and injury.

Boating

Catamaran sunset cruises out of Waikiki and Honolulu may not be particularly active, unless you count drinking as sport, but there are other boating options around the island.

Whale Watching

Catching a view of a whale on O'ahu isn't a fluke. Between December and May, humpback whales and their newly birthed offspring visit the harbors of northern and western O'ahu. Hawaiian spinner dolphins are year-round residents of the Wai'anae Coast in leeward O'ahu. Whale- and dolphin-watching boat trips depart from Honolulu, Hale'iwa on the North Shore, and from Kapolei, Ko Olina and Wai'anae on the Leeward Coast. (For cautions about swimming with dolphins, see p299.)

Learn more about Hawaii's humpback whales and find out how to volunteer to participate in one of three annual whale counts at the **Hawaiian Islands Humpback Whale National Marine Sanctuary** (http://hawaiihumpbackwhale.noaa.gov). Note that you don't always need a boat; look for whale sightings from land along the North Shore at Turtle Bay or from Ka'ena Point, and from Makapu'u Lighthouse in southeast O'ahu.

Fishing

Why order dinner when you can catch it? There are a number of sport-fishing operations around the island that'll take you out on the sea for the day and help you land the big one. Do respect the ocean, respect marine preserves and practice catch-and-release. There are outfitters operating out of Hawai'i Kai in southeast O'ahu and from Wai'anae Small Boat Harbor in leeward O'ahu.

Hiking

Even though O'ahu is Hawaii's most populous island, nature sits right outside Waikiki's door. About 25% of the island is protected natural areas. The entire coastline is dotted with beaches, while the lush mountainous interior is carved by hiking trails.

Trails

Even if you don't have a lot of time, there are plenty of hikes that can be accessed near Waikiki. The island's classic hike, and its most popular, is the short but steep trail to the city overlook at the crater's summit in Diamond Head State Monument in southeast O'ahu. It's easily reached from Waikiki and ends with a panoramic city view. Also in the

Responsible Diving & Snorkeling

Of the 700 fish species that live in Hawaiian waters, nearly one-third are found nowhere else in the world. Divers can also often see spinner dolphins, green sea turtles and manta rays. The waters hold hard and soft corals, anemones, unusual sponges and a variety of shellfish. The popularity of underwater exploration is placing immense pressure on many sites. Please consider the following tips when diving to help preserve the ecology and beauty of reefs.

Don't touch the turtles Minimize your disturbance of marine animals. It is illegal to approach endangered marine species too closely; these include whales, dolphins, sea turtles and the Hawaiian monk seal. In particular, do not ride on the backs of turtles, as this causes them great anxiety.

Please don't feed the fish Doing so disturbs their normal eating habits and can encourage aggressive behavior; besides, you might feed them food that is detrimental to their health.

Be conscious of the coral Take care not to touch coral with your body (never stand on it) or drag equipment across the reef. Polyps can be damaged by even the gentlest contact. If you must hold on, only touch exposed rock. Be conscious of your fins; even without contact, the surge from heavy strokes near the reef can damage delicate organisms. When treading water in shallow reef areas, take care not to kick up clouds of sand. Settling sand can easily smother delicate reef organisms.

Take only pictures Resist the temptation to collect coral or shells from the seabed. Buy an underwater camera and take pictures instead.

Pack it out Ensure that you remove all your trash and any other litter you may find. Plastics in particular are a serious threat to marine life. Turtles can mistake plastic for jellyfish and eat it.

Practice proper buoyancy Major damage can be done by divers descending too fast and colliding with the reef. Make sure you are correctly weighted and that your weight belt is positioned so that you stay horizontal. Be aware that buoyancy can change over an extended trip.

Care for caves Spend as little time in underwater caves as possible; your air bubbles may be caught within the roof and thereby leave previously submerged organisms high and dry.

island's southeast corner, investigate the Kuli'ou'ou Ridge Trail: the views are worth the sturdy climb.

In Honolulu, the less-trodden Manoa Falls Trail is another steep but rewarding excursion. Two miles further is the Nu'uanu Pali Lookout, which has a similar flavor and makes for a good double shot. Also only a few miles from downtown Honolulu, the forested Tantalus and Makiki Valley area has extensive trail network, with fine overlooks of Honolulu and surrounding valleys. Wa'ahila Ridge Trail provides a different perspective on the area and good bird watching possibilities.

Just to the west of Honolulu in the Pearl Harbor area, 'Aiea Loop Trail is popular with both hikers and mountain bikers. It's contained within Kea'iwa Heiau State Recreation Area, which also allows an opportunity for an ancient temple visit.

Traveling a bit further afield to the Windward Coast, the Maunawili Trail System in Kailua provides a varied walk that covers a lot of different territory, including a waterfall, along with up to 10 miles of travel. Outside Kailua, a short, tree-shaded climb will take you to lesser-known Likeke Falls. For an excellent beach stroll, take to the sands outlining Kailua Bay. North up the coast, there are several quiet upland hikes in Ahupua'a o Kahana State Park and above Hau'ula; all take you deep into the forest and are worth exploring.

On the North Shore, the mixed sand-and-rock coastline at Turtle Bay makes for a pleasant trek. Further west, above Pupukea, Kaunala Loop Trail was considered sacred by Hawaiian royalty – it's no wonder, since the view is awesome.

Far from anywhere else, one of the most stunning of the island's hikes starts in Ka'ena Point State Park at the northwestern edge of leeward O'ahu. The trail hugs the coastline, as blue ocean crashes against dark volcanic rocks below and craggy cliffs rise above. Expect to see shorebirds, and maybe monk seals, in the windswept natural reserve on the uninhabited tip of the island.

Note that other ridge climbs and more challenging trails exist; ours is not meant to be a comprehensive list. Search the excellent website administered by **Na Ala Hele Trail & Access System** (☏587-0062; http://hawaiitrails.ehawaii.gov) for trails, printable topo maps and announcements of recently developed or reopened paths. Maps by the **US Geological Survey** (www.usgs.gov) are available in some island bookstores and can be ordered, or downloaded free online. Pay attention to the map dates, as some may have been drawn decades ago.

Guided Hikes

Local guided hikes provide entry onto otherwise inaccessible private land in the valleys of Kualoa Ranch on the Windward Coast, and out of Hale'iwa and in Waimea Valley on the North Shore. The latter is highly recommended. Hawai'i Nature Center in the Makiki Forest Recreation Area, near Honolulu, leads family-oriented hikes by reservation. Island-wide, clubs arrange group hikes that you can meet and join up with; no transportation provided. Outfitters offer guided hiking tours, the main advantage being that bus transport from Waikiki is included. On tours, it's always a good idea to ask what, if any, food or water is provided. Group hikes are also listed in the *Honolulu Weekly* (http://honoluluweekly.com) calendar; alternatively, contact one of the following.

The Best...
Diving & Snorkeling Spots

1 Hanauma Bay (p162)

2 Shark's Cove (p215)

3 Offshore at Makaha (p256)

4 Three Tables (p216)

5 Ko Olina lagoons (p247)

Hawaiian Trail & Mountain Club (http://htmclub.org; group hike per person $3) Volunteer community group that organizes informal hikes every weekend.

Sierra Club (www.hi.sierraclub.org; group hike per person $5) Organizes weekend hikes around O'ahu; provides volunteer opportunities to rebuild trails and restore native plants.

O'ahu Nature Tours (☎924-2473; www.oahunaturetours.com; tours $30–55) Hiking-oriented options include two waterfall treks and a Diamond Head crater climb.

Hawaiian Escapades (☎366-0400; www.hawaiianescapades.com; tours $65–120) Wander through a botanical garden or hike Manoa Valley with these tours.

Hiking Preparation & Safety

It's advisable to hike with at least one other person; at the very least, tell a reliable individual where you are going and when you are expected back. Pack four pints of water per person for a full-day hike, carry a whistle to alert rescuers should the need arise, wear sunscreen and, above all, start out early. Sturdy footwear with good traction is a must here, where it often gets muddy.

Overall, O'ahu is a very safe place to go for a hike. You won't find any poison oak, snakes, poison ivy or many wild animals to contend with. There is the rare chance you might encounter a wild boar – as exciting and death defying as that sounds, unless

Camping on O'ahu

O'ahu has no full-service campgrounds with swimming pools and wi-fi as on the US mainland, but you can pitch a tent at many county and some state parks around the island. Expect basic facilities: restrooms, open-air showers and some picnic tables or grills. The Windward Coast contains the best camping option. Two beach parks down in Waimanalo are well recommended; you can camp in the shadow of the majestic Ko'olau Range at a botanical garden in the Kane'ohe Bay area; and Malaekahana State Recreation Area has both a public and a private campground. On the North Shore, camping options are extremely limited, but there is a church camp in Mokule'ia that accepts campers when it's not group-booked. We don't recommend camping on the Wai'anae Coast in leeward O'ahu, where some homeless islanders have set up permanent tent cities. There are no suitable campgrounds near Waikiki.

Note that all county- and state-park campgrounds on O'ahu are closed Wednesday and Thursday nights (from 8am Wednesday to 8am Friday) and some are only open on weekends. Permits are required for all; you must apply in advance from one of the following.

City and County of Honolulu (☎768-3440; www1.honolulu.gov/parks/camping.htm; Permits Section, Frank F Fasi Municipal Bldg, 650 S King St, Honolulu; tent sites free; ◷8am-4pm Mon-Fri). Administers beach parks and their campgrounds across O'ahu. Apply for your free permit in person, no sooner than two Fridays prior to the requested date.

Division of State Parks (☎587-0300; www.hawaiistateparks.org; Room 131, 1151 Punchbowl St, Honolulu; tent sites $18; ◷8am-3:30pm Mon-Fri) Administers state parks and recreation areas. You can apply for the required permits in person or online up to 30 days in advance.

cornered they are rarely a problem. However, flash floods (see p324) and the following are potential hazards:

Landslides Be alert to the possibility of landslides and falling rocks. Swimming under non-maintained waterfalls can be dangerous, as rocks may dislodge from the top. Be careful on cliff edges as rocks here tend to be crumbly.

Nightfall Darkness falls fast once the sun sets, and ridge-top trails are no place to be caught unprepared at night. Always carry a flashlight just in case.

Cycling & Mountain Biking

Though challenging, it's possible to cycle around O'ahu; for more see p328.

Mountain biking is still an emerging sport on the island and opportunities to rent the appropriate off-road bikes are limited to Kailua on the Windward Coast and Honolulu. Having said that, there are some trails worth seeking out. In Hau'ula, the loop trail is a fun track (if only it were a little bit longer!); Maunawili Trail System is a scenic 10-mile ride that connects the mountain Nu'uanu Pali Lookout with sea level in Waimanalo – both are on the Windward Coast. In southeast O'ahu check out the Kuli'ou'ou Ridge Trail for great views and a staunch climb, and in Pearl Harbor there's the 'Aiea Loop Trail that is part of Kea'iwa Heiau State Recreation Area.

Hawaii Bicycling League (☎735-5756; www.hbl.org; group rides free) Local bicycle club holds group road-cycling rides most weekends, from 10-mile jaunts to 60-mile travails.

Bike Hawaii (☎734-4214; www.bikehawaii.com; tours $60–120) Tours offered by this adventure outfitter include mountain biking alone, and in conjunction with hiking, snorkeling and kayaking. A 5-mile rainforest road ride cruises downhill on pavement.

Cyclists at Sunset Beach Park (p213)
ANN CECIL / LONELY PLANET IMAGES ©

Horseback Riding

Saddle up, pardner. There are several opportunities for exploring rural parts of the island by horseback. Ride through a valley ranch in Kualoa or La'ie on the Windward Coast, or trot beachside at the polo club in Mokule'ia, canter the coast at Turtle Bay or plod along the mountainside above Pupukea on the North Shore. A 1½-hour trail ride costs between $60 and $90.

Golf

Some say that a round of golf is the perfect way to ruin a good walk, but if you disagree, O'ahu could very well be paradise. With more than 40 courses to choose from you're spoiled for golfing choice. You'll find PGA-level courses with the atmosphere of a private club, resort courses, and municipal greens with lower fees, a relaxed atmosphere and similarly spectacular surrounds.

The most highly rated courses include Ko'olau Golf Club in Kane'ohe on the Windward Coast; Ko Olina Golf Club in leeward O'ahu; and at Turtle Bay Golf on the North Shore. For a full list of O'ahu courses, log on to www.islandgolf.com. Green fees run from about $85 to $185 for 18 holes. Discounted rates are often available if you don't mind teeing off in the afternoon or reserve in advance online.

City and County of Honolulu (☏ 733-7386 golf reservations; www1.honolulu.gov/des/golf/; **green fees $50**) runs six 18-hole municipal golf courses. Reservations for out-of-state visitors are accepted up to three days in advance, and can be made online.

Yoga & Massage

The outdoorsy lifestyle of O'ahu is an ideal setting for rejuvenation. Yoga classes are offered all over the island. Look for sessions in Waimanalo and Kailua on the Windward Coast and in Hale'iwa and Waialua on the North Shore, among other towns.

Kayaking off Lanikai Beach (p181), near the windward town of Kailua

Therapeutic massages can also be had in a number of locations, including Kailua and Hale'iwa. For more on spa pampering in Waikiki, see p108.

Bird Watching

Most islets off O'ahu's Windward Coast are sanctuaries for seabirds, including terns, noddies, shearwaters, Laysan albatrosses, boobies and 'iwa (great frigate birds). Moku Manu (Bird Island), off the Mokapu Peninsula near Kane'ohe, has the greatest variety of species, including a colony of 'ewa'ewa (sooty terns) that lays its eggs in ground scrapes. Although visitors are not allowed on Moku Manu, bird watchers can visit Moku'auia (Goat Island), offshore from Malaekahana State Recreation Area on the Windward Coast. In Kailua, the Kawai Nui Marsh is another place to see Hawaiian waterbirds in their natural habitat.

On the edge of the North Shore, James Campbell National Wildlife Refuge encompasses a native wetland habitat protecting some rare and endangered waterbird species.

Hikers who tackle O'ahu's many forest-reserve trails, especially around Mt Tantalus, can expect to see the 'elepaio (Hawaiian monarch flycatcher), a brownish bird with a white rump, and the 'amakihi, a yellow-green honeycreeper, the most common endemic forest birds on O'ahu. The 'apapane, a bright-red honeycreeper, and the 'I'iwi, a scarlet honeycreeper, are rarer.

For birding checklists and group field trips, contact the **Hawaii Audubon Society** (528-1432; www.hawaiiaudubon.com). **O'ahu Nature Tours** (924-2473; www.oahunaturetours.com) offers custom bird watching tours.

Running

In the early hours of the morning you'll see joggers aplenty in parks, on footpaths and on beaches all around the island. Running on O'ahu is huge. Kapi'olani Park and the Ala Wai Canal are favorite jogging spots in Waikiki.

O'ahu has about 75 road races each year, from 1-mile fun runs and 5-mile jogs to competitive marathons, biathlons and triathlons. For an annual schedule of running events, check out the **Running Room** (www.runningroomhawaii.com) and click on 'Races.'

The island's best-known race is the Honolulu Marathon, which has mushroomed from 167 runners in 1973 into one of the largest in the US. Held in mid-December, it's an open-entry event, with an estimated half of the roughly 25,000 entrants running

Alternative Adventures

Sick of swimming and surfing? Though we don't see how you could be, there are other adrenaline-fueled options. Hawai'i Kai in southeast O'ahu is alternative water sports central: parasail, waterski, ride a banana boat...even journey below the sea in a submersible scooter and above it with a water-borne jetpack (a la Buzz Lightyear).

Prefer sky to sea? Head up to Dillingham Airfield, in Mokule'ia on the North Shore. From there you can take a glider ride, fly in a biplane, help operate a powered hang glider or simply jump out of a plane (tandem, with a chute).

in their first marathon. For information, contact the **Honolulu Marathon Association** (www.honolulumarathon.org).

Tennis

O'ahu has 181 public tennis courts at county parks throughout the island; for locations, log on to www1.honolulu.gov/parks/programs/tennis. If you're staying in Waikiki, the most convenient locations are the courts at the Diamond Head Tennis Center in Kapi'olani Park; and at the Kapi'olani Park Tennis Courts, opposite the Waikiki Aquarium. The courts at Ala Moana Beach Park in Honolulu are also close.

Canoe paddlers at sunset on the North Shore
ANN CECIL / LONELY PLANET IMAGES ©

Survival
Guide

Nu'uanu Pali (p172) at sunrise
JOHN ELK III / LONELY PLANET IMAGES ©

A-Z

Directory

●●●

Accommodations

RATES

In this guide, unless otherwise stated, reviews indicate high-season rates for a double-occupancy room:

$	under $100
$$	$100 to $250
$$$	over $250

Quoted rates generally don't include taxes of almost 14%. Unless noted, breakfast is *not* included and bathrooms are private.

RESERVATIONS

A reservation guarantees your room, but most reservations require a deposit, after which, if you change your mind, the establishment may not refund your money. Note cancellation policies and other restrictions before making a deposit.

SEASONS

○ During high season – mid-December through late March or mid-April, and to a lesser degree, June through August – lodgings are more expensive and in demand.

○ Certain holidays and major events command premium prices, and for these, lodgings can book up a year in advance.

○ In low or shoulder seasons, expect significant discounts and easier booking.

AMENITIES

○ Accommodations offering online computer terminals for guests are designated with the internet icon (@); an hourly fee may apply.

○ In-room internet access is often wired (not wireless); a daily fee may apply.

○ When wireless internet access is offered, the wi-fi icon (📶) appears. Look for free wi-fi hot spots in common areas (eg hotel lobby, poolside).

○ Where an indoor or outdoor pool is available, the swimming icon (🏊) appears.

○ Air-conditioning (❄) is a standard amenity at most hotels and resorts and some condos. At many hostels and some condos, B&Bs and vacation rentals, only fans may be provided.

○ For more icons and abbreviations used with reviews in this book, see How to Use This Book.

B&BS & VACATION RENTALS

B&B accommodations on O'ahu are usually spare bedrooms at residential homes. With restrictive local regulations that make it impossible to license new businesses, the majority of B&Bs and vacation rentals are technically illegal. Officials know this, and usually turn a blind eye unless there's a complaint. A recent statewide crackdown did result in closures and forfeited guest reservations, so this de facto policy of acceptance is subject to change at any time.

Contrary to their name, most B&Bs do not offer a full breakfast; they provide supplies – coffee, juices, fruits and breads or pastries, usually – stocked in the unit's refrigerator. Unless they have a state-approved restaurant kitchen, they can be fined if caught making hot meals for guests.

Because B&Bs and vacation rentals discourage unannounced drop-ins, they sometimes do not appear on maps in this book. Same-day reservations are hard to get – always try to book B&Bs in advance, especially since they tend to fill up weeks or months ahead of time. Many B&Bs have minimum-stay requirements of a few nights, though some will waive this if you pay a surcharge.

Typically, a vacation rental means renting an entire

Book Your Stay Online

For more accommodations reviews by Lonely Planet authors, check out http://hotels.lonelyplanet.com. You'll find independent reviews, as well as recommendations on the best places to stay. Best of all, you can book online.

apartment, duplex, condo or house (with no on-site manager and no breakfast provided), but many B&Bs also rent stand-alone cottages. Often all these kinds of properties, which typically have kitchens, are handled by the same rental agencies. Ask about added cleaning fees, commonly for stays of less than five nights.

Most B&Bs and vacation rentals are found in Kailua, as well as elsewhere along the Windward Coast and on the North Shore. This book reviews B&Bs and vacation rentals that can be reserved directly through the owners or through local real estate agencies listed in the destination chapters earlier. Also try:

Affordable Paradise Bed & Breakfast (www.affordable -paradise.com)

Bed & Breakfast Hawaii (www.bandb-hawaii.com)

Air B&B (www.airbnb.com)

Craigslist (http://honolulu. craigslist.org)

Hawaii Beach Homes (http://hawaii-beachhomes. com)

Hawaii's Best Bed & Breakfast (www.bestbnb. com)

HomeAway (www.homeaway. com)

Vacation Rental by Owner (www.vrbo.com)

Practicalities

○ **Electricity** 110/120V, 50/60Hz

○ **Magazines** Monthly *Honolulu Magazine* (www. honolulumagazine.com) is a glossy lifestyle mag, while *Ka Wai Ola* (www.oha.org/kwo) covers Native Hawaiian issues.

○ **Newspapers** *Honolulu Star-Advertiser* (www. staradvertiser.com, www.honolulupulse.com) is Hawaii's major daily. *Honolulu Weekly* (http://honoluluweekly.com) is a free alternative tabloid.

○ **Radio** O'ahu has more than 45 radio stations; for Honolulu, see p88.

○ **Smoking** Prohibited in enclosed public spaces, including airports, bars, restaurants, shops and hotels (where smoking rooms are rarely available).

○ **Time** Hawaii-Aleutian Standard Time (HAST) is GMT-10. Hawaii doesn't observe Daylight Saving Time (DST). The euphemism 'island time' means taking things at a slower pace, or occasionally being late.

○ **TV** All major US networks and cable channels available, plus 24-hour tourist information.

○ **Video Systems** NTSC standard (incompatible with PAL or SECAM systems); DVDs coded region 1 (US and Canada only).

○ **Weights & Measures** Imperial (to convert between metric and imperial, see the inside front cover).

CAMPING & CABINS

For public and private camp-grounds, camping permits and cabin reservations, see p312.

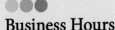

Business Hours

Unless there are variances of more than a half-hour in either direction, the following standard opening hours apply throughout this book:

Banks 8:30am-4pm Mon-Fri, some to 6pm Fri & 9am-noon or 1pm Sat

Bars & clubs To midnight daily, some to 2am Thu-Sat

Businesses 8:30am-4:30pm Mon-Fri; some post offices 9am-noon Sat

Restaurants Breakfast 6-10am, lunch 11:30am-2pm, dinner 5-9:30pm

Shops 9am-5pm Mon-Sat, some also noon-5pm Sun; major shopping centers keep extended hours

Climate

Hale'iwa

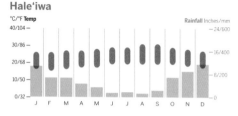

Windward O'ahu

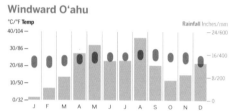

Honolulu

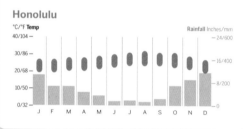

- 200 cigarettes (one carton) or 50 (non-Cuban) cigars (if you're over 18)

- Amounts higher than $10,000 in cash, traveler's checks, money orders and other cash equivalents must be declared. For more information, check with **US Customs and Border Protection** (www.cbp.gov).

- Most fresh fruits and plants are restricted from entry into Hawaii (to prevent the spread of invasive species). At Honolulu's airport, customs officials strictly enforce both import and export regulations (see p327). Because Hawaii is a rabies-free state, pet quarantine laws are draconian. Questions? Contact the **Hawaiian Department of Agriculture** (http://hawaii.gov/hdoa).

●●●
Electricity

120V/60Hz

●●●
Courses

Hawaiian language, arts-and-crafts and cultural classes are most plentiful in Honolulu (p61) and Waikiki (p106). To learn how to surf, windsurf, kitesurf (kiteboard), stand-up paddle or scuba dive, browse the Activities listings in the destination chapters of this book.

Road Scholar (☎ 800-454-5768; www.roadscholar.org) Top-notch educational programs for those aged 50 or over focusing on Hawaii's

people and culture and the natural environment. One- to two-week programs cost from $1600 to $3300, including accommodations, meals, classes and activities, but not airfare to/from Hawaii.

●●●
Customs Regulations

Currently, each international visitor is allowed to bring into the USA duty-free:
- 1L of liquor (if you're over 21 years old)

120V/60Hz

Food

In this book, restaurant prices usually refer to an average main course at dinner (lunch is often cheaper, sometimes half-price):

$	mains under $12
$$	most mains $12-30
$$$	mains over $30

These prices don't include drinks, appetizers, desserts, taxes or tip (see p323).

Lunch is generally served between 11:30am and 2:30pm, and dinner between 5:30pm and 9pm daily, though some restaurants close later, especially on Friday and Saturday nights. If breakfast is served, it's usually between 6am and 10am, with weekend brunch until 2pm.

For more about Hawaii's cuisine, see p278.

Gay & Lesbian Travelers

The state of Hawaii has strong minority protections and a constitutional guarantee of privacy that extends to sexual behavior between consenting adults. Same-sex couples also have the right to civil unions. But showing affection toward a same-sex partner in public isn't common.

Waikiki is without question the epicenter of O'ahu's LGBTQ nightlife (see p111), but this laid-back 'scene' is muted by US mainland standards. **Honolulu Pride** (www.honoluluprideparade.org), in early June, celebrates with a parade from Ala Moana's Magic Island to Waikiki's Kapi'olani Beach Park.

The monthly magazines **Odyssey** (http://dysseyhawaii.com) and **eXpression!** (www.expression808.com), both distributed free at LGBTQ-friendly businesses in Waikiki, cover O'ahu's gay scene. The national monthly magazine **OutTraveler** (www.outtraveler.com) archives gay-oriented Hawaii travel articles online.

Helpful DIY resources include the website **Gay Hawaii** (www.gayhawaii.com) and **Purple Roofs** (www.purpleroofs.com/usa/hawaii/oahu.html), an online accommodations directory. **Pacific Ocean Holidays** (http://gayhawaiivacations.com) arranges package vacations.

Insurance

Getting travel insurance to cover theft, loss and medical problems is highly recommended. Some policies do not cover 'risky' activities such as scuba diving and motorcycling, so read the fine print. Make sure your policy at least covers hospital stays and an emergency flight home.

Paying for your airline ticket or rental car with a credit card may provide limited travel accident insurance. If you already have private US health insurance or a homeowner's or renter's policy, find out what those policies cover and only get supplemental insurance. If you have prepaid a large portion of your vacation, trip cancellation insurance may be a worthwhile expense.

Worldwide travel insurance is available at www.lonelyplanet.com/travel_services. You can buy, extend and claim online anytime – even if you're already on the road.

For car-rental insurance, see p330.

Internet Access

◦ In this book, the @ symbol indicates an internet terminal is available, while the 🛜 symbol indicates a wi-fi hot spot; either may be free or fee-based.

◦ Most hotels and resorts, and many coffee shops, bars and other businesses, offer public wi-fi (sometimes free only for paying customers).

International Visitors

ENTERING HAWAII

- Visa and passport requirements change often; double-check *before* you come.

- For current info, check the visa section of the **US Department of State** (http://travel.state.gov) and the **US Customs & Border Protection** (www.cbp.gov/travel).

- Upon arrival, most foreign visitors must register with the **US-Visit program** (www.dhs.gov/us-visit), which entails having electronic (inkless) fingerprints and a digital photo taken; the process usually takes less than a minute.

PASSPORTS

- A machine-readable passport is required for all foreign citizens to enter Hawaii.

- Passports must be valid for six months beyond expected dates of stay in the USA.

- Any passport issued or renewed after October 26, 2006, must be an 'e-passport' with a digital photo and an integrated biometric data chip.

VISAS

- Currently, under the US Visa Waiver Program (VWP), visas are not required for citizens of 36 countries for stays of up to 90 days (no extensions).

- Under the VWP you must have a return ticket (or onward ticket to any foreign destination) that is nonrefundable in the USA.

- All VWP travelers must register online at least 72 hours before arrival with the **Electronic System for Travel Authorization** (https://esta.cbp.dhs.gov/esta/), which currently costs $14. Registration is valid for two years.

- Travelers who don't qualify for the VWP must apply for a tourist visa. The process is not free, involves a personal interview and can take several weeks, so apply early.

CONSULATES

O'ahu has no foreign embassies. Honolulu has only a few consulates, including:

Australia (☏ 529-8100; Penthouse, 1000 Bishop St)

Japan (☏ 543-3111; 1742 Nu'uanu Ave)

Korea (☏ 595-6109; 2756 Pali Hwy)

Netherlands (☏ 531-6897; ste 702, 745 Fort St Mall)

New Zealand (☏ 595-2200; 3929 Old Pali Rd)

MONEY

- All prices in this book are quoted in US dollars. See p31 for exchange rates.

- Foreign currency can be exchanged for US dollars at larger banks only in Honolulu or Waikiki; airport exchange booths are convenient but expensive.

- Most ATMs are connected to international networks and have OK exchange rates.

- Large hotels, restaurants and stores accept US-dollar traveler's checks as if they're cash, although smaller businesses and fast-food chains may refuse them.

- Honolulu, Waikiki and a few island towns have cybercafes or business centers with pay-as-you-go internet terminals (typically $6 to $12 per hour) and sometimes wi-fi.

- Hawaii's **public libraries** (www.librarieshawaii.org) provide free internet access via their online computer terminals, but you will need a temporary nonresident library card ($10). A few library branches now offer free wi-fi (no card required).

Language

Hawaii has two official languages: English and Hawaiian. There's also an unofficial vernacular, pidgin, which has a laid-back, lilting accent and a colorful vocabulary that permeates the official tongues. While Hawaiian's multisyllabic, vowel-heavy words may seem daunting, the pronunciation is actually quite straightforward. To learn the basics, including some Hawaiian and pidgin terms, visit www.lonelyplanet.com/hawaiian-language for our free Hawaiian Language & Glossary download.

Legal Matters

If you are arrested, you have the right to an attorney; if you can't afford one, a public defender will be provided free. The **Hawaii State Bar Association** (☏ 537-9140; www.hawaiilawyerreferral.com) can make attorney referrals.

- If you are stopped by the police while driving, be courteous. Don't get out of the car unless asked.

- It's illegal to have open containers of alcohol (even empty ones) in motor vehicles; unless containers are still sealed and have never been opened, store them in the trunk.

- Bars, nightclubs and stores may required photo ID to prove you're of legal age (21 years) to buy or consume alcohol.

- Drinking alcohol in public anywhere besides a licensed premises (eg bar, restaurant), including at beaches and parks, is illegal.

- In Hawaii, anyone caught driving with a blood alcohol level of 0.08% or greater is guilty of driving under the influence (DUI), a serious offense that may incur heavy fines, a suspended driver's license, jail time and other stiff penalties.

- The possession of marijuana and nonprescription narcotics is illegal. Foreigners convicted of a drug offense face immediate deportation.

- Public nudity (as at beaches) and hitchhiking are illegal, but sometimes police ignore them.

Money

- Major banks, such as the **Bank of Hawaii** (www.boh.com) and **First Hawaiian Bank** (www.fhb.com), have extensive ATM networks throughout O'ahu.

- Some B&Bs, condominiums and vacation-rental agencies will not accept credit cards, instead requiring cash, traveler's checks or personal checks drawn on US bank accounts.

- Hawaii has a 4.17% state sales tax tacked onto virtually everything, including meals, groceries and car rentals. Accommodations taxes total nearly 14%.

TIPPING

In Hawaii, tipping practices are the same as on the US mainland, roughly:

Airport and hotel porters $2 per bag, minimum of $5 per cart.

Bartenders 15% to 20% per round, minimum of $1 per drink.

Hotel maids $2 to $4 per night, left under the card provided; more if you're messy.

Parking valets At least $2 when your keys are returned.

Restaurant servers 18% to 20%, unless a service charge is already on the bill.

Taxi drivers 15% of the metered fare, rounded up to the next dollar.

Post

The **US Postal Service** (USPS; ☏ 800-275-8777; www.usps.com) is inexpensive and reliable. Mail delivery to/from Hawaii usually takes slightly longer than on the US mainland.

●●●

Public Holidays

On the following holidays, banks, schools and government offices (including post offices) close, and transportation and museums operate on a Sunday schedule. Holidays falling on a weekend are usually observed the following Monday. For major annual festivals and events, see p26.

New Year's Day January 1

Martin Luther King Jr Day Third Monday in January

Presidents' Day Third Monday in February

Easter March or April

Prince Kuhio Day March 26

Memorial Day Last Monday in May

King Kamehameha Day June 11

Independence Day July 4

Statehood Day Third Friday in August

Labor Day First Monday in September

Columbus Day Second Monday in October

Veterans Day November 11

Thanksgiving Fourth Thursday in November

Christmas Day December 25

●●●

Safe Travel

In general, Hawaii is a safe place to visit. Because tourism is so important, state officials have established the **Visitor Aloha Society of Hawaii** (VASH; ☎ 926-8274; www.visitoralohasocietyof-hawaii.org), which provides non-monetary emergency aid to short-stay visitors who become the victims of accidents or crimes.

THEFT & VIOLENCE

O'ahu is notorious for thefts from parked cars, both locals' and tourist rentals. Thieves can pop open a trunk or pull out a door-lock assembly in seconds. They strike not only at remote trailheads when you've gone for a hike but also in crowded beach parking lots where you'd expect safety in numbers.

Try not to leave anything of value in your car anytime you walk away from it. If you must, pack things well out of sight *before* pulling up to park; thieves watch and wait to see what you put in your trunk. Some locals always leave their cars unlocked with the windows rolled down to avoid paying for broken windows.

Stay attuned to the vibe on any beaches at night, even in Waikiki where police patrol, and in places like campgrounds and roadside county parks where drunks, drug users and gang members hang out. In rural areas, there may be pockets of resentment against tourists, particularly on the Wai'anae Coast, where homeless encampments have taken over a few beaches (see p243).

FLASH FLOODS & WATERFALLS

No matter how dry a stream-bed looks, or how sunny the sky above is, a sudden rainstorm miles away can cause a flash flood in minutes, sending down a huge surge of debris-filled water that sweeps away everything in its path. Always check the weather report before starting a hike; this is crucial if you're planning on hiking in valleys or swimming in natural pools or waterfalls. Swimming underneath waterfalls is always risky due to the danger of falling rocks.

Tell-tale signs of an impending flash flood include sudden changes in water clarity (eg it becomes muddy), rising water levels and/or floating debris, and a rush of wind, the sound of thunder or a low, rumbling roar. If you notice any of these signs, immediately get to higher ground (even a few feet could save your life). Don't run downstream – you can't beat a flash flood!

TSUNAMI

On average, tsunamis (incorrectly called tidal waves – the Japanese term *tsunami* means 'harbor wave') occur only about once a decade in Hawaii, but they have killed more people statewide than all other natural disasters combined. The tsunami warning system is tested on the first working day of every month at 11:45am for less than one minute, using the yellow speakers mounted on telephone poles around the island. If you hear a tsunami warning siren at any other time, head for higher ground immediately; telephone books have maps of evacuation zones. Turn on the radio or TV for news bulletins. For more information, visit the **Pacific Disaster Center** (www.pdc.org) and **Hawaii State Civil Defense** (www.scd.hawaii.gov) online.

●●● Telephone

CELL (MOBILE) PHONES

Check with your service provider about using your phone in Hawaii. Among US providers, Verizon has the most extensive network; AT&T, Cingular and Sprint get decent reception. Cell coverage may be spotty or nonexistent in rural areas, on hiking trails and at remote beaches.

International travelers need a multiband GSM phone in order to make calls in the USA. With an unlocked multiband phone, popping in a US prepaid rechargeable SIM card is usually cheaper than using your own network. SIM cards are available at any major telecommunications or electronics store. These stores also sell inexpensive prepaid phones, including some airtime.

DIALING CODES

○ All Hawaii phone numbers consist of a three-digit area code (☏808) followed by a seven-digit local number.

○ To call long-distance from one Hawaiian island to another, dial ☏1-808 + local number.

○ Always dial '1' before toll-free numbers (☏800, 888 etc). Some toll-free numbers only work within Hawaii or from the US mainland (and possibly Canada).

○ To call Canada from Hawaii, dial ☏1 + area code + local number (international rates apply).

○ For all other international calls, dial ☏011 + country code + area code + local number.

○ To call Hawaii from abroad, the international country code for the USA is ☏1.

USEFUL NUMBERS

○ Emergency (police, fire, ambulance) ☏911

○ Local directory assistance ☏411

○ Long-distance directory assistance ☏1-(area code)-555-1212

○ Toll-free directory assistance ☏1-800-555-1212

○ Operator ☏0

●●● Tourist Information

In the arrivals area at the airport there are tourist-information desks with helpful staff. While you're waiting for your bags to appear on the carousel, you can leaf through racks of tourist brochures and magazines, such as **101 Things to Do** (www.101thingstodo.com), **This Week** (http://thisweekmagazines.com) and **Spotlight's O'ahu Gold** (www.spotlighthawaii.com), which are packed with discount coupons. For pre-trip planning, browse the information-packed website of the **Hawaii Visitors & Convention Bureau** (☏800-464-2924; www.gohawaii.com), which has a business office in Waikiki.

●●● Tours

If you're short on time, the following tours give a quick overview of island highlights. For more local tours, anything from historical walks to organic farm visits, see the destination chapters earlier in this book, especially Honolulu (p61), the North Shore (p223) and the Windward Coast (p199). For guided hikes, see p311. For older-adult learning vacations, see p320.

Hawaiian Escapades (☏888-331-3668; www.hawaiianescapades.com; tours $65-120) Waterfall walks, circle-island adventures and, most popularly, *Hawaii 5-0* and *Lost* TV location tours that pick up and drop off in Waikiki.

E Noa Tours (☏591-2561, 800-824-8804; www.enoa.com) O'ahu-based tour company utilizes smaller buses and knowledgeable local guides, with standard circle-island tours (adult/child from $73/60) that include Waikiki hotel pick-ups/drop-offs.

Roberts Hawaii (☏539-9400, 800-831-5541; www.robertshawaii.com) Conventional bus and van sightseeing tours of O'ahu, such as marathon full-day 'Circle Island' trips (adult/child from $53/29) that include Waikiki hotel pick-ups/drop-offs.

●●● Travelers with Disabilities

○ Bigger, newer hotels and resorts in Hawaii have elevators, TDD-capable phones

325

and wheelchair-accessible rooms (reserve these well in advance).

- ◦ Telephone companies provide relay operators (dial ☎711) for hearing impaired.

- ◦ Many banks provide ATM instructions in Braille.

- ◦ Traffic intersections have dropped curbs and audible crossing signals in cities and some towns, as well as all along Waikiki's beachfront.

- ◦ Honolulu's **Department of Parks and Recreation** (☎768-3027; www1.honolulu.gov/parks/programs/beach/) provides all-terrain beach mats and wheelchairs for free (call ahead to make arrangements) at several beaches, including Ala Moana, Hanauma Bay, Sans Souci, Kailua, Kualoa and Poka'i Bay.

- ◦ Guide dogs and service animals are not subject to the same quarantine requirements as pets; contact the Department of Agriculture's **Animal Quarantine Station** (☎808-483-7151; http://hawaii.gov/hdoa/) before arrival.

TRANSPORTATION

- ◦ All public buses on O'ahu are wheelchair-accessible and will 'kneel' if you're unable to use the steps – just let the driver know that you need the lift or ramp.

- ◦ If you have a disability parking placard from home, bring it with you and hang it from your rental car's rearview mirror when using designated disabled-parking spaces.

- ◦ Some major car-rental agencies offer hand-controlled vehicles and vans with wheelchair lifts. You'll need to reserve these well in advance.

USEFUL RESOURCES

Access Aloha Travel (☎545-1143, 800-480-1143; www.accessalohatravel.com) Local travel agency can help book wheelchair-accessible accommodations, rental vans and sightseeing tours.

Disability & Communication Access Board (www.hawaii.gov/health/dcab/travel) Online 'Traveler Tips' brochures provide info about airports, accessible transportation, sightseeing, and medical and other support services.

Volunteering

For volunteering opportunities on O'ahu, see p297.

Transport

Getting There & Away

✈ AIR

Most visitors to O'ahu arrive by air. Honolulu is a major Pacific hub and intermediate stop on many flights between the US mainland and Asia, Australia, New Zealand and the South Pacific. Flights can be booked online at www.lonelyplanet.com/bookings.

AIRPORTS

US mainland, interisland and international flights arrive at **Honolulu International Airport** (HNL; Map p38; http://hawaii.gov/hnl), a modern facility with all the usual amenities such as currency-exchange booths, duty-free shops and fast-food eateries, as well as flower lei stands. You'll find visitor information desks, car-rental counters and courtesy phones in the baggage claim area. Free **Wiki-Wiki shuttle buses** (⏱6am-10pm) connect the airport's public terminals.

To get through airport security checkpoints, you'll need a boarding pass and photo ID. Airport security measures restrict many common items (eg pocket knives, any liquids or gels over 3oz) from being carried on planes. These regulations often change, so get the latest information from the **Transportation Security Administration** (TSA; ☎866-289-9673; www.tsa.gov).

TICKETS

Air fares to Honolulu vary tremendously, depending on the season and day of the week you fly. Competition is highest among airlines flying from major US mainland cities, especially with **Hawaiian Airlines** (www.hawaiianair.com) and **Alaska Airlines** (www.alaskaair.com). Generally speaking, return fares from

Agricultural Inspection

All checked and carry-on bags leaving Hawaii for the US mainland must be checked by an agricultural inspector using an X-ray machine. You cannot take out gardenia, jade vine or Mauna Loa anthurium, even in lei, although most other fresh flowers and foliage are permitted. With the exceptions of pineapples and coconuts, most fresh fruit and vegetables are banned. Also not allowed to enter mainland states are plants in soil, fresh coffee berries (roasted beans OK), cactus and sugarcane. For more information, contact the **USDA Honolulu office** (☏ 861-8490) or go online to http://hawaii.gov/hdoa.

the US mainland to Hawaii cost from $400 (in low season from the West Coast) to $800 or more (in high season from the East Coast).

Offered by major airlines and online travel booking sites, vacation packages that include airfare, accommodations and possibly car rental, tours and/ or activities may cost less than booking everything separately. **Pleasant Holidays** (☏ 800-742-9244; www. pleasantholidays.com) offers competitive vacation packages from the US mainland.

Within Hawaii

Fast, frequent flights connect Honolulu with the Neighbor Islands. Interisland fares vary wildly; expect to pay from $60 to $180 one way. Round-trip fares are usually double the one-way fare with no additional discounts. The earlier you book your interisland ticket, the more likely you are to find a cheaper fare. Buy tickets on airline websites, which often post online-only deals.

○ Of the two main interisland carriers, **go! Mokulele** (www.

iflygo.com) tends to be cheaper, but **Hawaiian Airlines** (www. hawaiianair.com) has far more flights and reliable service.

○ Commuter airlines such as **Island Air** (www.islandair. com) and **Pacific Wings** (www.pacificwings.com) use smaller turboprop aircraft that almost double as sightseeing planes – tons of fun!

Getting Around

O'ahu is a relatively easy island to get around, whether you're traveling by car or public bus. Compared with US mainland cities, island traffic is fairly manageable, although traffic into, out of and through Honolulu jams up during weekday morning and afternoon rush hours.

TO/FROM THE AIRPORT

Honolulu International Airport is on the western outskirts of the metro area, approximately 10 miles from Waikiki via Ala Moana Blvd/Nimitz Hwy (Hwy 92) or the H-1 (Lunalilo) Fwy. An airport taxi to Waikiki costs approximately $35 to $45,

depending on where your hotel is exactly. Major carrental agencies have booths or courtesy phones in the arrivals baggage-claim area.

AIRPORT SHUTTLE

Of a few door-to-door airport shuttle companies, **Roberts Hawaii** (☏ 441-7800, 800-831-5541; www.airportwaikik ishuttle.com) operates buses to Waikiki hotels around the clock. Shuttles depart frequently from the roadside median on the airport's ground level outside baggage claim. Reservations for airport pickups are helpful but not always required; for the return trip to the airport, you must call 48 hours in advance. The ride to/ from Waikiki averages 45 minutes, depending on how many stops the shuttle makes. The one-way/round-trip fare is $12/20, with surcharges for bicycles, surfboards, golf clubs, strollers and other oversized or excess baggage.

BUS

Buses 19 and 20 travel to downtown Honolulu, Ala Moana and Waikiki, taking anywhere from 45 to 80 minutes. Buses stop at the roadside median on the airport's second level, upstairs from baggage claim and outside the airline check-in counters. Buses fill up fast, so catch them at the first stop outside the interisland terminal; the next stops are outside the main terminal's Lobby 4 and Lobby 7. Buses run every 20 minutes from 6am to 11pm daily; the regular one-way adult fare is $2.50. Luggage is restricted to what you can hold on your lap or stow under

Climate Change & Travel

Every form of transport that relies on carbon-based fuel generates CO_2, the main cause of human-induced climate change. Modern travel is dependent on airplanes, which might use less fuel per mile per person than most cars but travel much greater distances. The altitude at which aircraft emit gases (including CO_2) and particles also contributes to their climate change impact. Many websites offer 'carbon calculators' that allow people to estimate the carbon emissions generated by their journey and, for those who wish to do so, to offset the impact of the greenhouse gases emitted with contributions to portfolios of climate-friendly initiatives throughout the world. Lonely Planet offsets the carbon footprint of all staff and author travel.

the seat (maximum size: 22in x 14in x 9in). In Waikiki, buses stop on Kalia Rd, Saratoga Rd and every couple of blocks along Kuhio Ave.

CAR

The easiest driving route to Waikiki is via Hwy 92, which starts out as the Nimitz Fwy and turns into Ala Moana Blvd. Although this route hits local traffic, it's hard to get lost. For the fast lane, take the H-1 Fwy eastbound, then follow signs 'To Waikiki.' Returning to the airport, beware of the poorly marked interchange where H-1 and Hwy 78 split; if you're not in the right-hand lane at that point, you could easily end up on Hwy 78 by mistake. It takes about 25 minutes – if you don't hit heavy traffic – to drive from Waikiki to the airport via H-1, but give yourself at least 45 minutes during weekday morning and afternoon rush hours.

BICYCLE

Cycling around O'ahu is a great, nonpolluting way to travel. Realistically, as a primary mode of transportation, cycling can be a challenge. Bicycles are prohibited on freeways, so take the bus (p328) to get beyond Honolulu's metro-area traffic. Every public bus is equipped with a rack that can carry two bicycles. Let the driver know that you'll be loading your bike, then secure your bicycle onto the fold-down rack, hop aboard and pay the regular fare (no bicycle surcharge). Hawaii's **Department of Transportation** (http://hawaii.gov/dot/highways/Bike/oahu/index.htm) publishes a *Bike O'ahu* route map, available free online and at local bike shops.

RENTAL

- Rental rates start at $20 to $40 per day (up to $85 for high-tech road or mountain bikes); multiday and weekly discounts may be available. A hefty credit-card deposit is usually required.

- You can easily rent beach cruisers and hybrid commuter bikes in Waikiki (see p137), Kailua (p193), Hale'iwa (p228) and Wai'anae (p253).

- For high-end road and mountain bikes, visit specialty bike shops, including in Honolulu (p60) and Kailua (p193).

- Some B&Bs, guesthouses and hostels rent or loan bicycles to guests.

ROAD RULES

- Generally, bicycles are required to follow the same state laws and rules of the road as cars. Bicycles are prohibited on freeways and sidewalks.

- State law requires all cyclists under age 16 to wear helmets.

- Any bicycle used from 30 minutes after sunset until 30 minutes before sunrise must have a forward-facing headlight and at least one red rear reflector.

BUS

O'ahu's extensive public bus system, **TheBus** (☎ 848-5555; www.thebus.org; ⏰ infoline 5:30am-10pm), is convenient and easy to use, but you can't set your watch by it. Besides not getting hung up on schedules, buses sometimes bottleneck, with one packed bus after another passing right by crowded bus stops (you can't just flag a bus down anywhere along its route).

As long as you don't try to cut your travel time too close or schedule too much in one day, the bus is a great deal. All buses are wheelchair-accessible and have two front-loading, fold-down bicycle racks (let the driver know before using them). One caveat: with arctic blasts of air-con, a public bus in Honolulu is probably the coldest place on O'ahu, regardless of the season.

Don't Get Lost

Directions on Oʻahu are often given by using landmarks. If someone tells you to 'go ʻEwa' (an area west of Honolulu) or 'go Diamond Head' (east of Waikiki), it simply means to head in that direction. Two other commonly used directional terms are *makai* (toward the ocean) and *mauka* (toward the mountain, or inland).

Street addresses on some island highways may seem random, but there's a pattern. For hyphenated numbers, such as 4-734 Kuhio Hwy, the first part of the number identifies the post office district and the second part identifies the street address. Thus, it's possible for 4-736 to be followed by 5-002; you've just entered a new district, that's all.

FARES & PASSES

○ The regular one-way fare is $2.50/1 for adults/children aged six to 17.

○ Pay upon boarding with coins or $1 bills; bus drivers don't give change.

○ For each paid fare, one free transfer (two-hour time limit) is available from the driver.

○ A $25 visitor pass valid for unlimited rides during four consecutive days is sold at Waikiki's ubiquitous ABC Stores and TheBus Pass Office (☏ 848-4444; 811 Middle St; ⊙ 7:30am-4pm Mon-Fri), far west of downtown Honolulu.

○ A monthly bus pass ($60), valid for unlimited rides during a calendar month (not just any 30-day period), is sold at TheBus Pass Office, 7-Eleven convenience stores, UH Manoa Campus Center and Foodland and Times supermarkets.

○ Seniors (65 years and older) and anyone with a documented physical disability can buy a $10 discount ID card at TheBus Pass Office, which entitles you to pay $1 per one-way fare,

or $5/30 for a pass valid for unlimited rides during one calendar month/year.

ROUTES & SCHEDULES

More than 100 bus routes collectively cover most of Oʻahu, but leave some popular viewpoints, parks and hiking trails beyond reach. Most routes run fairly frequently throughout the day from around 6am until 8pm (or later in Honolulu and Waikiki), with reduced night and weekend schedules. The Ala Moana Center shopping mall is Honolulu's central transfer point.

Confusingly, the same numbered bus route can have different destinations, even though buses generally keep the same number when inbound and outbound. For instance, bus 8 can take you into the heart of Waikiki or away from it toward Ala Moana, so take note of both the number and the written destination before jumping on. If in doubt, ask the driver.

For a table of useful bus routes to/from Waikiki, see p137; for Honolulu, see p89.

 CAR

Most visitors on Oʻahu rent their own vehicles, but if you're just staying in Waikiki and Honolulu, a car may be more of an expensive hindrance than a help. Free parking is usually plentiful, except in Honolulu and Waikiki. When parking on city streets, bring change for the meters, beware of color-coded curbs and read all posted restrictions to avoid being ticketed and possibly towed.

AUTOMOBILE ASSOCIATIONS

AAA has reciprocal agreements with some international automobile associations (eg Canada's CAA), but bring your membership card from home.

American Automobile Association (AAA; ☏ 593-2221; www.hawaii.aaa.com; 1130 N Nimitz Hwy, Honolulu; ⊙ 9am-5pm Mon-Fri, to 2pm Sat) Members are entitled to discounts on select car rentals, hotels, sightseeing and attractions, as well as free road maps and travel-agency services. For emergency roadside assistance and towing, members can call ☏ 800-222-4357.

DRIVER'S LICENSE

○ Foreign visitors can legally drive in Hawaii with a valid driver's license issued by their home country.

○ Car-rental companies will generally accept foreign driver's licenses, but usually only if they're written in English. Otherwise, be prepared to present an International

...rmit (IDP) along with ...ne license.

...as prices on O'ahu ...rrently range from $3.85 to ...4.10 per US gallon, averaging 70¢ higher than on the US mainland.

RENTAL

Agencies

Avis, Budget, Dollar, Enterprise, National and Hertz have rental cars at Honolulu International Airport. Alamo and Thrifty operate a mile outside the airport off Nimitz Hwy (free courtesy shuttles provided). All things being equal, try to rent from a company with its lot inside the airport. On the drive back to the airport, all highway signs lead to on-site airport car returns, and looking for a lot outside the airport when you're trying to catch a flight can be stressful.

Rental cars are also available at agency branch offices in Waikiki (see p137), although rates may be higher than at the airport. Independent car-rental agencies in Waikiki are more likely to rent to younger drivers under age 25 (surcharges may apply) and/or offer one-day deals on 4WD vehicles. To rent eco-friendly 'smart' cars and hybrid sedans and SUVs, see p137.

When you pick up your vehicle, most agencies will request the name and phone number of the place where you're staying. Some agencies are reluctant to rent to anyone who lists a campground as their address; a few specifically add 'No Camping Permitted' to rental contracts. Alternatively, **Hawaii Campers** (☎ 222-2547; www.hawaiicampers.net) rents pop-top VW camper vans, equipped with kitchens, (from $125 to $155 per day, weekly discounts available).

Major car-rental agencies on O'ahu, some of which offer 'green' hybrid models:

Advantage (☎ 800-777-5500; www.advantage.com)

Alamo (☎ 877-222-9075; www.alamo.com)

Avis (☎ 800-331-1212; www.avis.com)

Budget (☎ 800-527-0700; www.budget.com)

Dollar (☎ 800-800-3665; www.dollar.com)

Enterprise (☎ 800-261-7331; www.enterprise.com)

Hertz (☎ 800-654-3131; www.hertz.com)

National (☎ 877-222-9058; www.nationalcar.com)

Thrifty (☎ 800-847-4389; www.thrifty.com)

Rates

◦ The daily rate for renting a compact car usually ranges from $35 to $75, while typical weekly rates are $150 to $300.

◦ When getting quotes, always ask for the full rate *including taxes, fees and surcharges*, which can easily add more than $10 a day.

◦ Rental rates usually include unlimited mileage, but ask first.

◦ If you belong to an automobile club or a frequent-flyer program, you may be eligible for discounts. Also check **Discount Hawaii Car Rental** (www.discounthawaiicarrental.com).

Insurance

◦ Required by law, liability insurance covers any people or property that you might hit.

◦ For damage to the rental vehicle, a collision damage waiver (CDW) costs an extra $15 to $20 a day.

◦ If you decline CDW, you will be held liable for any damage up to the full value of the car.

◦ Even with CDW, you may be required to pay the first $100 to $500 for repairs; some agencies also charge you for the rental cost of the car during the entire time it takes to be repaired.

◦ If you have collision coverage on your vehicle at home, it might cover damage to car rentals; ask your insurance agent before your trip.

◦ Some credit cards offer reimbursement coverage for collision damage if you rent the car with that card; check before you leave home.

◦ Most credit-card coverage isn't valid for rentals over 15 days or for 'exotic' models (eg convertibles, 4WD Jeeps).

Reservations

Always make reservations in advance. With most car-rental companies there's little or no

Driving Distances & Times

DESTINATION	MILES TO/ FROM WAIKIKI	AVERAGE DRIVING TIME
Diamond Head	3	10min
Hale'iwa	37	55min
Hanauma Bay	11	25min
Honolulu Airport	10	25min
Ka'ena Point State Park	49	70min
Kailua	17	30min
Ko Olina	31	45min
La'ie	38	65min
Nu'uanu Pali Lookout	11	20min
Pearl Harbor	15	30min
Sunset Beach	43	65min
Waimanalo	20	35min

cancellation penalty if you change your mind before arrival. Walking up to the counter without a reservation will subject you to higher rates, and during busy periods it's not uncommon for all cars to be rented out (no kidding). If you need a child-safety seat ($10 per day, maximum $50), reserve one when booking your car.

ROAD RULES

Slow, courteous driving is the rule on O'ahu, not the exception. Locals don't honk (unless they're about to crash), don't follow too closely (eg tailgate), and let other drivers pass. Do the same, and you may get an appreciative *shaka* (Hawaiian hand greeting sign) in return.

◉ Talking or texting on a cell phone or mobile device while driving is illegal.

◉ Driving under the influence (DUI) of alcohol or drugs is a criminal offense (see p323).

◉ The use of seat belts is required for the driver, front-seat passengers and all children under age 18.

◉ Child safety seats are mandatory for children aged three and younger; children aged four to seven who are under 4ft 9in tall must ride in a booster seat or be secured by a lap-only belt in the back seat.

MOPED & MOTORCYCLE

Surprisingly, a moped or motorcycle can be more expensive to rent than a car. Mopeds cost from $40/175 per day/week, while motor-

cycles start around $125/500 per day/week (hefty credit-card deposit usually required). Both are rented in Waikiki (see p138), but you'll have to contend with heavy urban traffic.

ROAD RULES

◉ You can legally drive a moped in Hawaii with a valid driver's license issued by your home state or country. Motorcyclists need a specially endorsed motorcycle license.

◉ The minimum age for renting a moped is 16; for a motorcycle it's 21.

◉ Helmets are not legally required, but rental agencies often provide them free – use 'em.

◉ By law, mopeds must be ridden by one person only and always driven single file at speeds of 30mph or less. They're prohibited on sidewalks and freeways.

TAXI

Taxis have meters and charge a flag-down fee of $3.25, plus another $3 per mile and 35¢ per suitcase or backpack. Taxis are readily available at the airport, resort hotels and shopping malls, but otherwise you'll probably need to call for one. In Honolulu and Waikiki, try:

Charley's (☏ 233-3333, from payphones 877-531-1333; www.charleystaxi.com)

City Taxi (☏ 524-2121; www.citytaxihonolulu.com)

TheCab (☏ 422-2222; www.thecabhawaii.com)

Behind the Scenes

Author Thanks

SARA BENSON

Thanks to Margo Vitarelli for the tour in Manoa Valley and to Jan Pickett for helpful Kailua and Lanikai tips. Without Emily Wolman, Alison Lyall, Anna Metcalfe and everyone else at Lonely Planet, this book wouldn't have had such smooth sailing. *Mahalo nui loa* to Lisa Dunford for being a rock-star coauthor – let's run away and go back to Hawaii immediately!

LISA DUNFORD

My deepest gratitude goes to Theresa Longstreet Renalds, who first introduced me to O'ahu. Thanks, too, to Lisa Keaney, Jennie Lee, Terri Cozette and Ku'uipo for the insight. Julie and Gerry Mansell, *mahalo* for sharing your home and your friendship with me. And a big ditto of my coauthor's thanks to Emily and other Lonely Planet staffers; Sara, I'll meet you there tomorrow!

Acknowledgments

Climate map data adapted from Peel MC, Finlayson BL & McMahon TA (2007) 'Updated World Map of the Köppen-Geiger Climate Classification', *Hydrology and Earth System Sciences*, 11, 1633–44.

Cover photographs: Front: Waikiki Beach at sunset, Giovanni Simeone/4Corner; Back: Waikiki Beach and Diamond Head, Travel Pix Collection. Many of the images in this guide are available for licensing from Lonely Planet Images: www.lonelyplanetimages.com.

This Book

This guidebook was commissioned in Lonely Planet's Oakland office, and produced by the following:
Commissioning Editor Emily K Wolman
Coordinating Editors Sarah Bailey, Kellie Langdon
Coordinating Cartographers Karusha Ganga, Andy Rojas
Coordinating Layout Designer Joseph Spanti
Managing Editors Brigitte Ellemor, Anna Metcalfe, Martine Power
Senior Editor Andi Jones
Managing Cartographers Shahara Ahmed, Anita Ba Alison Lyall
Managing Layout Designer Chris Girdler
Assisting Editors Kate Evans, Amanda Williamson
Cover Research Naomi Parker
Internal Image Research Nicholas Colicchia

Thanks to Sasha Baskett, Valeska Canas, Erin Corriga Laura Crawford, Ryan Evans, Larissa Frost, Suki Gear, Trent Paton, Kirsten Rawlings, Raphael Richards, Johr Taufa, Gerard Walker

Index

See also separate sub-indexes for Activities (p413), Beaches (p411), Drinking (p419), Courses (p415), Eating (p417), Entertainment (p419), Shopping (p420), Sights (p412), Sleeping (p416) and Tours (p416).

000 Map pages

INDEX BEACHES

Sights

....

Activities

Courses

Eating

Shopping

How to Use This Book

These symbols will help you find the listings you want:

- 🏖 Beaches
- ◉ Sights
- ✪ Activities
- ⊜ Courses
- 📷 Tours
- ✪ Festivals & Events
- 🛏 Sleeping
- ✘ Eating
- 🍷 Drinking
- ✪ Entertainment
- 🔒 Shopping
- ⓘ Information/Transport

These symbols give you the vital information for each listing:

- 🎵 Telephone Numbers
- ⊙ Opening Hours
- P Parking
- ⊜ Nonsmoking
- ❄ Air-Conditioning
- @ Internet Access
- 🛜 Wi-Fi Access
- 🏊 Swimming Pool
- ✔ Vegetarian Selection
- 🍴 English-Language Menu
- 👪 Family-Friendly
- 🐾 Pet-Friendly
- 🚌 Bus
- ⛴ Ferry
- M Metro
- S Subway
- 🚊 Tram
- 🚆 Train

Reviews are organised by author preference.

Look out for these icons:

- **FREE** No payment required
- ✔ A green or sustainable option

Our authors have nominated these places as demonstrating a strong commitment to sustainability – for example by supporting local communities and producers, operating in an environmentally friendly way, or supporting conservation projects.

Map Legend

Sights
- ⊙ Beach
- ⊜ Buddhist
- 🏯 Castle
- ✝ Christian
- 🕉 Hindu
- ☪ Islamic
- ✡ Jewish
- ⊙ Monument
- 🏛 Museum/Gallery
- 🏛 Ruin
- ⊛ Winery/Vineyard
- 🐾 Zoo
- ⊙ Other Sight

Activities, Courses & Tours
- ⊜ Diving/Snorkelling
- ⊜ Canoeing/Kayaking
- ⊕ Skiing
- ⊕ Surfing
- ⊜ Swimming/Pool
- ⊛ Walking
- ⊛ Windsurfing
- ⊕ Other Activity/Course/Tour

Sleeping
- 🛏 Sleeping
- ⛺ Camping

Eating
- ✘ Eating

Drinking
- 🍷 Drinking
- ☕ Cafe

Entertainment
- ⊙ Entertainment

Shopping
- 🔒 Shopping

Information
- ✉ Post Office
- ⓘ Tourist Information

Transport
- ✈ Airport
- ⊗ Border Crossing
- 🚌 Bus
- ⊶ Cable Car/Funicular
- ⊛ Cycling
- ⊝ Ferry
- 🚝 Monorail
- P Parking
- S S-Bahn
- ⊜ Taxi
- 🚆 Train/Railway
- 🚊 Tram
- Ⓤ U-Bahn
- • Other Transport

Routes
- Tollway
- Freeway
- Primary
- Secondary
- Tertiary
- Lane
- Unsealed Road
- Plaza/Mall
- Steps
-)= = Tunnel
- Pedestrian Overpass
- Walking Tour
- Walking Tour Detour
- Path

Boundaries
- — — — International
- — — — State/Province
- — — Disputed
- — — Regional/Suburb
- Marine Park
- Cliff
- Wall

Population
- ☻ Capital (National)
- ◉ Capital (State/Province)
- ● City/Large Town
- ◉ Town/Village

Geographic
- ⊙ Hut/Shelter
- ⊕ Lighthouse
- ⊚ Lookout
- ▲ Mountain/Volcano
- ⊙ Oasis
- ⊙ Park
-)(Pass
- ⊙ Picnic Area
- ⊙ Waterfall

Hydrography
- River/Creek
- Intermittent River
- Swamp/Mangrove
- Reef
- Canal
- Water
- Dry/Salt/Intermittent Lake
- Glacier

Areas
- Beach/Desert
- Cemetery (Christian)
- Cemetery (Other)
- Park/Forest
- Sportsground
- Sight (Building)
- Top Sight (Building)

Our Story

A beat-up old car, a few dollars in the pocket and a sense of adventure. In 1972 that's all Tony and Maureen Wheeler needed for the trip of a lifetime – across Europe and Asia overland to Australia. It took several months, and at the end – broke but inspired – they sat at their kitchen table writing and stapling together their first travel guide, *Across Asia on the Cheap*. Within a week they'd sold 1500 copies. Lonely Planet was born.

Today, Lonely Planet has offices in Melbourne, London and Oakland, with more than 600 staff and writers. We share Tony's belief that 'a great guidebook should do three things: inform, educate and amuse'.

Our Writers

SARA BENSON

Coordinating Author, This Is O'ahu, Top Experiences, Top Itineraries, Honolulu, Waikiki, Southeast O'ahu, O'ahu Today, History, People of O'ahu, Hawaii's Cuisine, Survival Guide After graduating from college in Chicago, Sara jumped on a plane to California with just one suitcase, and $100 in her pocket. She then hopped across the Pacific to Japan, eventually splitting the difference by living on Maui, then the Big Island of Hawai'i and O'ahu, as well as trekking all over Kaua'i, Moloka'i and Lana'i. Sara is an avid hiker, backpacker and outdoor enthusiast who has worked and volunteered for the National Park Service. The author of more than 50 travel and nonfiction books, including *Top Trails Maui*, Sara has also contributed to Lonely Planet's *Hawaii* guide. Follow more of her adventures online at www.toptrailsmaui.blogspot.com, www.indietraveler.blogspot.com, www.indietraveler.net and @indie_traveler on Twitter.

Read more about Sara at:
lonelyplanet.com/members/Sara_benson

LISA DUNFORD

Get Inspired, Month by Month, Need to Know, Pearl Harbor, Windward O'ahu, North Shore, Central & Leeward O'ahu, Hawaii's Arts & Crafts, Family Travel, Green O'ahu, Outdoor Activities & Adventures Lisa first landed on O'ahu in 1994 when her best friend moved to the island. She was immediately entranced by the history, the culture – and the quilting – and has been returning as often as possible ever since. Though she's tried her hand at appliqué, and her hips at hula, she's mastered neither. What she has figured out is that among her favorite pastimes is pretending to live on the Windward Coast, hiking the hikes and strolling the sand. Lisa has been contributing to Lonely Planet titles for more than 10 years.

Read more about Lisa at:
lonelyplanet.com/members/Lisa_Dunford

Published by Lonely Planet Publications Pty Ltd
ABN 36 005 607 983
1st edition – Sep 2012
ISBN 978 1 74220 466 6
© Lonely Planet 2012 Photographs © as indicated 2012
10 9 8 7 6 5 4 3 2
Printed in China

Although the authors and Lonely Planet have taken all reasonable care in preparing this book, we make no warranty about the accuracy or completeness of its content and, to the maximum extent permitted, disclaim all liability arising from its use.